# DANCE –

## An Illustrated History

## By Helene Andreu

*AuthorHouse™*
*1663 Liberty Drive*
*Bloomington, IN 47403*
*www.authorhouse.com*
*Phone: 1 (800) 839-8640*

*Published by AuthorHouse 07/31/2015*

*ISBN: 978-1-5049-2046-9 (sc)*
*ISBN: 978-1-5049-1981-4 (e)*

authorHOUSE®

# Preface

DANCE – An Illustrated History is meant for anyone interested in dance, the general reader or the student. It explores the dances of many people including those too often omitted in books on dance: Native Americans, Alaskans, Hawaiians, Japanese, Indians, Indonesians, Turkish, Cambodians, Mexicans, and Chinese. It searches into the background of the dances of today: tap, modern, ballet, and jazz dance in musicals and concerts, and looks ahead to their future.

This book developed from an abbreviated course in dance history that I gave for the IRPE – Institute for Retirees in Pursuit of Education – (now named Brooklyn Lifelong Learning) at Brooklyn College and from courses in dance – modern, tap, jazz, ballet, folk, ethnic – which I gave in colleges, continuing education classes and studio classes, and had previously taken myself as a late-starting but avid student of dance.

After studying ballet at The School of America Ballet, I performed with the Brooklyn Civic Ballet Company under Alan Banks, appeared as choreographer-dancer-singer in numerous musicals at the Ephrata Star Playhouse, PA, and in operettas and operas with the American Savoyards, and performed in summer stock.

In writing this book I have drawn largely on the research and writings of Richard Kraus, Joseph Mazo, William Grimes, Camille Forbes, Nancy Reynolds, Lynne Fauley Emory, Riordan Fienup, Helen Brennan, Brenda Bufalino, Tyler Anbinder, Walter Sorell, Ruby Lal, Selma Jeanne Cohen, Lillian B. Lawler, Brenda Dixon Gottschild, Wendy Buonaventura, Constance Valis Hill, Marshall and Jean Stearns, Gus Giordano, and others. For current reviews and dance criticism I have gone to Alastair Macauley, Claudia La Rocco, Jack Anderson, Gia Kourlas, Brian Seibert, and Roslyn Sulcas of "The New York Times."

On many occasions I reverted to the Google Search Engine. I am grateful for the countless sources it provided for each search, allowing me to read and compare these and also to see dance on the Internet.

I am in awe of the Brooklyn Public Library and wish to congratulate it on letting me look at some of the books on its Website before deciding to put them on hold; the maximum seems to be front cover, information on the author, summary about the book, and sometimes reviews; very helpful.

If you, the reader, are looking for something specific from this book, do not forget to delve into the index at the end of the book for the exact pages for what you need.

I am indebted to my friends for any hints and suggestions they offered.

To my sister and friend, Denise Andreu, I wish to convey my special gratitude for her time, dedication, and patience in editing and proofreading both the manuscript as well as the galleys for this book, for her invaluable assistance in searching for appropriate illustrations, and for putting together the end-of-the-book credits and acknowledgments for the numerous images in this book. A million thanks to a priceless sister and friend.

# Table of Contents

# Introduction

Many people have thought that dance, for early man, was a form of communication. Stéphane Mallarmé, a French 19th century poet, felt that the dancer, writing with the body, conveyed things that the written work could articulate only by using many paragraphs of dialogue or descriptive text. Dance was a universal language that could often relate emotion more directly and effectively than words because the gestures were very closely connected to those of ordinary life and could be understood both visually and kinesthetically. Of course, the culture of the particular persons interpreting the movement affected their interpretation of it.

Explorations in dance history have revealed much more concerning our world than just dance steps. An important aspect of dance history is to show how the essence of the times has shaped the dancing. As you read on about the art of dance you will be exposed to fascinating bits of information pertaining to people's interests, styles, music, art, relationships, ideals, education, beliefs, and culture. These are uncovered or mirrored in their dances. Dance has been and still is an important part of all cultures.

Each chapter in this book deals with a special type of dance or a different period in its development. Examine the Table of Contents at the beginning of the book; gaze at the images for each chapter; then decide how to continue with the book – the usual way from beginning to end, or starting with whatever interests you most. However, you may prefer to just flip through the book and read something that catches your eye at that moment – a very good way to enjoy a book such as this. Each time you look at the book you'll discover something else that will arouse your curiosity.

You will notice that in this book the creative works, such as dance pieces, books, paintings, songs, are written in *italics*, and the names of dancers and dances (especially the first time they are mentioned in a chapter) are in **bold print** except in the Photo Plate captions and in the index.

The images for each chapter are interspersed within that chapter. Further related material is located in the bibliographies near the end of the book, with a separate one for ballet, for modern, for jazz, for tap, and one for Chapter 3: Native American, Hawaiian, and Alaskan dance. They include the books used by me while doing research for this book and also other very enjoyable ones on the subject of dance.

Writing this book on dance was a wonderful experience. Everything regarding dance is exciting – exploring its past and dreaming of its future. I hope you will get as much pleasure from this book as I had in the writing of it. Enjoy reading, looking at the images in the book, seeing DVDs and YouTube displays of various kinds of dance as you read about them, and watching live performances. Have fun.

# 1

# Early Dance

# to the Middle Ages

Early man may not have written books but he found ways to tell posterity about his life and dancing through paintings in caves, on rocks, pottery, or animal skins.

The earliest signs of dancing were revealed over 20,000 years ago as paintings in caves. These were figures dressed in animal skins, the outfits of that time. Between 8,000 and 12,000 years ago the first drawings of dance were created on the walls of the Trois Frères cave in France. Dancing was a body language, a form of communication. The cave paintings found in France and in Spain were prehistoric dance-like images of rituals for hunting, fertility, entertainment, or education. A Neolithic rock painting of dancers can be seen in the ravine of Oued Mertoutek in the Sahara. All of nature: the stars, the moon, the sun, the day, the night, the seasons, the birds, the animals, inspired people's dances and influenced their spiritual beliefs.

The Neolithic Age was the last part of the Stone Age; the Stone Age started about 2.5 million years ago and terminated from 40,000 to 10,000 years ago, depending on the area. During this period the human species evolved into the true Homo sapiens and entered the Neolithic Age, also called the New Stone Age.

The New Stone Age was the first period known for its human culture and the making of stone implements. It began in or around 9500 BC in the Middle East and as late as 5000 BC in other areas. By then people had changed from being hunter-gatherers (hunting meat and gathering berries and edible wild plants), living in nonpermanent settlements, to being food growers, raising a narrow range of plants such as millet, wheat, barley, and an ancient grain called spelt, domesticating and keeping dogs, pigs, sheep, goats and cows, living in permanent settlements, and using pottery. This period lasted until about 2500 BC, into the Bronze Age, when metal tools were used, and led to the rise of towns, cities, and states and the Iron Age.

The medium used to represent the current dances of the time, whatever time, whether the year 3000 BC or last year, depends, naturally, on what is available and on the latest technology. Now it is videos on the Internet, but much earlier it was sketches on pottery. A piece of Iranian pottery dating from about 3000 BC illustrates a **circle dance,** while a painting of two opposing lines of dancers decorates a water jar made around 700 BC. More recently, paintings of Native Americans from the Plains tribes and the Sioux were found on buffalo hides. Much later, in the mid-nineteenth century, oil paintings and then still photography captured some of the new dances of that period.

The shapes that dance took varied in each country and throughout the centuries and were affected by all aspects of life. Primitive man observed the animals around him; he hunted them for food and noticed their habits, strength, cunning, colors, and dance-like movements and he imitated them too. Some male birds at mating time were observed to perform very intricate mating dances to attract females. Other bird couples did synchronized movements together.

There were many dances in which the human male, too, showed off his virility and vigor to please the women by performing leaps, kicks, and acrobatics, and by lifting the woman way up as a finale. The **Bavarian-Austrian schuhplattler** was one of these. A dance that still survives in the 21st century, it is thought to be from before 3000 BC and of Neolithic, stone-age, origin. Similar stamping and leaping movements by the men occurred in the **Norwegian halling** and the **Caucasian Lezghinka**.

The **Lezghinka** dance got its name from the Lezgin people and was performed by many who lived near the Caucasian Mountains: Azerbaijanis, Georgians, Lezgins, Turkish, and others. This dance is still done today. Try to watch a wedding group from Azerbaijan performing this dance on a video on the Internet. The footwork was and still is incredible and especially impressive when the dance is performed on a chair.

**Halling**, a dance originally from Norway and parts of Sweden, is another dance that has survived. It is performed today by the Friskar Dance Co. of Norway, which has traveled to over 20 countries with that dance. **Hallgram Hanselgard**, Friskar's founder, developed the traditional halling dance in a contemporary setting with a song written by Norway's pop singer Rybak. This song, the singer, and the Friskar dancers were chosen to go to the Eurovision song and dance competition in Moscow in 2009 and they won the international finale. In this new, up-to-date version of the halling dance, the women also do the acrobatics and fancy leaps. The old version had the men doing the solos, followed by a dance for couples. (Hanselgard has now also included a halling dance in a computer game.)

In ancient times the future existence of a group was of prime importance to tribes everywhere, therefore most of them did **fertility dances** at the ceremonies related to the beginning of adolescence, to marriage, and to the birth of a child. Even today people like to go dancing to show off their grace, skill, coordination, and assets to the opposite sex while they are having a good time.

It was believed in pre-state societies that rituals, such as dancing, also helped in the task of integrating and organizing people, especially during tasks that had a delayed reward, like farming. Hunter-gatherers, by comparison, had immediate rewards. During the planting or harvesting season some communities of farmers would get together and dance. The next day all would go to work to plant or harvest crops.

Photo Plate 1-1

"Dragon in The City". Dragon Dance. Photo: Maita Ru.

"Musicians and the dancing girls from the banquet scene," 18th Dynasty, Egypt, at the tomb of Nebamun, c. 1370 BC.

"Dancing Krishna," ca. 11th century, bronze; Chola period, Asian art. Brooklyn Museum Photograph.

"Los Voladores de Papantla." Photo of Ceremonia del Volador, pre-Hispanic ritual, Mexico. Photo by Alberto Loyo.

"The Flying Men dancing on a pole." Photo of the Flying Men of Papantla. Photo by Afagundes.

Before the existence of schools or writing, rituals and dance were tools used to impart education and knowledge to the community from one generation to the next or to coordinate the activities of a community. Some examples are mentioned below:

In Australia, skilled members of aboriginal tribes performed mime and acrobatic dances to instruct and entertain.

The Chaldeans from Babylonia, now part of Iraq, exhibited their interest in astronomy and taught it in a **Dance of the Stars**. They were given credit for being the first to have started the science of astronomy. On a chosen day all would gather together and, to the sounds of gongs and bronze horns, adults would replicate the motion of the stars as the children gathered to watch. Much of this was similar to the formation of ancient Native American dances in North and Central America, although the time and place made it impossible for the Babylonians and the Native Americans to have communicated. Joseph Campbell (1904-1987), the philosopher and mythologist, found that people in widely disparate places had surprisingly similar customs and mythologies.

In Egypt, by 4000 BC, lengthy **dance-dramas** were performed to communicate with people and gods. At first this was done through hieroglyphs and tombstone frescos such as the one *(Photo Plate 1-1)* portraying dancing girls, beauteous maidens in topless bikinis, and flutists in a fresco from a mural painting from the tomb of Nebamun, a nobleman in the 18th dynasty of ancient Egypt, c. 1350 BC in Thebes, Egypt, artist unknown. Egyptian culture was advanced and complex, with knowledge of architecture, engineering, and geometry. A varied class structure existed: royal family, workers, slaves, priests, and later, professional entertainers. Judging from the hieroglyphs and paintings, their dance movements varied from simple dignified walking steps to splits, turns, somersaults and acrobatic positions such as handstands.

Live dramatic dances were performed at festivals in Egypt to educate young people about agriculture and religion. They recreated the death and rebirth of the god Osiris, the search for his bones by his wife, Isis, and his resurrection. They also represented the seasonal rising and falling cycle of the Nile River, as well as the rituals of planting and harvesting. This was a highly ritualized form of worship concerned with death and rebirth. Gradually, trained dancers assisted the priest or first dancer.

There were other dances in Egypt including a **Dance of the Stars** that was similar to that of the Chaldeans. This dance was essential for the Egyptians when planning their control of the dikes that fertilized the land. Professional pygmy dancers were imported from the interior of Africa and were known for their artistry. The Middle Eastern **belly dance** of Egypt was also of African origin. It was described in a report of 4th century dance from Memphis, Egypt, as a **rhumba-like** couples dance of exotic character. A tomb painting from Shaykh 'Abd al-Qurnah, presently in the British Museum, shows almost nude dancers who were intended to amuse the dead as they had done in their lifetime.

Egypt was unquestionably influential in spreading its culture and dancing to the Mediterranean area.

On the other side of the Mediterranean, Turkey, as it is now called, was another country possessing a wealth of **folk dances** reflecting a complex culture. Turkey is on the border between Europe and the Middle East, facing three seas and with many trade routes. Because of its location there had been invasions, conquests, and migrations since the beginning of history. At various times it was the home of diverse civilizations: the Kingdom of the Hittites (c. 1700-1180 BC), the Thracians, and the Phrygians. Alexander the Great conquered it (334-33 BC), then it was absorbed into the Roman Empire in the 1$^{st}$ century BC, invaded by Arabs, Crusaders, Mongols and the army of Timur before the Ottomans took full control in the 15$^{th}$ century *(Photo Plate 1-4)*. (Its history since 1923 is that of modern Turkey.)

Each of Turkey's regions had a different dance style that stemmed from various aspects of its culture: weddings, births, and events of rural life, love, sadness, and harvesting. In the Aegian locale the **zeybek**, a dance symbolizing courage and heroism, was popular. It varied from very slow to very fast and was in measures of 9/8, danced as a solo or by a group, and accompanied by a drum and zurna (a kind of double reed oboe).

**Bar dances**, linear dances performed outdoors in groups in the northeastern area, were different for men and women, were performed in a side-by-side formation facing the audience, and were also in the 9/8 and 5/8 measures characteristic of much Turkish folk music. Bar dances were accompanied by a duval (a kind of drum) and a zurna.

The **horon** or round dance's most usual rhythm was in 7/16. A small zurna and drum were the accompaniment. The **kolbasti** dance was popular among teenagers. The **samah** used only vocal accompaniment, no instruments. The **kaşik oyunlah** or wooden-spoon dance (wooden spoons were the accompaniment) was in measures of either 2/4 or 4/4.

And the **halay** was a dance that had all the measures of Turkish folk music and was performed in the Eastern, South Eastern, and Central regions. The costumes for Turkish dances were very colorful and the dances, even now, are varied and enjoyable to watch on the Internet.

Another group of people whose earliest dances have been traced back to the Neolithic period were the Chinese. Their dances go back to a period before the writing of Chinese characters. Colorful dancers are depicted on ceramic pots from the Sun Chia Chai excavation site in Ta-Tung County of the Chinese province of Chinghai. These are believed to be people of the Neolithic Yang-shao culture of the 4$^{th}$ millennium BC. On these ceramic pots people are depicted with locked arms and doing a group dance.

During the Shang and Chou eras of the first millennium BC there were two types of dances. The civilian ones with feathered banners represented the fruits of the day's fishing and hunting. These dances gradually evolved into religious rituals. The second type was a large-group **military dance** with coordinated forward and backward movements and the carrying of weapons. Dances not only expressed love for heavenly spirits and features of daily life but were also performed for the joy of dancing

7

Photo Plate 1-2

"A scene of a Shinto shrine dance Kagura." Author; Katsushika Hokusai (1760-1849) an ukiyo-e painter and print maker best known for his woodblock series, "Thirty-six views of Mount Fuji."

"Female figure," Egyptian, a priestess or goddess, possibly dancing at a funeral ritual. Date: 3650-3300 BC. Brooklyn Museum photograph.

"Japanese Sumo Wrestler Performing Bow Ceremony." Photo: © H. Buchholz.

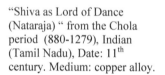

"Shiva as Lord of Dance (Nataraja) " from the Chola period (880-1279), Indian (Tamil Nadu), Date: 11th century. Medium: copper alloy.

"Hard-to-Beat Musashigawa sumo wrestlers at morning training doing ritualized dance that emphasizes teamwork." Photo: Kit Nagamura.

During the Han Dynasty (206 BC to 220 AD) the Music Bureau collected folk songs and dances, but by the 3$^{rd}$ century AD the dances of the Han people were gradually mixed with those of neighboring groups that were entering China: the Hsiung-nu, the Sienpi, and the Western Chang people. With the Tang Dynasty (618-907 AD) came greater stability and glorious dancing as the imperial court founded the Garden Academy, the Imperial Academy, and the T'ai-ch'ang Temple. The best dancers in the country performed the sumptuous **Ten-Movement Music dance** encompassing some elements of dance from China, Sinkiang, Korea, India, Persia, and Central Asia into one tremendous dance. It was the predecessor of contemporary Chinese opera and had colorful costumes and props, poetry, plot, music, and complex body movement *(Photo Plate 1-4)*.

The two most popular traditional Chinese dances, from the Han Chinese people, were the **lion dance** and the **dragon dance** *(Photo Plate 1-1)* that required from ten to fifty dancers, depending on the length of the mock dragon. The dancers used poles to support, raise, and lower it. The dragon represented wealth, power, and dignity. The lion dance used only two persons, one for the front and one for the rear, with the performers imitating a lion's movements in a lion costume. In Northern China the lion symbolized ferocity and agility; in Southern China it was a guardian, sometimes against evil spirits. In China these two dances are performed for all festive occasions and to celebrate the Chinese New Year.

The **court dances**, from the royal court of Emperor Qin of the Qin Dynasty (221-207 BC), were performed either to relate a successful battle in which the present emperor participated or just for entertainment.

In the 21$^{st}$ century, Chinese dance students often begin with ballet and/or modern and then try to take a fresh look at Chinese dance, keeping an open mind about experimentation. There are now numerous Chinese dance groups of modern Chinese dance: The Cloud Gate Dance Troupe of **Lin Hwai-min**, the New Classical Dance Troupe of **Liu Feng-haueh**, and The **Hsu Hui-mei** Dance Society which collects traditional folk dances and creates new ones with the spiritual values of the past. The **Shen Yun** Chinese Dance is a company that presents classical Chinese dance with ethnic and folk dance included for variety, using ancient instruments like the erhu and the pipa and lovely colorful costumes. The TAO Dance Theater is China's newest choreographic voice. This company was founded in 2008 by **Tao Ye** who believes in letting the audience use its imagination and in not giving away anything in the titles of his works, such as *"2,"* and *"4"* except perhaps the number of performers in a given work. The Chinese reach out to other countries in relation to the arts so that there is a constant involvement and exchange.

Music and dance have always served psychological purposes. It was found that work could be made more agreeable when accompanied by a chant, rhythm, or a rhythmic movement. In the case of Japanese rice planting, for example, Buddhists introduced chants to Japanese vocal music during the 7$^{th}$ and 8$^{th}$ centuries; ancient chants are still used by the workers while working the rice fields in a farming district like Okinawa. **Dengaku** was the name of the folk dance ritual used while planting rice. In the 14$^{th}$ century the dengaku came to the city and Japanese playwrights incorporated it into the Noh Theater performances.

Among some Native American tribes, dancing was sometimes used by medicine men to lead to trances, to altered states of consciousness, possession by spirits, the healing of others, or the performance of great feats of strength and endurance. Such a trance dance was the **sun dance** performed by Native Americans; more about them will be found in chapter three.

A West Indian **voodoo** dancer could sit on a metal frame over a hot fire without getting burned. When Indonesian **trance dancers** thrust sharp daggers against their bare chests the daggers were bent from all the force that was used, but they did not go through the chest.

Groups used dance as an element of their social life. Both men and women in Assyria (presently a division of Iraq) included dance as a component of their social life and their religious practice. In Babylonia, also a part of Iraq, **circle dances** were performed around the idol of the god being honored, with musical accompaniment. The hill and tribal people of India danced all night to celebrate community festivals and weddings.

The Etruscans from the north of Rome and up to Florence made it evident in their tomb paintings of the 5$^{th}$ and 7$^{th}$ century BC at the Tomb of the Lionesses in Tarquina, Italy, that dance was a part of their life. The women performed **funerary chain dances** and also energetic couples dances (with a courting attitude to them) as seen in those frescos.

Early Christian missionaries discovered that all people had similar dances: fertility rites, dances to ward off evil and promote goodness, fighting dances to assist warriors in battles, and some dances expressing the joy of life *(Photo Plate 1-5)*. The missionaries thought these dances were signs of the devil. People showed their knowledge about life and the world through dances. They also related to their gods through their dances and asked them for favors.

Some people created highly unusual **ceremonial dance rituals** to perform when asking the gods for favors. According to some ceramics found in Nayarit, Mexico, very attractive and potentially dangerous ceremonial dance rituals existed there, having survived from Mexico's pre-classic period (2500 BC to 200 AD).

In Mexico, besides the Aztecs and the Maya there were also the Olmecs, the Toltecs, the Zapotecs, and the Totonacs, among others. The earliest Mexicans may have been descendants of Stone Age hunter-gatherers who reached North America around 12000 BC after crossing the Bering Strait or of earlier explorers from Asia. By 10000 BC Mexico was populated, and it was involved with agriculture and with the domestication of animals soon after 5200 BC. The Egyptian pyramids had not yet been built. The Olmecs had developed a system of writing, and a calendar, and the Maya perfected this, while the Zapotec civilization, with its art, architecture, religion, and mathematics, was at its height between the third and eight centuries AD.

The Totonacs, rivals of the Aztecs, had a **ceremonial dance ritual** for communicating with the gods and nature. It was performed to ask the gods to end a drought. Supposedly the gods had not sent rain because they felt neglected by the people. This ceremonial performance was meant to make amends. The ritual, which originated with the Nahua, Huastec, and Otomi people, consisted of four men dancing on the ground, and then climbing a 30-meter pole (originally a tree selected for this purpose and with its branches removed). The four men, each with a rope tied to the pole as well as to an ankle, climb the pole, and then each man winds the rope thirteen times around his ankles. A fifth man climbs the pole, remains on a stand *(Photo Plate 1-1)* at the top of the pole, and plays a drum or flute and dances there. (Originally the four dancers, **voladores** or flying men, were dressed as birds, macaws, parrots, quetzals and eagles and represented the gods of fire, earth, water, and air.) The four voladores then launch out, backwards, away from the top of the pole, headfirst. Since the ropes are wound around the ankles of the four voladores, the men turn in the air as they descend. Each volador circles the pole 13 times, the total of 52 representing the weeks of the year. Each volador swings from the rope tied to his ankles and goes around a pole that is 100 feet high as he gradually descends to the ground. At the end of these men's descent, the fifth man descends from the top of the pole and then there is a final dance on the ground to end this performance. At one time this dance had spread as far as Nicaragua, but today it is mainly the Totonac people of Papantla who perform it.

To help the dance survive, UNESCO has named this ceremonial dance ritual an Intangible Cultural Heritage, thus obliging Mexico to promote it and keep it alive. Mexico has done so by establishing a school for children of voladores. They start at ages 8 to 10 and prepare for 10 – 12 years to become voladores. Groups have performed this ceremonial dance for cultural events in cities such as Monterey, Milwaukee, and Barcelona. (For those of you who may not consider this to be a dance, please reconsider the works of post-modern dance choreographer **Elizabeth Streb,** as well as **Trisha Brown's** *Walking on Walls*.)

There are several indigenous Aztec dances that are still performed in Mexico City during holidays, using flutes, maracas, drums, seashells and voices as accompaniment. But now European instruments often replace these.

The best known of Mexico's numerous folk dances is, of course, the **jarabe tapatío (Mexican hat dance)**, a dance of love and courtship with lots of flirting. It consists of many hopping steps as well as heel and toe tapping movements and was originally choreographed in the 19th century to celebrate the end of the Mexican Revolution. **Anna Pavlova** popularized this dance even more when she created a version of it in pointe shoes. In 1924 the Mexican Secretary of Education, José Vasconcelos, declared it the national dance of Mexico to be taught in all Mexico's public schools as a means of tying together Mexico's diverse ethnic groups. On the other hand, the Catholic Church at that time considered it lustful and scandalous.

Another region where people love to dance is the Punjab area overlapping India and Pakistan where the **bhangra dance** originated. It was related to ancient harvest celebrations as well as to social issues. The movements in the bhangra reflected the way the farming was done. People beat the drum, the dhol, and the smaller drum, the dholki, played a single-stringed instrument called the iktar, sang, and danced for special occasions. There still exist several varieties of bhangra dances: **daankara**, a celebratory wedding dance in which sticks are tapped together in time to the rhythm of the drum; **dhamal**, a folk dance with arms high overhead, head and hands shaking, and much yelling; **luddi,** a dance in which participants circle around the drummer in a snakelike manner, and many others. All of the bhangra dances are high-energy, and colorful costumes are worn. These too are worth watching on the Internet.

Dance has always been a part of Hindu rituals: farmers danced for a good harvest; the community danced to celebrate a birth or a wedding.

The Chola period in India was outstanding for its bronze sculpture and also for its architecture *(Photo Plate 1-1)*. The sculptures of the 11th and 12th centuries showed much grace and classical form, as did the bronze statue of the **Lord of the Dance, Shiva Nataraja** shown here *(Photo Plate 1-2)*, from Tamil Nadu, India, from the Chola period in the 11th century, artist unknown. In this statue, Shiva is executing the dance **ananda tandava**. Surrounded by a flaming aureole, Shiva is shown in his incarnation as Nataraja, or the Lord of the Dance, dancing at the center of the universe on the powerless demon-dwarf Apasmara who represented ignorance and materialism. Shiva is holding a two-sided drum to keep time; the flame stands for destruction since Shiva is the god of both destruction and regeneration. His lower hands show hope and protection. His hair is fanning out to the sides from all the energy in his dancing and turning, connecting him to the universe. The purpose of his dance was to create, to protect, to embody, to release and to destroy the primary forces of the universe at regular intervals.

The lost wax technique was used in making these sculptures in the Chola period. Bees' wax was mixed with a little oil, kneaded and used to fashion wax models. These were then coated with clay from termite hills, dried, and fired in the oven with cow dung cakes; the melted wax flowed out; melted bronze was then poured into the empty clay mold. When the bronze had filled the crevices, hardened, and cooled, the mold was broken off. It could only be used once. No exact copies could be made. Shiva, lord of the cosmic dance of creation and destruction, has had many bronze casts made of him. For festivals these statues were decorated with garlands, jewels, and silk cloth. Holes at the bottom at the base of the statues were used for inserting poles for greater effortlessness in carrying the heavier statues during festivities.

Finally people started writing about dance. One of the earliest texts about dances was the *Natya Shastra* believed to be by the Muni (sage) Bharata and written sometime between 200 BC and 200 AD. It was an ancient Indian treatise on the performing arts, written in Sanskrit, encompassing theater, drama, and dance. It mentioned various **mudras**, or hand gestures, as well as gait and movements of limbs and had four categories: secular, ritual, abstract, and interpretive. Each and every Indian dance and all mudras, body positions, and expressive acting were rooted in this text. The distinct hand gestures were used to convey to the onlookers what the dancer was trying to get across. Percussive instruments and ankle bells provided accompaniment for the dance.

"Relief of Carved Apsaras," Angkor Wat, Cambodia, 12<sup>th</sup> century.  Photo by Scott Dunbar.

Terracotta "Statuette of a veiled dancer;" Hellenistic period, Greek pontic period. Metropolitan Museum photograph.

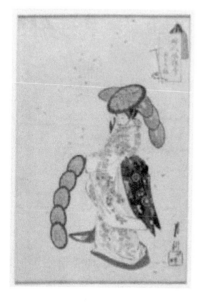

"Odori Dancer," woodblock print, from "Pictures of customs of Elder Sisters,' by Ogata Gekko, 1850-1920. Odori dance, a traditional Japanese dance, started about 220 years ago. It varies from an Odori sparrow dance  to  Bon Odori to welcome the spirits of the dead.

"Terpsichore, Muse of Dance and Music," 1730, by Jean-Marc Nattier (1685-1766), French painter who specialized in portraits.  Oil on canvas.

The origin of **kagura dances**, the foundation for all Japanese dance forms, was described in the *Kojiki* (*Records of Ancient Matters*), an old Japanese historical document dating back to the 8th century (711-712) and composed by Ö no Yasumaro at the request of the Empress of Japan. It begins with the origin of the world, the creation of the islands of Japan, and the descent of the gods and goddesses to Japan. These ritual and formal kagura dances were executed in a variety of sacred locations on numerous special occasions *(Photo Plate 1-2)*. The artist of this scene is Katsushika Hokusai (1760-1849), an ukiyo-e painter and print-maker best known for his wood block series, *Thirty-six views of Mount Fuji*.

Kagura dances were performed at important shrines, for court music festivals, and during harvest. Kagura dance also included several folk dances, such as the lion dance, **shishi kagura**, in which participants wore lion masks and costumes and danced through the town. Kagura dances were a reenactment of the dances that were performed in Japanese mythology to entice the sun goddess, Amaterasu, out of her cave to bring the sunlight back to the universe. An 1857 painting of the Japanese sun goddess, *Amaterasu emerging from a cave,* is by Utagawa (Toyokuni III) Kunisada (1786-1865). The kagura dances were over 1,500 years old and were accompanied by flute, drum, and brass. Modern kagura dances are still performed at festivals and shrines to honor local gods to the music of pipes and drums by dancers wearing brightly colored kimonos.

Geishas, meaning performing artists, also used these ageless traditional dances of Japan years later in their profession. A geisha had to know how to sing, dance, and play traditional instruments and had to be a skilled conversationalist (*Photo Plate 1-5)*. The art of being a geisha originated in the 17th century. Young girls and women were trained to provide light entertainment for a man or a group of men. They learned many of their skills by being apprenticed to trained geishas for several years and also from the housemother of the geisha house. *Geisha with Fan,* 1894, by the artist Edward Atkinson Hornel (1864-1933) is a lovely painting of a geisha's performance *(Photo Plate 7-6)*. In the 1920's there were approximately 80,000 geishas while now there are just a few thousand, all in the Kyoto and Tokyo regions of Japan. Low economy, lack of interest in traditional arts, and the huge expense of being entertained by a trained geisha caused this decline.

Dance in one country was affected by dance in other countries, either neighboring ones or those through which its armies had traveled. Hand movements and the use of masks, for example, often varied from one area or country to another. Dance in much of Southeast Asia included movements of the hands as well as the feet, so that Sri Lanka, due to its geographical location, was easily influenced by the traditions in South Asia. Masks were used in ritual exorcism and in **dance-drama**. South Asian dance comprised many types of dance; they might be based on the martial arts, or be executed in deep knee bent position, or have whirling movements or very complex hand positions. In South Asia, dance and acting were inseparable, therefore an actor, whether classical or folk, had to be able to sing, dance and do mime. The **lion dance**, originating in China, could be found in Korea, Japan, India, Sri Lanka, and Bali.

In Indian temples, as well as in those of Indonesia and Indochina, bas-reliefs of gods as dancers can be seen. Cutting the figures or scenes into the walls of stone, unknown artists made bas-reliefs so the sculpted images stood out and were practically detached from the wall. These bas-reliefs were of **apsaras**, very beautiful female celestial beings gifted in dance, different from the devatas who just stood and guarded the temples. The apsaras, wives of the court servants of Indra who were dominant in the ancient religion of the Veda, danced to the music played by their husbands, usually in the palace of the gods. There, each of the twenty-six apsaras represented a different element of the performing arts. They were also the guardians of fallen heroes. They were similar to Greek sirens in that they too could entice men to their death. However, in Hindu and Buddhist mythology, apsaras were the spirit of the clouds and waters. Apsaras can also be found in Balinese dances and in the Javanese court dances of Bedhoya. In the 8th century Borobudur temple of Java, Indonesia, apsaras and devatas can be seen flying to heaven. The 12th century Angkor Wat temple at Angkor *(Photo Plate 1-3)* in Cambodia shows three apsaras in the bas-relief in the temple called the Bayon; the artist is unknown. The temple has at least 1,860 apsaras carved on high towers, pillars, or walls, often holding lotus flowers.

The Royal Ballet of Cambodia, formerly called the Khmer Classical Dance Company *(Photo Plate 1-4)*, was inspired by the dance of the celestial apsaras of mythology. This dance was often called **apsara dance**, and it descended from the **court dances** of the Angkorian monarchy. The apsara dance is an important part of the culture of Cambodia and its neighbors, Thailand and Laos. Its graceful movements convey classical myths and religious stories. UNESCO declared the dance to be a masterpiece of culture and was planning for its regeneration when in 2003 the Khmer Rouge almost caused this dance tradition to be destroyed. Presently The Royal Ballet of Cambodia is still performing scenes of dance influenced by the apsaras in the Angkor Wat temple.

Dance in Bali and Indonesia dates as far back as written history; its heritage originated in Java but after the 16th century it became important in Bali, especially in religious ceremonies where it served to mollify and entertain the gods and goddesses. The epic of the Ramayana, an early story written in Sanskrit between the 5th and the 4th century BC gave us the teachings of Hindu sages as well as philosophical elements. Its influence can be seen in the multiple versions of dance as the story is told in Balinese dance, Javanese dance, Thai dance, Burmese dance, Jain dance and Nepal dance, among others, and often with completely different endings.

The Old Testament mentioned the singing and dancing by the Jewish people as being joyous, with leaping and turning movements. The types of dances that were done were **circular ring-dances** or **processional marches** as well as hopping and **whirling dances**. Although the prohibition of graven images explains the lack of visual art, there is a very attractive piece of art depicting *Miriam's dance (Photo Plate 1-5)* based on Exodus 15:20, *Then Miriam, the prophetess, Aaron's sister took a timbrel in her hand and all the women followed her with timbrels and dancing*. The Old Testament mentions that dancing occurred on special occasions, after the Israelites crossed the Red Sea (Ex. 15:20), for example, and (Psalms 149.3) to show joy and praise God.

Photo Plate 1-4

"Artists in Khmer Classical Dance" performing apsara dance in Siem Reap, Cambodia, in traditional costume. Photo by Det-anan.

"Female Dancer;" China, Western Han dynasty (206 BC-AD 9); Earthenware with pigment. The unknown artist conveyed a feeling of motion in his sculpture. Date: 2$^{nd}$ century BC.

"Relief with a dancing Maenad." Early imperial Augustan ca. 27 BC-14 AD (adaptation of a work attributed to Kallimachos). Photo by Schecter Lee.

Greek-Attic "Hydria," early 4$^{th}$ century BC Ceramic.

"Kocek dancer with Tambourine," an aspect of the Ottoman Empire from the 17$^{th}$ to the 19$^{th}$ century. Artist unknown.

At Orthodox Hassidic Jewish weddings men and women also danced, but not together, and this is still true today. The men dance with the bridegroom, and the women dance with the bride. Later a piece of cloth or a handkerchief was used to separate the sexes as the bride and groom each held on to opposite corners of the cloth. Folk dances from other cultures also occasionally used a handkerchief to connect the dancers.

Dance was highly regarded by the ancient Greeks. According to their beliefs, nine muses guided the arts and two gods presided over dancing: Apollo, the sun god who also looked after philosophy and art, and Dionysus, the god of wine, revelry, fertility, and wild abandon. One goddess, **Terpsichore** *(Photo Plate 1-3),* was the sole goddess or muse who supervised dancing and inspired the creators of dance. She was often shown accompanying a dance on the lyre with her music. She was the mother of the mythological Greek sirens. The word muse meant the one who inspired a creative work. **George Balanchine**, the master choreographer of the 20th century, had several "muses" in the course of his long career.

Mainland Greeks loved dancing and would burst into dance for no apparent reason *(Photo Plate 1-3, 4, and 5)*. Greek **folk dance** traveled with the army and could be found in several countries. In Sparta, Greek warriors had to learn to dance **pyrrhic war dances** as part of their training. These fell into four categories: one had rapid shifting movements of the feet to prepare for hand-to-hand combat; another was a mock battle but in dance-like formation; also there was one with leaps and vaults in preparation for scaling fortresses; and last was the one in dignified formation to meet the enemy as a group, or with interlocked shields for protection. Socrates, a philosopher, said that those who honored the gods most beautifully in dance were the best in war. He felt that dance was the best training for a warrior, perhaps because both warriors and dancers had to think on their feet.

Early Greek theater had a chorus of dancers, all male, who would play women's roles in dramatic performances. The Greek chorus used gesture and dance to accompany words. The dance included heroes and subjects from Homer's legends. In comedies, the **kordax**, a lewd masked dance, was popular. In the tragedies the chorus executed an imposing dance with flute accompaniment. Greeks also danced to pay respect to their gods, such as Apollo, Artemis, and Dionysus. The **choral dances** included some that were dedicated to Apollo. These came to Athens by way of Crete and included one in which naked boys imitated wrestling. Women took part in a regal **round dance** in honor of the deities; it was a chorus of virgins and consisted of women stamping the ground as they turned around in recurring convulsive movements. As in many primitive dances, these showed signs of demoniacal possession. This ecstatic dance belonged to the cult of Dionysus. Many of the earliest Greek dances dated back to ancient mystical rites and the worship of mother earth.

You probably remember hearing about teenagers' reaction to Elvis Presley and the Beatles in the twentieth century; seeing Presley or the Beatles or hearing their names would cause the youngsters to scream excitedly. Would you believe ancient Greeks did the same thing, but with regard to Dionysus? In the tragedy *Bacchae* Euripides described how female worshippers of Dionysus would sing and dance in a state of exhilaration and

Photo Plate 1-5

"Traditional Cretan Dancers in colorful Cretan Greek outfits." Photo by Crete TOURnet.

"A Kyoto Geisha," 1796. Artist: Yamaguchi Soken, Japanese (1750-1818). Edo Period. Hanging scroll; ink and color on silk.

"Miriam's Dance," Art Quilt (after Hodler) by Marilyn Belford. Part of her Bible Series.

"Painting of a Dancer," Early 19th century, Iran. Oil and gold on canvas. Artist unknown.

delight. In Rome these women were called **bacchantes**; in Greece they were called **maenads** as seen here in a relief created between 27 BC and 14 AD *(Photo Plate 1-4)*. This is a Roman copy of a Greek relief attributed to Kallimachos, ca. 415-400 BC. The maenads sometimes dressed in animal skins and went to the mountains in a state of extravagant madness brought about by their spiritual wedding to the god Dionysus, performing rites of music and dance. They carried an object typical of his followers, the thyrsos, that contained a fennel stalk topped with a pinecone and ivy berries. The relief shown here with a dancing maenad was made of pentelic marble, a very fine marble obtained from the quarries of Mount Pentelikos near Athens. In the 4th and 5th centuries this marble was used for all the important monuments and statues near Athens.

Many of the old Greek folk dances, such as the **hasapikos**, went from one region to another as people adopted what they saw in their travels, or wars. That explains why some dances, with slight variations, are found in several different places. The geography influenced these dances too. People living near the sea had rolling movements resembling the men working on a boat at sea, or the motions of life on the Black Sea, or the movements of a fish, as in the **tik dance**. People living on mountains had dances with movements imitating someone leaping from one mountain ledge to another, as in the **tsamiko**.

It is easy to find references to Greek dance. The Greeks themselves had a lot to say about it. Homer mentioned the dance in the *Iliad* and in the *Odyssey*. Aristotle stated in the *Poetics* that dance was rhythmic movement whose purpose was to represent men's characters as well as what they did and suffered. And, in fact, that is exactly what the dance did in the Greek theater and what **Martha Graham,** a modern dancer, choreographed later. Plato (c. 428-348/47 BC), another philosopher, said in *Laws*, that to sing well and dance well was to be well educated.

Xenophon (430/1-355 BC), a historian, described a narrative dance of his time about the union of the legendary heroine Ariadne with Dionysus. The arts, to the Greeks, represented man's spirit, mind, and body and were an indispensable part of him.

Greek philosophers, statesmen, and generals used to do solo dances before an audience of thousands on important occasions or after a victorious military campaign. Can you imagine a similar situation today?

Proficient amateurs such as Sophocles, the poet, or Aristophanes, the playwright, performed these dances till the end of the century, when a class of acrobats, jugglers and dancers took over.

Illustrations of Greek dancing can be seen on lovely Greek vases *(Photo Plate 1-4)*. They show running and skipping movements done with effortlessness. The Greeks encouraged dancing.

By comparison, Romans who danced were looked upon with suspicion and considered to be effeminate and dangerous. In 150 BC the Roman emperor, Scipio Africanus, ordered the many dancing schools in Rome to be closed. The Romans did not really care to dance; they preferred to watch others doing it. Cicero (106-43 BC) truly stated the Romans' opinion when he said that no one danced unless he was insane.

For the Romans, although dance was a necessary part of festivals, pantomime was much more important. The Romans had conquered Algerians, Gauls, Greeks, Iberians, Syrians, and Teutons; that was a large variety of languages, so pantomime proved useful. The two **dancer-mimes, Bathyllus of Alexandria** and **Pylades of Sicily,** became star performers of Augustan Rome. Although the Romans used professional dancers as traveling entertainers, dance suffered under Rome. The citizens of Rome wanted spectacles that were vicious and brutal. The Circus Maximus in Rome could hold an audience of three hundred and fifty thousand. There were all sorts of performers, acrobats, singers, dancers, and jugglers to entertain the public while at the same time showing some very cruel shows.

One could say that in Rome the punishment for criminals was death by dancing. Plutarch recorded one of these events: criminals, confined in an enclosed arena, were dressed in costumes specially treated with a material that would make their costumes burst into flames after the prisoners had danced for a certain length of time. They would die an excruciating death while the audience watched. Dance had certainly degenerated in Rome. Two Roman emperors, Caligula and Nero, were especially identified with these atrocious types of games.

# 2

# Dance in the Middle Ages

Now came the years of the great Roman Empire's decline, followed by the Dark Ages from the 2$^{nd}$ to the 9$^{th}$ centuries AD, the Early Middle Ages – the 10$^{th}$ and 11$^{th}$ centuries AD, and then the Middle Ages – 12$^{th}$ to 15$^{th}$ centuries AD. Life seemed dismal. Warfare, barbarism, and violence came with the expansions and conquests by the Vikings, Huns, Barbarians, and Muslims in the 7$^{th}$ and 8$^{th}$ centuries, and with the Crusades from the 11$^{th}$ through the 13$^{th}$ centuries AD. Religious persecutions were certainly in the air (and forget about "do unto others as you would have them do unto you!" The point of the Crusades was to get rid of everyone whose religious ideas differed from yours.) There was a tremendous drop in population, partly caused by frequent invasions, but also due to the cold period of the Dark Ages from 300 to 700 AD that caused farmers, already greatly overburdened, to leave their farms because of the low agricultural yields caused by the declining temperatures. There was famine. Cities were overcrowded, with the resultant consequence of shortages of water and food and of many diseases. (Any remaining Roman public water baths increased the propagation of infectious diseases at this time.)

One might think that no one could have wanted to dance, but quite the opposite occurred. The peasants, and others, were used to their pagan dances and wished to indulge in them. The Church was primarily concerned with saving souls, nevertheless they did try to oblige and find a place for **pagan dance** in Christian worship while attempting to maintain their authority and forbid any dances involving what they considered to be movements of ecstasy or lasciviousness such as the ones the Romans and Greeks had sometimes used. The Church was not always successful, partially because opinions about dancing were so mixed. In 350 AD, for example, St. Basil of Caesarea said that dancing was the most dignified action of the angels, and that was exactly what Dante said about it almost 1,000 years later. St. Augustine (354-430 AD) was against dance. But in spite of St. Augustine's usual influence in the medieval church, dancing as part of church rituals went on for centuries. It was not till the Reformation (Martin Luther and the Calvinists) in the 16$^{th}$ century that dance was completely removed from worship. (However, in the 20$^{th}$ century dance again began making its appearance in Catholic and Protestant churches as liturgical dance, the idea being that prayer, worship, praise of the Lord, and joy could be shown with the whole body and not just with words. Various sects differed in their attitude toward this thought. Modern dancers Ruth St. Denis and Ted Shawn both advocated a church service that included liturgical dance (see chapter seven).

During the Dark and Middle Ages the clergy even performed dances inside the church for Mass at Easter, All Saints' Day, and Christmas while the congregation watched. Also, people performed popular **sacred dances** during All Saints' Day, weddings, funerals, and religious festivals. These were either processions or round dances. When there was heavy drinking for these occasions during the Dark Ages and the Early Middle Ages, then the church disapproved. Inasmuch as **round dances**, especially, seemed to imply equality, bishops who had originally joined in the dancing at these festivities gradually stopped doing so since participation in the dancing threatened the hierarchy of the new developing church. And so, most of the time the church censored such dancing, but not always. They seemed undecided, and besides, people simply did not follow the church's dictates.

The festival for the Summer Solstice, the longest day of the year, was another popular festival with dancing, leaping over fires and through bonfires while holding burning brooms. The church may not have approved, but this festive occasion went on till the late 15th century.

The yearly Feast of Fools, which started in the 5th century and lasted through the 16th when Charles VII (Charles of Ponthieu) of France and the Church put a stop to it, actually dated back to the Romans who had the habit, once a year, of allowing slaves and owners to more or less change places. In Europe this had eventually become a burlesque of church service, in which the lower clergy and church members made fun of the bishops while singing bawdy songs and dancing.

In the 9th century, the Holy Roman Emperor, Charlemagne, opposed dance in general and banned it. However, many people disregarded the ban. The Teutons had a tradition of dancing to celebrate the end of winter and the beginning of spring with its longer days and increased daylight, and they continued to do so; simply changing the name of the occasion and secularizing the dance often made it more acceptable. This was probably the case with the popular Traunstein sword dance.

The **Traunstein sword dance** of Germany was such a dance, celebrating the beginning of spring and the end of winter through dance. Sword dances have been recorded throughout history since the **pyrrhic war dances** of ancient Greece. They existed in the Middle East, Pakistan, India, China, Japan, Korea, England, and Scotland. In Germany, the Traunstein sword dance, dating to 1530, depicted Spring symbolically, winning the battle with Winter, in dance, and then the person representing Spring was held high up on a platform of horizontal swords.

But sword dances, usually performed by men, were not all the same. Some tested a man's agility by having him perform difficult steps quickly between highly sharpened swords that were placed on the ground (*Photo Plate 2-2*). Other dances were executed in round dance formation with each man holding his own sword in his right hand and that of the person in front of him in his left hand. The dance called for the men to leap over or pass under the swords, turning or twisting as necessary.

Dance continued to be indulged in by those newly converted to Christianity who had previously followed pagan rites that included dancing.

Photo Plate 2-1

"Dance of Death," Woodcut by
Michael Wolgemut, illustration
for Hartman Schedel's
"Chronicle of the World,"
1493.
.

"Napoli Tarantella" by Giorgio Sommer. It is a collage of images shot
by Sommer himself.

Muffin Cat. In Medieval times
cats were considered to be
associated with Satan.
Hundreds or more were killed;
rodents multiplied and spread
diseases, and people went on
dance crazes as a form of
escapism. Photo: Helene
Andreu

"Masquerade Dance with Torches." Woodcut by Albrecht Dürer,
probably 1516.

Kempe performing Morris Dance,
Cover of book: "Kempe's Nine Daies
Wonder," 1600, by  William Kempe.

For example, ancient Ukrainian dances were really **agricultural dance games** done in a circle and connected to the cult of that life-giving power, the sun. In early autumn the dances imitated agricultural activities – harvesting by the women, and using the scythe by the men. These dances, in a circle, led to solo and pair dances and to dances dealing with daily life, like serfdom. Then came the traveling professional dancers who performed at public squares and for the nobility in their castles. Music was gradually added to keep the rhythm; the choreography was based on the meaning of the lyrics. Different regions of the country had slightly different dances.

In the early centuries there were the Germanic and Frankish Kingdoms, and in the east, Byzantium. Dance was often a part of the religious service in eastern churches as it had been in the early Christian church.

Feudal lords returning from crusades in the east came back with silks and damasks. Until the 12th century, garments had been short-sleeved tunics, loose trousers, and a wide cloak for the men; women had worn long shapeless dresses over an under-bodice with tight-fitting sleeves. But after the Crusades men had close fitting hose to show off their handsome legs and wore embroidered garments that revealed the shape of the body; women also had colorful garments and long gowns with a décolletage. The city of Paris led the world in fashion. The lowest of the vassals, however, still wore the simple pre-Crusades garments.

By the middle of the 12th century there were three classes – the nobility, the peasants, and the clergy. These can be seen in the manuscript illuminations and tapestries of the Middle Ages.

The feudal lords and the Church were the authority for education and morals. The Church disapproved of dancing and theatrical entertainment, nevertheless dancing was part of the worship in the 4th and 5th centuries and until the 12th century. In Spain the clergy were forbidden to dance, but for important occasions religious dances continued. In general, when dance was performed to honor the Church it was praised, but if a dance was irreverent, such as the **Dance of Death, Totentanz,** from Germany, or the **Witch's Dance**, then the Church condemned it.

In the ritual of the Dance of Death *(Photo Plate 2-1)* the leader, representing death and costumed as a skeleton, danced in an unattractive manner and compelled all, regardless of rank, to follow him as he led them in a dance around and back to the graves in the cemetery. It was considered to be the beginning of democracy; death leveled all ranks. Paintings of this ritual were common on the walls of the churchyards and cemeteries. The earliest depiction, now lost, was a mural for the Cimetière des Saints Innocents in Paris, 1424-25. Long after, a set of seventeen woodcuts of the Dance of Death based on these mural paintings was published in several editions. Holbein the Younger (1497-1543), a Northern Renaissance German painter, was thought to have been the artist until people realized that he had not yet been born. In any case, Holbein's Dance of Death Alphabet was first published as wooden sheets with Bible guides in 1524. (The woodcutter was Hans Lutzelburger; The Trechsel Brothers published both Holbein's Dance of Death and the Old Testament with his woodcuts, for the Frellon Brothers in Lyons, France, in 1538.)

Michael Wolgemut (1434-1519), a late Gothic painter and printmaker of Nuremberg, Germany, was discovered to have been the artist who created *The Dance of Death* in 1493 for a German printed edition for *Liber chronicanum* by Hartmann Schedel and then for a Latin edition that same year, 1493. Various depictions of this ritual were to be found. They served to remind people, including those unable to read, that death could occur at any moment from famine, disease, fire and wars, and to be penitent and ready; what better way to go than while dancing. *The Dance of Death* even inspired Saint Saens, a French composer, to write a piece of music, *Danse Macabre,* much later, in the nineteenth century.

At the beginning of the 12th century, legends of vampires, werewolves, and ghosts existed, and sometimes dances were performed during wakes or after a burial to prevent the dead from coming back to life. Conversion to the new religion did not do away with the old superstitions.

Due to the numerous epidemics, deaths, and acts of violence that had followed the decline of the Roman Empire into the Dark Ages and the Middle Ages there was a great preoccupation with death. Cats were believed to be associated with Satan, so hundreds of cats, if not more, were killed with the consequence that rats were free to roam and propagate without predators like cats to do away with them *(Photo Plate 2-1)*. This resulted in the spread of diseases such as the Black Plague, anthrax, typhoid, cholera, and the death of millions of people who were infected and died; the population of Europe went down from 450 million to 365 million in 1400.

The mood was dark with disease, famine, fires, and wars destroying whole villages in Europe. Meanwhile the living went on dance crazes as a form of escapism, relieving their emotions and living life to the fullest. These frenzied **dance manias** reached their highest point in the Middle Ages during the 14th and 15th centuries; they were considered to be dance epidemics and continued through the 17th century.

The height of the dancing mania **(danseomania)** occurred at the time of the Black Plague in 1349. However, it began in the 11th century and affected children as well as adults. In 1237 a group of German children danced from village to village with many dying as they went. In 1278 a bridge at Marburg, Germany, collapsed from the weight of the people dancing across it; they all drowned. The dance craze was also called **St. Vitus's dance** in Germany, Italy, and the Lowlands; it spread from city to city. People danced as though bewitched, foaming, making ear-piercing sounds, and leaping until they collapsed on the ground; all the rites of exorcism had no effect in getting rid of their demons. Some thought the dancing mania was due to a fear of death and the plague, or that it was a result of having had the plague, or that these people were suffering from ergotism, a toxic condition due to eating grain products infected with the ergot fungus that made its victims react with fitful, uncontrollable movements. In Italy it was thought to be from the bite of the Apulian spider and was called tarantism, supposedly cured by dancing the **tarantella** to tarantella music *(Photo Plate 2-1 and 2-2)*. The rhythm, rapid and ever more so, was believed to cause the poison to spread throughout the body and the body to "sweat it out" in the dance.

Photo Plate 2-2

A participant takes part in the sword dancing event while a piper provides the musical accompaniment at the Ballater Highland Games in Aberdeenshire. Photo: Paul Tomkins.

"Tarantellatänzer und Mandolinenspieler" (Tarantella Dancer and Mandolin Player), by Anton Romako, Austrian (1832-1889), watercolor over pencil on paper.

"
.

"The Gavotte, a Country Dance," pen drawing by Randolph Caldecott for "Breton Folk, an Artistic Tour of Brittany" by Henry Blackburn, 1880. The gavotte became popular in courts in France and England in the 17th and l8th centuries. It was referred to later in the musical "1776" and in the 1967 movie "How to Succeed in Business Without Really Trying."

"Morris dancers with maypole, pipe and taborer," page 631 of Chambers' "Book of Days," Vol. I, 1869, Robert Chambers, editor.

"Figure des Sereines," by Jacques Patin, designer/engraver, 1581, from the chariot (designed like a fountain) used by Catherine de Medici to take Queen Louise, the ladies and musicians to "Le Ballet Comique de La Reine."

The fact that people felt compelled to dance uncontrollably reinforced the Church's opinion of dance as something pagan. The Bishop of Paris forbade dance in general; but the Church sold dance indulgences, and the Church was disinclined to enforce the laws prohibiting dance; they made money selling these indulgences, which were exemptions or dispensations from a Church law. In later years the Church's disapproval of any particular dance proved to be an incentive for more people to indulge in that dance. Hence, dance, despite or due to the church, managed to continue into the Renaissance and through to the 21st century.

At this time folk dancing was an important part of the life of the common people. They amused themselves by dancing. **Folk dance** was their dance and it provided a diversion and an outlet for their emotions.

The Lithuanians had never written down their folk dances. Many years later they lost them when their country was occupied by the Soviet Union and by Germany, which meant that several generations had no opportunity to learn them. They felt the loss to such a point that countless years after, when they were finally free of occupation, they wrote folk songs and dances for their people to learn, even though these were not their original traditional dances.

In the Transcarpathian region south of the Carpathian Mountains, a lot of the older dances were also lost, and ethnographers and choreographers were used to figure out what a number of these could have been and to put them together again.

The formation for folk dances, usually performed outdoors and by peasants at that time, was as follows: a long chain of dancers would dance while holding hands and moving in an open or closed circle or a line *(Photo Plate 2-3)*, the idea being to keep the good spirits in and to let the bad ones out. Everyone seemed to know that the spirits would not go in the opposite direction; that is, the good spirits always stayed in while the bad ones always remained outside the circle.

The **round dances** of the peasants were noted for the joy, passion, pantomimic expression, stomping, cavorting movements, and for the singing by the participating dancers. This can be seen in *Round Dance at Aninoasa (Photo Plate 2-5)*, painted in 1890 by Theodore Aman (1831-1891), a Romanian painter whose style was considered to be a predecessor of Impressionism in Romania.

A popular dance that was executed either in a line or a closed circle was the **branle**, called **brawl** by the English, and **brando** by the Italians. It consisted of a sideward balancing movement and a chainlike joining of hands. It had many variations to suit young and old.

**Couples dances** using pantomime also existed but were considered somewhat scandalous. **Courtship dances** that included pantomime were based on courtship gestures. These included the **Austrian landler** and the **Spanish fandango.** The **landler**, originating in Bavaria, involved the lady being turned rapidly under the man's hand while in a close position.

The Spanish fandango *(Photo Plate 2-3)* is thought to have been of either African, Moorish, West Indian, or Latin American origin. Carlo Blasis (1803-1878), author of *The Code of Terpsichore* (1830), said the moors had received that dance from Africa and that it resembled the African **chica** dance.

The Philippines, a Spanish colony for over 300 years, had a fandango dance called the **pandango**. They did not use castanets but had glasses with candles inside and would swirl these over their heads while dancing.

In Portugal the **fandango** is usually done with two male dancers facing each other, showing off how light they are on their feet and how extensive their repertoire of foot movements is, somewhat like what tap dancers might do.

The Brazilians also had a **fandango** *(Photo Plate 2-5)*, probably because they had been under Portuguese rule for many years – from 1500 to 1820.

The Spanish **fandango** became popular in Europe in the 18th century and is still danced today in Spain, Portugal, southern France, Latin America, and Mexico. The men  can snap fingers, clap hands, stamp feet, or play castanets to keep the rhythm.

Because folk dance was of a social nature, dancers changed partners frequently and so the dance provided communication between people. It also developed rhythmic and motor skills as well as poise and self-confidence.

The Scottish had the **Highland fling** with arms flinging up in the air, and the Irish had their step dance with fancy footwork, stiff upper bodies, and arms down at the sides. These dances were believed to have stemmed from religious rituals.

Folk dances also reflected the climate, music, beliefs, and history of the people. Frigid climates had strong, energetic movements; warm climates had more fluid, slow movements while temperate climates had a mixture of energetic and quiet movements. People who lived on plains had dances that traveled and covered space. Those from isolated mountains tended to dance in one place.

**Sufi whirling** (dance of the Whirling Dervishes) was not actually a folk dance but a form of meditation that was physically active and that originated in the 12th century in Konya, Turkey, inspired by the Mevlevi Sufi sage and mystic Jalaluddin Rumi (1207-1273). As he whirled he repeated the name of God until he fell into a trance. The dancer whirled from left to right *(Photo Plate 2-5)*, to the sound of flutes. It is now performed throughout the world and is also found in the works of the American postmodern dancer **Laura Dean** who has similar spins, without focusing, in much of her work.

Of great importance in dance was the attire of the dancer. The costume of a people was determined by climate and geography. It protected the body from the elements and suited the work of its owner. The variety of dance movement was limited, depending on the material and cut of the footwear, skirt, trousers, and jacket worn by the dancer. The barefoot dancer of Southeastern Asia had greater freedom and balance than dancers of the **Austrian landler** wearing nonflexible, heavy nailed boots.

28

Photo Plate 2-3

"Performances by Kocek acrobats, singers, dancers and a tightrope-walker," from "Surname-i Vehbi," (The Book of Festival by Vehbi), illustrations by Abdulcelil Levni Celebi in 18th century Istanbul.

A Spanish folk dance, "the Spanish Fandango," ca. 1810, by French painter Pierre Chasselat (1753-1814).

"Local residents do Attan Dance," a traditional line dance of Afghanistan. Photo by Rahmat Alizada, Ghazni.

"Three couples in a circle dance," pen and brown ink with watercolor. Artist unknown, German, ca. 1515.

La Bourrée d'Auvergne," ca. 1906. Artist unknown. Here shown in a postcard.

Some of the earliest folk dances were **hobbyhorse dances**, as seen in Basque folk dances that were performed during carnivals, as well as in some of the English **morris** dances.

The **morris dance** was one of the earliest English folk dances. It was based on a Spanish dance, the **moresca** or **morisca,** which probably came from the Spanish word morisco, meaning Moor. The performers would put on blackface, especially in an old French version that was meant to represent the Christians fighting the Moors, who would be the ones in blackface. The **moresca** dance can be seen at the end of Monteverdi's opera *Orfeo* and near the beginning of Mozart's *Don Giovanni,* depending on the current choreographer. But by the 15th century the moresca became known in England as the morris dance, a lively dance in two-quarter time in which the dancers wore jingly bells attached to their legs. It was done in May to celebrate spring and therefore at some time it was probably linked to the Druids and dancing around a maypole *(Photo Plate 2-1 and 2-2).*

In 1538, at May Day celebrations, young and old would go dancing in the woods at night around a maypole. This was a pagan celebration dedicated to the tree spirit. The Church and Puritans frowned on this celebration.

Early German dances were done in closed or open circles *(Photo plate 2-3)* or in rows, one reason being that couples dances, like the one shown in Bruegel's work *(Photo Plate 2-5)*, were considered scandalous and became popular only in the 15th century.

Peasants were earthy, boisterous, and heavy-footed, with large movements that were probably affected by their clothes and by the fact that they danced outdoors on the earth *(Photo Plate 2-3 and 2-4)*. Their clothes were weighty and bulky. The men's shirts were long and covered their buttocks; then they had a jacket that extended a bit below the waist. The leg wear was also bulky but it was not unwieldy and it revealed the shape of the calves and sometimes the thighs too. The women wore sturdy ankle-length dresses with long sleeves and aprons. *The Peasant Dance (Photo Plate 2-5),* painted in 1568 by Pieter Bruegel the Elder, a Netherlandish Renaissance painter and printmaker, is an excellent example of peasant clothes and dance. The participants seem to be having fun, and there appears to be much individuality and enthusiasm in their dancing in this couples dance.

In the 14th and 15th centuries, the royal courts of France, Italy, and Burgundy all had impressive entertainment as the lords tried to outdo one another and amaze their vassals and peasants. In Europe these diversions were held for almost any occasion.

In 1393, King Charles VI of France held a festival at which he and his noble friends participated and danced. The Duc d'Orléans, holding a lit torch, happened to lean forward to see better and, regrettably, set everyone on fire. King Charles had disappeared to flirt with a maiden, otherwise he too would have died. The Duc would then have inherited the throne, but he claimed the fire was not started on purpose; it was just an incident, an accident, whatever.

At the wedding of the Duke of Milan in 1489, there was a lavish ballet arranged by the Italian dance master, **Bergonzio di Botta**, in which each part of the ballet matched one of the courses of the elaborate dinner for the marriage of the Duke of Milan to the daughter of King Alfonso II of Naples, Isabella of Aragon. This was just the beginning. Many memorable and intriguing festivities followed it.

Soon these festivals became more intricate productions with scenery, costumes, plotlines, and orchestras. King Charles VIII of France had crossed the Alps in 1494 to get to Italy. In 1496 he saw a production put on by the Duke of Milan with costumes, stage effects, and machinery all designed by none other than Leonardo da Vinci. That is not surprising because in those days these pageants were even more sumptuous and extravagant than our modern-day opening ceremonies at the Olympic games.

During the Middle Ages France set the trend in **court dance**, but it was Italy that would soon share the spotlight during the Renaissance. It was an epoch of personal fortunes, mixed social classes, and an appreciation of worldly pleasures and of the human body. The itinerant jugglers of the Middle Ages became highly sought after to teach not only dance but also deportment and etiquette, and to stage splendid festivities.

This led to the professional dance master or choreographer. These were educated men, and many were of Jewish heritage from a group of medieval Jewish entertainers.

**Domenico da Piacenza** (1400-1470) was a famous dance master who worked for the powerful Estes family among others. Although music had already been notated since about 800, not till 1400 was dance notated for the first time. Domenico indicated in 1450 exactly how his steps were to be performed and in 1463 he wrote the first paper on dance, *De arte saltandi et choreas ducendi.* His pupils, **Antonio Cornazzano** and **Guglielmo Ebreo da Pesaro,** notated Domenico's other dances; these had stories based on mythology. Cornazzano (1430-1484), poet, writer, and dancing master, and Ebreo (1425-1480), choreographer, dance theorist, and dancing master, both worked for rich families in Milan. The latter was Jewish but converted to Christianity around 1463 due to the pressures of court life and his contact with the dancing daughters of the aristocracy who were closely linked to the church. He was even knighted in Venice by the Holy Roman Emperor.

When European folk dances were adapted as **court dances** *(Photo Plates 2-3 and 2-5)* by the nobility, they were then performed indoors, they stressed manners and coquetry, and the attire included fancy headdresses, long gowns and trains. The dancing was gliding, curtseying, posing, executed in very precise formations and on smooth wooden floors. Dancing master became a very special new profession. It was the dancing master who accompanied the prince or courtier to instruct him in matters of propriety, how and when to bow, how to stand with good posture, how to look poised, and he also became his confidant. It became essential for courtiers to take daily dance lessons to achieve the necessary precision in all the dances' details: intricate floor patterns, proper deportment, and exact steps.

Photo Plate 2-4

"Peasant Dance in Front of a Tavern," 1652, an etching by Adriaen van Ostade (1610-1685), a Dutch painter and etcher.

Chennai, India-Traditional Indian Dance Drama, "Kathakali Dancer, " Often deals with religious themes, uses hand gestures (mudras) to tell the story. This Traditional Dance Drama dates back to the 17th century and involves elaborate makeup and costumes. Only now are women beginning to appear in Kathakali dance dramas.

"Performance of the Ballet Comique de la Reine," 1581, by Balthazar de Beaujoyeulx. Representation of a ballet before Henri III of France and his Court in the Gallery of the Louvre.

The court dances consisted of two types, those without jumps, the **danse basse**, and those with a few light skips and jumps, the **danse haute**. The latter were a bit unbecoming for noblemen since these steps included many jumps and antics copied from joyous peasant dances, so it became customary for the noblemen to wear masks when doing these dances. From that time the habit of wearing masks began for all ballet and theatrical dances.

By the end of the 16<sup>th</sup> century, rules were introduced for each dance and included the proper music to be played. Well-known dances of this period were the pavane, gigue, courante, allemande, galliard, and the sarabande. All these popular court dances were described in great detail in the *Orchésographie* (1588) of **Thoinot Arbeau**, the pen name of a priest named Jehan Tabourot. As a general rule, torso and arms were held in a predetermined position while the legs moved. There were just a few basic steps, and the first letter of the step was indicated in the musical score and thus gave the movement its rhythm. The illustrations in Arbeau's book showed positions resembling the five classic positions of the feet that were later to become the foundation of ballet. Arbeau declared that dance was a kind of silent rhetoric.

From 1530 to about 1670, musicians joined the **pavane**, a very dignified dance, and the subsequent **galliard, also called the cinqpas**, a lively courtship dance, often with five steps followed by kicks, high leaps and turns, making the dance become a two-part suite. In 1620, as musicians and court dancers became more skilled, a four-part suite replaced this suite. The **allemande** *(Photo Plate 2-5)*, named from a simple, ancient German dance that became more flowing in France, was followed by the **courante**, a couples dance from Italy and France, with running and gliding done in triple time, which then became more solemn in later years. The third dance in the four-part suite was the **sarabande**, from Spain, often danced with castanets, and with couples advancing, retreating, and passing between the lines of the other dancers. The fourth and last dance in this suite was the **gigue**, lively exuberant, found in many European countries where it was often danced by itself to fiddle music. Also popular as isolated dances were the **bourrée** *(Photo Plate 2-3)*, a light, fast dance in which a line of men faced a line of women, and the **gavotte** *(Photo Plate 2-2)*, a French dance with gay, hopping movements. The early ballets utilized many of the steps from these court dances.

Some of the many composers who wrote in these forms were Henry Purcell, George Frideric Handel, Johann Sebastian Bach, François Couperin, Jean-Baptiste Lully, and later, Maurice Ravel, Eric Satie, Claude Debussy, Arnold Schoenberg, and Sergei Prokofieff.

The early dances were set in interesting patterns. Many of the dances were of Spanish origin and were borrowed, refined, and elaborated to become the basis of ballet technique, and they became definitely French. Courtiers were trained to participate in formal balls. These dances were not difficult, but movements in court procedure were expected to be elegant, confident, and to show excellent bearing based on a turned out leg and the deportment of fencing.

One dance that could never be considered elegant or dignified, however, was the **volta**. It was done to the same music as the galliard, but was a controversial dance requiring much turning and leaping. While dancing, the couple transitioned from the position of the galliard, side by side with each partner facing the opposite direction, to the position of the volta, directly in front of and face-to-face with one's partner. The consistent turning movement in the volta made the dancers dizzy. But the leaping in a close dance position with one of the gentleman's hands on the lady's back just above her hip and the other in front at the bottom of her busk (stiff corset), his free left thigh under her right thigh for a higher leap, and the lady's gown flying upwards while exposing her knees (especially if the gentleman also decided to leap while lifting the lady), was considered highly immoral and controversial. It reached the courts of Paris in 1500, and England much later. Queen Elizabeth I enjoyed dancing it with the Earl of Leicester. The volta is still danced in Provence, France, as a folk dance.

The courtiers' attire, however, usually made it practically impossible to perform intricate steps or to jump off the ground. Some of the costumes weighed as much as one hundred and fifty pounds. Both men and women wore heels and gigantic headdresses; women had corsets, heavy skirts held out by hoops, and layers of underskirts and pantalettes; the men had fancy waistcoats with trousers buttoned at the knee and hose covering the calf. The garments were stiff, and so were the movements; but men were given more complicated steps than women since the movements made by their legs could easily be seen.

**Formal dancing**, an amateur art until 1661, was performed within a ballroom, with the king and his family sitting at one end of the hall and everyone else on the other three sides; the audience was close to the performers. By 1663 the general public was also allowed to attend these performances *(Photo Plate 2-4)*.

It was not considered ladylike for a woman to dance on stage, although a dance ball was proper, hence it was only men who took part in stage performances and they wore masks and dressed as women if the role required. In fact, to correct the shortage of dancers, Louis XIV passed a royal decree allowing noblemen to dance on stage without losing their noble rank or being tormented by social dishonor. In the 1680's this started to change, and women appeared on stage, wearing masks and hoop skirts called panniers.

Gradually, with the coming of the Renaissance, creativity was dominated not by the Church but by Kings and Queens and wealthy nobility. The comic art from Rome was revived in the commedia dell' arte by traveling players who did variations on stock characters such as Pulcinella, Punch, Columbine, Pierrot, and Harlequin all over Europe.

Ballet originated from the pageantry at Italian courts and the expensive celebrations for the weddings of the aristocrats. No special costumes were worn, just the elaborate outfits that the nobility usually wore.

Catherine de Medici, the mother of Henry III of France, introduced the new Italian pageantry to France toward the end of the 16th century, when she produced that marvel, *Le Ballet Comique de la Reine*, on October 15, 1581, to honor the marriage of her sister to the brother of Henry II, her husband. The ballet was choreographed by

"Negro Fandango Scene," Campo St. Anna, Rio de Janeiro, Brazil, ca. 1822, Artist: Augustus Earle, English painter, (1793-1838), watercolor on paper.

Detail of a miniature of the Carolle (round dance with music) in the garden of Sir Mirth. "The Dance in the Garden," illumination from the" Roman de la Rose," early 16th century. Origin: Netherlands.

"The Whirling Dervish," ca. 1889. Artist: Jean-Léon Gérôme (1824-1904), French painter, draftsman, and sculptor. Oil on canvas.

"Round Dance at Aninoasa" by Theodore Aman, 1890. Romanian painter (1831-1891).

"The Peasant Dance." Oil on oak panel. c.1567. Artist: Pieter Bruegel the Elder (1525-1569).

"The Allemande Dance." 1772, Creator: James Caldwell (1739-1819), printmaker; etching and engraving, hand colored, 1772.

**Balthazar de Beaujoyeulx**, an Italian, at the court of Henry III in Paris. Beaujoyeulx was Catherine de Medici's valet, a skillful violinist and choreographer who became her ballet master. His intricate patterns were best seen from the gallery around the stage floor; the gallery was where the audience sat *(Photo Plate 2-4)*. The performance was excessively long and lasted five hours, from ten o'clock in the evening until three in the morning, with Italian opera, music, singing, dancing, complex scenery, and mechanical effects. The word ballet came from the Italian and Latin, ballare, to dance.

When Catherine de Medici had come to France to marry Henry II in 1533 she had brought many outstanding Italian dancers and musicians from Florence, Italy. These were part of her entourage in Paris as she planned *Le Ballet Comique de la Reine*. Beaujoyeulx was very creative in his mixing of medieval forms of court entertainment, masquerades, and court social dances. The story may have been based on ancient Greek mythology *(Photo Plate 2-2)*, but the dance steps were not. They came from the social dances of the Renaissance. The various parts of this spectacle – poetry, music and dance – were all fused and its success guaranteed the future of dance.

It was the first ballet as we think of ballet today, with a combination of original music written for the occasion, dancing, plot, and design. It was limited to a single major dramatic theme, based on Circe, the Greek enchantress who turned men into beasts. The story was based on the Circe from Homer's *Odyssey* and the ballet involved the taming of man's emotions and the establishment of order and harmony by means of reason and moral virtue. The King had to step in to aid in the struggle. This type of plot was prevalent at that time, to glorify the monarch. Art, dance, verse, and music were all supposed to instruct the audience. The intent was to present a performance that would give pleasure but also instruct at individual levels, something for everyone. Over 10,000 spectators saw the show. When it was over the performers invited the audience to join them in dancing, as was done in those days.

Thanks to the invention of Gutenberg's moveable-type printing earlier in about 1440, copies of this performance's music and poetry were sent to all the courts of Europe and impressed them greatly. As a result Henry III was considered to have the most refined and musical court in Europe. The invention of the printing press meant that dance books and music could now be printed. One of the problems with dance as an art had been that it was preserved in the dancers' bodies, not on paper. Now this was no longer true.

Under patrons of the dance such as Henry IV and Louis XIII of France, many ballets were performed. They consisted of a series of dances, from ten to thirty of them, by different groups of dancers. At the end, general dancing took place and all members of the court were included. After that, these groups went to the palace of another nobleman and repeated the entire ballet. The evening then ended with yet another performance on a platform in front of the City Hall, with the townspeople watching, and finally, all the King's company stepped down and danced with the wives and daughters of the townspeople. The King's company was all male, since women courtiers did not dance in formal court ballets. Women's roles were performed not by women but by boys who wore fancy wigs.

Meanwhile, in Kerala in southern India during the 16th century, a very stylized classical form of dance-drama originated, called **kathakali**. It entailed elaborate makeup, very colorful costumes *(Photo Plate 2-4)*, detailed hand gestures or mudras, expressive body movements, and footwork. Percussion instruments accompanied it. **Kathakali** dances are still performed today and are developed to re-enact tales from Hindu epics, the Ramayana and Mahabharata. There is also a more feminine version of **Kathakali**, lyrical, softer and with hip movements, called **Mohiniattam**. **Kathakali** appears to be a great tourist attraction today. Two 21st century Canadian choreographers of Indian descent who use multicultural influences in their works are **Deepti Gupta** and **Roger Sinha**. Two of **Sinha's** works are *Loha* (2001) and *Thok* (2001). **Gupta** uses masks depicting birds, animals, and mythological heroes as well as **Kathak** (classical dance from North India), with intricate footwork and with ankle bells to stress the rhythm.

During the reign of the Mughal monarchy in the 16th and 17th centuries, the culture and art of northern India thrived more than ever. It was the longest-lasting Muslim dynasty to rule India. The Mughals were descended from the great Mongol warriors Ghengis Khan and Timur whose cavalry swept across and dominated all Eurasia in the 13th and 14th centuries. The harem was the residential quarters of the women of the royal household. The women here had both very traditional and contemporary characteristics. They tackled anything, including dancing. The Mughal women were more liberated than most for that time although they usually did wear veils whenever they were outside of the harem. They lived in a complex society in which, depending on their individual skills, they took part in business dealings, constructed buildings and gardens and supervised them, handled family life and education, pursued literary activities and an artistic life that included writing poetry, playing music, and dancing. They had an excellent education and were entertained in the harem by professional singers, dancing girls, and musicians.

In Turkey too, handsome young men who had trained since the age of seven for about six years in dancing and in playing percussion instruments were employed as entertainers and often cross-dressed in feminine attire. At first this art form, **kocek dancing**, took place only in palaces and harems, but gradually independent troupes of entertainers took this dance throughout Turkey and the Balkans. **Kocek** dancers performed for weddings, circumcision ceremonies, feasts, and to entertain the sultans. These young dancers were also sought among the non-Muslim people of the Ottoman Empire, the Greeks, the Jews, the Armenians, and they had a career that lasted as long as they looked young and beardless.

The Ottoman Turks captured Constantinople (now Istanbul) in the middle of the 15th century and scholars from the Eastern capital of the Holy Roman Empire fled to the West and influenced European countries such as Germany, France, and Italy with their knowledge of the classical cultures of Greece and Rome.

After the fall of Rome and of Greece, dance had declined even though it still existed. It was an age of darkness, and when resurgence appeared after many centuries, when all the various gods had disappeared and the new era was established, people unexpectedly turned back to mythology, to gods, goddesses, nymphs, fauns, and rituals as stories for their dance.

The result was that the asceticism and preoccupation with the spirit of the Middle Ages gave way to the Renaissance, an age of artistic elegance and classical learning, and wealthy men rather than wealthy churches were to become the patrons of the arts.

# 3

# Early American Dance

The dances of the Native American tribes, Native Alaskans, and Native Hawaiians came from ancient ceremonies. Pantomime was a part of the Hawaiian and Native Alaskan dances. Their myths and legends were told through dances and chants. Their feet kept the rhythm and the song told the story.

The Native Americans, like many other people, were utilitarian; success in battle, in the search for food, in obtaining rain, and in successful procreation were common requests made to the Great Spirit through dance. Native American dancers represented the spirit of all creatures and of all natural phenomena such as the sun or the rainbow, for example.

When Native Americans returned from a hunt they told about it in a dance; therefore their dances were often story dances. Traditional dances were centuries-old Native American stories such as the one about the Native American maiden, her father and the buffalo, the **Sioux buffalo dance**. The traditional **snowshoe dance** of the Ojibwa tribe, a Native American people of the region around Lake Superior and westward, was performed each year upon the appearance of the first snow of the season, accompanied by chanting and singing to thank the Great Spirit for the return of snow. Artist George Catlin (1796-1872) captured the **Snowshoe dance** in his painting in 1837 *(Photo Plate 3-2)*. Men and women did not dance together. Only the men performed the dance, but the women could join in the chanting and singing. The women performed some dances, such as the **women's medicine dance**, but separately from the men *(Photo Plate 3-1)*, or sometimes the women were in a circle outside the men. Native American dances were either line or circle dances and represented a prayer between the people, the environment, and the Great Spirit.

The Native Americans were keen observers of nature so that when rain was needed and was imminent they performed rain dances with great success. Occasionally they even did **rain dances** for the settlers in exchange for goods. For them, dancing accompanied by singing, chanting, and drumming was so much a part of life that they had dances for all occasions, trivial or important, such as for curing, for initiation rites, courting, hunting, planting and harvesting, death, sacrifice, prayer, life-cycle rituals, and marriage. The **hoop dance** symbolized the cycles of creation. This dance *(Photo Plate 3-3)* was one of the ones performed by the Iroquois tribe, a Native American confederacy originally of New York and consisting of the Cayuga, Mohawk, Oneida, Onondaga, and Seneca tribes, and later including the Tuscarora tribe, all in New York State. The Native Americans, like the Native Alaskans, also had **animal dances,** the actual dance depending on where the tribe came from and what animals lived there. Some of these dances were the **bear dance, bison dance** *(Photo Plate 3-5)*, **buffalo dance** *(Photo Plate 3-1)*, and the **eagle dance** *(Photo Plate 3-5)*. These dances, close to the earth and with small steps, were usually performed by a group rather than by one human being except in individual competitions. In the painting *Bison Dance of the Mandan (Photo Plate 3-5)* you see members of the Mandan tribe wearing bison heads and skins and holding spears, rifles, shields, as though a hunt for bison was occurring.

Many primitive groups have similar ways of moving, such as the Native Americans had when hunting and also in their hunting dances: barefoot, with crouching positions imitating animals that are stalking prey. Agnes De Mille believed this was a means of protecting the hunters' vital organs.

The **sun dance**, as it was originally done by the Mandans, a gentle tribe, and by many other Native American tribes, such as the Cheyenne, Crow, Hidatsa, Sioux, Plains Cree, Gros Ventre, Assiniboine, Arapako, Shoshone, Kiowa, Blackfoot, Plains Ojibwa, the Omaha, and others, was one of the most painful ways of testing a young warrior. It involved secret rituals to prepare him, followed by self-inflicted torture – a piercing of the skin under the breasts through which a skewer would be placed and tied to a center pole with long ropes of woven hair. The participants were to dance, pulling away and leaning back from the poles till the skin broke away and the skewers pulled through and broke loose, a dance lasting several hours to prove their manhood. It took several days and many people to prepare for this spiritual dance and ritual. Not only was the dance performed to test the manhood of young warriors, it was enacted to fulfill a vow made at a time when help from the gods had been needed, to call for the regenerative powers of the sun, and to give thanks and show appreciation for the buffalo, which was their prime means of sustenance with regard to food, clothing, and utensils. When the ordeal was over, the medicine man would take care of the participants and let them rest. This dance was meant to reaffirm the connection and balance between man, nature, and the Great Spirit. It was considered to be a religious ceremony by many tribes. They each had distinct practices, but they also had several traits in common: songs, dances, sacred pipes, traditional drums, and piercing of the skin. Non-natives have been banned from the ceremony and the sun dance since 2003. Some aspects of the **sun dance** were banned in Canada (1895) and in the U.S. (1904), but since then, with a better understanding of Native Americans' customs and traditions, the ceremony is now legal in Canada (since 1951) and in the U.S. since the passage of the 1978 American Indian Religious Freedom Act.

The **grass dance**, one of the dances most often used in Native American cultures, originated among the Plains Indians and represents the connection between earth, nature, and the Great Spirit and the harmony between them. Any accessories, such as eagle feathers, are blessed and are considered to be sacred. The dancer focuses on his dance and performs it to honor his ancestors. Many tribes perform this grass dance, using their own distinct costumes and steps. Grass dance costumes often have long fringes, and as the dancer moves they suggest grass blowing in the wind.

The **stomp dance** is another dance performed by several Native American tribes: Southeastern tribes and communities such as the Cherokee, Chickasaw, Choctaw, Delaware, Miami, Shawnee, and Seminole. The name refers to the stomp and shuffle steps in this spirited dance. The stomp dance is a ceremony – both religious and social, and for some tribes it is connected to the Green Corn Ceremony. The order of the events in this ceremony is food, then stickball (the predecessor of the lacrosse game) and then the stomp dance. This dance is always preceded by a game of stickball.

Photo Plate 3-1

"Dance of the Mandan Women," 1839, depicting Indian women dancing in full Indian costume including headdress, by Karl Bodmer, Swiss painter (1809-1893); technique: aquatint on paper. From "Travels in the Interior of North America" by Prince Maximilian of Wied.

"Buffalo Dance at Hano," 1921. Artist: Edward S. Curtis, American, 1868-1952.

The **stirrup dance**, a social dance of the Caddo tribe, a Southern tribe, sounds like fun. A man and a woman walk side-by-side for 16 counts, starting with the inside legs, with knees relaxed and slightly bent, and moving in a counterclockwise circle. Then the man raises his inside foot up in front, knee bent, leg low; the woman places her inside foot, raised, on his foot as though on a stirrup. They both hop around for 16 counts in this foot-on-top-of-foot position, and then repeat the whole dance.

But probably the most important dance of the Native Americans, and one which all of them performed, was the **eagle dance**. The Native American artist of Kiowa descent, Stephen Mopope (1898-1974), painted a lively scene of the eagle dance in 1937, at a time when Native American art metamorphosed from being a subject for anthropologists to being an important part of modern American painting. Mopope's paintings are part of the New Deal Post Office Murals titled *Scenes of Indian Life* embellishing the walls of the Anadarko, Oklahoma, Post Office. They were painted in the 1930's. Fine arts prints that have been made of the murals are part of the American Postal Collection and can be purchased. (A Kiowa is a member of a Native American group located in what are now the States of Colorado, Kansas, New Mexico, Oklahoma and Texas.)

The **Native American eagle dance** (*Photo Plate 3-5)* was performed as a part of a ceremony that varied somewhat from tribe to tribe. Because of its ability to fly very high, the eagle was considered to be sacred and to have supernatural powers. It could carry requests, such as for rain, to the gods. The dance depicted the eagle family and the life cycle of the eagle from birth to death, how it learned to walk, fly, and hunt. The dance sometimes had two main dancers dressed to look like the male and the female eagle. They often had yellow paint on their lower legs, white on their upper arms, and blue bodies. There were short white feathers painted yellow on their chests. The dancers wore a cap and a wig made of white feathers that had a beak-like yellow protrusion. Bands of eagle feathers were on their arms. The two dancers imitated eagle movements by turning, swaying, and flapping. The eagle could fly closer to the Great Spirit than any man, so the eagle was considered to be a symbol of wisdom, power, and strength. It was a great honor to wear an eagle feather.

Two exceptional artists who depicted the life of Native Americans, their dances, as well as the grandeur and beauty of American nature in the nineteenth century were Karl Bodmer and George Catlin. They both admired Native Americans, noticed how badly they were treated, and wanted to paint various aspects of their lives as well as their dances in order to preserve them for posterity.

Karl Bodmer (1809-1893) was a Swiss painter of the American West. Bodmer and his patron, the German Prince Maximilian (1782-1867), came from Germany in 1832. This was a time when many intellectuals in Europe were interested in the romantic notion of the noble savage. Maximilian was interested in botany and nature; he had already explored the flora, fauna (a few were named after him) and indigenous people of Brazil (1815-1817), written two volumes about them, and proceeded to do the same for more of the Americas. Maximilian's journal, *Travels in the Interior of North America in the Years 1832 to 1834,* which contained aquatint prints of sketches and paintings by Karl Bodmer, considered an extraordinary artist, provided us with a look at the botany, animals, and Native American cultures and dances in nineteenth century America from 1840 to 1843. Bodmer's paintings of Native American dance included: *Dance of the*

*Mandan, Bison Dance of the Mandan (Photo Plate 3-5), Dance of the Mandan Women (Photo Plate 3-1),* and many others. Prince Maximilian was especially interested in the Mandan and Hidatsa tribes. Maximilian's journal has a map of the route that he and Bodmer took in their travels as well as eighty-one aquatints by Bodmer. An aquatint is an engraving produced by a process of etching in which spaces are bitten in with aqua fortis or nitric acid to create an effect resembling a drawing in India ink or watercolor.

George Catlin (1796-1872), an American born in Pennsylvania, was a self-taught artist eager to capture the American scenery and Native American tribes and their dances before they all vanished from the face of the earth. This is what he thought would happen from what he had heard about the trials and tribulations of the Native Americans and the unjust treatment they received when they were forced to relocate to areas (later to reservations) where the land was arid and worthless for agricultural purposes. The white man was unnecessarily killing buffalos, the primary food and source of materials for Native Americans for making tools, clothes, and tipis, and many Native Americans had died from lack of resistance to the many European diseases to which they were exposed, such as smallpox and whooping cough.

Catlin was an extraordinary draftsman and artist who sketched and painted many of the Native American dances that he saw during the nineteenth century: a *War Dance by the Ojibwa Indians,* a *Mandan Tribal Dance,* a *Dance to the Berdache – a celebration of the two-spirit person (Photo Plate 3-2),* a *Ball-Play Dance,* a *Snowshoe Dance (Photo Plate 3-2), The Sun Dance,* and a *Bear Dance,* among numerous others.

When early European explorers discovered the continent that was later named America, they thought they had reached India and hence named the natives "Indians" whereas we now call them Native Americans, First Nation, or Native American Indians. Actually they were not a homogeneous population at all but members of hundreds of diverse tribes with different languages, cultures, and dances.

In difficult colonial times the dances were a means of cultural survival for the Native Americans. The colonizers repressed these ceremonies as time-consuming pagan rituals that ran against the Christian work ethic of the settlers. The unifying aspect of these dances worried European settlers, educators, Spanish governors, missionaries, and the United States Army.

The **powwow dance** came from a Narragansett (Algonquin) term Powwaw, meaning spiritual leader, and was a word used by settlers for any Native American Indian gathering, especially in the warrior tribes like the Pawnee, the Omaha, and the Kansa of the Plains. Gradually there were fewer of these tribes and the powwow dance became a more social event and included children and women. The powwow could last from five hours to three days. After World War II, modern powwows were celebrations of life, community, and identity, with each tribe stressing this in dress, dances, and traditions. The drummers would sit around a large drum and sing songs in their native language: intertribal songs, songs of welcome, grass dance songs, and others. There were also contest dances with cash prizes for the winners. The powwow now means different things to different people. Some believe it is too commercialized, with prize money and fancy sequined costumes. Others believe not only in the spirituality behind all the dances and songs that make them feel more connected to the Native American religions, cultures,

43

Photo Plate 3-2

"The Snowshoe Dance. An Ojibwa tradition," performed at the first snowfall every year since time immemorial, 1835-1837. Artist: George Catlin.

"Dance to the Berdashe" (1835-37) drawn by George Catlin (1796-1872) while on the Great Plains among the Sac Fox Indians. The sketch depicts a ceremonial dance to celebrate the berdashe, the two-spirit person. From George Catlin's "Letters and Notes on the Manners, Customs, and Condition of the North American Indians."

and traditions, but they are also interested in the hand beading on the costumes, and they are especially interested in a revival of Native American languages. Since many reservations are extremely poor, the powwow prize money is very welcome and so are the tourists who attend them.

The Indian Office, as it was then called (now called the Bureau of Indian Affairs), passed regulations banning Indian dances in 1904. The regulations stated that Indian dances, such as the sun dance, would be considered an "Indian offense" and any Indian found guilty could be punished by incarceration or by having his rations withheld. Only in 1934 were these regulations entirely repealed except for laws against the sun dance, which were not abrogated until 1978 by the passage of the American Indian Religious Freedom Act. By then, however, many reservations had lost their knowledge of traditional life and had to turn to other nearby Native American Indian communities for assistance in reviving these dances. Those Native Americans who were over forty years of age had been exempt from this ban in 1904 and so could perform in Wild West shows, as Sitting Bull had done, or on tours that traveled throughout the country and abroad. Youngsters, however, had no opportunity to learn the many dances of their native tribes. They were punished at school if they were seen doing Native American dances. What had been a way of life for generations of Native Americans – dancing and singing for any and every occasion – was completely lost to them. Presently things have changed for the better. Native American culture is being promoted on reservations, and native crafts, dancing, and singing are encouraged. Native Americans can once again take pride in their heritage. (The intricate Navaho tribe language is the one that was used as a code in World War II to help us win the war in the Far East.)

The water drum used by Native American tribes (the Eastern Woodland tribes: the Mohawk, Seneca, Cherokee, and Creek, and the Apache of the Southwest) is the only native instrument on the United States mainland. It is frequently the property of religious or ceremonial persons and is the most sacred of the drums, having the status of a person, not an object. About five to eight inches high and four to seven inches in diameter, these are small hand-held drums tuned according to the amount of water they contain and the dampness of the drumhead. About one inch of water is placed inside. Water gives the drum a distinctive sound. The more water, the higher the pitch; the vibrating air space is decreased, the vibrating frequency becomes more rapid, and the pitch goes higher. The drumhead is made of soft tanned animal hide, sometimes wetted so as to make it easier to stretch and tie it onto the top of the drum. These drums can also be found in Africa and Southeast Asia.

Early explorers coming to America had told about seeing dance everywhere: Jacques Cartier from his ship, in 1534, saw natives doing **dances of greeting**; De Soto in the Southeast; Champlain in the Northeast; Captain Cook in Hawaii in 1778. And in 1880 Hubert Howe Bancroft saw the Eskimos (now usually called Native Alaskans) dancing.

The Danish-born officer of the Russian navy, Vitus Jonassen Bering (after whom the Bering Sea and the Bering Strait were named), first noticed the Aleuts, natives of West Alaska and the Aleutian Islands during an expedition in 1741. Their language belongs to the Eskimo-Aleutian family. The Aleuts are racially similar to Siberian people. At that time their population was between 20,000 and 25,000. However, they were excellent at hunting sea mammals and this skill led to altercations with Russian traders so that by the end of the 18th century the Aleuts had dwindled to one-tenth of their former number. But Alaska became a part of the United States and by 1990 the Aleut population had again increased to almost 24,000.

Native Alaskans used to have outdoor **pantomimic dances** for whale catches with a woman enacting the role of the whale. Songs were sung when leaving shore, when sighting the whale, and when throwing the spear at the whale. Then the men and boys wore wooden masks and danced naked as their boat towed in the whale. But this dance was not exactly the same throughout Alaska. At Cape Prince of Wales on the Bering Strait it was the wife of the whaler who came to meet the boat in ceremonial garb, singing and dancing. Inside a circle of either stones or bones all the participants danced, sang, and feasted. The men had strong angular gestures and the women had curved swaying movements of torso and arms. They sat or stood. This was later replaced by **contra dances** or **square dances**.

The **contra dance**, sometimes referred to as a New England style of folk dance, was done in Alaska and throughout the world and was actually a term used to describe many partnered folk dances in which couples danced facing each other in long lines called sets. A set usually ran the length of the hall. The top or head of the set was the end closest to the caller and the musicians. The foot or the bottom of the set was the end farthest from the caller. Contra dances were popular in Europe from the end of the 17th century until the middle of the 19th century. Contra dance events were very sociable because traditionally the participants changed partners after every dance, so one could feasibly have danced with everyone present by the end of the session. Usually the caller would instruct the participants in a dance, have them "walk it through" as he called out the next step and then dance it several times, change partners, and proceed to do the same for the next contra dance or square dance. Contra dance events were open to all regardless of expertise or lack of it. Contra dancing was revitalized in the 1940's and 50's. In 1976 traditional dancing such as contra dancing and square dancing made its first appearance at the 2nd Annual Alaska Folk Festival. Contra dance as a whole has adapted to new choreography, less traditional music, and social changes, and so has kept its dance members evolving and has maintained the interest of younger dancers too. It remains popular in Alaska to this day, hence those wishing to indulge in it can easily find schedules on the internet listing the numerous contra dance events in Alaska.

The Yup'ik were one of the Alaskan groups often called Eskimos. The Inupiaq and Cupik lived to the west and north, while the Yup'ik lived in southeastern Alaska. They were semi nomadic. In the winter all the males, including male children over five years of age, lived in a men's house or community center called a qasgiq and learned male skills such as working with wood and hunting. The females and all the children up to age five lived in a community house called an enu and learned female skills such as cooking and sewing. In the spring, summer, and fall they all lived in fishing camps, to fish and collect berries. (Native Alaskans from the north lived in igloos.) Many of the traditional ways of living in Alaska changed gradually through the introduction of electricity, which many houses now have.

Photo Plate 3-3

"Nunivak Drummer," 1929 February 28. Depicts an Eskimo man wearing a fur parka beating a large hand-held drum made of walrus stomach or bladder. Creator/Photographer: Edward S. Curtis. The drum is held either in a vertical or horizontal position and is beaten with a slender wand-like stick.

"Nunivak Maskette," 1929, Photographer: Edward S. Curtis (1868-1952). Shows Eskimo man wearing headdress consisting of a protruding headband around the crown of his head, feathers, and a wooden bird head in front. Photo was published in "The North American Indian" by Edward S. Curtis.

"Thunderbird Transformation Mask," by Namgis, Native American, Kwakwaka'wakw, British Vancouver, Canada 19th century.

"Hanasilahl-Qagyuhl, British Columbian ceremonial dancer," wearing a mask and fur garment during the Winter Dance Ceremony. Photo by Edward S. Curtis, 1914.

"Native American Dancer Competing in World Championship Hoop Dance Contest." Photo by Paul B. Moore.

The Yup'ik made a wonderful variety of wooden masks, all different, for use in their dances *(Photo Plate 3-3)*. These were made from spruce and cottonwood that were easily shaped and comfortable to wear. No two were alike. Once a mask was made and used just one time it had served its purpose and could be discarded; many were found and put in museums. The story being depicted in the dance and the vision of the carver determined the design and shape of the mask. The **Yup'ik dance** as well as the mask were part of a prayer and related to the way of living, tradition, and culture of the Yup'ik (meaning real people). The dances were rhythmic, flowing, and energetic. Traditionally the dances were executed with complicated pulleys used to enliven some of the performances. In their group dances only the upper bodies and arms moved. Dance fans were used that were sometimes referred to as finger masks. Masked dances were an important part of the Yup'ik ceremonies, but masks are not worn very often today.

Native Alaskans from Nunivak Island also made and wore masks, but these were called maskettes since they covered only the crown of the head. A photograph by Edward S. Curtis taken between 1927 and 1929 shows a Native Alaskan from the north wearing a headdress that is a protruding headband around the crown of his head with a wooden bird head in front (*Photo Plate 3-3)*. At first the masks from Nunivak Island were traded for essentials for survival. Then they were used later in dances and healing rituals. The walrus and the loon were represented on these masks because they were vital for the survival of the Nunivak people. Shamans used masks to represent animals in personalized form in rituals or in ceremonies dealing with spirits. Masks reflected the unity between people and animals. When used in storytelling or dances, masks helped the participant to represent the animal or objects.

Edward Sheriff Curtis (1868-1952) was an American photographer who captured many of these Native Americans, Native Alaskans, their dance masks, and their traditions in the numerous photographs – over 7,000 – taken by him between 1907 and 1930 that were published in Seattle, Washington, in 1929 in his book, "The North American Indian." The Nunivak are shown in Volume 20. Curtis, too, wanted to document the Native Americans before their way of life disappeared; he took over 40,000 images of over 80 tribes.

As you read about the history of dance, you will notice how many cultures have used masks in their dances, sometimes to more easily take on a new identity or to capture a more spiritual interpretation, or to personify an animal or an object.

The Savoonga Eskimo dancers of Savoonga, St. Lawrence Island, Alaska, and the King Island Dancers are among the groups that have performed native dances of the Alaskans regularly at the Alaska Native Heritage Center in Anchorage, Alaska.

In Hawaiian dance, the hands and face told the story. The **hula** began as a means of worship and slowly developed into a form of entertainment. The color of the pa'u, the skirt of tapa cloth originating from the bark of a tree called the paper mulberry tree, that made up the hula costume together with leis (wreaths) around the neck and head, and bracelets and anklets of shell, dog teeth, or whale bone, was determined by the story of the chant or "mele" *(Photo Plate 3-4)*. This chant dealt with the poetry and history of Hawaii.

A hula dance can be performed either while sitting or standing and is a visual interpretation of the chant (oli or mele) that it accompanies. Numerous hand gestures are used to signify nature's movements, swaying trees, breezes, ocean waves as well as

Photo Plate 3-4

A Hura, or Native Dance, Performed In Presence of Governor Kuakini at Kairua.

"Governor John Adams Kuakini viewing a Hula dance at Kairua." Illustration: in Missionary William Ellis' "Narrative of a Tour through Hawaii," ca. 1827.

Sheet Music Cover: "Farewell to Thee: Aloha Oe;" Composed by Queen Lili'uokalani; Publisher: The Popular Music Publishing Co. 1913.

Sheet Music Cover:" Fair Hawaii," a popular song of that time; Words and Music by James Fulton Kutz. Artist; L.E. Morgan. Publisher: San Francisco, California: Sherman Clay and Co., 1913.

"Queen Lili'uokalani," ca.1915, Hawaii's last monarch was also a creative and prolific songwriter. "Aloha Oe" was the favorite of her songs.

human emotions of love and yearning. Fluid, smooth, undulating movements (side to side or circular) of the hips and feet are also used. Men as well as women have worn a knee-length skirt since 1820 (due to missionaries' objection to the loin cloths previously worn by the men).

Pele, the volcano goddess, was the inspiration of the "mele" of many of the favorite hulas. The volcanoes of Hawaii, besides inspiring the stories of the chants, have also stirred many painters and photographers.

After Captain Cook arrived in Hawaii in 1778, many artists were eager to sketch what they saw. One of these was the missionary William Ellis whose sketches illustrated his book, "Narrative of a Tour through Hawaii," 1827 *(Photo Plate 3-4)*.

Most of the missionaries who went to Hawaii were against all the native customs: the chants, hulas, and religion; they managed to convince the Hawaiian chiefs to react in the same manner. In 1830, after the queen regent of Hawaii became a Christian, the hula was forbidden under threats of imprisonment, fines, or hard labor.

It looked as though the hula was going to vanish, but **King Kalākaua** of Hawaii promoted the hula by starting his own Hawaiian Dance Company in the late 1800's and encouraging everyone to learn the old hula.

It was not till the 1870's that published Hawaiian music began to be seen, but thereafter a constant stream of Hawaiian music appeared, some authentic and much of it from Tin Pan Alley musicians doing their best to imitate it. Since people usually dance to music, it is difficult to write about dancing without including something regarding the music.

Queen Lydia Lili'uokalani (1838-1917), adopted at birth and the only reigning queen of the Kingdom of Hawaii, was recognized for her musical accomplishments. She played the guitar, organ, piano, ukulele, and zither. She also enjoyed writing songs about her native Hawaii *(Photo Plate 3-4)*, combining traditional poetic elements with western harmonics introduced by the missionaries. Two favorites were "A Daughter of the Sun" and "Farewell to Thee: Aloha Oe." She claimed writing music came to her very naturally. In 1999, The Lili'uokalani Trust published a collection of her works, *The Queen's Songbook*. As Queen she had felt that her aim was to preserve the islands for their native residents. However, she was forced to give up her throne in 1899 when Hawaii was annexed to the United States through a joint resolution of Congress.

When the play "Bird of Paradise" by Richard Walton Tully opened at Daly's Theater in New York on January 8, 1912, it was not just the star Laurette Taylor who received rave reviews but also the music. The play presented five Hawaiian musicians playing traditional Hawaiian music to an enraptured audience.

The Pan Pacific Exposition in San Francisco in 1915 showcased Hawaiian music and it became an immediate sensation all over America. Few had ever heard this music. By 1916, composers and lyricists were all writing melodies and songs with a Hawaiian theme. Hawaiian music and dance fever lasted for several years *(Photo Plate 3-4)*.

**'Iolani Luahine** (1915-1978), a native kuma hula dancer (a holder of the tradition of the ancient hula), teacher, and chanter, was considered to be the last great interpreter and champion of the sacred hula ceremony. The 'Iolani Luahini Hula Festival was established in 2003 in her memory to award a scholarship each year to enable a deserving student to continue the study of the hula; its aim is to perpetuate the hula, the memory of

Photo Plate 3-5

"Pueblo Indian Eagle Dance," New
"Mexico. Postcard published by
Southwest Arts & Crafts, Santa Fe,
New Mexico, "Tichnor Quality
Views."

"Bison Dance of Mandan Indians in
front of their Medicine Lodge," in
Mih-Tutta-Hankush, aquatint by
Karl Bodmer, illustration in
"Travels in the Interior of North
America" by Prince Maximilian de
Wied, London, Ackerman & Co.,
1842.

"Alutiiq Dancer"
Photograph by
Christopher
Mertl.

:

"Hopi Corn Dance" by Louis Lomoyesva, Hopi Pueblo Native
American, late 19th-early 20 century. Depicts the dancers and
drummers of the Hopi Corn Dance while omitting the
background. Medium: watercolor on paper.

'Iolani Luahine and her contributions to the preservation of the hula and the Hawaiian culture. It is held in Hawaii and draws participants from all over the world. The American modern dancer, **Ted Shawn**, in 1947 called 'Iolani Luahine an artist of "world stature." Her hula was likened to poetry. Both the hula and 'Iolani Luahine were named as America's First 100 Irreplaceable Dance Treasures in the year 2000.

There has been a revival of Hawaiian culture since the 1970's. The annual Merrie Monarch Festival is an international hula festival, named after Hawaii's last king, David Kalākaua (1836-1891), the Merrie Monarch, who preceded Queen Lili'uokalani. Now there are weeklong hula competitions and festivals each April and July in Hawaii.

Here are a few DVDs that you may enjoy watching:
- *Holo Mai Pele* DVD in Color, 2004.
- *Keepers of the Flame: The Cultural Legacy of Three Hawaiian Women* DVD in Color, 2005, Director Eddie Kamae.
- *Hula Girls* DVD in Color, 2006. Japanese with English sub-titles; it won many Japanese Academy Awards.

# 4

# Ballet and Other Dances
# from Louis XIV
# through the Renaissance

The Renaissance – from the 14th century through the 17th century – was a time of cultural rebirth of classical ideas and literature. Humanism, the interaction among people in politics and society, became important. Paper was readily available; the printing press proved a success and education was more democratic and accessible. The plague that swept Europe and decimated a third of its people had made workers more valuable and encouraged them to search for better wages and living conditions. People also became more involved with the here and now, considering the fragility of life, rather than with the spiritual aspects of their existence. Many historians found that the social factors from the Middle Ages – warfare, religious discrimination, poverty and political persecution – had worsened. Wars of Religion (as they were called) and witch-hunts were common. Explorations and scientific information, however, did serve to extend knowledge. Several historians have also thought of the Renaissance not as a period of rebirth but more as a bridge between the medieval times and modern times. Money was important during the Renaissance since rich rulers and noblemen sponsored explorations and were patrons of artists of all kinds. The idea of the Renaissance man, one interested in and knowledgeable in various facets of life and art, developed at this time.

In France **King Louis XIV** *(Photo Plate 4-5),* an accomplished dancer, took a class daily for over twenty years until he had become too heavy to continue performing in middle age. He had started to dance in public at the age of thirteen, in 1651, and continued as a leading performer until 1670. Among the many other men of importance who danced at that time were: **Pierre Beauchamp, Jean-Baptiste Lully, Jean-Philippe Rameau, Claude Ballon, Gaetan Vestris, Auguste Vestris, Jean Dauberval, Salvatore Viganò,** and **Jean-Georges Noverre.**

It was when King Louis XIV performed as the Sun god in the dance *Le Ballet de la Nuit* in 1652, that his nickname "the Sun King" ("Le Roi Soleil") originated, and it was also in his honor that the ballet step **entrechat trois** was renamed **entrechat royale.** (In a royale the calves are beaten together before the dancer does a **changement** with the feet.) In 1661 King Louis XIV founded The Royal Academy of Dance (the Académie Royale de Danse) that has survived to this day at the Paris Opera. He asked his ballet master, **Pierre Beauchamp** (1636-1705), also called "Charles" or "Charles-Louis" Beauchamp, to establish the rules for **ballet** and the positions of the feet that were to be used, with a turnout of the legs for ease of movement in all directions. These basic rules have lasted for centuries. At first, all the professionals who trained at the Academy were men.

Beauchamp, the Director of the Royal Academy of Dance, was himself an excellent dancer and invented the single **tour en l'air**; nowadays men do double and triple tours en l'air.

Since it was King Louis XIV of France who established a school where the names of the steps were learned and written down, French was the language that was used; ballet vocabulary was written in French, and still is. For example, the ability to jump with elevation and lightness is called **ballon** *(Photo Plate 4-1)* and comes from the name of a dancer with that quality who appeared from 1685 to 1710 and later became director of the Royal Academy of Dance: **Claude Ballon** (1671-1744, who is frequently and erroneously called Jean Claude Balon). French is the universal language of ballet and students throughout the world learn French names for the ballet steps they study. An **arabesque**, an **attitude**, a **pirouette**, or a **révérence**, for example, are basically the same throughout the world and are called by the same French name regardless of the height of the leg extension, the type or length of the costume worn, or where the steps are learned or performed.

By 1700 the notation of dance in **Arbeau**'s *Orchésographie* of 1589 was no longer adequate and a principal dancer, **Raoul-Auger Feuillet** (1653-1709), published *Choréographie, ou l'art de décrire la danse*, indicating mainly footwork, which did not include a turnout of more than 45 degrees. The five positions of the feet now enabled the dancer to move easily in all directions. The music to be used for each movement was notated at the top of the page and below it was the notation for the movement in abstract symbols, using circles, s-curves, and semicircles to signify the floor patterns that the dance should follow *(Photo Plate 4-2)*

Even in the American colonies there were dancing masters; in fact in 1685 two of them taught the **line dances** used in **social dances**. These line dances were called **contra dances** or **longways dances** and were all the rage in England in the 17th century. During the 16th and 17th centuries the English were known everywhere as the "dancing English." Queen Elizabeth I gave the office of Lord Chancellor to Sir Christopher Hatton supposedly because he performed the **pavane** flawlessly and wore little green bows on his dance shoes. In 1651, the English bookseller and musician John Playford published *The English Dancing Master – Plaine and Easy Rules for the Dancing of Country Dances, with the Tunes to Each Dance*. By 1728 there were about 900 different contras using all forms of complexities, but actually once you learned a few they were simple. Any number of people, few or many, could dance them at the same time, which was very convenient.

This was the situation regarding **country dancing** in the British Isles at the time that the English settled in America. The Puritans did not like dancing but there were many other settlers among the English, Scottish, and Irish who did. The Scots had excellent technique and precision in their contra dancing. It was customary in Scotland to dance all night long till the next morning, at weddings as well as after someone's death. The Irish influence was felt mostly in their music although they would dance a **jig** at any gathering of people. The most popular Irish music pieces that were used in American contra dances were: *The Irish Washerwoman*, *The White Cockade*, *The Girl I Left Behind Me*, and *Turkey in the Straw*. It was not surprising that **contra dances** were so popular in Maine, New Hampshire, and Vermont where many of these settlers went. Itinerant

"Mlle. Sallé," Paris, 1732. An engraving and etching by Nicolas de Larmessin, French, 1684-1753 or 1755.

Claude Ballon (1671-1744) of the Royal Academy of Dance in the typical heavy costume of that time (the men's legs could be seen but not the women's). Raoul-Auger Feuillet's book "Recueil de danses" (1704) contains dances performed by Mlle Subligny with M. Ballon.

Mlle MarieThérèse de Subligny dancing at the opera house in an unidentified ballet in the usual long costume of that period. Engraving, 1690's.

Ballon, the ballet term for a light, bouncy quality in a jump, was supposedly derived from the dancer Claude Ballon's name. The dancer jumps up lightly, pauses in mid-air and lands only to bounce up again with the smoothness of a bouncy ball. Dancer: Helene Andreu ca. 1960. Photographer: Denise.

fiddlers traveled around the country *(Photo Plate 4-4),* playing and then passing a hat around to get paid. A fiddler was a highly regarded individual at that time. He was asked to play for many weddings, dances, and other events. As word of a fiddler's presence got out, people came to hear and to dance. For larger occasions at a town hall, assembly, or a ball, more instruments were added such as the clarinet, cornet, violoncello, flute and later an organ and then a piano.

As for the differences between country dances and contra dances, there are a few; (both are still danced today, and schedules for dances and classes of these can be found on the Internet.) **Country dances** involve more intricate footwork, more variety of formations and dance figures, and a specific country dance is usually danced to a specific piece of music (as seen in John Playford's publication about *The English Dancing Master,* with dance directions and music for many, many country dances). **Contra dances**, on the other hand, consist of much dance walking, mostly only long line formation, and do not have to be danced to the same piece of music each time. It seems that the French were a bit upset that the English were so pleased with themselves for having invented country dancing, so as a result the French called it contredanse, and when the dance reached America it was called a contra dance.

The dancing masters in America went from one region to the next teaching the latest steps *(Photo Plate 4-3).* Puritan New England needed this for the very important Governor's Ball (especially since they did not usually indulge in dancing.) The **minuet** was popular in Philadelphia, but in the West it was the **quadrille squares**, with American Indian women as partners since female settlers were scarce in 1700. It was not until 1788 that a dance book was published in the colonies: *Collection of the Newest & Most Fashionable Country Dances & Cotillions, the Greater Part by Mr. John Griffith, Dancing Master in Providence.* During the 17th century, the population in the South came from a more aristocratic background than in the North, and they liked to dance. Those in the North had gone there mainly for religious reasons. Dancing, and certainly anything resembling dancing with a partner of the opposite sex, was risqué and was looked upon very unfavorably, especially in Philadelphia where many Quakers lived. The Quakers felt that their children would be corrupted, but upper classes considered dance to be good because, as the philosopher John Locke had said, it instilled confidence in children. By the 18th century this proved to be the case. A couple from the Paris Opera opened a school in Philadelphia (which was becoming a magnet for dance) and they and others produced talented American dancers such as **John Durang, Mary Ann Lee, Augusta Maywood,** and **George Washington Smith**, all from Philadelphia. (The Shakers included choreographed dancing as part of their services, so they did not disapprove of dancing.)

Back in France the transition to dance as a performance art was mainly due to the fact that King Louis XIV was no longer dancing. He built a ballroom with a wooden floor and a balcony for the audience all around the four sides. As the audience looked down at the performance, the patterns of the dances changed and became more appealing; think of a Busby Berkeley Hollywood movie. The interaction between dancers was also more obvious when seen from above.

"Trajes mexicanos, un Fandango," Chromolithograph by C. Castro, Artist, and by J. Campillo, Lithographer, 1869.

"Layout of Boreze (bourée) steps," page 3 in "An essay for the further improvement of dancing, being a collection of figure dances, of several numbers, compos'd by the most eminent masters; describ'd in characters after the newest manner of Monsieur Feuillet," by Edmund Pemberton, Published 1711.

"Baroque Dancing." Photo from Dancing Manual "The Art of Dancing Explained," published in London, 1735. Author: Kellom Tomlinson. Manuals by Feuillet and by Rameau also have baroque choreography. The baroque era (ca. 1600-1750) used exaggerated motion and easily understandable details to indicate exuberance, drama, and grandeur. It was a time of noteworthy scientific discoveries by Galileo Galilei and by Isaac Newton.

"Portrait of Francoise Prévost as a Bacchante," by Jean Raoux, early 18th century.

**Jean-Baptiste Lully** (1632-1687) was an Italian-born musician and dancer who assisted at The Dance Academy established by King Louis XIV. Lully became the court composer of the king and wrote operas, ballets, and dances *(Photo Plate 4-3)*. Lully composed music and also danced in the ballets that he introduced as a feature in the operas of that time. Molière, the dramatist, whose original name was Jean-Baptiste Poquelin, Molière being his stage name, collaborated with Lully to produce many successful ballets that pleased the court and the public. He helped create the **comédie ballet** like Molière's *Le Bourgeois Gentilhomme* with ballet numbers scattered among the dialogues; this may have been the predecessor to our present day Broadway musicals.

**Ballet** had gradually given up its song and speech and concentrated just on dance and mime. But in the meantime there were the comédie ballets of Molière and the composer Jean-Baptiste Lully, and the **opéra-ballets** of **André Campra** (1660-1744) and **Jean-Philippe Rameau** (1683-1764) *(Photo Plate 4-4)*. These were songs and dances to a specific theme. The first ballet without any song or speech was *Le Triomphe de L'Amour* (*The Triumph of Love*), 1681, choreographed by **Pierre Beauchamp** (1631-1719) to Lully's music *(Photo Plate 4-3)*. It was later revived for the stage with **Mlle de Lafontaine** (1655-1738) as the first professional ballerina and première danseuse of ballet. Until 1681 only men danced ballets, women did not.

The **ballet d'action**, such as the ballet based on the tragedy *Horace* (1640) by French playwright Pierre Corneille (1606-1684), was performed as a dance pantomime, *Les Horaces,* based on Corneille's play, with dance and mime, and without words. It was performed by **Claude Ballon, Marie Subligny** *(Photo Plate 4-1)*, and **Françoise Prévost** at the Paris Academy and it became popular, as well as the ballets of **John Weaver**. It foreshadowed the ballets with a plot of **Jean-Georges Noverre. John Weaver** (1673-1760), a British dancer, choreographer, and teacher, who worked mainly at the Drury Lane Theatre in London, wrote in 1721 that dancing was an elegant and regular movement, harmoniously composed of beautiful attitudes. On the whole, this indeed described the dance of his time with dignified bearing and no extreme display of emotion.

In 1717 Weaver produced *The Loves of Mars and Venus*, a ballet with no singing and no speaking. He thought that dance teachers should know anatomy, and in 1721 published his book *Anatomical and Mechanical Lectures Upon Dancing*. At about the same time, **Leipzig Gottfried Tauber** (a German) wrote *The Correctly Working Dance Teacher* (1717). These two books stressed the importance of dancing in education and seemed to have impressed the parents who tried to provide dance lessons for their children. Gaston Vuillier, the 19$^{th}$ century French historian, also mentioned grace, harmony, and beauty as distinguishing true dance from the unsophisticated dance improvised by early man.

Queen Elizabeth I is credited with having given dancing some momentum in England. She enjoyed watching English **country-dances – chain**, **round**, **branles** – and **folk dances,** as well as the noblemen trying them out. Lots of dancing schools existed in London and dancing became very popular.

After **Jean-Baptiste Lully** introduced the **minuet** in 1650 and Louis XIV danced it and made it the official dance, it became the dance craze of the 17$^{th}$ and 18$^{th}$ centuries. The name came from "pas menu" meaning small step. The years between 1650 and 1750 were known as the "Age of the Minuet." Voltaire at the end of the 18th century made fun of it saying that with their mincing steps, bows, and charm, the dancers still finished in just about the same place where they had started. The **minuet** was in three quarter time, conquered Europe, and did away with other dances like the **courante,** a couples dance with running and gliding steps, the **pavane,** a dignified court dance popular in the 15th century, the **bourrée**, and the **gavotte** at the French court.

With the growth of Spain's empire in America, there was an exchange of dances, and many American dances went to Europe, such as the **sarabande** and the **chaconne** from Central America and Mexico, brought over to Europe before 1600. Spanish writers such as Miguel de Cervantes (1547-1616) and Francisco Gómez de Quevedo (1583-1645) suggested a Mexican origin for these dances. Both were suggestive dances and became popular in the harbors of Andalucía. They had to be moderated and cleaned up before going to the French courts. The **sarabande** led to the **seguidilla,** the **canario** or **canary,** consisting of leaps, turns, and sole and heel stamps, and to the **jota** of Aragon. Afro-Cuban dances may have influenced the **fandango** *(Photo Plate 4-2)*. The fandango is in triple time and is danced by one couple at a time. It is accompanied, like many other Spanish dances, by a guitar, castanets, or the dancers' singing. It is believed to have come to Spain from the Moors.

Dance traveled both directions, to and from Europe, and to and from America. There was a blend of South American, Mexican, native, and European styles in these dances and the use of instruments of European derivation. When Native American Indians danced these dances they gave them their own native flavor, and their particular derivation can only be deduced from the style of the dance.

After the founding of The Dance Academy in Paris, ballet became a profession to be learned and mastered. **Beauchamps** became the Maître de Ballet at the Royal Dance Academy. And soon women too could be professional dancers.

Stage costumes mirrored the contemporary fashions of the time. Dancers wore heavy costumes, long padded skirts, tight bodices, enormous headdresses and wigs, high heels and masks. Props were used to indicate a period or style – a lyre for Greece, a fan for Spain and so on. The dances were more elaborate versions of the court dances – the **sarabande**, the **minuet**, the **gavotte** (a gay, lively, hopping couple dance of the 15th century), and of the rhythms found in suites by Bach. By the beginning of the 18th century, high standards of technique were developing but quick jumps were mostly executed only by the men, whose tights allowed their leg movements to be seen, whereas the women, with their long, heavy skirts, were not advancing in technique as were the men *(Photo Plate 4-1)*. But this soon changed.

When, during **Lully**'s time, performances were moved to a raked stage, one that slants down toward the front, Lully also used complex designs and no elevation in his steps; his traditional choreography made use of horizontal lines.

His successor, **Jean-Philippe Rameau,** wanted just the opposite. His dancers were required to jump off the floor in vertical designs and inventive choreography. The arguments continue to the present day between strict classicism and expressiveness, pure

" Ladies and Gentlemen Dancing," by Paul
Grégoire, 1780. Brush and gray wash with black
crayon, on ivory laid paper, laid down on card.

THE POSITION IN QUADRILLE.

"The Position in Quadrille," by Theodore Wüst,
Image plate between pages 20 and 21 of "The
Dance of Society, a critical analysis of all the
standard quadrilles, round dances…etc." by Wm.
B. de Garmo, published in New York, 1875.

"Jean-Baptiste
Lully" (1632-
1687), engraved
by Henri
Bonnart (1642-
1711).

Beadle's "Dime Ball-room Companion and
Guide to Dancing. Comprising rules of etiquette,
hints on private parties, toilettes for the ball-room.
Also synopsis of round and square dances,
dictionary of French terms." Published in New
York by Beadle and Co. in 1868.

"The Dancing
Master,"
engraving, from
Pierre Rameau's
1725 "Le maitre á
danser."
Translated by
English dancer
and writer John
Essex in 1732.

dance and story ballets, ballet and modern dance. Rameau's ballets often had imitations of dances from various countries – Turkey, Peru, Persia, and America. This was a change from the mythological characters of ballet that had existed previously. Rameau was an excellent musician. He was an organist, harpsichord teacher, music theorist and baroque composer of operas and ballets. The freshness of Rameau's ballet music set a standard copied by several countries like Italy and Germany. His best-known work was *Les Indes Galantes*, with the designer Giovanni Niccolò Servandoni creating an amazing erupting volcano for one scene. Rameau, along with Lully and Gluck, was one of the best-known pre-Revolutionary French opera composers *(Photo Plate 4-4)*.

Rameau used the 18<sup>th</sup> century French **quadrille** in an opera *(Photo Plate 4-3)*. This dance started out as a country-dance as did many other dances, became popular and was brought to America later by a French dancing master after the War of 1812. At that time the United States was leaning toward France rather than England; this dance used many French names for the steps such as **promenade** (a walking step done with a partner) and **do-si-do** (from the French dos-à-dos, or back to back). When it became the **cotillion** and went west after the Gold Rush of 1849, the caller and the calls for the steps or figures were important. Usually one of the musicians would be the caller. In 1858, the book *Howe's Complete Ball-Room Hand Book* appeared with the calls printed. The French word cotillion meant petticoat; it could be seen as the ladies did turns in the dance. The dance became the **square dance** in 1860 with many more steps from the **waltz** and more **figures** added to it. (A figure is a series of steps that then form a precise variation in a dance, such as **do-si-do**.)

The American National Association of Masters of Dancing was formed at about this time. There were many schools teaching European dances like the **mazurka**, the **schottisch**, and the **waltz** *(Photo Plate 4-4)*.

In Europe the peasants in Bavaria danced a form of the waltz, the **waltzer**, in 1750. The **landler**, a hopping dance in three-quarter time was popular in Bohemia and Austria with the country people. The **waltz** was both a folk dance and a ballroom dance in three-quarter time. It became more of a gliding and sliding dance as it moved to the city and was well liked by those bored by the minuet.

In those days there were very few career choices for women, in fact practically none. A woman working at the Paris Opera was actually working for the king; hence an abusive father, brother, or husband had no power over her. She had more independence than most women; she could keep her earnings. Some of the ladies were famous, well-liked dancers, who also had many lovers on the side. This tended to put every female dancer at risk of defamation.

In France, **Françoise Prévost** (1680-1741) *(Photo Plate 4-2)* was one of the first women of influence in ballet; she was very light and precise. She choreographed and danced a famous piece, *Les Caractères de la Danse*, in 1715 that consisted of solos based on popular dances of the day. Two of her pupils, **Marie Camargo** and **Marie Sallé**, became the best-known dancers of the time.

Photo Plate 4-4

"The Waltz," circa 1815. Detail from the frontispiece to Thomas Wilson's "Correct Method of German and French Waltzing," 1816, showing nine positions of the Waltz, clockwise from the left. The musicians are at far left. Engraver unknown, The waltz, a new dance in England in 1816, was not a traditional group dance, but a couples dance in which the gentleman placed his arm around the lady's waist, giving the waltz a dubious moral status.

"Portrait of August Vestris" (1760-1842) by Adèle Romany, 1793. He made his debut at 12 years in the Paris Opera and was the company's leading dancer for 36 years.

"Jean Philippe Rameau" (1683-1764); Artist: Jacques André Joseph Aved, 1728.

"The Fiddler." Artist: E. W. Kemble.," Century Magazine," May 10, 1887.

**Marie Camargo** (1710-1770) was a favorite ballerina in Paris. She preferred vertical dance and was a brilliant technician, with great strength and airiness. To gain strength she took classes with the men and did the steps they did. She had shown a sense of rhythm even at six months; when her father played the violin she would beat time on her crib. She made her debut at the Paris Opera in 1726 at the age of sixteen. She invented many new and difficult steps; she was a traditionalist as well and was interested in technique, not human and dramatic elements *(Photo Plate 4-5)*.

She shortened her heavy skirts to halfway between the ankle and knee so the audience could see her legs in **entrechats-quatre** and high **cabrioles**. (For **an entrechat-quatre** starting in 5$^{th}$ position, if the right foot is in front, jump up and beat the calves together with the right leg in back, open the legs slightly and land with the right foot in 5$^{th}$ position front. For a **cabriole devant** (front) or derrière (back) the working leg is raised to the desired height and is beaten from below by the supporting leg. The landing is made on the supporting leg with the knee bent in **demi-plié**.) The height of **Camargo**'s jumps necessitated the wearing of a "caleçon de precaution," emergency drawers, since the skirts would billow and show off more of the leg than was considered proper. This was the first step toward the adoption of the 19$^{th}$ century tutu – the bell-like tarlatan skirt that is the classic dancer's outfit.

Camargo started doing these jumps when she daringly stepped in to replace an absent male dancer. She is also said to have done away with heels in her dance shoes, so she could get a better spring from the floor. She was a powerful influence in shaping the course of dance. She proved that women were as capable of great elevation and of doing fast footwork as men. Until her time, dance was only horizontal movement even when the music was quick. Paris adored her. There were dresses à la Camargo, and shoes, hats, and hairdos à la Camargo.

**Barbara Campanini** (1721-1799), known as La Barberina *(Photo Plate 4-5)*, was a fiery, typically strong Italian ballerina who could do even more entrechats (**entrechat-huit**) than Camargo. She had many love affairs, later repented and became the abbess of a convent.

(**Entrechat-huit**: Start in 5$^{th}$ position, R foot front, knees bent in demi plié. Jump and open the legs, beat the R leg behind the L, open the legs and beat the R leg in front of the L, open the legs and beat the R leg in back of the L, open the legs and finish with the R foot in front in a 5$^{th}$ position demi plié. This is counted as eight crossings. Each crossing, which is very quick, counts as two – one for each leg.)

**Marie Sallé** (1707-1756), Camargo's rival, was a dramatic dancer who believed in spiritual rather than technical elevation; her accent was on nobility of posture and a dramatic characterization. She did not believe in dance simply for dance's sake. Her most popular role, which she created for herself, was that of Venus in her ballet *Pygmalion*. She first presented it in London in 1734. It was the story of a sculptor who fell in love with the statue of Venus that he had created. The dance was a ballet pantomime, completely different from the rigid, formal ballets of the Paris Opera.

Sallé let her hair down and wore just a muslin dress (over her corset and petticoat) in the style of a Greek statue or of the future modern dancer, **Isadora Duncan**, instead of the usual heavy costume and fancy wig *(Photo Plates 4-1)*. This gave her a greater freedom of movement. It was very radical and rather shocking for a period when cumbersome skirts, wigs, feathers, and jewelry were worn on stage. But she was actually mirroring the fashions of the times that were softer and more feminine than before and led to the Romantic era. Her steps were simple but very expressive.

Crowds would line the streets and start riots to get tickets to her performances. At seventeen, the famous Shakespearean actor, David Garrick, saw Marie Sallé in **Pygmalion** and was so overwhelmed that he always remembered her amazing dance acting. One season she even danced under the management of the great composer Handel. She always analyzed all her roles carefully, as an actor would. She also practiced daily after she retired, so she was at all times ready to appear on the spur of the moment as she did in 1752 when she danced with the new rising star, **Gaetan Vestris**, "the God of the dance," as he was later called.

**Louis Dupré** (1697-1744), known as "the Great Dupré," was another "god of the dance." He was considered to be unsurpassed in grace and allure and gave the male dancer a greater status than he had previously had. He was an exemplary danseur noble, and was also a renowned dance teacher (in an unbroken line of renowned dance teachers from the era of Louis XIV through the 20th century.)

It was during the Renaissance that men became the organizers of the dance: the teachers, choreographers, innovators, dance notators, and the analysts of dance movements, such as Beauchamps, Lully, and Rameau, and the women: Camargo, Sallé, La Barberina, and Prévost became its stars. As more and more dancers developed at the Paris Academy, they traveled all over Europe from court to court: Italy, Russia, England, and Denmark, and started their own schools and companies under royal subsidies or as part of an opera company. The future of ballet was secure.

But after Rameau's death, ballet was uninspired; each aspect – music, story, and spectacle – seemed to exist by itself. Technique existed without considering the music, drama, or the great performers such as **Gaetan Vestris** (1729-1808), **Jean Dauberval** (1742-1806) who choreographed *La Fille Mal Gardée,* still popular today, or **Charles Didelot** (1767-1837), Swedish but French-trained, and **Salvatore Viganò** (1769-1821), an Italian dancer and choreographer.

However, **Jean-Georges Noverre** (1727-1810), an excellent choreographer who danced in London, Vienna, and Milan complained about numerous aspects regarding ballet productions in his *Lettres sur la Danse et sur les Ballets* and became a force in the rebirth of ballet. Some of his suggestions were:

- Plots of ballets should be unified; all unrelated solos should be omitted.
- Technique should not only be brilliant, but should move the audience through dramatic expressiveness.
- Scenery and costumes should be related to the theme and should be appropriate to the theme.
- Music should be written specifically for a ballet. The choreographer should explain to the composer in detail what he would need as music. (**Noverre**, as choreographer, explained to the famous composer Christoph Willibald Gluck (1714-1787) the characters (of the savages) in the ballet *Iphigenie in Tauride,* their steps, gestures, and attitudes.)
- Pantomime should be made simpler and more understandable.

Photo Plate 4-5

"Louis XIV of France" in the role of Apollo, the sun god (Le Roi Soleil), in "Le Ballet de la Nuit" (The Ballet of the Night) c. 1653. Artist unknown, costume designed by Henri Gissey (1621-1673).

Barbara Campanini, "La Barberina," oil on canvas, 1745. She could do entrechat huit (more than Camargo). Artist: Antoine Pesne (1683-1757), court painter of Prussia, in the collection of Frederick II the Great (1712-1786), King of Prussia (1740-1786).

"Maria Anna de Cupis de Camargo," a ballet star of the Paris Opera c.1730. Artist Nicolas Lancret (1690-1743) painted several versions of this. Lancret's weaving of nature and figures in a cur-vilinear design is typical rococo.

"Merrymaking at a Wayside Inn." Artist: (formerly attributed to Pavel Petrovich Svinin's water-color of rural PA in 1812). He was a Russian who visited the U.S. as secretary to the Russian representative, during which time he painted watercolors of life in America, later publishing a book "Voyage Pittoresque Aux Etats Unis de l'Amerique par Paul Svignine en 1811, 1812, et 1813. Presently attributed to John Lewis Krimmel (1786-1821) .Watercolor and graphite on white laid paper.

"The Shepherds," 1717-1719, oil on canvas, by Jean-Antoine Watteau (1684-1721). The painting shows the pursuits of the idle rich such as flirting, dancing, playing at being peasants, a popular activity in France since the early 15th century.

65

- Masks should not be worn. (And gradually performers like Vestris, Dauberval, and Didelot eliminated the heavy, unwieldy headdresses and masks, especially if a dancer had been replaced, so that the audience would know who was actually dancing. The audience preferred the absence of masks, therefore they were no longer used.)

**Noverre**'s choreography was much admired by David Garrick, who tried to have Noverre's ballet, *Chinese Festival*, performed in London, but in 1755 France and England were on the verge of war and when Noverre's ballet opened in London a mob tried to destroy all the scenery and to set the theatre on fire. However, Garrick and Noverre remained friends.

Voltaire was a great admirer of Noverre, as was the Grand Duke of Stuttgart, who, being wealthy, furnished him in Stuttgart with one hundred dancers, twenty soloists from the leading Italian and German companies, as well as a costume designer, and an architect to design theatrical devices. Later, Noverre revived several of his ballets in Vienna. He proved to be an outstanding instructor and developed many great dancers. He remained in Vienna from 1767 to 1774, presenting seven to eight new ballets each year. After his glorious season in Milan, someone of his generation compared him to Raphael, the great painter, for expression and design.

Finally in 1776 Noverre became ballet master of the Paris Opera, thanks to Marie Antoinette whose dancing teacher he had been. Later he fled from France, worried that his friendship with Marie Antoinette could cause him problems during the French Revolution. He produced ballets in London but later returned to live in France.

**Gaetan Vestris** (1729-1808) and the Vestris family were exceptional male dancers. **Gaetan** was an excellent dancer, as were his sister and brother, and he was arrogant. Critics said they could really feel as though it was Apollo dancing when he appeared. He was not a good choreographer but refused to believe this. **Auguste Vestris** (1760-1842) (*Photo Plate 4-4*), his son, and his grandson, **Auguste Armand**, carried on the family tradition and outdid him. They also inherited some of their talent from Gaetan's wife, **Anne Heinel**, Auguste Vestris' mother and Auguste Armand's grandmother, who was the first female dancer to perform a pirouette. They had their father's great technique, and also had exuberance. Auguste Vestris' teaching methods enlarged the vocabulary of ballet. What had previously been the domain of the **danseur noble** now formed the **adagio** section of a class – the slow, fluid, graceful movements that develop the dancers' balance and sense of line; the quick, complex jumps, previously the domain of the **demi-caractère** dancer, also became a part of each class, as did the even more athletic movements that the **comic dancer** had previously used, along with a turnout of the legs of 180 degrees. An aim for virtuosity may not have been what Vestris had in mind when he taught, but greater virtuosity was what ensued in ballet. Auguste Vestris was an unparalleled performer and teacher at the Opera, with Taglioni and Fanny Elssler as his outstanding pupils.

By 1770 there were no wigs, no masks, no long flamboyant costumes, but shorter looser skirts and more unified plots as suggested by ballet masters **Jean-Georges Noverre** of France and **Gasparo Angiolini** of Italy in 1750-1760. They created the **ballet**

**d'action**, a unified ballet telling a complete story, but not as a part of an opera or a musical. Both claimed to have been the originator of the ballet d'action and disputed the other's assertion to having been the first. This led to a long and bitter controversy. Angiolini (1731-1803) created dances for Gluck's operas such as *Don Juan ou Le Festin de Pierre* (*Don Juan or The Stone Banquet*) and also went to Russia to start the ballet tradition under Catherine the Great while his pupil **Vincenzo Galeotti** did the same for the Royal Danish Ballet in Copenhagen. Noverre also worked with Gluck, who could not get his singers to move with the music as he wished. Noverre told him to have the singers sing from the wings and have real dancers on the stage to dance. Both of these men, Noverre and Angiolini, wanted costumes similar to the ancient Greeks – no wigs, no shoe heels, no shoe buckles, no large skirts, no hoops for the sides of the skirts, no tonnelets (short hooped skirts that men wore for women's roles).

An outstanding male dancer was **Salvatore Viganò** (1769-1821) of Naples, a pupil of Noverre; **Viganò's** mother had also been Noverre's pupil. He had a true understanding of Noverre's principles of dance and was an exceptional choreographer, but his young wife Maria was so delicate and lovely in a Grecian tunic with her black hair falling on her shoulders that courtiers adored her, which caused the jealous Empress, Marie Antoinette, to forbid the courtiers from attending the theatre when Viganò's wife danced. Maria was known to be a flirt and Viganò had to put up with it. When she was pregnant, women imitated her by wearing false stomachs.

Viganò was so well liked that people did things à la Viganò. He was excellent at pantomime, at handling large groups of people, and at giving each dancer in the chorus a character, just as Noverre had suggested. In 1801 Ludwig van Beethoven wrote his only music for a ballet, *The Creatures of Prometheus,* which Viganò choreographed. Viganò also choreographed at La Scala, in Milan, which had started a Dance Academy early in 1812. The French author Stendhal (1783-1842, the pen name of Marie-Henri Beyle) wrote very flattering words about Viganò. When Viganò died, thousands followed his funeral procession to the grave. He was adored.

With the French Revolution in 1789 came the overthrow of royalty. Many were executed, ballet felt challenged. It had been considered a form of entertainment for aristocracy, but the dancers were adaptable and so ballet survived. There were many festivals of a patriotic nature, with dancing and large choirs singing patriotic hymns and the Marseillaise outdoors. Maybe the Parisians danced to forget the number of ruthless executions that had taken place, because there were about twenty three theatres and eighteen hundred dancing schools that were open every evening, according to a writer of that time, Gaston Vuillier. When ballet performances again took place, the ballet stories were about the revolution, about political and social democracy, or about the American Revolution; it was the beginning of the Romantic Revolution and the Golden Age of Ballet.

Photo Plate 4-6

"Figure of a Dancer,"
bronze, ivory, marble base;
designed by Demetre Chiparus,
ca. 1925.

"The Elegancies of Quadrille Dancing," etching by George Cruikshank,
British, 1817.

"A Dancing Couple Celebrating New Year's Day.," from
"The London Illustrated News," 1848, artist unknown.

A "Reverence" is executed by a
dancer to acknowledge the
audience's applause at the end of
a dance and is a done in a style
that is appropriate to that
particular dance. Photo ca. 1958,
by Denise. Dancer: Helene
Andreu.

# 5

# Ballet's Golden Age

The Golden Age of Ballet was the Romantic Era when Romanticism prevailed (1820-1870). Romanticism was an artistic, literary and philosophical movement that originated in the 18th century. It was a reaction against the importance of reason in the Age of Enlightenment. There was a stress on imagination, intuition, feelings, and a melancholy state of mind. Romantic ballets were involved with the supernatural and with ill-fated love, as in *Giselle* and in *La Sylphide*. In literature and operas, the heroes and heroines usually died by the end of the work. There was an increased interest in nature and nationalism as well as in emotions, especially unattainable love, despair, and sadness.

Furthermore, technical inventions in the theater during the Romantic Era made possible a great change in scenic effects:
- House lights could be lowered during the performance.
- Curtains could be drawn between scenes.
- Gas illumination permitted a greater facility in changing the intensity of onstage lighting.
- Mechanical contraptions enabled spirits and sprites to appear to be flying through the air.

The supremacy of the ballerina was on its way from 1830 through the 1850's. Ethereal, exotic, and unattainable women, sprites, spirits, and supernatural creatures, were often the subject of ballets. The fabric of women's dance dresses and everyday dresses reflected one another and was now gauzy and light. Elements of fantasy and mysticism appeared in the ballets *La Sylphide*, *Ondine,* and *Giselle*. Character dance (national dancing) and advances in dancing en pointe (on the tips of the toes) took place during the Romantic Age. **Jules Perrot** choreographed the delicate ballet *Pas de Quatre (Photo Plate 5-4)* for the four great female dancers of the Romantic Age – **Marie Taglioni, Fanny Cerrito, Carlotta Grisi**, and **Lucille Grahn. Charles-Edmond Duponchel**, who later became director of the Paris Opera, started the custom of throwing flowers from the audience to honor a favorite ballerina.

In the early 1800's, ballerinas began to rise up en pointe and seemed to float across the stage. It may have been **Geneviève Gosselin** at the Paris Opera, or **Amalia Brugnoli** in Vienna who was the first to dance en pointe, but it was **Marie Taglioni** (1804-1884) who got credit for making it an art, especially in the ballet *La Sylphide*, choreographed by her father, **Filippo Taglioni**. The choreography and music did not survive; the version seen today is the **August Bournonville** choreography for the Royal Danish Ballet with music by the Norwegian composer Herman Severin Løvenskjold.

The opera *Robert le Diable*, composed in 1831 by Giacomo Meyerbeer, a German composer, also had ballet choreography by Filippo Taglioni for his daughter Marie as an integral part of the opera, not as a separate art form. During a particularly upsetting performance, a falling gas lamp hit one of the ballerinas, Marie jumped out of the way of some crashing scenery, and a tenor fell through a trap door by mistake. What a night. It was actually a very successful opera.

The ballet *La Sylphide*, not to be confused with the ballet *Les Sylphides*, was in keeping with the Romantic Movement. It dealt with supernatural creatures, the devil, sylphs, fairies, strong emotions, passion, unhappy love, and the death of a sylph. It was a perfect role for **Marie Taglioni**. She had not seemed promising in her teens, but her father, Filippo, a ballet master who traveled to Stockholm, Copenhagen, Vienna, and Munich, took over her training in Paris before her debut. She amazed the crowds in all her performances. She invented leg warmers by simply cutting off the sleeves of her sweater and wearing them on her legs when they were cold during a rehearsal.

Marie was part of a famous Italian dance family of the nineteenth century started by **Carlo Taglioni** in the late 1700's with his wife **Maria Petracchi Taglioni**. Their sons, **Filippo** (1777-1871) and **Salvatore** (1789-1868) choreographed extensively, the latter for the Teatro San Carlo in Naples, and the former for his daughter Marie whom he trained along with her brother Paul (1808-1884). Paul settled in Berlin as choreographer. **Salvatore, Filippo**, and **Paul Taglioni** all had daughters who were prima ballerinas in London, Paris, and Naples.

**Marie Taglioni** appeared in *La Sylphide* in 1832, in a multilayered white skirt that reached just below her knees; her hair was tied back in a bun. Her dancing and appearance caused a sensation. She looked delicate and lovely with her light floating way of dancing *(Photo Plate 5-1, 5-2, and 5-4)*. The women in Paris copied her looks, and a group of fans even bought a pair of her pointe shoes, cooked them in a delicious French sauce, and ate them. At that time new pointe shoes were not as solid and hard as now and it took a lot of energy to stay up en pointe.

Taglioni did not show emotions on stage, but she did not need to do so. The role of La Sylphide was ideal for her. It is about the winged ethereal Sylphide who awakens James, a Scottish youth asleep in an armchair. Later, while trying to capture the Sylph, he throws a scarf on her shoulders. He does not realize that a witch had given him the scarf and he is horrified when he sees the Sylphide's wings fall off. As the other sylphides carry her off to the sky, James, a role created by **Joseph Mazilier**, falls lifeless. It is a typical story of the Romantic Era. It is still performed today.

**Joseph Mazilier** (1801-1868), a French dancer, ballet master, and choreographer, was best known for his choreography of *Paquita* (1844), *Le Diable à Quatre* (1845), and *Le Corsaire* (1856) *(Photo Plates 5-2)*.

The only choreography **Marie Taglioni** ever did was *Le Papillon* for her favorite pupil, **Emma Livry,** who had many of her qualities as a dancer.

**Emma Livry** (1842-1863), a protégé of Marie Taglioni, was a young and very promising dancer who greatly resembled Taglioni in her delicate style. She created the principal role in *Le Papillon,* which Taglioni had choreographed for her and in which she was soon compared to Taglioni and to her contemporary, **Fanny Elssler** (1810-1884). Emma had always wanted to dance, and she could rise on the tips of her toes, shoeless, when she was six years old.

Photo Plate 5-1

Carlotta Grisi and Jules Perrot in" La Polka,"
lithograph by Augustus Jules Bouvier, published in
1844.

The Three Graces, representing the ballerinas
Taglioni, Elssler, and Cerrito, lithograph from a
drawing by A. E. Chalon, 1844.

Fanny Cerrito in "Alma," from the ballet, "Alma ou
La Fille de Feu," by Jules Perrot, lithograph by
Augustus Jules Bouvier, published in 1842.

Sheet music cover for "Valse de Giselle" from the
ballet "Giselle," danced by Carlotta Grisi and Marius
Petipa, 1841.

71

Once an author who was writing a novel concerning a ballet dancer asked **Emma Livry** to describe the ballet *La Sylphide* which he wanted to mention in his book. He told her that in his book the ballerina would be burned alive at the conclusion of the novel.

Not long after that, Emma Livry was rehearsing for a ballet, *La Muette de Portici*. She had the title role, and everyone was eager to see her. Suddenly screams were heard. Emma was terrified and kept running back and forth; her tarlatan skirt had caught fire from an open gas jet as she climbed onto the scenery, a make-believe mountain. Finally a stagehand caught her, put her on the ground, and smothered the flames but her body had already been badly burned. Her condition became worse; she died just a few months later at the age of twenty-one. Open gas jets were a big problem at that time, and management's advice was to dip costumes in a special fire retardant liquid, but Emma had not done so because she thought it made the dress look too limp.

A more pleasant story is one about **Marie Taglioni**. Once, in Vienna when she had just danced, forty Austrian noblemen detached the horses from her carriage and pulled the carriage themselves to take her to her hotel. That is how much she was loved. Johann Strauss II (1825-1899) composed the *Marie Taglioni Polka* (Opus 173) in her honor using music from ballets in which she had appeared. Taglioni later moved to Russia (overwhelmed with jealousy of her rival Fanny Elssler – more about her later). Taglioni inspired the Russian dancers, then the Italians, and then the British, in her travels.

The **polka** originated in the mid-19th century in Bohemia and from there spread to Vienna, Paris, and then to London and America where it replaced the waltz and gave way to the **ragtime dances**. There were many styles of polka. The French polka was slow and graceful while others, like those by Joseph Strauss, were of a quicker tempo, like a **galop**. (The polka consisted of a hop on "and", then a quick step on count 1 and also on count 2, followed by a slow step on count 3, and a pause on count 4.)

In London **Jules Joseph Perrot** (1810-1892) had the idea to choreograph *Pas de Quatre* for the four leading ballerinas of the day, Carlotta Grisi, Fanny Cerrito, Lucille Grahn, and Marie Taglioni *(Photo Plate 5-1 and 5-4)*. The presentation of this masterpiece was almost impossible when each of them complained about the order of her appearance on the program. Taglioni was given the last solo, the place of honor. But to get the others to agree, Benjamin Lumley, the manager, said the place of honor should go to the oldest. Finally the order was settled according to the age of the performer, beginning with the youngest and ending with the oldest. Taglioni was the oldest.

A garland of flowers around the hair, which came over the ears before being caught up in a bun, and the gracefully undulating long white tutu with a simple white bodice and puff sleeves of net held in with elastic became the traditional outfit for the ballet blanc (white ballet) of the Romantic Ballets. Even today the ballet blanc is still seen, often as the first ballet in the program. Some of these ballets blancs include *Giselle,* by **Jean Coralli** 1841 *(Photo Plates 5-3)*, for the Paris Opera, and *Les Sylphides* with its original plotless choreography by **Michel Fokine** 1907, in Russia, based on music by Frederic Chopin.

As for the male dancer who previously had silk hose even for everyday apparel, he now wore white tights from toes to waist. A full-sleeved, billowy blouse worn with either a jacket or vest completed his costume and is still the attire of a male classical dancer.

Photo Plate 5-2

Giuseppina Bozzacchi as Swanhilda in the first performance of "Coppélia," Paris, 1870, choreographed by Arthur Saint Leon, photographer unknown.

Sheet music "Mlle Fanny Elssler's Quadrilles," arranged for The piano by Chas. Jarvis, 1840.

Joseph Mazilier, dancer/choreographer of "La Tempète," ca. 1860. Artist unknown.

Sheet music cover, "La Gitana" (The New Cachoucha), danced by Marie Taglioni, 1838. Music arranged for the piano by Charles W. Glover, c. 1838.

Ballet shoes no longer had heels, became even softer, and were made of leather that fit the foot like a glove, allowing the foot to stretch and arch completely. The flexibility of shoes and the soft leather of the shoes allowed for quiet landings in jumps, more complicated footwork, and a more ethereal appearance. They were also a protection from the floor and allowed for ease in turns since the bare foot can stick to the floor. Before long, ballerinas were rising to a very high **demi pointe** (ball of the foot), and some who had strong toe muscles even rose up to full toe in the early 1800's without wearing toe shoes. This was so effective that women were trying to find ways to prolong the length of time that they could stay "sur les pointes" and look like sylphs and spirits. The ballerinas seemed to float across the stage and appeared even more inaccessible.

Several companies had ventured across the Atlantic Ocean even before the American Revolutionary War. **Henry Holt**, from England, came with his group in 1735, presented three ballets but did not start a company, due to the Puritan attitude against dance.

In America, after the Revolutionary War (1775-1783), there were patriotic spectacles such as *Liberty Asserted* or *The Patriot* that had a good amount of dancing. There were also extravaganzas, burlesque, vaudeville, striptease, and ballet influences in both the theatre and the dance.

**Alexander Placide** and his common-law wife, Susanne Théodore Taillandet, or Mlle Théodore, performed in Charleston, South Carolina, in 1791, and then in New York for an entire season with **John Durang** (1768-1822), a hornpipe dancer. (The hornpipe, popular during the 16th to 18th centuries, imitated sailors' movements – hauling in an anchor, rigging ropes, and was originally danced solely by men.) They presented *The Bird Catcher, The Return of the Labourers,* and *The Philosophers or the Merry Girl.* **Mme. Placide,** as she was called when she appeared on stage with **Alexander Placide,** became Prima Ballerina of the New Orleans Theatre, performing in ballets by **Noverre** and **Dauberval**. She later staged many original ballets, thus becoming America's first female choreographer.

Marie Taglioni's brother, **Paul Taglioni**, danced in *La Sylphide* with his wife **Amélie** at the Park Theatre in New York City in 1839. That same year **Marius Petipa** and family also performed in America before he became famous for his choreography.

In 1835 two members of the Paris Opera Ballet, **Paul H. Hazard** and his wife, settled in Philadelphia, opened a ballet school, and became the teachers of three talented dancers: **Mary Ann Lee**, **Augusta Maywood**, and **George Washington Smith,** who all became successful dancers.

**Augusta Maywood** (1825-1876) won acclaim in America for her performance in 1837 in *The Maid of Cashmere* together with Mary Ann Lee. In 1838, Augusta Maywood's parents took their daughter to France where, in 1839, she became the first American to dance with the Paris Opera Ballet. She spent most of her life in various European countries. She studied with **Joseph Mazilier** and **Jean Coralli** *(Photo Plate 5-1)* and acquired an exuberant jump. She went on to dance in Marseilles and in Vienna and was Prima Ballerina Assoluta at the La Scala Opera for twelve years; this was quite an achievement at that time, especially for an American. She was compared to many

Photo Plate 5-3

Statue of Mercury, bronze, after sculptor Giambologna (also called Giovanni da Bologna) c. 1780-ca. 1850).

Jean Coralli, French dancer and choreographer (1779-1854)

Attitude front, a pose derived by Carlo Blasis from the statue of Mercury, showing attitude back. In attitude front the knee is well bent and the foot is raised as high as possible. Dancer: Helene Andreu; Photographer: Denise.

"The Five Positions of Dancing" from Thomas Wilson's "Analysis of Country Dancing" (1811). "Containing also directions for compounding almost any number of figures to one tune, with some entire new reels together with the complete etiquette of the ballroom." Illustrated with engravings on wood by J. Berryman, Wilson, Thomas, dancing master. Created/published, 3rd ed., London: J.S. Dickson, 1811.

prominent ballerinas of that era. She formed her own company and then retired in 1858 to open a school and teach in Vienna. Her lifestyle – three children each from a different father – did not make her popular in the United States.

Her colleague **Mary Ann Lee** rushed to Paris from America in 1844 after the opening of *Giselle* in Paris, learned the ballet from **Carlotta Grisi**, and brought it back to America in 1845 as a ballet for herself, her partner, **George Washington Smith**, and her company. In 1846 they were the first to dance *Giselle* in the United States at the Howard Atheneum in Boston and they toured in America for two years. While in Europe she had studied with Jules Perrot and Jean Coralli. She retired but **Smith** went on to tour with the Irish dancer, **Lola Montez**, to teach, to choreograph, and even to perform with the young **Enrico Cechetti** while dancing with the Ronzani Ballet Troupe in their American tour. The present day version of *Giselle* is the one revived by **Petipa** in 1884 and still performed by the Kirov/Mariinsky Ballet in Russia.

Ballet made its first appearance at the Bowery Theatre in New York City's Five Points neighborhood when a French ballet dancer, **Mme. Francisque Hutin**, performed there in *The Deserter* in 1827; some ladies in the lower box seats left when they saw the skimpy attire of the dancers. One report said it was only tights and a tutu.

(The American dancer-author **Lillian Moore** (1911-1967), a frequent contributor to *Dance Magazine* and to *The Dancing Times,* did extensive research on dance in America during the 18th and 19th centuries. The Lillian Moore Dance Research Files are available in the New York Public Library of the Performing Arts.)

**Fanny Elssler** (1810-1884), Marie Taglioni's principal rival, was a forceful and precise dancer. Born in Vienna, Elssler had traveled to Naples where the example set by the Italian ballerina, **Amalia Brugnoli**, encouraged her to be expressive in her dancing. Fans were divided as to their preference for Taglioni or for Elssler. Elssler could dance any character dance; she was very versatile. Some of her most famous dance performances were *The Cachucha*, *The Cracovienne*, and *The Tarantella*, but audiences hissed her if she attempted to perform Taglioni's roles.

Fanny Elssler's sister **Therese Elssler**, also a dancer, was the first woman choreographer to have a work produced at the Paris Opera. It took place in 1838 as a benefit for the two sisters, with Therese playing the part of a young man, something often done in those days when male dancers were not as popular as previously and were practically disappearing from the stage in western Europe.

**Fanny Elssler**'s adventurous spirit made her eager to visit America. Her reputation had already reached America before she arrived in 1840. Elssler stayed in the United States three years instead of two as planned. She arrived with only her manager and three dancers and had to engage and train a corps de ballet for her American appearances *(Photo Plate 5-1, 5-2, and 5-4)*. When she visited Washington, Congress adjourned on the evenings when she performed because so many Senators were playing hooky and attending her performances. In Baltimore, seats for her performances were auctioned, the demand was so high. She extended her American tour and danced in New England, Richmond, Wilmington, Charleston, Frederick, Baltimore, New York, and even went to Havana, Cuba.

Photo Plate 5-4

Sheet music cover for "Beauties of the Ballet – La Mazurka," danced in the ballet "La Gitana" by Mme. Taglioni, 1838. Music arranged for the piano by Charles W. Glover, c. 1838.

Fanny Cerrito and Arthur Saint Léon in "La Redowa Polka," 1844. Lithograph by Augustus Jules Bouvier.

Sheet music cover for" La Cracovienne," dance by Fanny Elssler. Arranged for the piano by L. Gomion,1840.

"Pas de Quatre," ballet by Jules Perrot as danced at her Majesty's Theatre, July 12th, 1845, by the four ballerinas, Grisi, Taglioni, Grahn, and Cerrito.

**Fanny Elssler** had a way of using her entire body to express her emotions in dance, all with much energy and spirit. When she danced *The Tarantella*, based on the reactions to the bite of that spider, reviewers loved her and so did the audience; they packed the theaters for each performance. Tradesmen in America profited from her popularity by naming hats, cuffs, boots, horses, whiskey, and even boats after Fanny Elssler. Her joy of life, and her warm, vivacious temperament came out in her dancing *(Photo Plate 5-2)*.

Elssler had broken her contract with the Paris Opera in order to extend her American trip and was not allowed to dance at the Paris Opera after that. When she went to Russia, after visiting Germany, Austria, and England between 1842 and 1847, the Russians were delighted to receive her. Before her last performance in Moscow her fellow artists there gave her a bracelet inscribed: À Fanny Elssler, les artistes de Moscou – Au Coeur le plus noble, au talent le plus beau. (To Fanny Elssler, possessor of the noblest heart and greatest talent, from the artists of Moscow.)

**Carlotta Grisi** (1819-1899) was discovered by another great dancer of that era, **Jules Joseph Perrot**. Taglioni had caused him to be banned from the Paris Opera, not wishing to share her applause with him. Jules Joseph Perrot was very well liked, although at that time the male dancer was becoming unpopular. Perrot took his exquisite pupil, Carlotta Grisi, to London where he danced every summer. They danced in *Le Rossignol* and eventually this led to a career rivaling that of Taglioni and Elssler. They married, and he continued to be her teacher, but they separated after seven years *(Photo Plates 5-1 and 5-4)*.

In London, Milan, and Munich, audiences threw bouquets at them and applauded – but not just her – Perrot had great legs and the audience loved to watch his easy grace and rhythm. Perrot had meant to create *Giselle* for the Paris Opera Ballet for Carlotta Grisi and himself, but the Paris Opera did not ask him to dance and gave the choreographic job to **Jean Coralli** in 1841. Giselle became Grisi's signature role. **Lucien Petipa** (1816-1898), the brother of **Marius Petipa**, created the role of Giselle's partner, Albrecht. London admired Jules Perrot's work and made him ballet master from 1841 to 1848. He created *Ondine* and also *Esmeralda*, based on *Notre Dame de Paris* by Victor Hugo, first danced by Carlotta Grisi and later by Fanny Elssler. Perrot's best romantic ballet was *Pas de Quatre* created for Taglioni, Cerrito, Grisi, and Lucille Grahn, a Danish dancer who was compared to Taglioni *(Photo Plate 5-4)*. Théophile Gautier (1811-1872), the French poet who wrote the scenario for the ballet *Giselle*, greatly admired Grisi and thought her to be the love of his life, but since she did not reciprocate his love he married her sister, Ernestina, a singer.

**Carlotta Grisi** had started as a singer–dancer, but concentrated on dancing after meeting Perrot. In the Coralli choreography of *La Peri* she was required to make a rather dangerous leap from a high piece of scenery into the arms of her partner, Lucien Petipa. It was a type of acrobatic adagio used later by Léonide Massine and George Balanchine. She retired early, while still an excellent dancer, and at thirty-five she lived in Geneva doing needlework and caring for her young daughter *(Photo Plate 5-1 and 4)*.

**Fanny Cerrito** (1815-1870) was the fourth great ballerina of the Romantic Age. She was Italian, vivacious, and temperamental. Her energy and good spirits infused her dancing with gaiety. She was tiny, rounded, and very pretty, but especially so while dancing. She introduced the full circle of turns (**tours chaînés déboulés**) that is still very popular. In 1840 she became a favorite in London. Taglioni was in Russia; Elssler was in America; and Grisi was getting attention in Paris. Cerrito's style was more like Elssler's than like Taglioni's. In 1838 at the La Scala Theatre, she had met and studied with **Carlo Blasis**, known to be an excellent instructor. In Vienna, Cerrito also attempted choreography, something not usually done by ballerinas. She choreographed *Alma, the Daughter of Fire* (1842). It suited her and her dancers perfectly and was found to be highly original and striking in design *(Photo Plate 5-1 and 5-4)*.

She met her future husband, **Arthur Saint-Léon** (1821-1870), in London when she danced with him in *Ondine*, her favorite ballet, about a sea nymph who loved a mortal, a perfect vehicle for Fanny Cerrito, especially in the shadow dance, full of childish happiness, whimsicality, and exuberance. (There is a delightful video of **Margot Fonteyn** in that role.) Although most of the choreography of *Ondine* was by Jules Perrot, the ballet was partly choreographed by Cerrito. She also choreographed *Rosida,* for which Saint-Léon had arranged the plot. After 1847 it was **Saint-Léon**, and not Fanny Cerrito, who choreographed their ballets *(Photo Plates 5-4)*. After he and Cerrito separated she went to Russia where a piece of scenery caught fire during a performance and fell. This was such a shock to her that it affected her heart and she retired from the stage.

Saint-Léon's first ballet was *The Little Humpbacked Horse* (1864) based on Russian folklore, which was unusual since he was French, not Russian; in it he included many Russian folk dances. Audiences loved it. He also wrote a book of dance notation in 1852, *La Sténochoréographie*, which was decoded in 1970 by **Pierre Lecotte** of the Paris Opera Ballet and **Anne Hutchinson** of the Dance Notation Bureau in New York. Saint-Léon's notation was the first to write down choreographed movements of the arms, head, torso, and feet. His work *Pas de Six* from *La Vivandière* (1846) can now be accurately restaged; he notated it in 1848 but was too busy doing choreography to notate all his other works. He was very cultured and spoke many languages. At the age of fourteen he had made his debut in Munich as a dancer and solo violinist. At a time when male dancing was out of favor, the audience had always applauded and loved Saint-Léon for his effortless jumps and vigor. Later he turned to writing about dance.

Saint-Léon succeeded Jules Perrot as Maitre de Ballet at the Bolshoi Theatre in St. Petersburg from 1859 to 1869, after which Marius Petipa became the next Maitre de Ballet. The last ballet choreographed by Saint-Léon was *Coppélia* (1870) with music by Leo Delibes. **Giuseppina Bozzachi**, a sixteen-year-old, danced it with charm and outstanding technique *(Photo Plate 5-2)*; she died in the terrible smallpox epidemic that swept Paris after the Franco-Prussian war broke out (7/19/1870 – 5/10/1871). *Coppélia* later became a favorite of **Anna Pavlova** and remained in the repertoire of many companies.

Ballet declined at the Paris Opera after Cerrito left, and Russia became the leader in dance, greatly due to its wealth at that moment. During the era of the Romantic Ballet, the best dancers of Europe, Elssler, Taglioni, Grisi, Perrot, and Saint-Léon, spent much time in Russia during which period the Italian and French ballet techniques were absorbed by Russian dancers.

Photo Plate 5-5

"The Rehearsal of the Ballet Onstage," oil painting by Hilaire-Germaine-Edgar Degas, 1874.

Poster showing a scene from the Karalfy Bros. production of "Black Crook," lithograph created and published in New York by Central Litho. and Eng. Co, 1866.

Carlo Blasis (1797-1878) was an Italian who had studied with **Salvatore Viganò**, became head of the Ballet School at La Scala, and in turn had pupils coming from all over to study with him. He was an excellent instructor. Several of his students then went to America to perform in *The White Faun* and in *The Black Crook*, including **Maria Bonfanti** (1845-1921) who performed in the latter until 1891, then opened a school and taught the Carlo Blasis ballet technique until she died.

*The Black Crook*, with its book written by Charles M. Barras (1826-1873), an American playwright, became an American musical, a sensational extravaganza, when its producers William Wheatley, Henry Palmer, and Henry C. Jarrett combined a stranded ballet chorus, whose theatre had burned down, with Barras' metaphysical melodrama. The dancers' flesh-colored tights did much to increase the musical's popularity. It opened on September 12, 1866, and closed on January 4, 1868; it was revived on Broadway in 1870-71 and many times afterwards. It had songs, music and lyrics by Thomas Baker and others, dances (choreographed by **David Costa**) in a semi-classical style interspersed throughout and performed by the actors, ornate production numbers, elaborate costumes, provocative songs, chorus girls, and large production numbers *(Photo Plate 5-5)*.

**Carlo Blasis** discovered **spotting**, doing turns without dizziness by focusing on one spot while turning. He wrote *Notes on Dancing* and, in 1839, *The Code of Terpsichore*, which showed practice costumes that resembled the Greek style. He analyzed ballet movements and passed this knowledge on to his students, which is why the students were so good.

He adopted the pose of *Mercury* by the Flemish-Italian sculptor Giambologna (1529-1608, also known as Giovanni da Bologna), considered to be one of the greatest of Italian Renaissance sculptors. His sculpture of *Mercury* of 1581 has a feeling of action that inspired Blasis to use it as the **attitude back** position in ballet *(Photo Plates 5-2)*. (Standing on one foot, the other leg is raised in back with the knee bent at a 90 degree angle, well turned out so the knee is higher than the foot; the arm on the same side as the raised leg is held over the head and rounded with the other arm out to the side.)

Among Blasis' ballet students were the first ballerinas to do thirty-two consecutive **fouetté** turns: **Pierrina Legnani** (1863-1923), who was prima ballerina assoluta of the St. Petersburg Imperial Theatre, and **Malvina Cavallazzi** (1852-1924), the Metropolitan Opera's first prima ballerina. In 1909 **Cavallazzi** was asked to start and direct the Metropolitan Opera's Ballet School. She taught Italian ballet exercises known for building strength and retired in 1913. Other excellent Italian ballet teachers followed her to America. These included **Rosina Galli** (1896-1940), **Maria Gambarelli** (1900-1999), and **Vincenzo Celli** (1900-1988).

Italian ballerinas in Russia included **Virginia Zucchi** (1849-1930) and **Carlotta Brianzi** (1867-1930), the original Sleeping Beauty. The Italians commanded excellent technique and a dazzling style but without the nuances and taste to make their dancing an art; that's what the Russians added.

The Father of Classical Ballet, the most influential choreographer until that time, **Marius Petipa** (1818-1910), and the Petipa family came next. **Petipa** was a Frenchman who adopted Russia in an era when no Russian dancer held any of the important dance positions in the world of ballet. His young wife and their daughters became outstanding through his coaching and carried on the tradition of the Petipa family.

# 6

# Ballet

## from Petipa to the 1960's

The Father of Classical Ballet, **Marius Petipa** (1818-1910), a Frenchman who adopted Russia, was a wonderful choreographer. He stressed grace for women, had a gift for arranging solos, and excelled at mime; the *Bluebird Variation* and the adagios from *Swan Lake* (1895) with **Lev Ivanov**, *Sleeping Beauty* (1890), and *The Nutcracker* (1892) were and are still favorites. Everyone admired his works for their formal design and elegance. He used chess pawns on a table in his home to plan the movements of dance groups. He gave detailed instructions to Pyotr Ilyich Tchaikowsky, the composer, regarding the music desired for *The Nutcracker*, such as: soft music – 64 measures; the tree is lit up – sparkling music for 16 measures; entrance of the children – joyful and exciting music for 24 measures. Other remarkable ballets by Petipa were *Don Quixote* (1869, to music by Ludwig Minkus), *La Bayadère* (1877, to music by Minkus), *Giselle* (originally choreographed by **Jean Coralli** and **Jules Perrot** to music by Adolphe Adam in 1841 and rechoreographed by **Petipa** in the 1880's), *Raymonda* (1898, to music by Alexander Glazunov), and *Le Corsaire* (1856, to music by Adolphe Adam).

Through **Petipa**'s effort and that of both **Lev Ivanov** (1834-1901) and **Christian Johansson** (1817-1903, Swedish and a pupil of **August Bournonville**), a new generation of exceptional Russian dancers was developed – **Olga Preobrajenska***)*, **Vera Trefilova, Tamara Karsavina, Anna Pavlova** *(Photo Plate 6-2)*, **Vaslav Nijinsky** *(Photo Plates 6-1and 6- 4)*, and **Michel Fokine**.

Notation made it possible to stage **Petipa**'s works outside Russia. This was the dance notation created by **Vladimir Ivanov Stepanov** (1866-1896), a dancer of the Imperial Ballet in St. Petersburg, in his published work, *The Alphabet of Movements of the Human Body* (1892), continued by **Nikolas Sergeyev** (1876-1951) and improved upon by **Alexander Gorsky** (1871-1924). Complex movements were now broken into simpler ones, notated by using musical notes to record them. The Sergeyev Collection, as it is called for short, has been at Harvard University since 1969. It has been utilized for reconstructions of Petipa's works by the Royal Ballet in London, the Kirov/Mariinsky Ballet, the Bolshoi Ballet, the Pacific Northwest Ballet School in the U.S., and the Ballet Company of the La Scala Theatre, Italy.

By the year 1860 soft ballet shoes no longer had heels and pointe shoes were made of satin. Before this time, women had stuffed the tip of the slippers with cotton to make them harder. (I remember once seeing a young dancer do a circle of chaînée turns on pointe in her soft ballet shoes. I was amazed at her ease in executing this.) How high up on her toes a dancer could go depended on the strength of her toe muscles; the early ballet shoes offered little support, if any. How light and ethereal the dancer appeared, however, depended on her ability to project the quality of lightness, which is what **Marie Taglioni** did so well.

Gradually women's pointe work improved as the toes of the shoes were blocked with layers of glue and resin to make them easier to stand on; ribbons were sewn on the shoes to hold them on securely; the tips of the shoes were darned; a hard leather sole was used to give better support; and a second pair of pointe shoes was kept available in case the first pair became soft or worn out during a lengthy ballet. Soft ballet shoes were used only in ballets in which pointe work was not required.

As women became more expert and versatile en pointe, the role of men became less interesting to the audience and declined to that of supporting the ballerina and carrying her around. At the premiere of *Coppélia* a woman danced the role of the young man, Franz, and in Paris this custom continued until the mid-1950's.

The Royal Danish Ballet where **August Bournonville** (1805-1879) choreographed was an exception. Men and women were about equal; women were expected to be competent at doing most of the men's steps. There was not an excessive amount of partnering or pointe work. The man and woman performed side-by-side. The men were commended for their **ballon**, elevation, and cheerful style and the women for their charm and technique. It was **Bournonville** who choreographed the present-day version of *La Sylphide* for **Lucille Grahn** (1864-1901), a Danish ballerina known as the Taglioni of the North.

The Imperial Ballet of the Russian Empire and the Royal Danish Ballet, both founded in the 1740's, flourished and grew. In the 20th century ballet expanded greatly and began to spread to many parts of the world: London – The Royal Ballet in 1931; New York – The American Ballet Theatre in 1933; Australia – The Australian Ballet in 1940; The New York City Ballet in 1946, The National Ballet of Canada in 1951, The Delhi Ballet in 2002, and many, many others.

However, ballet at the Paris Opera had declined. With its emphasis on star ballerinas, the corps, rendered unimportant, was pushed into the background. Ballerinas like the Italian **Carlotta Zambelli** and the Danish **Adeline** (or **Adelaide) Genée** *(Photo Plate 6-2)* did not have the qualities of Taglioni, Elssler, Camargo, or Sallé. France had been supreme since Louis XIV; then came Italy, which had contributed the virtuoso dancers Fanny Cerrito and Amalia Brugnoli, the Taglioni family, and instructors like Carlo Blasis and Salvatore Viganò.

By 1844 Paris's interest had strayed away from ballet, which was becoming dull, and had shifted to the **can can** (a scandalous dance with kicks, splits, and the sight of underwear) performed at the Moulin Rouge with the latest favorite dancers, **La Goulue,** her partner, **Valentin,** and **Jane Avril** *(Photo Plate 6-3),* and also to the new ragtime dances, the **turkey trot**, the **cakewalk**, and the Brazilian **maxixe**.

The **maxixe**, sometimes called the **Brazilian tango**, began in Rio de Janeiro, Brazil, at about the same time that the **Argentine tango** was developing. The music for this dance was in a rapid two-quarter time and even included folk dance elements.

Sheet music cover," Down to the Folies Bergère,"
Words and music by Vincent Bryant, Irving Berlin, and
Ted Snyder. Published by Ted Snyder Co., New York,
1911. Cover artist F. Pfeiffer, NY.

Helene Andreu doing a piqué with the working foot in
raccourci derrière, a position in back of the knee, ca.
1958. Photographer: Denise Andreu.

Nijinsky in "Danse Siamoise" from the ballet
"Orientales," Photographed in 1910 by Eugene Druet,
French (1868-1917).

Photograph of Michel Fokine as Prince Ivan and Tamara
Karsavina as the Firebird in "Firebird," 1910.

But by 1900 the majority of the dances in a ballroom program were **waltzes**. Regardless of the variations in styles, they remained a favorite. The waltz was in three-quarter time with the strong accent on the first beat. It was popular in the 19<sup>th</sup> century. Tchaikovsky wrote waltzes in his ballets: *Nutcracker, Swan Lake*, and *Sleeping Beauty*.

The beautiful waltzes of Johann Strauss became ever more popular in 1830, especially the fast waltzes. Queen Victoria loved the waltz, so its popularity increased. A Boston dance master, **Lorenzo Papanti**, introduced it to America in 1832. The turns and closed dance position with faces almost touching, and the man's hand around the lady's waist made it seem indecent and the waltz was denounced (especially in Puritan America) but then was accepted whenever a more suspect dance came along. The waltz led to the creation of many other ballroom dances and became even more well liked in the 20<sup>th</sup> century when it was used in operettas by Franz Lehar or by Jacques Offenbach, in Richard Strauss's operas, and became Maurice Ravel's *La Valse*. Pierre Auguste Renoir (1841-1919) painted a lovely waltzing couple in *Bal à Bougival* (1883) *(Photo Plate 6-5)*.

Poets and philosophers wrote about dance: Stéphane Mallarmé, Théophile Gautier, Paul Valéry, Martin Buber, and Friederich Niezsche. In the 1860's dance images were everywhere. Dancing inspired many artists, Hilaire-Germain-Edgar Degas (1837-1917), Jules Chéret (1836-1932), and Henri de Toulouse-Lautrec (1864-1901), to paint dancers of ballet, the **can-can** with its many high kicks and splits, the **bolero** *(Photo Plate 6-5)* and many others.

The bolero was a national dance of Spain that had been introduced in 1780 by **Sebastian Zerezo**. It resembled the fandango and was of Moroccan origin, was in either two-quarter or three-quarter time, and could be danced as a solo (as seen in Lautrec's painting) or with a partner. The accompaniment was vocal, guitar or castanets, or the voices of the dancers. Probably the best-known bolero is the piece by Ravel, *Bolero*, that was beautifully used by skaters **Jayne Torville** and **Christopher Dean** for their free ice dance at the 1984 Winter Olympic Games.

Degas depicted ballet dancers hard at work in class, stretching at the barre, and then in performance. The French painter Georges Seurat (1859-1891), who used a pointillistic style comprised of dots, Everett Shinn (1876-1953), who was often called the American Degas, as well as the German Expressionist August Macke (1887-1914), preferred to paint dancers on stage and included some of the audience and musicians to give us a better picture of the entire atmosphere. Others like the German Expressionist Ernst Ludwig Kirchner (1880-1938) and the Norwegian Expressionist painter, Edvard Munch (1863-1944), sometimes painted couples dancing.

Benjamin Lumley, the producer of English ballet at that time, was saddened by the decline of ballet as serious art, claiming that only legs, not brains, impressed audiences.

Russia had taken the lead in ballet from the middle to the end of the 19<sup>th</sup> century. The Russian Imperial Ballet dated back to 1738, when French Ballet Master **Jean-Baptiste Landé** asked Empress Anna Ivanovna to grant him twelve students to start a school in St. Petersburg. This was the basis of the St. Petersburg Imperial Ballet School. Dancers were often children of serfs, orphans, or serfs who had performed in serf theaters at the manors of exceedingly rich Russian noblemen. These theaters gradually disappeared. With the economic problems of the War of 1812 (the invasion of Russia by Napoleon), serf theaters were sold or transferred to the state. Excellent teachers were imported to train the dancers. Young dancers were educated, nourished, sheltered, and received respect and luxuries that few others in the country could ever have. Hence they were not too likely to complain about the system. When they graduated, dancers owed ten years of work to the state. In 1801 Tsar Paul I had invited French-trained choreographer **Charles Didelot** (1767-1837) to join the company. When the tsar Alexander I returned from Paris, victorious after the Battle of Paris (1813), Russian folk dances became stylish, and in 1823 Didelot began a Russian style of ballet with his choreography based on Russian literature, for example the poem *The Prisoner of the Caucasus* by Alexander Pushkin, but with a happy ending. However, after the Decembrists' coup of 1825 in which the new tsar, Nicholas I, censored many former activities, Didelot was forced to resign. **Taglioni** performed in St. Petersburg, and **Jules Perrot** staged *Giselle* for **Grisi**. In the 1890's came sumptuous productions of four-act classical ballets with excellent technique, the result of very good teaching methods.

Ballet masters, dancers from France and Italy, had gone to Russia and it could be appreciated that **Petipa**'s choreography had stressed the attributes of his dancers, **Ekaterina Vazem, Virginia Zucchi, Pierina Legnani, Mathilde Kschessenskaya**, and others. This could be seen when dancers later joined the Diaghileff Ballets Russes Company. Leg extensions gradually became shoulder high, tutus were saucer shaped, not bell shaped, and exposed the legs. The tutu had a stiff bodice attached to the stiff skirt, all in one piece with a little panty. This tutu was very convenient for partner work; it was out of the way for shoulder sits, fish dives, and other lifts. The ballerina's hair was worn high on top of the head in a bun with a tiara for the classical look. Partner dancing was at a new height; a set formula was: entrée, adagio, solo variations, coda, finale (*Photo Plate 6-1*). This formula is still used.

Pyotr Ilyich Tchaikovsky composed music for *Sleeping Beauty, The Nutcracker*, and *Swan Lake*, the three most popular ballets, while at the same time keeping a government job and writing six symphonies (seven if the Manfred Symphony is included), four concertos, and eight operas. By that time, the Kirov/Mariinsky Theatre in St. Petersburg and the Bolshoi Theatre in Moscow had excellent reputations in ballet performances. **Arthur Saint-Léon, Carlo Blasis, and Marius Petipa** had all staged ballets at the Bolshoi. Both companies survived the Russian Revolution of 1917.

The Bolshoi style, called "the Moscow style," was more spontaneous and more influenced by folklore than that of the traditional Kirov where **Agrippina Vaganova** later developed her system of teaching classical technique and where **Galina Ulanova** would perform *Romeo and Juliet* (1940) so beautifully with her wonderful dancing and acting skills. The Bolshoi had commissioned *Swan Lake* in 1894. It was not a success. But after **Marius Petipa** redid the choreography in 1895 into the version we now see, with one ballerina doing the roles of both Odette and Odile, the mistaken identity became more convincing. **Olga Preobrajenska** (also spelled **Preobrajenskaya**) and **Anna Pavlova** were excellent Russian ballerinas in that stunning role.

Photo Plate 6-2

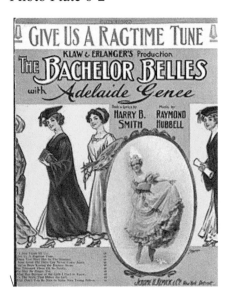

Anna Pavlova as Nikiya in the "Grand Pas Classique of the Shades" From Act III of the Petipa/ Minkus "La Bayadère" Photograph, ca. 1902.

Sheet Music Cover: "Give Us a Ragtime Tune," from "The Bachelor Belles" with Adelaide (or Adeline) Genee, Danish ballerina of the Empire Theater in London for 19 years, who starred in several musicals in America: "The Soul Kiss" in 1908, "The Silver Star" in 1910, "The Bachelor Belles" in 1910; Book & Lyrics: Harry B. Smith; Music: Raymond H. Hubbell. Publication: NY, Jerome H. Remick & Co.

Photograph of Bronislava Nijinska as the Street Dancer in "Petruchka," with Ludmilla Schollar and Michel Fokine as Petruchka, 1911.

Illustration from the original "Souvenir Petruchka Program," Paris, 1911, showing several dancers. Artist unknown.

Photograph of Lubov Tehernichnova in "Petruchka," 1916. Photo by Jean de Strelecki.

Both of these ballerinas, stars of the Russian Imperial Ballet, had been pupils of **Enrico Cechetti** (1850-1928), a prominent Italian dancing master who had numerous outstanding pupils; he taught **Tamara Karsavina, George Balanchine, Serge Lifar**, and **Léonide Massine** *(Photo Plate 6-4)*; and in London: **Margaret Craske, Ninette de Valois,** and **Alicia Markova** *(Photo Plate 6-3)*. He danced many roles, especially character and mime, in the Diaghileff Ballets Russes Company, and he introduced **thirty-two turns à la seconde** for the male dancer **(grande pirouette à la seconde)**; he was outstanding at turns.

(For a grande pirouette à la seconde, the preparation may be taken in fourth or second position. The raised leg remains up at the side during all the consecutive turns. Each time the dancer finishes one revolution he does a plié on the standing leg, then relevés, rises up on the ball of the standing foot while doing the next turn and continues till he has accomplished the required number of pirouettes, often 32.)

**Cechetti**'s accomplishments were highly regarded. As a guest performer in Russia he convinced the performers that excellent makeup was preferable to masks. In 1881 Cechetti appeared in *Excelsior* choreographed by an Italian, **Luigi Manzotti** (1835-1906). This was a very unusual, big, lavish, stunning, first ballet based on spectacular, up-to-date material: the opening of the Suez Canal, with gangs of Italian and Chinese laborers building the transcontinental railroad; the ballet was revived, revised, and successfully updated many times. Before this, Cechetti had also directed the Warsaw School of Ballet till the beginning of the Polish Revolution (1863). He so greatly impressed the Russians when he staged a version of *Excelsior* for them that they asked him to be a principal dancer and second ballet master to Petipa at the Russian Imperial Theater in St. Petersburg, where he remained for 15 years, until 1902.

In 1910, Sergey Diaghileff (also spelled Diaghilev) engaged Cechetti to instruct his corps de ballet. After that, Enrico Cechetti returned to the La Scala Theatre in Italy to teach. The order of the exercises he gave was the same every day, and the center steps were on a schedule as well: Monday was **assemblées**; Tuesday was **battements** and **entrechats**, etc. He collapsed while teaching a class and died the next day. Students and dancers all mourned him. He was known to be an outstanding instructor.

**Sergey Diaghileff** was an impresario who happened on the ballet scene just at the right time; he had a gift for finding and choosing creative talent *(Photo Plate 6-3)*. Paris was disenchanted by the ballet, but the ballet again became popular in Paris due to Diaghileff and his Ballets Russes; the Ballets Russes stunned Paris in 1909 and in 1911, and continued to amaze audiences till Diaghileff's death in 1929. The music by Russian composers was new to Paris; the artists were creating spectacular effects in set designs and costumes. The collaborators in the Diaghileff Ballets Russes Company were all exceptional: the composers: Maurice Ravel, Sergei Prokofiev, Igor Stravinsky, Claude Debussy, Eric Satie, and Francis Poulenc; the artists: Pablo Picasso, Henri Matisse, Coco Chanel, and Joan Miró, who made costumes, set designs, backdrops, and stage curtains; and the dancers, most of whom were Russian: **Serge Lifar, Ida Rubenstein, Anton Dolin, George Balanchine, Alexandra Danilova, Léonide Massine, Vaslav Nijinsky, Adolph Bolm, Mikhail Mordkin, Tatiana Riabouchinska, Tamara Toumanova, Irina Baronova, Boris Romanoff, Michel Fokine**, and **Alicia Markova** *(Photo Plate 6-3)*. At that time non-Russian dancers often changed their names to sound Russian. Hence Alice Marks became Alicia Markova.

**Michel Fokine** (1880-1942) *(Photo Plate 6-1 and 6-2)* was an exceptionally innovative choreographer who rebelled against 19<sup>th</sup> century conventions. When he left the Imperial Russian Ballet to join the Diaghileff Ballets Russes group in 1909 (the company began performing in 1911), pointe work technique, made easier by blocked pointe shoes and shortened tutus, often had nothing to do with the plot of the dance. Fokine felt that pointe shoes should be used only if appropriate, such as for ethereal creatures. An appearance of supernatural lightness was the aim when pointe work started during the Romantic Era but now the aim had become simply spectacular technique en pointe.

There was much travel and interest in foreign countries in the early 20<sup>th</sup> century. The Russian Revolution (1917) caused many artists to scatter to other countries, like England, Australia, and the United States, to develop ballet. There were varied cultural influences on dance at about that time; for example, dancers from Japan and India had appeared at the Expositions in London and Paris. Michel Fokine, in Russia, was interested in all things Greek at the same time as was Isadora Duncan, but the Russian Imperial Ballet rejected Fokine's barefoot ballet based on the story of Daphne and Chlöe. He choreographed *Chopiniana* (to become *Les Sylphides*) with Frederic Chopin's character sitting at a piano in the wings, and then *Cléopatre* (1909), using authentic Egyptian costumes and wigs for the Diaghileff Ballets Russes Company.

Fokine wrote to the *London Times* in 1914:
- Mime and ballet dancing should express the dramatic action of the story.
- Mime should be used only if appropriate.
- Individual dancers and groups should all have expressive faces. New steps should be invented for each dance work.

Fokine was chosen as ballet master of the Diaghileff Ballets Russes Company and he choreographed *Prince Igor* with barbaric rhythms by Alexander Borodin and sets by Nicolas Roerich depicting camps of the Polovetsk warriors. All his ballets were triumphs: *Schéhérezade* (1910) had music by Alexander Borodin, costumes by Léon Bakst. Dancing the favorite slave was **Vaslav Nijinsky** (1889-1950), and also in *Schéhérezade* was the actress-dancer **Ida Rubenstein.**

In 1910 Fokine created his masterpieces *Firebird*, a Russian folk tale with Igor Stravinsky's music, and *Carnaval*, danced to Robert Schumann's music. *Petrouchka* (1911) had music by Igor Stravinsky, costumes and settings by Alexandre Benois, and excellent characterization by the incredible dancer **Vaslav Nijinsky** as a puppet with human emotions. After these works came *Le Spectre de La Rose* (1911) *(Photo Plate 6-4)* to Carl Maria von Weber's *Invitation to the Waltz*, with **Vaslav Nijinsky** dancing as the spirit of the rose and **Tamara Karsavina** as the young woman dreaming of the rose she had worn. This array was an impressive variety of dance works, many of which have lasted to this day. All have **Fokine**'s artistic and imaginative genius. For **Pavlova** he even created a one act solo dance, *The Dying Swan* (1907, with music by Camille Saint Saens) that stood on its own and was not part of a longer ballet. It consisted of simple movements; it was a lyrical, almost improvisational piece that suited Pavlova perfectly.

However, **Fokine** found that his pieces were given too little rehearsal time and that Diaghileff was trying to get Nijinsky interested in choreography. As a result, Fokine left. He went to New York City in 1919, stayed there and taught. In America he helped start a New York company in the 1920's and 1930's for which he choreographed *Thunder Bird*, based on Aztec mythology. He produced his last work, *Le Coq d'Or*, for the De Basil Ballets Russes Company in 1937, based on Rimsky-Korsakov's opera.

**Tamara Karsavina** (1885-1978) was a great dancer who grasped and interpreted each character's depth; her book *Theater Street* is a gem *(Photo Plate 6-1)*.

**Anna Pavlova** (1882-1931) brought beauty and poetry to many as she toured Egypt, South Africa, Australia, and the American Middle West. Her dancing in *Giselle* and *Coppélia* made them favorites. Stockings and perfumes were named after her. She joined the Diaghileff Ballets Russes Company in 1909 but remained no more than one season. She and Diaghileff did not get along; she had refused to dance in *Firebird*. She was a stickler for detail and would not dance a role that she did not believe she could perform exceptionally well. Her movements were always very expressive. She went to London, formed her own company, toured with it, went to America during World War I and toured there from 1912 to 1925, often with the fabulous **Mikhail Mordkin** as her partner. She convinced **Cechetti** to teach her for three years. There was only one Anna Pavlova and she was loved wherever she went.

**Vaslav Nijinsky** (1889-1950) was a fantastic dancer with high leaps and numerous pirouettes, and an actor renowned for the power and force of his characterizations. He created choreography that outraged audiences because the dance and music were too unusual: *L'Après midi d'un faune (Afternoon of a Faun*, 1912, with music by Claude Debussy) had a 2-dimensional look, a rejection of traditional form, and sexual movement *(Photo Plates 6-1 and 6-4)*; *Le Sacre du Printemps*, or, in English, *The Rite of Spring* (1913, with music by Stravinsky), called *massacre du printemps* by opponents, had as its theme the adoration of the earth and the sacrifice of the chosen one. The music for these sacrificial spring rites of early pagan Russian tribes was Igor Stravinsky's new, unappreciated music with strange rhythms, to movements that were turning in, jerking, earthbound, and grotesque, according to the critics at that time. This ballet, *The Rite of Spring*, had a great influence on **Martha Graham, Pina Bausch**, and the Israeli choreographer **Moshe Efrati** due to its unusual rhythms and movements.

**Nijinsky** was as interested in new kinds of dance movements as were the modern dancers of the 1920's, but he never abandoned classical ballet. However, the ballets that he choreographed for others to dance were anything but classical. His audiences whistled loudly, booed, hissed, and rioted; the dancers could not hear the music; he had to count the music beats for them while standing offstage in the wings.

It was necessary for Diaghileff to take his entire ballet company to **Emile Jacques Dalcroze** for the dancers to go over the music with him and understand its rhythm. Dalcroze (1865-1950) often worked with orchestra conductors and musicians, using his system of eurythmics to increase their sense of musical rhythms.

Nijinsky had other problems in his life, too. Diaghileff and Nijinsky had been lovers until the South American tour in which Diaghileff was absent. **Romola Pulszky**, a

Hungarian in the corps de ballet, pursued Nijinsky, hoped to marry him and did. Diaghileff lost interest in him and took the young **Léonide Massine** as his new lover.

Nijinsky unsuccessfully started his own company, was interned in Hungary during World War I, and finished his life in a sanatorium. It is now believed that his illness was glandular and possibly inherited.

**Bronislava Nijinska** *(Photo Plate 6-2)* was Vaslav's sister and also very talented. She choreographed *Les Noces* (*The Wedding*, 1923, about a Russian peasant wedding) for the Diaghileff Ballets Russes Company, using impressive asymmetrical and angular groupings and new ideas. Bronislava Nijinska also choreographed *Le Train Bleu*, for **Alicia Markova** and **Anton Dolin**. Her revival of *Romeo and Juliet* featured **Tamara Karsavina** and **Serge Lifar** who later was to become the director of the Ballet Company at the Paris Opera for many years.

While with Diaghileff, the dancer-choreographer **Léonide Massine** (1895-1979) applied **Fokine**'s reforms with appropriate movements for the various characters, folk dances, and demi-caractère roles in his choreography for *La Boutique Fantasque* (1919). Afterwards he was known for *Le Beau Danube* (1924) which later became part of the repertoire of Sergei Denham's Ballet Russe where millions saw **Alexandra Danilova** perform the role of the Street Dancer, often with the remarkable **Frederick Franklin**. In 1938 Massine choreographed another audience favorite, *Gaité Parisienne*. He even choreographed symphonic ballets: *Les Présages* (1933) to Tchaikovsky's *Fifth Symphony*, *Choreartium* (1933) to Brahm's *Fourth Symphony*, and *Rouge et Noir* (1939) to Shostakovitch's *First Symphony*. He was the only one at that time to attempt choreographic pieces independent of stories. He also used music by Eric Satie, Manuel de Falla, and Ottorino Respighi. **Massine** was not a classical dancer, but was exceptional in mime and character roles. Throughout the time that the Diaghileff Ballets Russes stayed in Spain during World War I, Massine studied and absorbed the intricacies of **flamenco dance** and choreographed *The Three Cornered Hat* with music by de Falla, art of Pablo Picasso, as well as with inspiration from Diego Velasquez's painting *Las Meninas*. **Léonide Massine** *(Photo Plate 6-4)* believed in getting ideas from any dance movement appropriate for his work: modern dance, flamenco, film, mime, music hall, and also in suiting the role to the dancer who performed his choreography.

World events such as the Polish Revolution of 1863-1864, the extreme poverty in Poland in 1890, the Russian Revolution of 1917 in which some families lost everything they had, World War I from 1914 to 1918, the Russian Civil War (1918-1922), and World War II (1939-1945), with the incarceration and execution of Jews in concentration camps, caused profound concern. (**René Blum,** a Frenchman who together with Colonel de Basil, a Russian, had founded the Ballets Russes de Monte Carlo after Diaghileff's death, was arrested in 1941 and sent to Auschwitz where he was killed.) All these events forced many dancers who had trained in Warsaw, Moscow, St. Petersburg, and Paris to go to South America or North America to teach or open their own studios. Some of these were: **Michel Fokine** and **Mikhail Mordkin** in New York, **Adolph Bolm** in Chicago, and later **Pierre Vladimiroff** (1893-1970), his wife, **Felia Doubrovska** (1896-1981), **Anatole Oboukhoff** (1896-1962), **Ludmilla Schollar** (1888-1978) *(Photo Plate 6-2)*, **Anatole Vilzak** (1896-1998), **Maria Swoboda, Vladimir Dokoudovsky** (1919-1998), and **Antonina Tumkovsky** (1905-2007) in New York

Photo Plate 6-3

English ballerina Alicia Markova. Portrait by Carl van Vechten, 1940.

Photograph of "Aurora's Wedding," 1921, ("Le Mariage de la Belle au Bois Dormant"), ballet in one act. Choreography by Marius Petipa, staged and with additional dances by Bronislava Nijinska, sets and costumes by Alexandre Benois, with additional costumes by Natalia Goncharova. Music by Tchaikovsky.

La Troupe de Mlle Eglantine, 1896 poster by Henri de Toulouse-Lautrec was done at the request of Jane Avril, Lautrec's friend, for the group's London appearance at the Palace Theater..

Photograph of the Official Program of May-June, 1922 of the Ballet et Opéra Russes de Serge Diaghilev with portraits of the ballerinas Hilde Bewicke, Leocadia Klementovicz and Felia Doubrovska. Photograph by Swaine et Albin, 1922.

Photograph of Serge Diaghilev, Impresario, ca. 1916. Photographer unknown.

Another country that gained with the exodus of dancers from foreign countries was Australia. **Kira Bousloff**, formerly of the Ballets Russes, founded The West Australian Ballet Company. **Edouard Borovansky** started the Borovansky Australian Ballet that became the Queensland Ballet. Many dancers in the corps de ballet as well as some of the principals stayed in Australia to start dance schools; they taught, danced, and did much to develop Australia culturally. **Dame Peggy van Praagh**, an English-born dancer who went to Australia in 1959, started the Australian Ballet Company in 1962, now the leading classical ballet company in Australia and acknowledged worldwide to be an excellent company.

**Mikhail Mordkin** (1880-1944) studied at the Bolshoi School in Russia and performed with the Bolshoi Ballet. He toured with **Pavlova**, with the Imperial Russian Ballet, and with his own company, the Mordkin Ballet, with **Pierre Vladimiroff** and **Felia Doubrovska** among the company's artists. He formed a new company in America in 1937, with **Lucia Chase**, a dancer who provided much of the financial backing. It later became The American Ballet Theatre. **Mordkin** inspired the growth of ballet in America.

While Diaghileff's Ballets Russes Company was performing, there were also a few other companies around. **Rolf de Maré** and the choreographer **Jean Börlin**, Swedish, performed only new works with their company, Les Ballets Suédois, or the Swedish Company. They tended to include the latest thing, such as snatches of film in their performances. **Börlin** unfortunately died very young, in 1930 at age 37.

**Boris Romanov** directed the Russian Romantic Ballet in Europe for five years from 1921 to 1926 with **Hélène Smirnova** and **Anatole Oboukhoff** as principal dancers. The music included oldies like Mikhail Glinka and Riccardo Eugenio Drigo but also George Gershwin's *Rhapsody in Blue*.

When **Sergey Diaghileff** died in 1929, many smaller Ballet Russe companies were formed: The Original Ballet Russe, The Ballets de Monte Carlo, The Ballets Russes de Monte Carlo, Ballets Russes de Colonel de Basil, Sol Hurok's Ballet Russe and Sergei Denham's Ballet Russe de Monte Carlo. Sergei Denham (1896-1970) formed this company from the Blum and de Basil companies. Innumerable dancers were able to work during the war years and after due to the several Ballets Russes companies. A few of these remarkable dancers not mentioned yet were: **Igor Youskevitch, Rosella Hightower, André Eglevsky, Ruthanna Boris, Roman Jasinski, Vera Nemchinova, Nana Gollner, Sono Osato**, an American of Japanese parentage, **Léon Woizikovsky, Agnes de Mille,** and **Vera Zorina**. Several of these dancers received film contracts, and movie audiences were also able to see outstanding dance performances by such artists as **Marc Platoff (or Platt, 1913-2014), Alexandra Danilova, Léonide Massine**, and **Frederick Franklin**.

**Frederick Franklin** (1914-2013), with his astounding memory, recreated ballets from the Ballet Russe era in many countries, and performed character roles in them even while in his 90's. He received an award from *Dance Teacher Magazine* in September 2007 for Lifetime Achievement in Dance. He certainly merited that award. Balletomanes all over the world have had memorable experiences seeing performances, both classical and otherwise, by **Franklin** and **Alexandra Danilova** or other ballerinas such as **Alicia**

**Alonso, Mia Slavenska, Rosella Hightower, Alicia Markova, Maria Tallchief,** in works by **Léonide Massine, Frederick Ashton, George Balanchine** or **Agnes de Mille**.

The de Basil Ballets Russes de Monte Carlo, which opened in New York in 1921, and Sergei Denham's Ballet Russe provided exuberant and excellent dancing with colorful sets and costumes. Le Grand Ballet du Marquis de Cuevas toured the United States from 1943 through 1947 then toured Europe till 1961. The impresario **Sol Hurok** did much for dance in the U.S. by enabling people to see Pavlova, the modern dancer Martha Graham, Sadler's Wells, Margot Fonteyn, the Stuttgart Ballet, the Bolshoi, and the de Basil Ballets Company. He provided extensive publicity for all his companies.

**Alexandra Danilova** (1903-1997) was always a favorite, first as a performer then as a master teacher. She had studied in Russia and had been a member of the Imperial Russian Ballet when she toured with **Balanchine** in 1924 and joined Sergey Diaghileff's Ballets Russes Company till Diaghileff's death in 1929 of diabetes. She was seen by millions as the prima ballerina of the Ballets Russes de Monte Carlo from 1938 to 1952. She always stood out not only for her dancing but also for her charm, elegance, and acting ability in her roles in **Massine**'s ballets, *Le Beau Danube* (1933), *Jardin Public* (1935), and *Capriccio Espagnol* (1937). She toured with her own company for a while. As a teacher she brought the classical traditions of Russian ballet to her students at the School of American Ballet for thirty years from the 1960's through the 1980's.

The many Ballet Russe companies had searched dance schools in America for talent for their companies and discovered five Native American ballerinas: **Moscelyne Larkin, Yvonne Chouteau, Rosella Hightower**, and **Maria Tallchief** (1925-2013) and her sister **Marjorie Tallchief** (b. 1926). The **Tallchief** sisters were descended from the Native American Osage tribe and performed classical roles with the Paris Opera Ballet **(Marjorie)** and the New York City Ballet **(Maria)** in the 1940's and 1950's.

**Moscelyne Larkin** (1925-2012) was of part-Shawnee-Peoria Indian descent, was married to Polish dancer **Roman Jasinski**, and toured with Col. W. de Basil's Ballet Russes and Sergei Denham's New York-based Ballet Russe de Monte Carlo. The Jasinskis retired to teach and started a small group that developed into the Tulsa Ballet, a company with a varied repertoire of classical ballets as well as contemporary pieces.

**Yvonne Chouteau** (b. 1929) is a member of the Shawnee Tribe and is partly of French ancestry. At 14 she became the youngest member accepted into the Ballet Russe de Monte Carlo. In 1962 she and her husband, **Miguel Terekhov**, founded a dance program, the School of Dance, at the University of Oklahoma. It was the first fully accredited dance program at a university in the U.S.

**Rosella Hightower** (1920-2008), of Choctaw heritage, danced leading roles with the Ballet Russe de Monte Carlo, Ballet Theater and other companies before starting a Centre de Danse Classique in 1962 in Cannes where she lived.

Also discovered was the lovely lyrical black American ballerina, **Raven Wilkinson** (b. 1935), the first black American ballerina hired by an important ballet company – the Ballets Russes de Monte Carlo. But in her third year the Ku Klux Klan gave her problems when the company traveled south so she left and went to Europe to perform. She danced in Holland with the Dutch National Ballet from 1966 to 1973. From 1974 to 1985 she performed in the New York City Opera Ballet.

(Much later, **Jock Soto** (b. 1965), another excellent ballet dancer of both Native American Navajo and Puerto Rican descent, was in the New York City Ballet Company; he retired in 2005.)

**George Balanchine** (1904-1983) was the last resident choreographer of the Diaghileff Ballets Russes Company. He had choreographed *The Prodigal Son* to a score by Prokofiev in 1929 for **Felia Doubrovska** and **Serge Lifar** and later recreated it for the New York City Ballet. He also choreographed *Apollon Musagète* (1928, now known as *Apollo,* to Stravinsky's music) and varied on the classical technique by using contractions and hip isolations. He died in 1983 of Creutzfeldt-Jacob disease.

At the dance studios in Paris of the famous Russian dance teachers, **Olga Preobrajenska** and **Mathilda Kchessinska** (also spelled **Kschessinskaya**) Balanchine found three exceptionally talented teenagers, **Irina Baronova, Tatiana Riabouchinska**, and **Tamara Toumanova** living and studying there. Dance critic Arnold Haskell named them "The Baby Ballerinas." While still in their early teens they danced principal roles with the Ballets Russes de Monte Carlo and later with other companies such as American Ballet Theater.

Eventually the earlier Mordkin Ballet became American Ballet Theatre (1940) with performances of works by American choreographers: **Agnes de Mille**'s *Rodeo* (1942, to Aaron Copland's music) and *Fall River Legend* (1948, about Lizzie Borden, the ax murderess, to Morton Gould's music), **Eugene Loring**'s *Billy the Kid* (1938, to music by Aaron Copland), **Jerome Robbins**' *Interplay* (1944, music by Leonard Bernstein), fun and jazzy, and *Fancy Free* (1944, music by Bernstein) about three sailors on leave in New York City, a light playful gem, a hit. Also present were psychological ballets by the British choreographer **Antony Tudor**, who gave his dancers exercises to prepare them to show self-doubt and inner conflicts in his ballets: *Lilac Garden* (1936), *Dark Elegies* (1937), and *Pillar of Fire* (1942), with **Nora Kaye** as the dramatic ballerina. She once received twenty-six curtain calls. In this Freudian age these ballets were popular but so were the classics, including *La Fille Mal Gardée* (1789) by **Dauberval**. **Balanchine** created *Theme and Variations* (1947) to Tchaikovsky's music. It was majestic and elegant, with **Alicia Alonso**, a prima ballerina and **Igor Youskevitch**, a premier danseur noble. In 1950 **Herbert Ross** created a masterpiece, *Caprichos*, inspired by etchings of the Spaniard, Francisco Goya. Wonderful dancers were **Hugh Laing**, **Sallie Wilson, Nora Kaye, Alicia Alonso**, and **Cynthia Gregory**. Ballet Theatre never had just one principal choreographer, but always several.

In America there had already been dance in New York at the Henry Street Settlement with **Irene Lewisohn**, in Chicago with **Ruth Page**'s Opera Ballet Company (Page had danced with the Diaghileff Ballets Russes Company in Monte Carlo), in Philadelphia with **Catherine Littlefield** (her company was the first American ballet company to perform in France and England). The Atlanta Ballet in Georgia had already existed since 1929 as the **Dorothy Alexander** (1904-1986) Concert Group and in 1940 became the Atlanta Ballet Company, the country's longest continuously performing company, with **Dorothy Alexander** as artistic director. In 1937 The Philadelphia Ballet had toured Europe. In San Francisco there were the Christensen brothers.

The **Christensen Brothers**, **William, Harold,** and **Lew,** were the first classical ballet dancers that many Americans had ever seen when the three toured in vaudeville on

Vaslav Nijinsky in" Le Spectre de la Rose," 1911, by Emil Otto Hoppé, printed 1913. Photogravure from the portfolio: "Studies from the Russian Ballet."

Scene from" La Boutique Fantasque" choreographed by Leonide Massine (1895-1979), Russian dancer and choreographer; photographer unknown, 1919.

" Great Russian Ball at the Academy of Music," New York, November 5, 1863, showing several dancers; wood engraving by Winslow Homer.

Katherine Dunham in "Tropical Revue" at the Martin Beck Theater, Oct. 16, 1943. Photographer: Alfredo Valente.

Marius Petipa, 1899, choreographer of numerous ballets such as " Swan Lake," "Sleeping Beauty," and "The Nutcracker." Photographer unknown.

the Orpheum Circuit, in Lincoln Kirstein's Ballet Caravan, or in Balanchine's American Ballet Company, the precursor of The New York City Ballet Company. **William Christensen** (1902-2001) established a ballet school at the University of Utah (1951), and in 1963 he formed the Utah Civic Ballet (later renamed Ballet West). He choreographed his version of *Coppélia* (1939), *Swan Lake* (1940), and *The Nutcracker* (1941), with the unforgettable **Janet Reed** dancing with the company from 1937 to 1941. She later danced with the New York City Ballet Company. **William Christensen** also choreographed *Sonata Pathétique* to Beethoven (1943). **Harold Christensen** (1904-1989) was director of the San Francisco Ballet School for 35 years, providing dancers for the San Francisco Ballet Company. **Lew Christensen** (1909-1984) choreographed over 100 works for the San Francisco Ballet Company.

**George Balanchine** was persuaded by **Lincoln Kirstein** in 1930 to come to America to open the School of American Ballet. And in 1934 with the assistance of Lincoln Kirstein and Edward M. M. Warburg, Balanchine did open a school. (It was in a studio that had once belonged to Isadora Duncan.) That same year his students premiered a new work of his that has been revised many times and is a signature work of the New York City Ballet Company – *Serenade.*

While Kirstein was doing his military service, Balanchine choreographed the films *The Goldwyn Follies* (1938) starring **Vera Zorina**, a German-Norwegian ballerina (Balanchine's wife from 1938 to 1946), *I Was an Adventuress* (1940) starring Zorina, and *Star Spangled Rhythm* (1942) also starring Zorina, as well as the Broadway musicals *On Your Toes* (1940) and *Louisiana Purchase* (1941).

Balanchine had a very creative two years with **Sergei Denham**'s Ballet Russe from 1942-44. He choreographed *Baiser de la Fée* (1940), *Night Shadow* (1946, later renamed *La Sonnambula*), *Danses Concertantes* (1944), *Mozartiana*, revised from 1933, and excerpts from Petipa's *Raymonda*, always popular with audiences and danced by **Danilova** and **Massine** and later with **Frederick Franklin**. The American dancers **Mary Ellen Moylan** and **Maria Tallchief**, in Denham's Company, began to stand out, as well as did the partnership of **Leon Danielian** and **Ruthanna Boris.**

**Lincoln Kirstein**, a rich and gifted lover of art and dance, had started a ballet company called Ballet Caravan with the American dancers **Lew Christensen, William Dollar, Marie-Jeanne, Erick Hawkins, Gisella Caccialanza**, and **Eugene Loring**. The company's most popular ballets were the American ones: *Billy the Kid* (1938) by **Eugene Loring** and *Filling Station* (1938) by **Lew Christensen** and also danced by **Christensen** and later by **Jacques d'Amboise**.

In 1941 Balanchine and Kirstein combined Balanchine's American Ballet Company and Kirstein's company, Ballet Caravan, and toured South America for a State Department tour after which the company disbanded.

For the South American tour **Balanchine** choreographed *Ballet Imperial* for **Marie-Jeanne**, an American-trained ballerina who had the speed and precision needed for a Balanchine dancer; this was a work for which brilliant jumps, turns, and batterie (beats) were obligatory. His second piece was *Concerto Barocco* to Bach's *Concerto for Three Violins*. It had syncopation of rhythm, hip isolations, hips askew, especially with legs in extremely high extensions over the head, angular movements, contracted torsos, jerky movements, turned in positions of the legs, and women en pointes, not in such a way that they seemed unearthly but, rather, so that they appeared to dig into the ground. All this could be seen as well as the weaving of the two principal dancers in and out of the arms of the corps dancers; these traits of Balanchine's are also obvious in his later works.

Several ballets on American themes also appeared in other American ballet companies: **Ruth Page** choreographed *Frankie and Johnny* (1938), later revived in 1945 by the Ballets Russes de Monte Carlo, and revived again in 1982 by The Dance Theatre of Harlem. Other American themes were *Pocahontas* (1936) by **Lew Christensen**, *Yankee Clipper* (1937) by **Eugene Loring**, and *Barn Dance* (1937) by **Catherine Littlefield.**

On the whole, however, American dancers were not doing well. There were no steady jobs for dancers and seasons were remarkably short. **Patricia Bowman** danced at the Roxy and at Radio City Music Hall (with shows 3-4 times a day). **Marie-Jeanne** danced with the Ballets Russes de Monte Carlo, **Harriet Hoctor** was in the Ziegfeld *Follies of 1936*, and **Paul Haakon** danced for **Balanchine**'s American Ballet and then at Jones Beach with **Fokine**'s group. The only American ballerina to reach international stardom was **Nana Gollner** who first danced with Ballet Theatre and then in London with the International Ballet.

Finances were not good for ballet companies and one-night stands were the usual. The repetitious bus and train schedules, incessantly looking for a hotel, living out of a suitcase, rehearsing, performing, searching for food at a late hour, finding a school in which to take a ballet class, all proved wearisome, but it provided a livelihood with performing and choreographic experience for many Americans. The Ballet Russes closed in 1962.

After Kirstein's discharge from the U.S. Army, he and Balanchine presented their students in *Symphonie Concertante* with Leon Barzin as conductor; Barzin remained with them for many years. In 1946 **Balanchine**'s *Four Temperaments* was presented – Melancolic, Sanguine, Phlegmatic, and Choleric. It was angular with high extensions, speed, and hip isolations – a new way of looking at classical dancing. From 1944-46 Balanchine was resident choreographer for the Ballet Russes de Monte Carlo, then in 1947 he choreographed *Symphony in C* for the Paris Opera. He had to wait several years before he could produce it as sumptuously and successfully in his own company. Then in 1947 came Balanchine's *Orpheus* for his new company Ballet Society (formed with Kirstein's help), to Stravinsky's score, with props and costumes by Isamu Noguchi, a Japanese-American who had made sculptures for Martha Graham's works. The result of this outstanding ballet was an invitation in 1948 by Morton Baum, chairman of the New York City Center, for the company to be the resident company of the City Center for Music and Drama. The company was now to be called the New York City Ballet Company, and **Janet Reed, Melissa Hayden** (1923-2006), and **Jerome Robbins** joined the company. In 1949 Balanchine rechoreographed *Firebird* for prima ballerina **Maria Tallchief** who was also his wife from 1946-1952. She made a brilliant and exotic firebird. It was a very popular ballet and it had the original sets and costumes by Chagall.

A product of Balanchine's school, **Tanaquil Le Clercq**, tall, slender, flexible, became another of Balanchine's muses and his next wife (from 1952-1969); she danced in his ballet *Prodigal Son* (1950, with Georges Rouault's sets and music by Prokofiev). **Jerome Robbins** was the prodigal son, a role later performed by **Edward Villella** in a ballet featuring **Yvonne Mounsey** (1919-2012). Robbins choreographed a timely *Age of Anxiety* (1950) based on W. H. Auden's poem about the atmosphere of the post atomic era. Music was by Leonard Bernstein and sets by Oliver Smith.

The addition of **André Eglevsky** to the company provided **Maria Tallchief** with a wonderful partner (and as a soloist he could do an endless number of very slow multiple pirouettes gorgeously). Then **Diana Adams, Hugh Laing,** and **Nora Kaye** joined the company. Kaye inspired Robbins to create *The Cage* (1951) for her to Stravinsky's *Concerto in D*.

**Balanchine** created many "leotard" ballets to be danced to difficult modern scores by Paul Hindemith and Igor Stravinsky. He preferred doing choreography for women rather than men, and demanded speed, energy, and high extensions from his ballerinas. For **Tallchief**'s lyrical quality he created *Scotch Symphony* (1952, Mendelssohn), for her virtuosity he created *Pas de Dix* (1955); for **Allegra Kent** he choreographed *Ivesiana* (1954) in which her feet seemed never to touch the ground, and for **Le Clercq**'s sophistication, *La Valse* (1951) to the music of Ravel. (**Le Clercq** contracted paralyzing polio in 1956 and Balanchine took some time off to care for her.) Three other American pieces by Balanchine are: *Western Symphony* for the whole company (1954), *Square Dance* (1957), and *Stars and Stripes* (1958).

In 1954 Balanchine choreographed a full length *Nutcracker* and included children in it (as had been done in Russia). **Le Clercq** had been the Dewdrop, and **Tallchief** the Sugar Plum Fairy. It was successful, was shown for several weeks, and was also on television. It inspired innumerable companies and dance schools throughout the country to put on a full length *Nutcracker*. Its success at the box office did wonders for the financial situation of these companies.

**Jerome Robbins** (1918-1998) choreographed some humorous pieces, *Pied Piper* (1951, to music by Copland) and *The Concert* (1956, to Chopin's music), also *Fanfare* (1953, to Benjamin Britten's *Young Person's Guide to the Orchestra*) in honor of the coronation of Queen Elizabeth II, and his version of *Afternoon of a Faun* (1956, with music by Stravinsky). Then Robbins left the NYCB Company to form his own company called Ballet U.S.A., for which he created *Moves* (1961) without any music and *N.Y. Export: Opus Jazz* (1958, to a score by Robert Prince, décor by Ben Shahn), and also to work on Broadway.

**Janet Collins**, trained by **Lester Horton** and **Carmelita Maracci** on the West Coast, made her debut in 1949 and became the first black Premiere Danseuse of the Metropolitan Opera in 1951, but she never went to the South when the Metropolitan Opera went on tour each year. When she returned to concert work she was replaced by her cousin, **Carmen de Lavallade**, also trained by **Lester Horton**, an excellent dance instructor. The Metropolitan Opera hired black dancers long before pressure called for equal casting. They also asked black American dancer-choreographer **Katherine Dunham** to choreograph *Aida* for them *(Photo Plate 6-4)*.

Meanwhile in Britain in 1920, **Marie Rambert**, Polish, had opened a ballet school in London. At that time Cechetti, Italian, was teaching in London, as was **Serafina Astafieva** (**Markova**'s teacher) and **Nikolai Legat**, a Russian-style dancer-instructor. **Rambert** must have been an excellent teacher, since several of her students later became directors of ballet companies: **Celia Franca**, the National Ballet of Canada, **Peggy van**

**Praagh**, the Australian Ballet, and others. **Frederick Ashton** (1904-1988) developed as a choreographer with the Rambert Ballet. Some of his early works that have lasted were the humorous *Façade* (1931), *Les Rendezvous* (1933), and *Les Patineurs* (1937). The attributes of the particular dancers creating his roles were always considered. **Alicia Markova**, light and delicate, was **Ashton**'s favorite ballerina and she proved to be versatile and capable of doing comedy and drama.

Antony Tudor (1908-1987), a late starter in dance, was the next choreographic find for Rambert. Tudor developed movements that revealed the characters' conscience, passion, or tension. In 1936 he achieved his masterpiece, *Jardin aux Lilas (Lilac Garden)* to Ernest Chausson's *Poème* for violin. His next great piece was *Dark Elegies* (1937) to Gustav Mahler's *Kinderstatenlieder*; it was plotless but mournful. **Tudor** gave ballet a subject matter that was very contemporary, dealing with repressed libido and his subjects' psychological attitudes. At the same time he shaped classical technique to this new material. Surprisingly, Tudor's subject matter also extended to comedy, as proven by *Judgment of Paris* 1938) and *Gala Performance* (1938) in which three ballerinas, French, Italian, and Russian, try to outdo one another.

At about this time, **Ninette de Valois** (1898-2001), an Irishwoman, founded the Academy of Choreographic Arts while also choreographing movements for dramas at the Abbey Theatre and occasionally her own works at two theatres owned by Lillian Baylis, the Old Vic, and Sadler's Wells. The Camargo Society, a group that had been founded in London by Arnold Haskell, a dance critic, and Phillip Richardson, editor of *The Dancing Times*, to promote ballet and nurture choreographers, proved to be helpful in producing classics: *Giselle, Swan Lake*, and **de Valois**' choreography of *Job* to music by Ralph Vaughn Williams, with de Valois' groupings inspired by William Blake's drawings. In 1931 the Vic-Wells Ballet (later renamed Sadler's Wells Ballet) moved to the Sadler's Wells Theater with Constant Lambert as music director. **Alicia Markova** (1910-2004) and **Anton Dolin** (1904-1983) were principal dancers but they left after two years to tour with their own company. **Markova**'s role in *The Rake's Progress* (1935) by de Valois confirmed Markova's versatility as she danced the Betrayed Girl. William Hogarth's paintings of 18th century London inspired this ballet, with **Robert Helpmann** (1909-1986) playing The Rake. Markova danced in de Valois' piece as well as in **Nikolas Sergeyev**'s reconstructions of the Russian classics, *Giselle, Nutcracker*, and *Coppélia*.

The young **Margot Fonteyn's** (1919-1991) first appearance in 1934 was an example of the wonders to come throughout her 45-year career. She became **Ashton**'s muse and inspired his *Baiser de la Fée* (1935), *Apparitions* (1936), and *Les Patineurs* (1937). In 1937 **de Valois** succeeded in producing a full length *Sleeping Beauty* for Fonteyn, with **Robert Helpmann** as her superb partner.

The release in the United States of the British movie *The Red Shoes* (1948) made by Michael Powell and Emeric Pressburger and starring **Moira Shearer** (1926-2006), **Robert Helpmann**, and **Léonide Massine,** aroused more interest in ballet than anyone had thought possible. The American film *The Turning Point* (1977), starring Anne Bancroft, Shirley MacLaine, and the ballet dancers **Alexandra Danilova,** ABT's **Leslie Browne**, and **Mikhail Baryshnikov**, directed by **Herbert Ross** with his wife, retired ballerina **Nora Kaye**, as co-director, was also a success, and besides the storyline there were lovely moments of classical dance by Leslie Browne and Mikhail Baryshnikov.

France had had a rigid system of exams to handle the promotions of dancers, but the leading dancers on the whole were outsiders. In 1894 **Carlotta Zambelli**, Italian, went to France and stayed for 36 years. **Jacques Rouché** was appointed director at the Paris Opera and he named the young **Serge Lifar** (1905-1986) as ballet master for a short term; Rouché revived an old French opera-ballet by **Rameau**, *Castor et Pollux*, and also had an all-Russian evening of dance with a revival of Fokine's *Daphne and Chlöe* in 1921. He persuaded **Olga Spessivtseva** to dance *Giselle*. Critics were enchanted with this divine dancer. Then came the 1929 crash in the Wall Street Market, a World War, and Zambelli's retirement. **Rouché**, a great administrator, got **Balanchine,** who was in Paris in 1929, to choreograph and **Lifar** to dance in *Les Créations de Prométhée,* but Balanchine became ill so Lifar finished the choreography, danced in the performances, and became director of the Paris Opera Ballet. **Lifar** accomplished many reforms, taught some classes himself, and encouraged the dancers to take classes from the many Russians teaching in Paris studios. During his tenure of thirty years he choreographed over sixty ballets. He respected his dancers and won their affection. Several excellent dancers emerged from his disciplinary methods: **Solange Schwartz, Lycette Darsonval, Yvette Chauviré, Nina Vyroubova**, and **Serge Peretti**. Not only was Lifar a prolific choreographer but he also provided many new dramatic ballets for his dancers. When Germany entered Paris on June 14, 1940, there was a short interval without performances. Paris was liberated on August 25, 1944, and the Paris Opera Ballet revived only in 1958 when **Nureyev** became director.

**Boris Kochno** (1904-1990), poet, dancer, and librettist for the ballet *The Prodigal Son*, together with Roland Petit, Jean Cocteau, and designer Christian Bérard, founded the Ballets des Champs Elysées in France after the war.

**Roland Petit** (1924-2011) choreographed an unforgettable piece, *Le Jeune Homme et la Mort* (in English *The Young Man and Death*), 1946, to music by Bach with **Jean Babilée**, a fabulous actor-dancer, portraying the main role and Babilée's wife **Nathalie Philippart** portraying the woman. (After using only jazz music for rehearsals, Petit substituted Johann Sebastian Bach's *Passacaglia* for performances.) For his own company, Ballet de Paris, Petit choreographed *Carmen* (1949, with a new eroticism, to music from Georges Bizet's opera) for his wife **Renée (Zizi) Jeanmaire** and himself as José, with decor by Antoni Clavé. Roland Petit's works were always dramatic and very popular. He also choreographed for films, *Hans Christian Anderson* (1952, with Jeanmaire and Danny Kaye), *The Lady on the Ice* (1953, in collaboration with Orson Welles), *Daddy Long Legs* (1954, with **Fred Astaire** and **Leslie Caron**), *Anything Goes* (1956, with Bing Crosby and **Jeanmaire**), and *Black Tights* (1960), consisting of several of Roland Petit's ballets, *La Croqueuse de Diamants*, *Cyrano de Bergerac, A Merry Mourning,* and *Carmen*.

In Denmark it was **Harald Lander** (1905-1971), when he was appointed ballet master in 1932, whose changes included Russian ballet training in all the classes. He felt Bournonville style was not demanding enough for the students. He did not attempt the classics; he felt the dancers were not yet up to that. He choreographed a few novelties based on foreign lands, *Quarrel of the Goddesses* (1933) as well as *Spring* (1942) to

Photo Plate 6-5

Programme Officiel des Ballets et Opèras Russes de Diaghilev (Theatre National de L'Opèra, Mai-Juin 1922, showing the costume by Natalia Goncharova for the ballet" Le Mariage de la Belle au Bois Dormant. "

"Marcelle Lender doing the bolero in Chilpéric," 1895-1896. Artist: Henri de Toulouse-Lautrec (1864-1901), oil on canvas.

Bal à Bougival,   Artist: Pierre Auguste Renoir, famous French Impressionist painter (1841-1919), oil on canvas. Woman seated at left is painter Suzanne Valadon.

Spanish Dance "El Jaleo," 1882, oil on canvas, by John Singer Sargent, 1856-1925, American painter.

Edvard Grieg's music, with emotional solos for his wife, **Margot Lander**, the first Danish ballerina of that time. His most creative work, *Qarrtsiluni* (1942), was about Greenland's Eskimos and their agony during a long winter of perpetual darkness. It finishes with a glimmer of the sun appearing at last. **Lander**'s most successful piece was *Étude* (1948, to Knudåge Riisager's arrangement of Carl Czerny's exercises for piano); it begins with children at the barre and progresses to a display of feats by a trio for two men and a ballerina. It became even more popular after Lander revised it in 1952. The new training proved to be excellent as seen in the dancing of **Erik Bruhn**, especially in *La Sylphide*. **Vera Volkova**, a renowned ballet dancer and teacher who had trained with **Agrippina Vaganova** in Russia, came to Copenhagen to visit in 1951; she was so impressed that she stayed till her death in 1975. **Flemming Flindt** became the next director in 1966.

In the Soviet Union, choreographers often had a difficult time trying to be innovative while adhering to the wishes of the authorities. **Alexander Gorsky** (1871-1924) became the stage manager and rehearsal director at the Bolshoi Theatre (now called The State Academic Bolshoi Theatre of Russia) in Moscow. The Bolshoi has both a ballet company and an opera company. Gorsky had studied **Laban** (see chapter 7), taught himself **Stepanov** notation, was inspired by Isadora Duncan, and believed in the Stanislavsky method of acting, as did many Soviet dancers (including **Galina Ulanova**). He valued acting skills more than showy technique. Thus when he staged *Don Quixote* (1900), *Esmeralda* (1912, based on *The Hunchback of Notre Dame*), or *Swan Lake* (1920), he added some realistic details. He did away with Petipa and Ivanov's symmetrical lines for the corps de ballet and included playful groups for *Don Quixote* as well as confused flocks of swans for *Swan Lake*. His stars, **Mikhail Mordkin** and **Ekaterina Geltzer**, were excellent as always. During World War I and the Bolshevik Revolution, dancers had a very difficult time: pay was in goods or food, theatres were unheated, free tickets were given to workers in the city. The avant-garde was encouraged in art works at that time, but later this was not always true.

In 1922, **Fyodor Lopukhov**, husband of the ballerina **Lydia Lopukhova,** was appointed director of the Mariinsky (recently renamed the Petrograd State Theatre of Opera and Ballet). He believed in studying the musical score and in devising new dance movements, one of which was a daring lift that foreigners raved about when the company toured. The authorities accepted his *Ice Maiden,* but even this ballet was removed from the repertoire when in 1928 his pieces were found to be controversial, causing them all to be removed. However, he continued working till the 1970's. His ballet of 1935, *The Bright Stream*, caused him to be accused of formalism in his choreography. Nevertheless he was appointed director of the choreographic faculty at the Leningrad Conservatory from 1962 to 1973.

Subsequently, **Kasian Goleizovsky**, a Russian who introduced acrobatics and high overhead lifts like Lopukhov's, created a work based on a biblical story, *Joseph the Beautiful* (1925, to music by S. Vasilenko). The subject displeased the authorities and so did the new ideas of using geometrically shaped movements. **Nikolais Foegger** was next; he too was denounced for his new and presumably decadent idea of using a machine-like style of dance.

Finally, *The Red Poppy* (1927), the collaborative effort of choreographers **Lev Lashchilin** and **Vasily Dmitrievich Tikhomirov**, to music by Reinhold Glière, was a very popular piece with the Bolshoi and the Leningrad companies. It dealt with the struggles of Chinese workers, Western imperialists, and a teahouse dancer who sacrifices herself to save a Soviet captain.

In their ballet companies the Soviets preferred to show extravagant works, usually with contemporary or historic content. Examples of these are: *The Flames of Paris* (1932) set during the French Revolution and Pushkin's *Fountain of Bakhchisarai* (1934), in which **Galina Ulanova** was memorable, dancing the leading role, or a short pas de deux such as *Spring Water* with amazing overhead lifts. The Mariinsky Ballet Company was renamed the Kirov Ballet Company or the Mariinsky/Kirov Ballet Company in 1935.

Folk music and folk dance were approved by the Soviet regime. Consequently, **Igor Moiseyev** created the State Folk Dance Ensemble of the USSR in 1937. His dances *Bulba* (1937) and *Kolkhoz Street* (1937) represented activities of the common folk – harvesting, collective farming, and the courage of the people of the Soviet Union during WWII. The company was extraordinary, especially the men, and found a very welcoming audience everywhere.

While the Nazis were invading the USSR in 1941, the Bolshoi Ballet was moved to Kuibyshev; the school was moved to Vasilsursk; the Kirov Ballet was moved to Tashkent, then to Perm (at that time called Molotov). Dancers either joined the Red Army Song and Dance Ensemble or danced for troops, hospitals, and factories. After the war many of the Soviet dancers became even more loyal to their country in recognition of the care it had given them during the difficult war years. However, what followed were several years during which newly composed music was considered offensive; ballets, even those with war themes, were likewise unacceptable until finally **Konstantin Sergeyev** (1910-1992), Ulanova's dance partner, and the husband of the prima ballerina **Natalia Dudinskaya**, became director of the Kirov on and off from 1946 to 1970, stuck to the classics, such as *Swan Lake*, and revised them when necessary to keep the authorities happy. After Stalin's death in 1953, the situation became somewhat better. **Leonid Yakobson**'s *Spartacus* was produced at the Kirov, and then in 1962 at the Bolshoi, rechoreographed by **Igor Moiseyev**. In 1961 *Petrouchka,* choreographed by Fokine, was at last given in Russia for the first time.

Other Russian experimental choreographers were the Kirov's **Yuri Grigorovich** who wanted more dance, less drama, as in his *The Stone Flower* (1957), *The Legend of Love* (1961), and in the 1968 production of *Spartacus* that he choreographed and that proved to be very popular; **Igor Belsky** choreographed *The Coast of Hope* (1959) and *Leningrad Symphony* (1961) but for the latter he was unfortunate to have chosen Stravinsky's music, which had dissonance, which was not approved, so Belsky lost his position at the Kirov; **Oleg Vinogradov** used modern dress (a first) in his full-length production of *Asel* (1967) about an ordinary Soviet girl. (Vinogradov became director of the Kirov in 1977). The many interventions, even with the classics, led to the defection of **Nureyev, Makarova**, and **Baryshnikov**. Nevertheless, the teaching standards in Russia remained high and the dancers were all brilliant.

**Agrippina Vaganova** had created better teaching methods with a knowledge of which muscles were needed to perform finer movements, and these methods produced exquisite dancers, including **Marina Semyonova** as Juliet in *Romeo and Juliet*. Even in their 50's **Galina Ulanova** was ever youthful, and **Maya Plisetskaya** had superb arms. In recognition of Vaganova's accomplishments, The Imperial Ballet School in St. Petersburg was renamed The Vaganova Academy of Russian Ballet, the associate school of the Mariinsky/Kirov Ballet Co. (The school had previously been called The Imperial Ballet School and then The Leningrad State Choreographic Institute during the Soviet era.)

Other companies that were formed in Europe after WWII included the Dutch National Ballet in 1961 under **Rudi van Dantzig**, **Hans van Manen**, and **Toer van Schayk** who all combined modern dance and ballet, and also the Nederlands Dans Theater in 1959 and the Ballet du XXe Siècle founded in 1960 by **Maurice Béjart**.

In Italy the ballerina **Carla Fracci** (b. 1936) danced for over thirty years and created a lasting impression on all who saw her, especially in romantic ballets such as *Giselle*. A Hungarian, **Aurelio Milloss** (1906-1988), danced and choreographed 200 works in Italy attempting to combine the avant-garde art of Italy with music and dance but without lasting results.

Balletomanes, when comparing the various companies, sometimes comment that the French have the loveliest arms; the Russians are the most flamboyant and energetic with the best fluidity because before quite finishing one movement they start the next one so that one movement melts into the next; the British are the most reserved, but precise with attention to detail; the Italians spring up onto their toes rather than rolling up; and the Americans have excellent feet and legs, move fast but the arms are neglected, and the hands are too fingery. I guess you cannot please everyone.

Ideas from choreographers and from people who move from place to place and start companies and schools are all influencing each other and producing original and innovative thoughts, or sometimes introducing old notions that are being reconsidered and utilized again but with a different intention. There seems to be enough variety to keep audiences happy.

Since you like dance and enjoy watching it, do what dance critics do and try to see many diverse kinds of dance. Attend a ballet performance one month, then the next month see modern dance. Or go more often. Don't forget tap, jazz, ethnic, ballroom and folk dancing. Also watch something with which you are unfamiliar on the Internet, on YouTube. You'll find books by a variety of authors listed in the Bibliographies at the end of the book They are listed by type of dance. You may want to read some of them.

# 7

# Modern Dance

## Soloists and New Techniques

Ideas introduced by modern dancers were often similar to those seen in new innovative ballets of the early 20$^{th}$ century. Ballet developed from folk and court dances and was based on the five established positions of the feet, whereas modern dance is based on many systems of dance and can even include tap, ballet, and non-dance activities. Modern dance derived from various ethnic sources: Greek, Asian, Native American, and African-American. By the beginning of the twentieth century, ballets were becoming mostly crowd pleasers; technique looked like tricks aimed at getting applause; music was a background for a feat of innumerable pirouettes. Of course this was an accomplishment for ballet, because certainly when dancers previously had to perform on a raked (slanted) stage these feats would have been almost impossible. But there were now no more or very few raked stages; technique had advanced, but emotions were often left behind.

By 1907 **Michel Fokine** had complained about the unnecessary use of toe shoes when it did not suit the story. He felt the steps should serve the dramatics of the ballet. His ballets, *The Dying Swan*, *Les Sylphides*, and *Firebird* show that he was convinced that steps should fit the dramatic or abstract aims of a particular ballet.

Ballet had already introduced many of the customs that one thinks of as having come from modern dance rather than from ballet: bare feet (when it suited the story), loose costumes instead of tutus, using the floor to recline on or kneel on as a new level of action (*Photo Plate 7-1)*, and commissioning music from a specific composer to suit a new choreography. The difference was that the modern dancers simply threw out everything about ballet that they did not like. Their audience either agreed with the modern dancers or did not attend the performances.

The 20$^{th}$ century saw female dance soloists who seemed to burst upon the scene with a new way of looking at dance that had nothing to do with ballet technique. These were **Isadora Duncan**, **Loie Fuller**, **Ruth St. Denis**, and **Maud Allan**. They danced in bare feet and without tight corsets.

Solo dances that were not part of a ballet were almost unheard of before the eighteenth or nineteenth century, except as a performance in a salon or drawing room for the benefit of guests. Loie Fuller had already given solo dance recitals that inspired Isadora Duncan and Ruth St. Denis to do solo programs of their own and use the term "artiste;" but it was the success of Isadora Duncan's recitals that established solo performances for the modern dancer. **Michel Fokine**, however, had already choreographed the dance solo *The Dying Swan* (1907) as a ballet solo for **Anna Pavlova**.

He used the floor freely whenever it suited his dramatic purpose just as some of the modern dancers would do later.

The dance style of **Isadora Duncan** (1877-1926) was a complete change *(Photo Plate 7-1)*. She danced from 1899 to 1926, she was American but her life centered in Europe. She had studied very briefly with **Marie Bonfanti**, former ballerina at La Scala, a pupil of **Carlo Blasis**, and performer in the popular musical of the late nineteenth century, *The Black Crook*. Isadora broke all the rules in dance and in life. Her technique was basically steps that almost anyone could do, skipping, light running, bending down, reaching up, using the arms and upper torso freely, and not holding the torso upright as in ballet. She moved with great fluidity. She reacted to the music and danced as the music moved her but with dramatic style, much expression, and to music that people did not necessarily consider to be dance music, such as *La Marseillaise* and music composed by Wolfgang Amadeus Mozart, Frederic Chopin, Richard Wagner, Alexander Scriabin, Christoph Willibald Gluck, and Ludwig van Beethoven. Her dance movements interpreted the rhythm of the music.

Her need to feel free and unrestricted led her to wear tunics resembling those seen on figures displayed on Greek vases; these robes revealed her figure underneath and flowed as she moved. She danced barefoot and wore no tights. Her arms were bare and her bare legs could occasionally be seen too. She admired the human body and soul; she was probably influenced by the teachings of **Francois Delsarte** on the meaningfulness of gesture and movement. She believed movement came from the solar plexus, and her favorite teacher was nature.

Her dance and life were dramatic. Her two children, out of wedlock, died when her car, with the driver, nurse, and the two children, fell into the river Seine. She tried to open schools for children of the poor several times but unsuccessfully. The only one that lasted was the one she opened in Russia in 1922 with that government's help; it lasted till 1949 under the direction of one of her "Isadorables," **Irma Duncan**. Isadora Duncan had adopted several of the orphan children that she taught (her "Isadorables"); she married a Russian poet, became a Russian citizen, and died by strangulation in Nice, France, when her scarf got caught in the wheel of her car. Germans called her "the Divine Isadora."

**Isadora** felt that everyone was imitating her, but actually there was at that time an awareness of all Greek art. **Fokine** and also **Maud Allan** were admirers of this art; Maud was loved by the public but did not do well historically compared to **Isadora Duncan**.

**Maud Allan** (1873-1956) was Canadian born, self-taught, a contemporary of Duncan's. She danced to Edvard Grieg's *Peer Gynt*, Felix Mendelssohn's *Spring Song*, and Frédéric Chopin's *Funeral March*. Her signature dance, *The Vision of Salome*, was a dance interpretation of *Salome's Dance of the Seven Veils*. It caused a scandal in Manchester, nevertheless it played in London's Palace Theater for over a year to a huge audience. She may perhaps have been taking advantage of the fads of the time rather than copying Isadora Duncan. She traveled to countries that Duncan never saw: China, New Zealand, South Africa, India, South America, Egypt, and the United States.

**Loie Fuller** (1862-1928), an innovator, was an American who danced mostly in France *(Photo Plates 7-2 and 7-5)*. She was a pioneer of modern dance and of theatrical and electrical lighting technique. As a child she gave temperance lectures. She would

Photo Plate 7-1

Ballet and modern dance were both using the floor as a new level of action. Photographer: Sal Terra-Cina, dancer Helene Andreu, ca. 1959.

Ted Shawn, American modern dancer, in "Invocation to the Thunderbird," (the Native American Indian Rain God), 1922.

J

Isadora Duncan in "La Marseillaise," 1916.
Photographer: Arnold Genthe (1869-1942).

José Limón (1908-1972, Mexican-born) was one of the greatest male modern dancer/choreographers. His best known work is "The Moor's Pavane," 1949.

never have called herself a modern dancer. She was an "artiste," not a dancer. Loie Fuller loved colors, and now that electricity had just been invented, she traveled with forty electricians who set lights under her stage. She cued them to change lights by tapping the floor with her foot. Loie danced on a glass stage for her *Flame Dance*. As part of the scientific and artistic revolution of her time, she revolutionized the art of theatrical lighting, became a great electrician and ran her own laboratory for experiments, one of which blew off a large chunk of her hair. Carbon arc lights, colored gelatins, and large magic lantern projectors with slides were part of her equipment. When she arrived in Paris in 1892, Loie contacted Pierre and Marie Curie to find out more about radium. Loie Fuller made use of phosphorescent salts to give her costumes luminosity.

When **Loie Fulle**r moved on the stage she had swirls of fine cloth, 100 yards in length, and long bamboo extensions that she held and swirled under yards of transparent silk fabric to augment her movements. She was strong and so was able to do this fluidly. Loie considered the cloth to be fine enough if it could pass through her ring. She danced to music of Maurice Ravel, Franz Shubert, Emile Saint Saens, Richard Wagner, Claude Debussy, and Wolfgang Amadeus Mozart. She did a *Serpentine Dance* (1891), *The Butterfly* (1892), *The Fire Dance* (1895), and many others. Paris loved her. Isadora Duncan in *My Life*, her autobiography, praised Fuller's performances; she went to see them several days in a row. Loie Fuller performed in *The Folies Bergère*, never learned French but stayed in Paris. She painted designs on her fine cloths, got in the habit of wetting the paintbrush in her mouth, and eventually died from this since much of the paint of that period was poisonous. Her last performance was in 1926; she died in 1928. "La Loie" was a creature of light. Artists such as Jules Chéret, who was considered to be the "Father of the Poster" through his numerous innovations in design and technology, and Henri de Toulouse-Lautrec adored her dance.

**Ruth St. Denis** (1877-1968) was an American who performed mainly in the United States; she toured in David Belasco's production of *Du Barry Was a Lady*. The theatrical impresario, Belasco (1853-1931), considered her to be so ladylike that he added St. to her name and she kept it. Passing by a store window one day she saw a poster for cigarettes with a picture of the goddess Isis. The owner of the store gave her the poster. She studied it and did further research on East Indian, Asian, and Egyptian costumes and music. This led her to choreograph several Asian pieces, *Radha* (1905), *The Cobra* (1906), *The Incense* (1906), *The Yogi* (1907), *Egypta* (1910), and *Nautch* (1919), all danced in bare feet. She changed her original dances to suit her audiences in the Western world *(Photo Plates 7-2, 4, and 5)*.

St. Denis toured the United States in 1909 and was very successful. Managers noticed that a different type of audience would appear in the vaudeville and variety theaters when she danced there. She had little training: a few movements developed by **Francois Delsarte**, some aesthetic dance, a bit of ballroom, and the flexibility to do high kicks. During the first decade of the 20th century Europeans were experiencing everything Asian and they were stunned by the delicacy of Japanese painting. Subsequently, when St. Denis went to London and Paris with her Asian dances she was well liked, and in Germany they would have built a theatre just for her, had she stayed. She returned to the United States in 1909 and doors were opened to her.

The second wave of new ideas in dance appeared with the **Denishawn Company**, the work of **Mary Wigman** (1886-1973) and of **Rudolph Laban** (1879-1958) in Germany and Switzerland.

**Ruth St. Denis**'s appearances had all been solo acts, but she considered getting a partner because audiences then seemed to like **Vernon and Irene Castle**, a dancing pair. When Ruth St. Denis met **Ted Shawn** (1891-1972) they formed a partnership that lasted twenty years. Their styles complemented each other. Early in life he had planned on becoming a minister, but illness had forced him to concentrate on bodybuilding. He had contracted diphtheria, and through an overdose of serum became paralyzed. Therefore he studied dance to gain strength, formed a small dance group, and met St. Denis. They both believed in having a spiritual basis for dance. They were married in August 1914.

In 1915 they established the Denishawn School in Los Angeles, which later led to a chain of schools throughout the country. They also hired other teachers for their schools. Their fame, unlike that of Isadora Duncan and Loie Fuller's, was in America. Most of the early modern dancers studied and performed with them: **Doris Humphrey** *(Photo Plate 7-4)*, **Martha Graham**, and **Charles Weidman**. The Denishawn School gave complete dance training: ballet, Asian, East Indian, flamenco, primitive dance, character dance (dances from various countries), eurhythmics, and visualization of music. Like Fokine before them, they believed that dancers who were well trained in all areas would be better able to express themselves. After meeting Shawn, St. Denis's interests spread, and she got involved in music visualization with each dancer representing a different instrument, as in her presentation of Shubert's *Unfinished Symphony* and of *Soaring,* 1920, a work created by her student, **Doris Humphrey**, with Ruth St. Denis' assistance, to Robert Schumann's music *Aufschwung*. It was Ruth St. Denis who started one of the first Dance Departments at a college, Adelphi University, in 1938.

**Ted Shawn**'s interest was in Native American sources and he choreographed *Invocation to the Thunderbird* (1917), *The Hopi Indian Eagle Dance* (1923), The *Osage-Pawnee Dance of Greeting* (1930), and *Xochitl* (1921, in which **Martha Graham** danced when she was a student at Denishawn). He also created dances based on American folk themes, such as *Boston Fancy* (1924), a popular suite. In 1923 he created and danced in the nude in *Death of Adonis,* a plastique based on poses of Greek sculpture. (Plastique is a technique of making extremely slow movements in dancing, like a statue in motion – *Photo Plate 7-4.)* Ted Shawn had trained his audiences to watch dance as art and consequently they were able to judge his dance from that point of view and not as something scandalous.

The Denishawn Company traveled mostly throughout the United States, not Europe. They appeared at Carnegie Hall in New York, at the Lewisohn Stadium in New York, in vaudeville, and in the *Ziegfeld Follies*. Like Isadora Duncan before them, they too wore rather revealing costumes, especially so for that era, to represent nudity. Their dances, based on ethnic sources, such as Australian aborigines, Native American *(Photo Plates 7-1, 3, 4, and 5),* and East Indian, appealed to audiences. When they toured Asia with their Asian dances they were very well received. They were the only dance company to survive well during the Great Depression of the 1930's. The   Denishawn Company often toured in the vaudeville circuit until 1932.

Loie Fuller Dancing, ca. 1900. Photographer: Samuel Joshua Beckett (British, 1870-1940).

Ruth St. Denis (1879-1968). Photographer George Grantham Bain (1865-1944)..

Portrait of Martha Graham and Bertram Ross, 1961.Photographer: Carl van Vechten (1880-1964).

Portrait of Martha Graham and Bertram Ross, as Clytemnestra and Orestes, June 27, 1961. Photographer: Carl van Vechten.

In her later years St. Denis believed even more than before in the spiritual purpose of dance. She founded the Society of Spiritual Arts. Both she and Ted Shawn choreographed church services in dance form. His was in 1917; hers was performed as a church service three times since its creation in 1934. In 1947 she established her Church of the Divine Dance in Hollywood, where she began building a dance liturgy suitable to the varied services conducted by guest churchmen and philosophers. She died in 1968 at the age of 91.

**Ted Shawn** devoted himself later to promoting dancing for men, and he started an all-male dance company in 1933 emphasizing male characteristics during work, as in his *Labor Symphony*, and showing feelings in response to emotional stress or depicting positive masculine energy as in *Kinetic Molpai* (1935, to music by Jess Meeker). Both pieces are in the repertoire of the Alvin Ailey Company, as are Shawn's dances of Native Americans and primitive people. Shawn's all-male company made it obvious that men, too, should dance. The company continued to perform until 1940.

Shawn and his company went each summer to Jacob's Pillow, founded by him in 1933, in the Berkshires, Massachusetts, to study, create, and watch others perform. King Frederick IX of Denmark knighted Shawn for having actively encouraged the Royal Danish Ballet by inviting them to perform at Jacob's Pillow. Jacob's Pillow promotes all forms of dance, continuing long after Shawn's death in 1972. Shawn also lectured and taught at universities and wrote several books, including *The American Ballet* (1926), *Gods Who Dance* (1929) based on his impressions of native Asian dances, and *Dance We Must* (1940). He sought to create dances that would convey ideas of both the mind and spirit and prove that dancing was a real profession for American men. He was a dedicated preacher-dancer.

The following three people greatly influenced the early modern dancers.

**Francois Delsarte** (1811-1871) divided movements into three categories – eccentric, concentric, and normal, expressions into three zones – head, torso, and limbs, and human behavior into three attitudes – mental, moral, and vital. He formulated a system for teaching control of body movements by analyzing the gestures of the human body as expressions of emotional states. He was a favorite instructor, for actors especially. His theories and those of Emile Jacques-Dalcroze greatly influenced many of the early modern dancers and others, as you will find out later in this book.

**Emile Jacques-Dalcroze** (1865-1950), a Swiss music teacher, developed a system that became known as eurhythmics. This system trained musical responsiveness through the translation of musical rhythms into movements of the body. His pupils included Hanya Holm, Mary Wigman, and Kurt Jooss, who all eventually left him to study with Rudoph Laban.

**Rudolph Laban** (1879-1958) invented a system of dance notation called Labanotation, used to this day, especially in the United States. The Germans considered his school to be anti-German, but luckily for him he managed to escape from Germany to London in 1937, where he worked during WW II as a consultant. He used his system of energy and movement notation to analyze the work of factory workers and increase their efficiency. In London, with co-worker Warren Lamb, he reviewed his analysis of human movement in terms of the effort/shape in controlling the dynamics and appearance of the body. This led to changes in both dramatic dance and the relation of the dancer to space. Actors, too, studied this. It involved movement in relation to the following: time (fast or slow), space (direct or indirect), and energy (strong or light); the basic movements were: punch, press, slash, wring, dab, glide, flick, and float. **Alwin Nikolais**, a modern dance choreographer, also used the qualities of movements in his choreography.

At about the same instant that modern dance appeared in the United States, it also appeared in Germany. The German dancer **Mary Wigman** (1886-1973), who studied with Laban and Dalcroze, began a school of movement in Germany (1920). It was closed by the Nazis and reopened by Wigman in 1948. She choreographed the *Witch Dance* (1914) portraying the wicked and witch-like trends in the human character. She believed that dance was a language to which people were born. It was a form made true by emotional experience. She did dramatic solos and choreographed pieces for her students using masks, as in the *Dance of Death* (1926), to underline the symbolic power behind the reality of the dancer, and every so often using no accompaniment, so her dances were not dependent on music; or she had her dancers play percussive instruments. She occasionally used levels in her dances and now and again employed weighty, heavy movements in her works.

Wigman believed that people needed each other and that dance was a form of communication. Dance had no limits. Everything about its expression – style, content, intellect, and emotion – was the representative image of its era. She believed that it had probably developed with one individual but was not invented solely by that person.

**Mary Wigman** toured the United States with her company in 1930. Seeing the Grand Canyon inspired her choreography about death for an opera on which she was working in Germany. She believed in the oneness of life and death and that one's feeling about death were a part of life. In dance, except for the ritual Dance of Death in the 12th century as described in Chapter Two, the figure of death did not appear until World War I, and in modern dance death appeared only in Mary Wigman's works and in **Kurt Jooss'** *The Green Table*. Wigman was known in Germany for her expressionistic dance and mysticism. Dance was a reaching out to someone or something beside oneself.

Several modern dance pioneers in Japan between 1886 and 1962 studied with **Mary Wigman** and **Emile Jacque-Dalcroze** and were greatly influenced by them. Dance in the twentieth century in Eastern Asia: Japan, Korea, China, and Taiwan took five directions: initiation of work influenced by the West; renovation of indigenous dance forms; inclusion of foreign styles of modern dance; introduction, incorporation, and creation of new works in the classical ballet field; and maintenance and continuation of new contents in traditional form.

Wigman's student, **Hanya Holm** (1893-1992), was sent from Germany to the United States to start a Wigman dance school in 1931. She was influenced by Wigman as well as by expressionism in German art. Her technique included dramatic and symbolic gesture as well as the use of percussion instruments, at least in class. **Hanya Holm**'s lighter side was seen in her choreography for *My Fair Lady* (1956). She also did choreography for *Kiss Me Kate* (1948) and *Camelot* (1960). Her dances were always integrated into the dramatics of the show.

Photo Plate 7-3

"Portrait of Alvin Ailey," 1955. Photographer: Carl van Vechten.

Ted Shawn, American modern dancer, "Invocation to the Thunderbird" (The Native American Indian Rain God), 1922. Photographer: Robertson.

Ruth St. Denis and husband, Ted Shawn, "Yardbirds," 1920, Photo by George Grantham Bain (1865-1944).

Portrait of Pearl Primus created by Carl van Vechten, Photographer, 1943. Primus was known for her energetic and exuberant jumps.

115

**Harald Kreutzberg** (1902-1968), of Austrian parents, was one of the few other outstanding male dancers of that moment. He studied with Wigman. When José Limón and Charles Weidman saw him, both were impressed by his performance, but 1939 was the last year the Germans allowed him to tour in the U.S. He performed with male energy and yet also with great sensitivity. He opened a school in Bern, Switzerland, in 1955. The ballets by him had a mixture of drama and humor. He appeared on television in the United States in an abridged German-American production of *The Nutcracker* that was shown several times in 1965; he danced in a dual role of Drosselmayer and the Snow King.

**Kurt Jooss** (1901-1979), a German choreographer, was ahead of his time in wanting ballet (the technique) and modern (the dance of the period) to merge and become accepted. Although much younger than Mary Wigman, he too had been influential on her work. His choreography was dramatic and had already been acclaimed before World War II. He used ballet and modern dance forms. His antiwar piece *The Green Table* (1932), his most enduring piece, was performed in ballet shoes and was in the repertoire of several ballet companies. His works were an analysis of current events. Kurt Jooss's choreography was concerned with the struggles of 20$^{th}$ century man: personal, social, and artistic. His works had a traditional, humanistic notion of art. Kurt Jooss had started a school in Germany, to which he returned in 1949 after his exile before and during World War II and where he remained until 1968. German choreographers **Pina Bausch** (1940-2009) and **Susanne Linke** (b. 1944) were among his students at the school.

The third distinctive phase in modern dance appeared in the 1920's and 1930's with **Doris Humphrey**, **Charles Weidman**, **José Limón**, and **Martha Graham**, all of whom created additional and new dance movement vocabulary that had never been used before.

**Doris Humphrey** (1895-1958*)* had studied ballet, clog, ballroom, folk, and aesthetic dance as a child and began doing choreography in 1920 while in the Denishawn Company *(Photo Plate 7-4)*. She and Ruth St. Denis cooperated to create a lyrical endeavor called *Soaring* (1920, to Robert Schumann's music) and included a parachute as a part of the dance. Humphrey felt she was not good at being Japanese or Egyptian in dance, as was sometimes required by the Denishawn Company, and preferred to be herself. Therefore in 1928 she formed a group with **Charles Weidman** (1901-1975) who had begun to study dancing at Denishawn in 1920. Humphrey and Weidman both felt that Denishawn was not doing anything particularly new but was just imitating others.

**Humphrey**'s choreography was done to Bach (1928, *Air for the G String*) as well as to contemporary music such as Aaron Copland's *El Salón México*, or to silence. She wrote a well thought out and instructive book on choreography called *The Art of Making Dances* which gave explicit rules on what to do and what not to do – don't make them too long, use a variety of levels in the groupings, use symmetry and asymmetry, for example. It was published posthumously in 1959 and is truly excellent.

She thought dance existed as "an arc between two deaths," that is to say, the muscular drama between balance and imbalance, between opposition to gravity and giving in to it, or between security and adventure. Her technique can still be seen in today's choreography in movements of swinging and falling. She also choreographed an Arnold Schoenberg production for the Metropolitan Opera as well as plays such as

116

Molière's *School for Wives* (1928). She taught at Bennington College. She felt dance should have very moving themes, not just beautiful movements. **Humphrey** and **Weidman** worked on Broadway shows and raised the standard of dancing there. Some of their company dances – *Water Study* (1928), *Shakers* (1931), *Piccoli Soldati*, also known as *Amour a la Militaire* (1932), were used in *Americana* in 1933. Weidman staged dances for *As Thousands Cheer* (1933), *Hold Your Horses* (1934), and *I'd Rather Be Right* (1937). Humphrey set dances for Molière's *A School for Husbands* (1933) in which she and Weidman both appeared.

After Humphrey/Weidman disbanded, **Charles Weidman** choreographed for Broadway, the City Center Opera, theatre productions, and established The Expression of Two Arts Theatre in New York with sculptor Mikhail Santaro in the early 1960's; it lasted until Weidman's death. Weidman's works provided comic relief from the serious works of most other modern dancers. He combined abstract movement with his original mime gestures. Some of his preferred dances in a satirical, comic style were: *And Daddy Was a Fireman* (1943), *The War Between Men and Women* (1954, based on James Thurber cartoons), and *A House Divided* (1945). Many consider his best pieces to have been *Flickers* (1941) and *Fables for Our Time* (1947). His most serious work, which provided no comic relief and was rather full of horror, was *Lynch Town* (1936). **Jack Cole** and **Bob Fosse**, two of his most innovative students, lived up to his work and went on to choreograph for Broadway with great success. Both Humphrey and Weidman taught at numerous places besides their own studios – The New School, New York University, Temple University, Columbia University, and Bennington College, among others.

**Doris Humphrey**, after the company was disbanded, joined **José Limón** (1908-1972), her former student, as artistic director of the José Limón Company. He choreographed *Danza de la Muerte* (1937) in opposition to the Spanish Civil War. He had been in Humphrey's company, had served three years in the U.S. Army in WW II, and then formed his own company. His group included **Alwin Nikolais**, **Lucas Hoving** (a pupil of Jooss'), **Pauline Koner**, and **Betty Jones**. For this company Humphrey choreographed *Lament for Ignacio Sánchez Mejías* (1946, based on Garcia Lorca's work, music by Norman Lloyd), *Day on Earth* (1947, music by Aaron Copland), *Ritmo Hondo* (1943, music by Carlos Surinach), and *Night Spell* (1951, music by Priaulx Rainier).

**Limón** turned to Mexico, his native country, for inspiration for *La Malinche* (1949, score by Norman Lloyd), involving the Spanish invasion of Mexico. Limón's most memorable work, *The Moor's Pavane* (1949, music by Henry Purcell) based on Shakespeare's *Othello,* was about the drama between four characters and has been performed by many ballet companies, including The Joffrey Ballet; **Rudolph Nureyev** also performed in *The Moor's Pavane* in the United States. Another of Limón's well known works was *There Is a Time* (1956, music by Norman Dello Joio). Limón's works were often dramatic and based on a story or legend, such as *The Emperor Jones* (1956, music by Heitor Villalobos) for an all-male cast and *The Unsung* (1970, performed without accompaniment), commemorating a different Native American tribe in each solo for the male dancers. **Limón** felt that the male energy had been neglected in this world of modern dance women. The Limón Company was chosen by the State Department for a tour abroad in 1972. After Limon's death, the company, under Carla Maxwell, who had danced in his piece *Carlotta* (1972) that used no music, toured the Soviet Union. Another piece by Limón, also from 1972, *Orfeo,* was in memory of his wife, to music of Beethoven. Limón won two *Dance Magazine* awards as well as one Capezio Dance award *(Photo Plate 7-1).*

José Limón's company survived the death of Limón and of Humphrey, and was later run cooperatively under the direction of some of its former dancers: **Ruth Currier**, **Pauline Koner**, **Betty Jones**, and **Lucas Hoving**. This was the first modern dance company to survive the death of its founder. Limón was second to Graham in box office appeal. His dignity and warmth were his incalculable possessions.

Another modern dancer who often used literary sources was **Valerie Bettis** (1919-1982). Some of these were *Yerma* by García Lorca (1946), and *As I Lay Dying* by Faulkner (1948, music by Bernardo Segall). Her best-known work was *The Desperate Heart* (1943, music by Bernardo Segall), a dramatic portrayal of a lonely woman. Bettis appeared on Broadway, in film, and concerts. She had danced in **Hanya Holm's** *Trend* in 1937.

**Martha Graham** (1894-1991) danced with Denishawn from 1916 to 1923. Graham thought the Denishawn style was too artificial and had nothing to do with human emotions *(Photo Plate 7-2).* She wished to give substance, in dance, to her beliefs and divulge the inner man so we could understand and know him. In *Letter to the World* (1940, music by Hunter Johnson) we saw the overt actions of Emily Dickinson, and through the movements of a second dancer, the figure of the secret self, the poetess' passionate inner self. Graham's dances were often stories about heroic or mythological women such as *Clytemnestra* (1958), which she herself danced, of course. Her work *Deaths and Entrances* (1943, music by Hunter Johnson) about the Bronte sisters, looked into their behavior from a Freudian aspect.

Graham collaborated with the sculptor Isamu Noguchi (1904-1988). His pieces were used at times maybe to be climbed on, to show power, to be wrapped seductively by the heroine, or to be carried as symbolic props. This was a bit new in dance. On occasion Graham's dancers even wore masks or large headdresses.

She collaborated with **Louis Horst** (1884-1964), her music teacher, who had previously collaborated with St. Denis. Horst composed music for several Graham dances, taught dance composition, and wrote two books, *Pre-Classic Dance Forms* (1937) and *Modern Dance Forms in Relation to Other Arts* (1960).

Graham was famous for her technique of "contraction and release," making the effort expended in a movement obvious and not concealed as ballet dancers were trained to do, and for using exaggerated breathing as a part of the technique.

*Cave of the Heart* (1946, music by Samuel Barber) about Medea, was followed in 1948 by *Night Journey* (music by William Schuman) with a Greek theme based on Jocasta's hopelessness. Eleven years later *Clytemnestra* (1958) *(Photo Plate 7-2),* also with a Greek theme, with sculptural works and sets by Noguchi and a score by an Egyptian composer, Halim El-Dabh, was an intricate study of the psyche of Clytemnestra. Graham redid a work about St. Joan of Arc, now naming it *Seraphic Dialogue* (1955, music by Norman Dello Joio); using Noguchi's décor and costumes in vibrant colors of stained glass windows, the work became a favorite piece. *Diversion of Angels* (1948) was unusual in that she had not choreographed a role for herself in it; it was a cheerful dance for three women with music by Norman Dello Joio.

Photo Plate 7-4

Katherine Dunham (1909-2006) in the ballet
"L'Ag'Ya" (1938) with choreography by Dunham.
This was her first outstanding creative work and it led
to many, many more.

Ruth St. Denis and Ted Shawn in "Dance of Rebirth"
from "Egyptian Ballet," 1916.

Students of modern dance at CUNY - New York City
College of Technology, ca. 1980's. Photographer:
Helene Andreu.

Ruth St. Denis with Edna Malone, Betty Horst and
Doris Humphrey in "Greek Veil Plastique."
Photographer: Witzel, 1918. Note: Part of the National
Endowment for the Arts Millennium Project.

She commissioned music from Paul Hindemith, Norman Dello Joio, and then from the American composer Aaron Copland (1900-1990) for *Appalachian Spring* (1944) for which he won a Pulitzer Prize in 1945. This work reminded people of spring, of Appalachia, and of Shaker life. This was not too surprising because Copland used folk melodies and tried to vary his style to suit the different occasions for which he was commissioned to compose a piece of music: *Rodeo* and *Billy the Kid* for ballet companies, or *Appalachian Spring* for Graham's Company, or for a film. That both **Nureyev** and **Baryshnikov**, magnificent Russian ballet dancers who defected from Russia, danced major roles in Graham's *Appalachian Spring,* is amusing considering how much against ballet she used to be. The dancers would otherwise have had to be trained in the Graham style. But great dancers are great dancers and one must bend the rules for them (and also for a large audience that wished to see them in her works). **Martha Graham**'s companies had long been integrated with Asian and black performers including the following excellent dancers: **William Louther**, **Dudley Williams**, **Clive Thompson**, **Mary Hinkson**, **Matt Turney**, and **Yuriko**.

There was a time, however, when it was quite obvious that Ballet and Modern dance were not getting along too well. For example, if a ballet dancer took a modern dance class and did a leap with a balletic arc to it instead of a straight line, there were no instructions on how to do it the "modern" way, only the admonition that the person had just executed a ballet movement, not a modern dance movement, in the Modern Dance Class.

In 1979 Martha Graham was chosen as a Kennedy Center Honoree. Graham's company lasted over fifty years. For a few years, however, there were not many performances by the Martha Graham Dance Company because of problems that arose when Martha Graham, the director of the company, died without proper choice of a person to run the company afterwards. Ron Protas owned Graham's works, or most of them, but the Board of Directors owned some of the costumes or most of them, and perhaps some of the works. By 2011, the 85th anniversary season of the Martha Graham Dance Company at Lincoln Center, the situation was much better; *Deaths and Entrances,* one of her most renowned works, was performed, along with a first showing of *Chasing* (2011) by choreographer **Bulareyaung Pagarlava** (from the Paiwan tribe of Taiwan) and **Robert Wilson**'s *Snow on the Mesa* (1995), an imaginative recreation of Martha Graham's art and life.

For the 2012 season at the New York City Center, **Diana Vishneva**, celebrated dancer of the Mariinsky Ballet and American Ballet Theater, joined the Martha Graham Dance Company. The company's performances of *Errand into the Maze* (1947), *Appalachian Spring* (1944), *Diversion of Angels* (1948), and the all-female war dance *Chronicle* (1936) were outstanding.

The dancer **Pearl Lang** (1921-2009) was a strong believer in the Graham technique; she felt it could serve all her choreographic needs, as in *The Possessed* (1975, music by Joel Spigelman and Meyer Kupferman), a full-evening dance drama with a Jewish orthodox community as background. It was based on *The Dybbuk*, a play by S. Ansky (pen name of Shloyme Zanvl Rappoport). Pearl Lang was the first dancer in Graham's company to take over one of Graham's roles. Outstanding male dancers who had been in Graham's company and went on to form companies of their own were: **Erick Hawkins**, **Merce Cunningham**, and **Paul Taylor**.

Another Graham dancer who formed her own company was **Jean Erdman** (b. 1916, married to philosopher Joseph Campbell). Her most distinguished work was her version of *Finnegan's Wake,* known as *The Coach with the Six Insides* (1962).

John Martin (1893-1985, dance critic) believed that dance was an art form or activity that used the body and the range of movement of which the body was capable. The qualities of self-expression, aesthetic pleasure, and entertainment might also be included. He felt that the movements of modern dancers, certainly the earlier ones, came from their everyday life experiences. He was a great influence on Martha Graham's career, wrote a number of books and received many awards for his exceptional work. He died of a heart attack in 1985. Some of his books include: *The Modern Dance* (1933), *Introduction to the Dance* (1939), *The Dance* (1945), and *World Book of Modern Ballet* (1952).

**Lester Horton** (1906-1953) went to the West coast from Indianapolis and was very influential through his teaching rather than through his choreography. He had studied ballet with **Adolph Bolm** (1884-1951), a Russian of Scandinavian descent, one of the male stars of the Diaghileff Ballets Russes who before settling in the United States had also assisted Diaghileff in organizing and preparing his company. Horton was especially interested in Native American dance, Aztec, Haitian, and African dance. He himself was white. His company, founded in 1934 in Los Angeles, produced several talented future choreographers and dancers, both black and white, such as **Carmen de Lavallade, Janet Collins,** and **Bella Lewitzky,** all of whose companies' homes were in Los Angeles, as well as **Judith Jamison** and **Alvin Ailey.** Horton's dance technique included elements of Native American dance and jazz dance. It stressed a whole body approach and incorporated flexibility, coordination, strength, kinesiology, and awareness of body and space. He did not want his students to have a common look but wanted them to be able to tackle all kinds of movements with fluidity. He died of a heart attack in 1953 at a young age, 47. His best known works are *The Beloved* (1948), a duet involving violence in a marriage, and *To José Clemente Orozco* (1952), a social protest work regarding Mexican peasants' wish for freedom. Horton's dance company was an interracial group, one of the few in the United States, especially then. He enjoyed the diversity that existed in people; his company included Asian Americans, black Americans, and Mexican Americans.

**James Truitte** (1923-1995, lead dancer in both **Horton** and **Ailey**'s companies) and **Joyce Trisler** (1934-1979, modern dancer-choreographer), both Horton's pupils, passed on his technology, replicated his dances, and were instrumental in the ability of the Alvin Ailey School, Alvin Ailey American Dance Theater in New York, to offer a class in the Horton technique.

**Bella Lewitzky** (1916-2004), a student of **Lester Horton**, was a dancer and prolific choreographer who received many honors during her 60-year career. She was known for taking good care of the dancers in her company, providing them with health insurance and year-round salaries regardless of their work schedules. When summoned before the House Un-American Activities Committee in 1951 she refused to cooperate in naming communists in the arts; she did not name anyone, stating that she was not a singer but a dancer. At the Idyllwild School of Music and the Arts in Los Angeles she taught the Lewitzky technique, which stressed line, flow, and articulation of the body, and she later started The Lewitzky Dance Company in 1966. It toured extensively in the U.S. She was awarded the National Medal of the Arts in 1997 for her contributions to American modern dance.

**Alvin Ailey** (1931-1989) *(Photo Plate 7-3)* became artistic director of Horton's Company when Horton died in 1953. Horton's company had always been multiracial. When Ailey formed his own company, The Alvin Ailey American Dance Theater, in 1958, it too was multiracial. He had studied dance with **Lester Horton**, **Martha Graham**, **Hanya Holm**, and **Charles Weidman**; he had also studied ballet and acting. He appeared in films and musicals: *House of Flowers* (1954), *Sing, Man, Sing* (1956), and *Jamaica* (1957). Two of the most popular dances that he choreographed for his company are *Revelations* (1960) to Negro spirituals, with *Rocka My Soul* and *Wade in the Waters* among the favorite sections, and *Blues Suite* (1958, set in a brothel) to Blues songs of the South. His company became the resident company, first at the Brooklyn Academy of Music in 1969, and then at the City Center in New York in 1972. **Ailey** also choreographed *The Mooche* (1975 to Duke Ellington's music) and *To Bird – with Love* (1984, as an homage to saxophonist Charlie 'Bird' Parker who died of a heart attack at age 34 in 1955, to jazz music that included Charlie 'Bird' Parker's).

Ailey was not one of those modern dancers whose company only used choreography by the person whose name was on the company name. He nurtured several black dance choreographers by giving them a chance to work out their choreography on his excellently trained professional company. It was a wonderful experience for them and a chance to get reviewed too: **Louis Johnson** (b. 1930) *Fontessa and Friends*, **Donald McKayle** (b. 1930) *Rainbow 'Round My Shoulder*, **Talley Beatty** (1928-1995) *Come Get the Beauty of It Hot, Road of the Phoebe Snow, Mourner's Bench*, and many other choreographers. The company's repertoire was varied and included works by **Ted Shawn**, **May O'Donnell**, **Katherine Dunham**, **Joyce Trisler**, **George Faison**, and **Louis Falco**. The State Department sent the company on a tour of the Far East in 1962, to several African nations in 1967, and then to the Soviet Union in 1970. **Alvin Ailey** was a Kennedy Center Honoree in 1988 and **Judith Jamison** in 1999.

Ailey died of AIDS at 58 in 1989. He had already chosen **Judith Jamison**, his star dancer, to be director; she was a good choice. The company continued to be very strong, with a varied repertoire and dynamic dancers.

**Talley Beatty** (1919-1995), who had danced in **Katherine Dunham**'s revues, often choreographed to jazz and Latin music. His most successful work, *The Road of the Phoebe Snow* (1959, the name of a railroad, music by Billy Strayhorn and Duke Ellington) was about the life of those living along the railroad tracks, a situation that was common not only to blacks in the United States but to many people in varied countries, and they related to this piece.

To support the unemployed during the depression years the government set up the WPA (the Works Progress Administration) program. It started in 1935 and was terminated after eight years in 1943. Its name was changed to the Works Project Administration in 1939. Artists were included in the labor force and considered for this program. This enabled modern dance to grow and find a place in universities where dance departments were started; even ballet began to take roots again.

One of the pioneers of dance in universities, **Margaret H'Doubler** (1889-1982), originated one of the first dance majors at the University of Wisconsin. Her technique was based on creating movements that would express emotions. The mind needed to be trained to allow the body to express and reveal the person's feelings through dance. (Anna Halprin was one of her students in 1938). H'Doubler explained her technique in her book *Dance: A Creative Art Experience*, published by the University of Wisconsin Press in 1940.

Bennington College in Vermont was another of the first colleges to offer a Bachelor of Arts degree in Dance when **Martha Hill** (1900-1995) was hired as the Chairman of the Dance Department in 1932. She recognized that dance was a theatre art and belonged on stage rather than in the gymnasium. In 1935 Bennington College started the American Dance Festival, a six-week summer festival of modern dance performances and a six-week and four-week school of dance. Martha Hill created opportunities there for many great modern dancers. (She had studied with Martha Graham and performed in her company.) The first choreographers to teach at the American Dance Festival and premiere their new works were **Martha Graham** *Letter to the World*, **Hanya Holm** *Trend*, **Doris Humphrey** *With My Red Fires* (1936, music by Wallingford Riegger), and **Charles Weidman**. Since then many of the modern dance greats have taught and performed there. However, although Bennington still has its dance program, the Dance Festival is no longer at Bennington but is now held at Duke University in Durham, North Carolina. Martha Hill became the first Director of Dance at The Juilliard School in 1951, remaining through 1985. This dance program trains dancers equally in ballet and modern while at the same time requiring instruction in music.

In the 2010's, with so many dancers interested in career transitions for dancers, as can be seen by Actors' Equity Association's regular announcements of lectures on this subject, some colleges are being very practical. Oklahoma City University has a BS in Dance Management, training dance majors for a second career to turn to after a performing career. California University at Long Beach goes into second careers in preventing and recovering from injury, and in how muscles work, for those interested in being personal trainers, becoming Pilates instructors, or going into physical therapy as a second profession. The University of North Carolina offers courses for those who might consider teaching later. Students can major in dance and minor in what might become their second profession. Drexel University and Goucher College also mention a double major or some sort of combination training to fit students' goals: performance, choreography, dance teacher, dance administrator, dance science, dance and theater, dance therapy, or dance history and criticism. However, some students might prefer not to go through four or more years of college but to take an intensive summer program and then go directly into a dance company, such as Taylor's second company, if Taylor saw them during the intensive course and offered them a contract. Others want to go to college but would be smart to go to a state college and save their parents from having to consider a second mortgage, especially since many of the state colleges are excellent. Why start your careers with a huge debt if you cannot get scholarships? Do not forget to look at all the dance magazines for information on scholarships, colleges, etc. These publications are probably available at your public library or on the Internet.

Many modern dance choreographers in the 1930's had lofty aims but the fact is that they had small companies made up of dancers who held daytime jobs, then took

Photo Plate 7-5

Poster for Festival of American Dance, Los Angeles
Federal Theatre Project, WPA, 1937. Artist unknown.

Loie Fuller (1862-1928). Painter: Jules Chéret (1836-
1932), Folies Bergère: Cabaret, 1893.

Ruth St. Denis and Ted Shawn in "The Abduction of
Sita," 1918. Photographer: Lou Goodale Bigelow.

Ted Shawn with dancer and wife Ruth St. Denis in
1916. Taken outdoors, in costume, for National
Geographic Magazine, April 1916. Reprinted in 1951.
Note: Part of the National Endowment for the Arts
Millennium Project,

classes, went to rehearsals, performed in the evenings, and were probably paid only for performances and not for rehearsals. Besides this, if they wanted the company to survive they had to lend a hand in getting the publicity out, making the costumes, and cleaning the floors in the rehearsal and performance space. Most of them danced in bare feet; they preferred to do so, and moreover, dance shoes were expensive. At that time the modern dancers seemed to be radical and attracted audiences who supported socialism, labor unions, and social themes.

**Anna Sokolow** (1910-2000), an exceptional teacher-dancer-choreographer, belonged to the group of modern dancers that was interested in the social problems of the day: the Great Depression, the holocaust, the alienation of youth in the 1960's, and the abuse of workers by their employers, among others. She studied with **Louis Horst** and **Martha Graham** at the Neighborhood Playhouse, performed in Graham's Company from 1927 to 1938 and formed her own company in 1936. She did the choreography for Kurt Weill's *Street Scene* on Broadway in 1947 and for Marc Blitzstein's *Regina* in 1949. She taught and influenced future generations of dancers in many schools including Juilliard (1958-1993) where she taught "method dance" and the School of American Ballet, where I studied and took my first modern dance class from this remarkable woman. **Sokolow** choreographed the original Public Theater production of *Hair* (1967) at Astor Place. Her extensive work in Mexico at the Ministry of Fine Arts led to the founding of the National Academy of Dance in Mexico. In Israel she worked with the modern dance companies Inbal and Batsheva. Two of her best-known pieces were *Rooms* (1965, to an original commissioned jazz score by Kenyon Hopkins) about alienation, and *Dreams* (1961) about the holocaust. She was always interested in social and political injustices and the resiliency of humanity in the face of misfortune. The Theatre Dance Ensemble, directed by **Jim May**, still performs **Anna Sokolow**'s repertory and also contemporary choreographies. Sokolow was inducted into the Dance Hall of Fame in Saratoga in 1998.

Several other modern dance choreographers of her time were likewise interested in social themes for their dances. Many of these dancer-choreographers had studied with and performed in **Martha Graham**'s or in **Lester Horton**'s companies. Both of these companies were racially integrated. Being interested in social issues and performing in these companies seemed to make many modern dance companies able to consider hiring performers solely for their ability, not their color, so many modern dance companies were the first to hire black dancers on an equal footing with white dancers.

**Helen Tamiris** (1905-1966) used jazz music and spirituals for several of her works, as she did for *How Long Brethren*, a dance for the Federal Dance Project of the WPA. This work dealt with problems facing African-Americans. She also went on to choreograph several Broadway shows: *Annie Get Your Gun* (1946), *Fanny* (1954), and *Plain and Fancy* (1955).

Helen Tamiris had been the principal choreographer for the Federal Dance Project (FDP) *(Photo Plate 7-5)* that lasted from 1936-1939, mainly through her energy and work and her love of the idea of bringing dance to masses of people who had had little opportunity to see theater or dance. The FDP was part of Franklin Delano Roosevelt's New Deal. It received federal funds and gave employment to professional dancers, choreographers, musicians, designers, and technicians with the goal of producing socially important dance pieces for a new dance audience.

**Daniel Nagrin** (1917-2009), Tamiris' husband as well as her assistant in Broadway shows, was multitalented: a teacher, choreographer, and great soloist, often to jazz music. Some of his best roles were in *Strange Heroes* (1948, music by Stan Kenton and Steve Rugolo), about a gangster type pursued and killed by his enemy, and *Man of Action* (1948), about a white-collar worker. In his *Peloponnesian War* (1968, music by Eric Salzman), accompanied by a reading of *The Thucydides*, he used varied characters in mime, and dance, and he interacted with the audience. He also wrote *How to Dance Forever: Surviving Against the Odds* (1988).

**Sophie Maslow**'s (1911-2006) dance *Dust Bowl Ballads* (1941, music by Woody Guthrie, the songs of migratory workers) dealt with the Depression of the 1930's and how the people of the Southwest endured it. **Jane Dudley** (1912-2001) choreographed a few works dealing with social dissent; some of these were: *In the Life of a Worker* (1934), *Songs of Protest* (1936), and *Under the Swastika* (1937). Together with **William Bales** they formed the **Dudley-Maslow-Bales trio** with the aim of making modern dance more appealing to all. They tended toward folk material rather than intellectual content. American folk songs and Carl Sandberg's *The People, Yes* inspired **Maslow**'s *Folksay* (1942).

**Sybil Shearer** (1912-2005), a pupil of **Doris Humphrey**, depicted the troubles of factory workers and their degradation in her choreography of *In a Vacuum* (1941). "Liquid acting" is what she called her work; it consisted of pantomime-like impersonations of nature, people, and events. She is said to have been a very independent-minded choreographer, and she inspired many future choreographers.

Another development of the depression was the New Dance Group in 1932. It offered classes after working hours at a nominal fee for working people to enable them to study dance. Classes were given in all the modern dance techniques – **Graham**, **Limón**, **Horton**, **Hawkins**, etc. The New Dance Group still exists.

In the dance concert field in the 20th century, two black American dancers, both trained in anthropology and influential in their insertion of African and Caribbean dance in their modern dance concerts, were **Pearl Primus** and **Katherine Dunham**. They both brought much validity to these concerts, which made us aware of some of the roots of American jazz dance, and they did so with charm, power, and theatricality.

**Pearl Primus** (1919-1994) was a groundbreaking teacher, dancer, choreographer, and anthropologist *(Photo Plate 7-3)*. She was a pre-med student at Hunter College and presented a dance concert at the 92nd Street Y (1943, to rave reviews). It offered a varied selection; among the dances were *Hard Time Blues* (1945) to a song by folksinger Josh White about sharecroppers, and *Strange Fruit* (1945) about lynching, based on a poem by Lewis Allan about black experience in the U.S. Her original dance company became the Pearl Primus Dance Language Institute in 1979. Besides her dance concerts she appeared in a revival of *Showboat* (1946, choreography by Helen Tamiris) and performed in the opera *The Emperor Jones* (1946) by Louis Gruenberg at the Chicago Civic Opera in 1946. In 1991 President H. W. George Bush awarded her the National Medal of the Arts.

Katherine Dunham (1909-2006), a beautiful black American dancer of French Canadian, black, and Native American heritage, a choreographer, author, song writer, educator, and activist, was called "Dance's Katherine the Great" by the *Washington Post* following her peak of success in the 40's, 50's, and 60's *(Photo Plate 7-4)*. She had appeared in **Ruth Page**'s *La Guiablesse* (1933). She became involved with the Federal Dance Theater under the WPA in Chicago. In NY she performed *Tropics* (1938) and *Le Jazz Hot: From Haiti to Harlem* (1940). She appeared in the films *Stormy Weather* (1943) and *Cabin in the Sky* (1943), both of which she co-choreographed with **George Balanchine**. In 1930 she formed Ballet Nègre, the first Negro Dance Company. She choreographed *Pins and Needles* (1939), and presented shows that were theatrical and glamorously costumed (by her husband John Pratt): *Tropical Revue* (1943) and *Carib Song* (1945). She incorporated Afro-Caribbean influences into her modern dance choreography. In 1963 she was asked to choreograph Verdi's opera *Aida* at the Metropolitan Opera House.

(The resident ballet company of the Metropolitan Opera House was dismantled in May, 2013. Individual choreographers will henceforth choose the dancers they prefer for their productions. Many opera companies throughout the world have a resident ballet company to dance in the operas and also give separate dance performances. )

**Dunham** also choreographed works of social protest such as *Southland* (1950) about a black man incorrectly accused of raping a white woman. Her New York City school attracted all sorts of performers as well as musicians and choreographers. Courses for them were offered in anthropology, languages, and the dance movements that were the basics of Caribbean and African dance. **Dunham**'s Performing Arts Training Center in East Saint Louis was mainly for the poor. She was honored with the Albert Schweitzer Music Award in 1979 and was a Kennedy Center Honoree in 1983.

"Geisha Holding a Fan," 1921-25, by Edward Atkinson Hornel, (1864-1933), Scottish painter of flowers, foliage, and landscapes, interested in rich colors and dense patterns.

Sheet Music Cover, "Dar's Ragtime in Da Moon," lyrics by Maurice Shapiro, music by Seymour Firth, Sunday World Music Album Supplement to the New York World, Sunday, July 15, 1900.

Matteo and Carola Goya performing a Spanish dance at Jacob's Pillow where they often taught and performed beween 1957 and 1966. Photo by John Lindquist.

Poster, Le Vrai Cake Walk au Nouveau Cirque, ca. 1901-1902; lithograph By Franz Laskoff (German, 1960-1918).

# 8

# Tap Dance

## Its Birth and Development

Another form of dance born in the United States during the 19th century was tap dancing. The first time the phrase "tap dance" appeared in print was in 1928. Before that time **tap dance** was called **clogging**, **buck dance**, or **flatfooting**. The name tap dance came from the tapping sound made when the small metal plates on the dancer's shoes, under the toes and the heel, touched a hard floor. This lively and rhythmic sound made the performer a percussive musician as well as a dancer. Many dance forms have had a hand (or should I say a foot) in its development, from African dance to West African drum rhythms, Irish and English clog, **step dancing**, and also **Spanish flamenco dance**, particularly the **bulería**. People saw others dancing, tried out a few of the new steps, mixed them in with theirs, created more varieties, and gradually tap dancing evolved. Today tap dancing is popular throughout the world and is danced by people of all ages – from the very young to senior citizens.

The **bulería** *(Photo Plates 8-1 and 8-5)*, the liveliest part of **flamenco** dance, like tap, required strength and speed to execute rhythmic combinations of sounds with the heel, sole, and toe of the foot (zapatear). Although written in 12 beats, this dance, which is based on Andalusian music, allows for improvisation and variation in rhythm, the same as tap does. The word flamenco may have come from an Arabic expression. Important in the Spanish flamenco dance are the Middle Eastern influences of the Moors, the Sephardic Jews, the Gypsies, and the Byzantine. These elements coalesced with time and the flamenco reached its Golden Age from 1869 to 1910. In a Spanish flamenco performance, the **bulería** is the flashy finale where the dance company forms a semi circle and each dancer steps forward one at a time to dance, returns to his/her place, and the next one comes forward. The bulería is quick, fun, flashy, sometimes humorous, and tests the skills of both dancers and guitarists. It is thought to have developed in the nineteenth century but to have been inspired by earlier dances of Spain.

Now for the Irish influence on tap. The Irish people loved to dance and took their dances with them whenever they traveled *(Photo Plate 8-1)*. The Irish **sean-nós** dance probably influenced percussive dances such as the **buck dance**, **clogging**, **flatfooting**, and of course **tap dancing** in Canada and America, wherever the Irish went. The sean-nós style of Irish dance emerged in the late 18th and early 19th century as dance masters traveled through various counties in Ireland, setting the standards for upright torsos, relaxed arms down at the sides (some counties actually disagreed with the dance master and preferred more leniency in the arm positions, with arms higher up and clicking fingers as in flamenco), percussive sounds with the toe, executing the dance in a limited space – on a dime – doing the steps twice, once with the right foot, then with the left, for proficiency with both feet. Dance masters taught **jigs**, **reels**, and **hornpipes** in Ireland since about 1713 with such steps as the **roll down**, the **double roll down**, the **pushing step**, the **spring and flourish**, the **upset and curl** and the **salmon leap**. But they did not all have the same steps nor did they have the same names for the steps. Also, the dance masters did not teach difficult steps to the girls. They would have to learn them from their brothers.

Counties with no dance masters tended to have more spontaneous, individualistic dancing and may have included steps from family members. In County Cork in southern Ireland the feet were close together while in Limerick County they were "loose" to allow for a better display of difficult steps. But there were still different dance styles in the north and in the south. In Munster County, in the north, the foot with the weight on it had to have the heel 2 inches off the floor, as was seen later in the performances of *Riverdance*. In the south there were more varieties of tempos and of forms.

The olden style in Connemara County used the quick heel and toe work and arm movements reminding one of the Spanish flamenco; there was also more flatfooting. This style led some to believe that west Ireland had not always been so remote but had been connected to both Europe and North Africa by former trade routes and political ties since the middle ages.

Dancing was always competitive in Ireland. Often rival dancers would challenge one another to endurance dances and to see which dance would last the longest and have the greatest variety of steps. At other times they would take a door off its hinges, soap it up to make it slippery, put it over a barrel on the ground and dance on it, or place a smaller board on top, also soaped and slippery, and dance, or even place the door on the chimney of a house and dance there. It took skill, energy, and nerves of steel to compete. When the Irish came to America, often as indentured farm workers, or as workers in railway building and maintenance, they brought these styles of dance with them and influenced all who saw them.

In America, slaveholders in the South were always afraid of revolt. There had been one in South Carolina, called the Cato Conspiracy because a slave called Cato had led the revolt. In 1740, laws were passed forbidding the use of drums once it was discovered that the slaves could communicate with one another through drums; they had memorized certain sounds, tones, and rhythms and could tell what these stood for. When they were in Africa, if an African tribe knew another tribe was getting ready for battle it could alert a third tribe with drum sounds. Africans had been used to dancing barefoot to the intricate West African drum rhythms, so now the African-Americans held onto their rhythms by tapping them out with their feet *(Photo Plate 8-1)*. This became a complex and very physical form of expression for them.

Slave owners hired out their slaves to work as stevedores on the levees when the season on the plantation was slow. On the levees these stevedores would make brushing and shuffling movements with their feet. **Levee dancer** was the name given to black dancers who would beat out rhythms on riverboats on the Mississippi River. The black performer was so popular that white performers imitated many of their intricate steps

"Warspite" cadets dancing the hornpipe. Author: Associated Press, 1928, National Maritime Museum. The hornpipe began in the 16th century on Great Britain's sailing vessels. The movements were all known by sailors: "looking out to sea first with the right hand then with the left, hauling in the anchor, lurching with the boat in rough weather." The dance was originally done by men only.

"Baile por Bulerías," oil on canvas, 1884, by José García Ramos (Sevilla, 1852-1912). A bulería is a form of flamenco dance.

Cover: "A Handbook of Irish Dances," by J. G. O'Keefe and Art O'Brien, 1934. The first Irish dances were ritual dances to the Druids. The circle dances survived in the round or ring dances of today.

Sheet music cover: "Africana." Composer: Leo E. Berliner; Lyricist: Monroe H. Rosenfeld, Publisher: New York, NY: Jos. W. Stern & Co. Cover illustrated by John Frew, 1904.

Since Africans had danced before coming to America, slave traders sometimes tempted blacks onto their ships near Africa with the promise that they would see the sailors do their typical **hornpipe** dances *(Photo Plate 8-1)*, and then the blacks would do their dances aboard the ship. Tired, they would all fall asleep on board; when they awoke the ship and slave traders were out in the middle of the ocean on the way to having the blacks sold as slaves. They had been abducted.

However, most slaves were not lured on board but were bought from slave dealers, or captured as prisoners of war and then sold by the winning African tribe, or abducted by white or black slave traders. The Portuguese, in 1441, were the ones who began the slave trading business in West Africa, but actually slavery began even much earlier. In the year 793 Norse raiders captured English people who were not as strong as they.

In an 18<sup>th</sup> century book, *An Account of the Slave Trade on the Coast of Africa*, Alexander Falconbridge, a ship surgeon, described how the slave trade was usually carried out. A ship that was meant to carry four hundred slaves often carried six hundred. A total of more than forty million Africans were shackled and kept in the crowded damp holds of ships as they went across the Atlantic. The journey took up to four months. A healthy slave would bring in more money for the slave trader than a sick one; thus every day the slaves were forced to go on the deck and dance as exercise to the accompaniment of bag-pipes, harps, or fiddles; it was called "dancing the slaves;" if they didn't move fast enough a cat-o-nine-tail flogging awaited them. And so they danced, not for the love of it at that time, but to escape a whipping.

African slaves were generally taken to the West Indies for a "seasoning" of three or four years before being brought to the United States. As a rule the French and Spanish slave owners in the West Indies treated the slaves better than the English or Americans did; the slaves were allowed to do their various dances for holidays and took these to America. In 1803, when there was an overthrow of the white ruling class in Haiti, they went to New Orleans with their slaves.

In West Africa there were **circular dances** to commemorate the many stages of life and the spiritual power of the forefathers. The group of dancers moved in a counterclockwise circle representing the phases of life while the feet close to the ground helped them to feel the spiritual authority of Mother Earth. The **challenge dance**, in which one person after another moved into the center and showed off his best steps, agility, and strong points while the others maintained the rhythm, progressed very easily from an African dance to tap. Many learned new steps from watching the dances. Each added something new to the steps he saw, rather than copying them exactly. In African dance the feet were bare, no shoes, but additional sounds could be made with tiny baskets woven from long leaves, filled with pebbles and attached to the dancer's wrists or legs. Some tribes wore long grasses or raffia over their costumes to make a shushing sound as they moved.

The **shout** or **ring-shout** in America was the blend of religious song and dance from the **African circle dance** that led to what were called **camp meeting hymns** and **work hollers** in the old south. The word "shout" derived from the Afro-Arabic word saut and referred to the counterclockwise pattern of the walk by the Muslim in their pilgrimage around the sacred Kabaa in Mecca, Saudi Arabia. (Twenty percent of the slaves were Muslim.) In 1807 the international slave trade had been banned. The Grand

Awakening, or the Evangelical revivalism, at this time, led to the conversion of blacks, especially to Baptist and Methodist sects in the South, and encouraged forms of worship adaptable to African rituals, including singing and dancing. People in America were not as interested in religion at that particular time as they had been earlier, so Christian religions were trying to adapt their religious service to the African people that they had enslaved, since they were an entirely new group that could be converted.

Some religious people felt that selling and buying members of the tribe that had fought and lost a war in Africa and enslaving them was wrong, whereupon others said that one should consider what the slaves were getting in return – they were being converted to Christianity (the religion of their enslavers). Of course, another group thought that this might not be good; the slaves might then believe themselves to be as worthy as their masters.

When camp meetings *(Photo Plate 8-3)* were instituted in America in the 19th century they consisted of religious services lasting several days, often in the woods with small tents to house the people and a larger tent, the tabernacle, in which the congregation would gather. Some congregations were interracial, with a larger number of blacks than of whites. There was singing, laughing and convulsive jerking movements of the body, which the participants seemed unable to stop. The dancer started by first walking in a **congo** pose and used the entire body while moving around in a counterclockwise circle; the feet slid and shuffled around as the hips wiggled and swayed, with the shoulders held stiff and an occasional stamping, singing, and clapping in syncopation as someone went to the center of the circle. They sometimes continued their dance-like movement to the same music for twenty to thirty minutes. For variety they just walked and sang and then returned to the dancing. The emphasis was on rhythm. The **walk-around**, in the later minstrel shows, was a parody of this dance.

The **congo step** was taught as follows by **Sevilla Fort**, a former member of **Katherine Dunham**'s Company and a renowned instructor of **African** and **Caribbean dance** at Teachers College, Columbia University: knees were bent, torso, arms, head, and shoulders were relaxed and went very fluidly where the movements led them, with care taken not to cross nor lift the feet, which would have been very unacceptable.

During the **ring-shout** the lead singer would narrate the story and the others would have a repetitive phrase to sing. The **ring-shout** survived for many years, probably because the experience was unifying, and as long as the feet did not cross it was not considered to be dancing (which was thought to be sinful in some areas) but a religious activity.

The **ring-shout** had many of the important characteristics of African dance: syncopation and polyrhythms, movement of all parts of the body including hips and shoulders, a lowered center of gravity that made for recognition of mother earth, a circular formation, and occasional improvisations by a participant who stepped into the center of the circle.

There were other dances that either were performed at plantations and were later used in tapping competitions or that influenced tap dance and its rhythms.

Dances done while carrying a bucket or a glass of water on the head seemed like a natural outcome of carrying almost anything on the head in Africa. The slaves would

William M. "Billy" Whitlock (1813-1878) in a lithograph of Eliphalet Brown, Jr., depicts "Billy" Whitlock of the Virginia Minstrels, as banjo player with his partner, either Frank Lynch or probably, John Diamond, at the Bowery Theatre in NY. as shown on sheet music cover of Whitlock's "Collection of Ethiopian Melodies" published by C. G. Christman, NY, 1846.

T.D. Rice ("Daddy" Rice), 1832, singing "Jump Jim Crow." Picture from 1832 playbill. Author unknown.

The blackface Virginia Minstrels, featuring fiddle, banjo, and bones, detail from the cover of "The Celebrated Negro Melodies, Jim Crow Polka," by A.F.Winnemore and Thos. Comer," 1843.

even have a **jig contest** with a glass of water on the head. The winner was the one who could jig, turn, and do the entire dance without a single drop of water falling out.

(Other countries have similar folk dances, but certainly some of the most notable are the graceful ones from the Philippines. The **Binasuan dance** from the Pangasinan Province of the Philippines is performed while holding a glass of wine on the head and on each hand. In another section of the Philippines, in Lubang Island, there is a lively **stepping dance** during which the participants balance an oil lamp on their head and on the back of each hand. These are performed for festive occasions.)

House slaves at a plantation were the ones who had had the most education and had the greatest awareness of the plantation owners' customs. The field slaves looked up to them for indications of proper decorum, especially when the dance being done was not of the hand clapping, circle variety but more like a **square dance** or a **quadrille**.

Then there were the dances for special occasions. **Corn shucking dances** took place a few times a year with mounds and mounds of corn to be shucked quickly. The slaves would choose two corn generals who would divide and select the participants for each group and check that the piles of corn were the same. Rhythm played a very important part in this activity. The group that shucked the most corn most quickly won. The corn generals led the singing for their group; their skill in picking a good rhythm in this call and response song speeded the action along. When this chore was finished, two strong slaves would raise the master onto their shoulders, carry him around the house three times, go over to the tables that were set out on the grass, and all would enjoy an excellent supper that had been prepared in the big house (the master's house). The fiddles and banjos came out and the dancing would go on till all hours with everybody dancing, the white folks in the master's house, and the slaves in a house that the master let them use for the occasion. As the years went on and the choice of dances changed, there were more **quadrilles**. This necessitated a caller-out to indicate the next step as well as how to do it.

There was also dancing at funerals. Sometimes the burial occurred the day after the death, whereas the funeral was from one to three months later with the minister sometimes officiating at several funerals on the same day. The **burial dance** was similar to the dance performed in many primitive cultures, back to the Dark Ages; the participants danced around the grave to keep away unwelcome spirits, but primarily to keep the dead person's spirit in the grave and not let it wander around.

A **wedding** also had a dance if the slave was a favorite; otherwise it often involved asking for permission to marry and simply "jumping over a broom" either singly or as a couple, but without touching the broom (or the marriage would be a failure).

The sale of a slave or of slaves was an occasion for a dance too: the dance showed that the slave was in excellent health, or that the slave had special talents of dancing or of playing the fiddle. Fiddle playing was important for all the dances at a plantation, whether for the master's entertainment or for the slaves'.

A formal dance was not a frequent occurrence at a plantation, which made it all the more memorable. Occasionally there would be a Saturday night dance at the plantation or at a nearby plantation; permission to go there was required. Dance and music were important aspects of a slave's life and the only available entertainment.

In the mid 1600's, Scottish and Irish indentured laborers came to the New World and brought their dances too. They lived and worked side by side with black Americans and saw each other's dances as well. Slaves in southern America imitated the quick toe and heel action of **Irish jigs** and the **Lancashire clog** and combined them with West African dances such as juba dances and the step dances of the "ring shouts." The **juba dance** was done in the United States since the early 19th century and was a style of making rhythm in which the dancer slapped his body in complex rhythms with the diverse parts of the body that were slapped making a slightly different sound. This was also known as **Pattin' Juba** and became well known by 1845 as a combination of European jig, reel steps, clog, and African rhythms.

The result of this exchange of styles of dancing was that African dances became more formal and watered down, and European movements acquired more fluidity and rhythm, and out of this came a uniquely American tap dance.

Strangely enough, the men and women who endured the long and dangerous Middle Passage (as the trip from Africa to America was called) on their way to the New World, and their descendants, had a great influence on the way Americans danced, and the music they played, no matter what their origin, whether Russia, France, Spain, Ireland, or elsewhere. (The only Americans who were not immigrants were the Native Americans.) The black dances: **ring shout**, **buck and wing**, jig, **buzzard lope**, **pigeon wing**, **cakewalk**, and numerous others inspired secular and sacred dances all through the United States. These led to several of the social dances such as the **turkey trot** and the **fox trot** of the 1900's and then the **Charleston** of the 1920's and others, as well as to later influences in movements, themes, and music in jazz, ballet, modern dance, and in dance in Broadway musicals

With the appearance of the minstrel shows *(Photo Plate 8-3)* in the late 1800's, tap took to the stage. In places without real theaters, the shows were often in tents. But it was only white dancers in blackface (faces blackened with burnt cork) who performed. They competed to see who had the most "authentic" interpretation of African and African American dance and music styles. Many white performers copied the complicated steps done by **levee dancers**; their shuffle dance style was used in minstrel shows as early as 1828 in the dancing of **Thomas "Daddy" Rice** (1808-1860).

"Daddy" Rice *(Photo Plate 8-2)* was a white performer and playwright who used black African American song and dance in his skits. He was the Father of American Minstrelsy. In his shows he used the vernacular dialect of blacks that he had heard in his travels in Manhattan and in Southern slave states for his impersonations of a character called Jim Crow This character was based on the real **Jim Crow**, a lame and black slave who danced and dressed in rags and old shoes. Rice sang and danced nimbly, his face and hands blackened. This was his signature act; every night he would make up a new verse about Jim Crow, and "Daddy" Rice's popularity grew. He sang his lyrics to an old English Morris dance tune, combining hops from Irish dance, shuffles, and a jumping-over-the-broom type of step. But "Daddy" Rice was ahead of the times. Successful blackface minstrel shows had not yet happened. Performers in blackface were more often

Sheet Music Cover:" At a Georgia Camp Meeting." Composer: Kerry Mills, Publisher: New York: F. A. Mills, 1897.

"Primrose & West's Big Minstrels". Creator: Strobridge & Co. Lith., 1896. Medium: print poster, lithography, color.

either part of a variety show or were used as a pause, an entr'acte, between two acts of a play.

Meanwhile, the term Jim Crow took on another connotation. It became part of our language and was synonymous with segregation of black Americans and with laws that oppressed them in the 19th and 20<sup>th</sup> centuries.

Minstrel shows were most popular from 1840 to 1890. The duo of **Jimmy Doyle** (1888-1927) and **Harland Dixon** (1885-1969) exemplified the **fast style** also called **buck and wing**, in wooden-sole shoes. The Irish American minstrel **George Primrose** (1852-1919) *(Photo Plate 8-3)* popularized the **soft shoe style**, a smooth, leather-sole style, in his dignified minstrel characters and on vaudeville. The material for these shows included jokes, songs, dance, and music. The dancers in minstrel-vaudeville shows were called "Song and dance men."

**William 'Billy' Whitlock** (1813-1878) *(Photo Plate 8-2)* was an American who started performing the banjo in circuses while wearing blackface. For a while he teamed up with **John Jack Diamond**, playing the banjo while Diamond danced. Then in 1843 he founded the Virginia Minstrels *(Photo Plate 8-2)* with fiddler Dan Emmett, Frank Brower playing the bones (asses' jawbones), and Richard Pelham on the tambourine. They also intermingled verbal comments with their dancing.

The four of them opened at the Chatham Theatre in the Five Points neighborhood of New York. They toured in New York and Boston and became well known. Whitlock also wrote music. Both the Virginia Minstrels and Christy's Minstrels sang *Miss Lucy Long*, one of his songs.

The performances in blackface presented the format used in future minstrel shows. The first part consisted of dance, jokes, and songs; the second act, called the olio, had a stump speech on social issues, politics, or just plain nonsense; it was the predecessor of today's standup comedy. The third and final act was either a slapstick plantation skit musical or a spoof of a popular play. There were several stock characters: a mulatto servant maid, an urban dandy, a mammy, an old black man, a plantation slave, and a black soldier. Blackface minstrelsy was decidedly an American theater form. The addition of jubilees, or spirituals, provided the first real black music to be used and was the basis of the growth of the American music and dance of the 1830's and 1840's.

Now, finally, black performers could appear on the American stage but only in all-black performances for an all-black audience and they had to put on blackface (burnt cork) makeup. They too would look like white performers trying to appear black.

Before the Civil War ended in 1865 black and white performers did not appear together. The exception was **Master Juba** *(Photo Plate 8-4)*, the stage name of **William Henry Lane** (1825-1852); he went to London to perform with a troupe in 1848. He died very young, at age 27, from malnutrition and overwork. He was born a free man, and had been a well-known dancer in New York since his teens. He had picked up all the movements of the Irish clog and step dances, did specialties of his own, and imitated the famous dancers of his day in all their outstanding routines. He was also an exceptional singer and tambourine player. The melting pot in the Five Points neighborhood in New

York City (presently the area northwest of South Street Seaport) from which William Henry Lane came, contributed much to his innovative dances.

There were many Irish people in the Five Points district. In Ireland, during the potato blight, the owners of the land were supposed to reimburse their tenant farmers for a portion of their loss. However, it was cheaper to put them all on a boat to America, and the majority of them found their way to the Five Points district where they hoped to earn enough to feed their families. The Five Points district, where at that time five streets met, was in the Lower East Side. (It is thoroughly discussed in the 2001 book, *Five Points*, by Tyler Anbinder. The 2002 film *Gangs of New York* was set in the Five Points district.) Many poor Irish had come to this neighborhood where they exchanged dance steps, fought with blacks, and intermarried. Both Irish and blacks worked as labor for the construction and maintenance of railroads. There were similar black-Irish ghettos in Boston, Philadelphia, and Cincinnati. The best tap moves were a mix of African shuffle and Irish clog. The **jig** was the most influential with its very rapid footwork.

Since the 1830's the Five Points had a fusion of Irish dancing and black African shuffle as a result of the various immigrant groups' competing and displaying their best tap dance movements. The Five Points neighborhood may have been an extremely poor section of New York but nevertheless it had two very well known theaters, the Chatham and the Bowery, where the contests sometimes took place. The Five Points was so well known that Charles Dickens mentioned it in his book *American Notes (Photo Plate 8-4)*.

**William Henry Lane (Master Juba)** created such amazingly complex and rhythmic dances with his footwork and body slaps that in 1844 he won three competitions against the famous Irish clog dancer **John Jack Diamond**, known as **Master Diamond** (1823-1857), who was said to be the best "jig dancer" of all time and who also excelled in black dance. But Master Diamond lost the competition and **Master Juba** won. Theatrical agents were the ones who arranged for these competitions, and in order to draw a very large crowd each contestant was paid the huge amount (in those days) of $500. Master Juba was proclaimed the King of All Dancers and was chosen to be the star of an all-white American company, the Ethiopian Minstrels, where he was treated like a star. And no one seemed to object to black Master Juba being in a group of all-white performers and getting the star billing he deserved. It was even said that he invented tap dancing.

Many black or mixed minstrel companies appeared. Black Americans, however, still had to wear blackface. Minstrel shows were extremely popular. The stereotypes and caricatures were racist, but the increasing popularity of minstrel shows denoted the increasing interest and influence of black culture – music and dance – in the United States.

There were several other well-known black dancers in the black minstrel shows and they were as popular as the white minstrel show performers. **Billy Kersands** (1842-1915) a singer, dancer, and comedian was one of them; all two hundred pounds of him did the **Virginia essence dance**, originated by him, to a slow four-four rhythm with a light-footed manner, a grace, and humor that made Queen Victoria laugh with gusto when he performed in England. The later **soft shoe** came out of the **essence**, with its graceful sliding steps devoid of flash or speed. **The Bohee Brothers** also went to

William Henry Lane ("Master Juba") dances in New York's Five Points District as Charles Dickens and a companion watch in the background. Engraving from "American Notes for General Circulation" by Charles Dicken*s* (1842). Engravings by Marcus Stone.

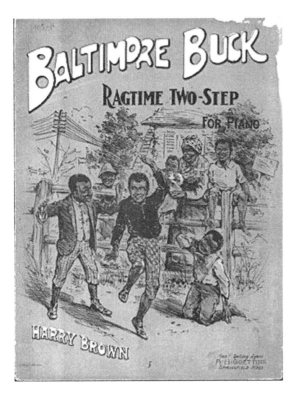

Sheet Music Cover: "The Baltimore Buck" ragtime two-step. Composer: Harry Brown. Publisher: Boston, MA: Vinton Music Pub. Co., 1905.

Dancer doing a toe tip tap to the back, a simple step used in more intricate combinations, in a Maxie Ford, and in turns. Photo by Enia.

England to dance and to teach the banjo to the Prince of Wales. They were the first to do both at the same time – the soft shoe while playing the banjo. A black performer named **Benjamin Franklin** did a specialty or **eccentric** dance, as these were called. It was danced to a waltz tempo while Franklin played the French horn with a pail of water on his head. Not a drop of water was spilled.

A **step dance** in those days was any dance style in which the footwork was the most important part of the dance. Body and arm movements were restricted. The dance was usually performed as a solo or group dance. At the other extreme of the spectrum were formation dances in which the patterns were the most important item.

English **clogging** began during the 18th century and the Industrial Revolution. Men sitting at weaving machines in the Lancashire cotton mills in England preferred to wear hard-sole shoes because the floors were kept wet to help keep the humidity high, which was important in cotton spinning. To keep their feet warm they would tap out the rhythms of the machines. At lunch and breaks they would have contests and the best rhythm pattern won.

The judges of clog competitions in the 19th century sat either under the floor or behind a screen so the performers' body movements would not influence them, for they would just judge the sounds. It was no wonder that Irish clog dancers did not use any arms but just concentrated on footwork. In America this became the black style known as **jigging** in which the body was bent forward and all the action occurred below the waist: springing, jumping, and winging. **Winging** was done with one leg up in the air while the other leg was responsible for all the tap sounds on the take-off and on the landing.

**Lancashire clog** was a complex Irish dance connected to **George Primrose**, who danced the clog with the usual wooden shoes that most clog dancers wore. (It was said that he was also the originator of the soft-shoe tap dance. Those who saw his show at the Fifth Avenue Theatre in New York in 1918 said he was 'the greatest soft shoe dancer in the world.') **Barney Williams**, in 1840, was the first professional clog dancer to come to the United States from Ireland, and the Irish Clog Dancers were the first professional group to come to the United States.

**Clogging** was also done in Wales where some contests had the dancers leaping over brooms. This also existed in American Appalachia, where settlers developed it in the 18th century, and in the French Canadian step dance. Clogging was the official state dance of Kentucky and North Carolina. Clogging was variously known as flatfooting, foot-stomping, buck dance, jigging, or other local terms. What these had in common was a stress on the downbeat of the music with animated footwork. This style of clogging was also noisier than the lighter forms of Irish jig dancing.

Irish jigs and hornpipes were the most difficult of the Irish clogs. In some of these the feet tapped the floor more than seventy times in fifteen seconds. In January 14, 1973, *The Guinness World Book of Records* entered as a record that **Roy Castle** did twenty-four taps per second or 1,440 taps per minute. The shoulders and arms in clog dancing were held down at the sides, motionless. This style was seen in the earlier black **buck and wing** variety of tap dancing. The **hornpipe**, from England, was an imitation of the movement of English sailors while tapping their feet to a tune. **John Durang** (1768-1822), the first white American-born professional dancer, mixed ballet steps with black American shuffles and winging steps in his solo dance of the hornpipe that he performed in blackface in 1784; his son **Charles Durang** described it in a book on new social dances.

The basic **chug** or brush step was done by pushing the ball of the foot across the floor while at the same time dropping the heel, with or without weight. The music was in two-quarter time, a syncopated march. This later developed into the **time step** and became a basic tap step along with **falling off a log**, **through the trenches**, and **shuffle off to Buffalo**.

Between the 1700's and 1800's tap dancing progressed. After the end of the Civil War (1861-1865) the tap vocabulary increased with the addition of the syncopated **stop time**, **soft shoe**, **waltz clog**, and **time step**. Dancers' postures were more relaxed and arms or shoulders were used for whimsical gestures.

Many cities had street tap performers. Street children who had no shoes found a way to get sharp sounds. They would place bottle caps between their toes. Those who had shoes could have the shoemaker put in small metal tips on the toes or heels. (Lots of people used these to conserve the soles of their shoes.)

The **soft shoe** was a form of tap done with shoes that did not have metal taps attached. All kinds of shoes were worn for soft shoe. The characteristics of soft shoe tap dancing was humor, wit, and a delicate style of tapping sometimes performed to classical music but always with a smooth and relaxed manner such as that of **Tommy Tune** (b. 1929) or **Paul Draper** (1909-1996). When sand was placed on the floor, it was called a **sand dance**. **Sandman Sims** (1917-2003) was famous for this.

In 1866 *The Black Crook* was the first white musical to feature minstrel and clog dancers. The dancer was known as a **pedestal dancer** since he went up on a marbled pedestal with a twenty-four inch base and performed a tap routine while posing motionless likes a statue.

By the mid nineteenth century the mixture of African-American footwork with Irish and British clogging was called **buck and wing**, portraying the African-American males, known as "bucks." The term "buck" can be traced back to the West Indies and to the French Buccaneer. Ship captains would have the male slaves dance on the ship's deck to keep up their morale and also as a form of exercise to keep fit; they could be sold for more at auction if they were fit. "Buck" was originally just a stamping of the feet to interpret the music. **Buck dancing** *(Photo Plate 8-4)* was the first tap performed to syncopated rhythm, the tribal rhythms from Africa.

**James McIntyre** (1857-1937) of New York supposedly invented the buck and wing routine and performed it on a New York stage in 1880. **Pigeon wing** is also known as **pistolets** and the **ailes de pigeon** in ballet. In the **can-can** the pigeon wing meant kicking the leg high, holding it up high against the cheek while hopping lightly on the other leg. In tap, wings were a step used in the 1900's, eventually becoming an "air" step, with the dancer springing up off the floor from one leg, doing one tap on the way up and two taps on the way down while the "winging" leg usually remained motionless; this was a three-tap wing. There were also five-and  seven-tap wings. The movement was done on

Photo Plate 8-5

"Andalusian Dance," 1893, by Spanish artist José Villegas Cordero (1844-1921).

"The Dancing Lesson (Negro Boy Dancing)" Date: 1878. Artist: Thomas Eakins (American, 1844-1916, Philadelphia, PA). Medium: watercolor on off-white wove paper.

.

the ball of the foot. The variations were: the five tap wing, the pump, with the winging leg going up and down, the pendulum, and others.

In the late 19th century, minstrel and showboat routines included either the fast style of **buck and wing**, typified by the duo of **Jimmy Doyle and Harland Dixon**, or the **soft shoe,** a smooth, leather-soled trend as executed by **George Primrose**.

There were occasionally female dancers who did buck and wing. **Mame Gerue** was featured at Brooklyn's Orpheum Theatre, dancing the Spanish fandango as well as the buck and wing. **Lotta Crabtree** (1847-1924, retired from the stage in 1891) likewise studied the Spanish fandango, Irish jigs, ballet and acrobatics and became well known for her dances of **breakdowns** and **jigs** for which she received excellent reviews.

The **breakdown**, a black-American slave dance, popular from 1800 to 1890, was later incorporated into jazz, swing, and tap dancing. There were different versions, the **Birmingham**, the **Cincinnati**, the **harmonica breakdown**, and others.

By the end of the 19th century, Irish clog dance had almost disappeared due to the combining of the clog and the black American tap dances. Modern tap dancing evolved from the years 1900 through 1920.

# 9

# The Beginnings of Jazz Dance

# and Minstrelsy

Looking back on the development of dancing, one cannot help noting that America, the place where people who were mostly uninterested in dancing went to live, was exactly where some future forms of dancing would have their foothold and growth. These included modern dance, tap dance and jazz dance. Native Americans had much dancing in their lives, but many of the settlers, especially the Puritans, the Calvinists, and a few other religious groups (except for two of them, the Shakers and the Holy Rollers) had no use for dancing. Dancing diverted man's thoughts away from God. It was quite a while before these groups accepted dance as a wholesome and healthy pastime for all men, women, and children.

The characteristics of **jazz dance** were the same as those of African dance: bent knees and thus a lowered center of gravity, movements that rippled out from the center of the body, use of the entire body in dance, not just the arms and legs, syncopated body rhythms and maybe even two or three different rhythms at a time, isolation of the various body parts, the ribs, head, hips, shoulders – in circles, in shifts to the sides, forward and back, or up and down – whatever movement that particular body part was capable of executing *(Photo Plates 9-1, 2, and 5)*.

For many years, in May, the Brooklyn Academy of Music (BAM) has presented a celebration of African dance called DanceAfrica, under the direction of **Chuck Davis**. For the duration of about one week many excellent African Dance companies perform traditional to contemporary dances such as African-Brazilian and hip hop, allowing us to appreciate the many sources of the basis of jazz dance. Chuck Davis (b. 1937) has had an important role in introducing Americans to African and African-influenced dance. DanceAfrica also appears throughout the country in such cities as Chicago, Hartford, Los Angeles, Miami, and Philadelphia. **Chuck Davis** was named one of the first 100 Irreplaceable Dance Treasures of the United States in 2000 for his dedication to dance.

The characteristics of **jazz dance** mentioned above were all movements found in African, Caribbean, and Latin dances, so they were not new. What was innovative, however, was their development into jazz dance as an art to be written about and to be used in theatrical dance. Before long, jazz dance had become the dance of the people, both rural and urban folks, reflecting the history, origins, economics, creativity and the music of their more recent environment. As these changed, so did jazz dance, along with our lifestyles, the speed and excitement of the city, our physical and mental needs, and the customs of the times. Before we were aware of it, we had **hip-hop, break dancing,** and variations of these such as **krumping** (an aggressive form of hip hop) as the latest trends.

From Brazil's slave era came **capoeira**, a fusion of fighting movements, kicks, and acrobatics. The slaves in Brazil originated it as a form of self-defense; since this was not permitted, it was transformed into a dance. It can be considered either as a form of martial arts or as a dangerous dance. DanceBrazil, a company under **Jelon Vieira** from Bahia, Brazil, performs an exhilarating combination of African dance, capoeira and contemporary dance in New York when they tour there. Brazilian dance has incorporated African, Portuguese, and European forms of dance. From 1500 to 1822 Brazil was a Portuguese colony and African slaves from Angola were brought to Brazil. These were not allowed to follow their own religion, so they disguised their worship into the rhythm of the **samba**. With the end of slavery in Brazil on May 13, 1888, the samba developed from a crude dance into a samba with many completely varied styles. The **capoeira** was often done within a circle that was formed with pairs taking turns going to the center to dance. The **samba de gafieira** was a partner dance of the 1940's and got its name from a nightclub in Rio de Janeiro. It included some of the **maxixe**, the waltz, and the entwining legs of the Argentine **tango**. The **samba axé** was a solo dance without any distinct steps. When a new piece of axé music was released, the choreography for its dance was released too. Then there was the **samba reggae,** popular in Bahia; the **samba de roda** was an African-Brazilian dance associated with the capoeira; and the **samba-rock** was playful and resembled the modern **salsa** and the **samba de gafieira**. All the sambas are highly flirtatious and lively dances. Movie audiences in the United States became familiar with the samba through the dancing of **Fred Astaire** and **Ginger Rogers** in *Flying Down to Rio* (1933) when they danced together in a movie for the first time with foreheads together, doing *The Carioca*, named after the Carioca River in Rio de Janeiro, and when **Carmen Miranda** danced the samba in the film *That Night in Rio* (1941, also starring Alice Faye and Don Ameche).

Another dance of African, Portuguese, and European descent was the sensual **carimbó**. Sometimes the woman would drop her handkerchief and the man had to pick it up with his mouth. The **lundu**, popular in the 17<sup>th</sup> and 18<sup>th</sup> centuries, was a partner dance that also used castanets and handkerchief. The **forro** was a party dance popular in Northeastern Brazil. The **lambada** with wave-like movements of the dancer's body was trendy in the 1980's. Brazilian dances have since gained worldwide popularity.

The African slaves who were brought to America from Africa and then from the West Indies, Cuba, Panama, and Haiti to the United States, also brought their dances. Many of these dances formed the basis of Latin jazz, and became known as the **cha-cha, mambo, pachanga, merengue, samba**, the **conga**, and the **salsa**. Once these dances had been adapted and freshened up for an audience, ballroom couples like **Irene** (1893-1969) **and Vernon** (1887-1918) **Castle**, or **Tony and Sally DeMarco** enjoyed teaching and doing the new dances of the early 20<sup>th</sup> century. And these became very fashionable. With time, the attitude toward one's body and toward dance changed, and in addition clothing become looser, largely influenced by modern dancer **Isadora Duncan** and by **Irene Castle**.

Photo Plate 9-1

NEGRO DANCE ON A CUBAN PLANTATION,

"Slave Dance, Cuba," 1859. From "Harper's Weekly," Jan. 29, 1859, Vol. 3, p.73. Depicts Negro men and women dancing.

THE LOVE SONG.

"Love Song." Artist: E. W. Kemble; Century Magazine, Vol. 31, 1886.

"The Bamboula dance," engraving by Artist E.W. Kemble in Congo Square, New Orleans, to illustrate the article "The Dance in Place Congo" by George Washington Cable, published in Century Magazine, February, 1886.

The European **waltz** survived as a result of being updated by infusions of black rhythm, artistry and humor, and became the **Charleston, black bottom, big apple, two-step, varsity drag, mooch, shimmy,** then **trucking, shag,** and the **Suzie-Q.**

Slaves were always regarded as more valuable if they could dance or play an instrument. Plantation owners would occasionally hold competitions in which dance couples "walked" against each other while someone played the African banjo or the fiddle. The couple with the most intricate steps, or the best rhythm, or the most elegance would probably win the cake in this **cakewalk** contest *(Photo Plates 9-2).* From there came the expression "that takes the cake." The contest was sometimes between different plantations, but a pass was needed in order for a slave to leave his plantation and go to another one. The plantation with the winning couple was proud to be the winner. For these festivals, which were sometimes held at harvest time, the slaves were dressed in their Sunday best. The Master and Mistress of the Big House would be there too and would often judge the contest and provide the cake for the winning couple.

The **cakewalk** started as a shuffling movement but gradually acquired a smooth walking step, and then a backward sway. An imitation and satire of the plantation owners' dance brought with it a prancing strut. As a rule, cakewalk music usually began in a minor key and ended in a major key. The cakewalk had so much possibility as a stage dance that it appeared in many shows: *The Creole Show* (1891), *The Octoroon* (1896); but it was left out of the show *Oriental America* (1896) where it was replaced by opera arias that were not as well-liked as the cakewalk, causing this show not to survive very long.

In the 1600's the Irish, who loved to dance and influenced much of our dancing, had a similar but different custom. On the patron saint's day of a parish the people would gather near the ale house in the afternoon on some convenient ground and dance for the cake prize, which was provided by the owner's wife. The couple that could continue dancing the longest around a bush made of apples and cake won the cake in Ireland, whereas in America it was the best dancing couple that took the cake.

Blacks in the U.S. danced to entertain either themselves or their masters with new dances or adaptations of what they saw. On their day off, slaves would go to Congo Square, near New Orleans, to dance *(Photo Plate 9-1).* This started in about 1805 and continued through 1880, during which time the black migration to the North began, Storyville, New Orleans, came into existence, and black dance halls were constructed. Whites, afraid of any large gatherings of blacks, had passed a law in 1817 saying that black slaves could gather at Congo Square, but only on Sundays, and not after sunset. There they could be watched to make sure they were not plotting anything. Their dances were the **chica,** the **bamboula,** the **calenda,** the **Congo,** often danced by the Congolese from Africa, as well as a variety of **voodoo dances.** In many of their dances the upper torso was often immobile while the hips moved. Since this was something completely different from European dance, it was considered improper and not favored although enjoyable to watch.

In the **calenda,** also spelled **calinda,** *(Photo Plate 9-5)* the dancers did jumps, turns, and steps with the arms held as though holding castanets. Whenever the drum would beat they would strike their thighs against their partners' thighs. The women had more languishing movements and the men were very energetic. One or more couples danced in the center. When the dancing couple was exhausted they left their spot in the center of the circle and another couple replaced them. The onlookers stood or sat in a large circle around them. These dances were also done in the West Indies and in the Caribbean.

The **chica dance** had flirtatious movements by the women as the men coaxed them. Here too, there were a lot of hip and thigh movements.

The **bamboula** *(Photo Plate 9-1)* was a frantic dance comprising leaps and chanting. A man went to the center of the ring of people, started to dance, then went over to a woman whom he led to the center and he danced for her as she watched; when he fell from exhaustion, another couple went to the center while he was pulled away to the side. It was a popular slave dance at Congo Square. The musicians sat around playing and varying the rhythms as they played.

The instruments used for accompaniment were the calabash, a gourd rattle, a triangle, an animal jawbone (scraped by an object or piece of metal and played by running a stick up and down the teeth), a banjo, and drums. All drums were prohibited in the United States but not in the West Indies. In spite of their prohibition in the U.S., these drums used in the West Indies seemed to have been prevalent in New Orleans. There was a long narrow drum, a square drum (a type of goomba drum), as well as a smaller drum called a bamboula, so named because it was made from one or two joints of very large bamboo.

Although many Americans did not care for the dances that were performed at Congo Square and found them dull, these Sunday dances actually became quite a tourist attraction and were danced for the benefit of tourists as late as 1885.

The religion of western Africa from where most of the slaves came was a part of their daily living. Song and dance were of prime importance in their ritual in which possession by a god, who spoke through the drums, was the end result and was considered the ultimate experience. A few of the dances were the **yanvalou,** done in an undulating, squatting position, and the **zepaule,** with much movement of the shoulders.

The influence of all these dances seen in Congo Square appeared again much later. Voodoo dances were seen on Broadway in *House of Flowers* (1954), a musical choreographed by **Herbert Ross** (1927-2001) and starring **Alvin Ailey** and **Carmen de Lavallade** *(Photo Plate 9-3),* beautiful in the dance *Gladiola.*

Several other black choreographers, like the dancer-choreographer **Rod Rodgers** (1938-2002) in his signature work *Tangents*, **Geoffrey Holder** *(Photo Plate 9-3)* (1930 – 2014, born in Trinidad) in his work *Dougla* (1974) and **Louis Johnson** (b. 1930) in *Forces of Rhythm* (1972), would interlace jazz rhythms with ethnic dance – African, Caribbean, and East Indian – or were interested in using the improvisational aspects of African dance and music in their works. The Dance Theatre of Harlem placed some of these pieces in its repertoire, a merging of classical ballet and ethnic dance.

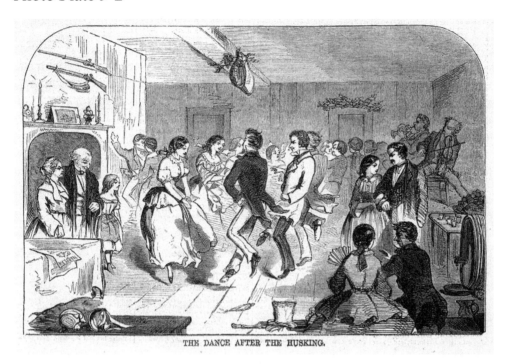

"The Dance After the Husking," engraving by Winslow Homer (1836-1910), published in Harper's Weekly on November 13, 1858. Signed lower left (on tablecloth) W. H.

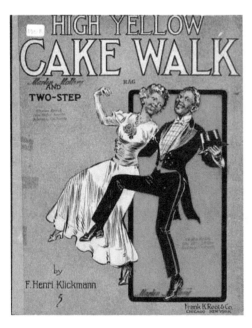

Sheet Music Cover: "High Yellow Cake Walk and Two-Step." Composer/Lyricist: F. Henri Klickmann (1885-1966), American. Published c. 1915 by Frank K. Root, Chicago.

.

"Walking for Dat Cake Songster, " compiled by Edward Harrington and Tony Hart, published by A.J. Fisher, New York, 1877. A songster was a collection of texts of songs (without the music) from vaudeville, minstrel shows, and traditional songs, as well as jokes, etc., of the day.

Back in the 19<sup>th</sup> century it was not surprising to find the dances and drums of the West Indies in New Orleans. Black slaves were in New Orleans with its first settlers, and the many occupants from the West Indies greatly increased the number of blacks in New Orleans. The result of the French Revolution was uprisings on the French-owned islands and in Haiti. In 1803 Napoleon sold the Louisiana Territory to the United States; in 1804, after Haiti declared her independence, 8,000 immigrants came to New Orleans from Santo Domingo, the Dominican Republic, where they had taken refuge, and in 1809 thirty-four ships came with over 5,000 more white slave owners and slaves.

Slaves in the Caribbean had been better treated than those in the United States. The result was that their music developed along traditional lines. It is said, moreover, that the self-education in music of the black people in the United States was what caused them to seek inside themselves and unearth the syncopated jazz music that developed and the jazz dance that came out of it. Very often they have more than one rhythm presented at one time. In dance these are body rhythms – heartbeat equals pulse rate.

The Caribbean influence was later seen and heard in many Broadway shows: *Alive and Kicking* (1949), a musical revue choreographed by **Jack Cole** (1914-1974) with a calypso style from Trinidad combined with East Indian dance, Latin motifs, and jazz rhythms. The *Benjamin Calypso* from *Joseph and the Amazing Technicolor Dreamcoat* (1982), with choreography by Tony Tanner (b. 1932), also had this mixture of dances and rhythms. Subsequently there was the jazz calypso number *I Left My Hat in Haiti* starring **Fred Astaire** and **Eleanor Powell** in the film *Royal Wedding* in 1951.

The Color Code was such that blacks and whites could not marry; if a white man had a child with a black slave it was customary for him to free the mother, and thus the child was automatically freed. (In some parts of the South, however, the owner sold his child.) These free women could only associate with their own class, or become a white man's mistress. But one drop of white blood permitted her to own property, to have freedom from slavery, and to become educated.

The complete opposite from Congo Square was another dance activity of New Orleans, the **Quadroon Ball**. In 1805 **Auguste Tessier** had the idea of holding dance balls two times a week, limited to white men, and available to free mixed or mulatto women, or quadroons, as they were called, to encourage these women to form liaisons with wealthy white men. This event was a total rejection of African heritage and a complete acceptance of white culture. The men who attended were all white (usually wealthy); the women, also called "gens de couleur," were of mixed blood, mostly white (and they appeared to be white), and beautiful; their mothers sent them to Paris to learn the dances done at Parisian salons and to become well educated.

The dances at the **Quadroon Balls** were not of African origin but the type of dances done at French salons, such as the **waltz** and **cotillion**. If a white gentleman desired to take a quadroon as a mistress, he asked her mother, not her, and prepared an apartment for her. If ever he changed his mind, she went back to her mother. If some other white gentleman paid her too much attention, a duel followed.

Photo Plate 9-3

Ada (Aida) Overton Walker, half length portrait, 1912, White Studio, NY. Photographer: Unknown. .

Sheet Music Cover: "Dancing On De Kitchen Floor." Composer: James Bland, black American, performer and member of the "all Negro" minstrel group headed by Billy Kersands; Pub: Boston: White, Smith & Co., 1880. Bland also wrote "Oh, Dem Golden Slippers" and "Carry Me Back to Old Virginny."

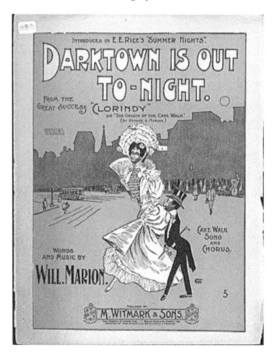

Portrait of Geoffrey Holder and Carmen de Lavallade, 1955, by Carl van Vechten.

Sheet Music Cover: "Darktown Is Out Tonight," from "Clorindy" Composer/Lyricist: Will Marion Cook, black American. Pub: NY: Chicago: M. Witmark & Sons. c. 1898.

Authors writing about the south often mentioned the quadroon balls in their novels.

The **cotillion dance** originated in the West Indies in the early 1700's, was refined in France in the 1750's, and became a French dance that went to England in the 1760's. It was a patterned dance with about four couples. The name came from the French word for petticoat, cotillion, which could be seen very briefly as the dance partners turned while changing partners in the dance.

The Color Code situation was not the same after the Civil War (1861-1865) and Jim Crowism. Before then, a single drop of white blood was enough to give the possessor special rights, but after Jim Crowism a single drop of black blood was enough to deprive the possessor of any privileges.

Jim Crow laws were state and local laws decreed between 1876 and 1965 in the United States. They authorized segregation of restrooms, public schools, public transportation, and the United States military. These were variously proclaimed unconstitutional in 1954, 1964, and 1966. (Jim Crow laws had nothing to do with the man **Jim Crow**, a lame and first-rate black dancer, although the laws bear his name.)

From 1862 to 1893, black minstrel shows were very popular. Black dancers performed in an all-black cast, wearing blackface, for an all-black audience. There also existed minstrel shows for white audiences. These had white performers in blackface doing the black dances such as the **buck dance**, the **pigeon wing** or, like white **Daddy Rice,** imitating **Jim Crow**.

When **Daddy Rice** (1808-1860) competed three times in dance challenges against black **Master Juba** (see chapter 8) in 1866, it was black Master Juba who won, got top billing, and then performed in minstrel shows with white men. Master Juba was an exceptional dancer, a black man in an otherwise white cast, performing for a white audience, and treated like a "star" – a very rare situation indeed at that time.

The result of minstrel shows was that many non-black people believed blacks to have the exaggerated look and characteristics that were depicted in these shows. This was regardless of the fact that sheet music covers would often have two sets of photos (*Photo Plate 9-5),* one with the performers in stage costume and exaggerated makeup and the other showing the performer in dignified everyday apparel and without burnt cork makeup. After the Civil War, blacks still wore blackface when performing in minstrel shows. This displayed the derogatory attitudes of the times and also influenced the way people saw blacks; but at the same time it did afford black Americans a chance to perform, albeit in blackface, and to develop their artistic endeavor in music, dancing, and acting.

**Bert Williams** (1874-1922), a black Bahamian immigrant, and **George Walker** (1873-1911), a black American, were always noteworthy for their **buck and wing** and their **cakewalking**. It was thought that they made the **cakewalk** popular and paved the way for other black dancers. Booker T. Washington felt that Williams' comedy skits helped people understand the blacks; W. C. Fields found Williams to be the funniest and saddest man he had ever seen on stage, while Walker was considered to be a great cakewalk dancer. As a vaudeville team, Williams was the comedian and Walker, an excellent dancer, often played the dandy.

Many performers did not like having to put on black burned cork makeup to perform. **Bert Williams,** however, had the same initial reaction to this that many previous dancers had had to the wearing of masks; that is, he felt protected and separate from the audience and better able to personify a character that was completely different from his own. Williams was actually a dignified, sensitive, and intellectual man but the characters he played were comedic, slouching, with worn-out shoes and ragged clothes.

At a time when some white performers in blackface were calling themselves "The Two Coons," **Williams and Walker** got theater agents' attention by calling themselves "The Two Real Coons." The term coon at first referred to the political party that had a raccoon as its emblem – the Whigs – and to the coonskin hats, made from raccoons, which everyone in America and Europe wanted to wear. But then "coon" songs spread as a result of the popularity of African American blackface performer **Ernest Hogan**'s song *All Coons Look Alike to Me* (1896), about a young lady (according to the lyrics) who already has a boyfriend and is not interested in other men – they all look alike to her – although the cover of that sheet music shows them all looking very different physically, in caricature. Even though Hogan claimed the word was meant to refer to the smartness of raccoons, it had a negative effect on the way blacks were represented. The song was catchy, had ragtime syncopation, vernacular dialect; it gained in popularity and, unfortunately, spread the use of the term "coon." Coon songs were extremely popular in the 1880's. By 1890 six hundred of them had been written. Blacks and whites all used the term in the lyrics of songs and in **minstrel shows**. Every composer wrote a coon song. People were used to hearing the word and did not react to it then, the way they would nowadays.

There was no radio, phonograph, or television. People owned pianos or player pianos and bought a lot of sheet music and player piano rolls. It was a chance for musicians to be appreciated and to earn a good living by providing people with the music they wanted. The music industry, with its attractive sheet music covers, had salesmen, called pluggers, pushing the songs on Tin Pan Alley, West 28th Street in Manhattan, where many of the music publishers had their offices. The inclusion of sheet music in newspapers also made sheet music available to millions on a weekly basis and at no extra cost. The music industry expanded greatly. But by 1910 the times had changed and not many coon songs were written anymore.

*A Trip to Coontown* (1898) written by black American composer/lyricist **Bob Cole** (1868-1911) was the first real black musical comedy; it was produced, organized, managed, and owned by blacks; it was not like a minstrel show, but was written with a complete cast of characters throughout the story plot; the cast was black; the star, **Sam Lucas** (1848-1921) was black, a former songwriter, composer, singer, minstrel player and then an actor.

Bent Creek Ranch Square Dance Team at Asheville Mountain Music Festival between 1938 and 1950.

Photo of Sam H. Harris (left) and George M. Cohan (right), 1917, photographer unknown.

"The Sandow Trocadero Vaudevilles," poster, Lithograph created by Strobridge & Co, Litho, New York, 1894..

Sheet Music Cover: "Great Ethiopian Songs," by James A. Bland, author of: "Oh Dem Golden Slippers," "In the Mornings," "De Angels Am a Coming," "In the Evening By the Moonlight," and many other minstrel show songs. Publisher: NY: Hitchcock's Music Store (B. W. Hitchcock), c. 1880. In 1940 his song, "Carry Me Back to Old Virginny," was chosen as the state song of Virginia.

At about the same time, another black musical opened, *Clorindy – The Origin of the Cakewalk (Photo Plate 9-3)*, with black writer, producer, and conductor **Will Marion Cook** (1869-1944). He was a composer and violinist who had studied at Oberlin Conservatory in Ohio, the National Conservatory of Music in New York, and in Germany. He was the first to use syncopated black music, ragtime, and to present it, as well as the **cakewalk,** with charm and grace and on the legitimate stage, the Roof Garden of the esteemed Broadway house, the Casino Theatre. The black American poet, Langston Hughes (1902-1967), saw the show and found it a joy to watch. **Cook** wrote and produced many other hit musicals and also became the musical director and composer for the **George Walker – Bert Williams** Company, Broadway's first top black performers.

Black performers, if they performed for black audiences and for white audiences, faced a dilemma. Black audiences wanted to see black performers portraying someone with a respectable image, someone of whom they could be proud. But white audiences enjoyed seeing the pre-Civil-War characters like **Jim Crow** and **Zip Coon** and the slavery and plantation skits. Black leaders like Booker T. Washington and W. E. B. Du Bois, as well as journalists, praised **Williams and Walker** for their move from minstrel shows to musical comedies and for setting such high standards for excellent comedy during the push of black musical comedy theater from 1890 to 1915.

*In Dahomey* (1902) *(Photo Plate 9-5)* was the all-black musical comedy in which **Williams and Walker** next appeared with great success on Broadway. The show was also popular in England where members of the royalty proclaimed the cast and the music by **Will Marion Cook** to be excellent. **Aida** (or **Ada**) **Overton Walker (1880-1914)**, George's wife, and George were recognized as superb dancers, Bert as a great comedian, his wife Lottie as a confident actress, and Aida was also an excellent teacher of the **cakewalk,** which started another **cakewalk craze** in London. All of this guaranteed the show's continued fame in America when they returned.

**George Walker** proved to be a very capable businessman, and as the Williams and Walker Company became more visible on a national level in America, George sought to get them first class theaters on Broadway. This was not the only accomplishment of Williams and Walker. Their recent annual earnings of $40,000 each placed them at a higher salary than many influential whites. Their managers, Hurtig and Seamon, sued Williams and Walker because Williams and Walker wanted to produce *Abyssinia*, another musical comedy with an African background but at a much higher cost than *In Dahomey*. **Williams and Walker** won the case in the New York Supreme Court. This was at a time when the NAACP did not yet exist, lynching was prevalent, and civil and social rights for black Americans were at a minimum. With new managers, Williams and Walker opened *Abyssinia* at the Majestic Theatre in New York on February 20, 1906; it was a blend of native African and black American melodies and incorporated some recent historical events into the musical, with music once more by **Will Marion Cook**. **Mrs. Aida Walker** was both a performer in it and its choreographer. *Bandana Land*, the next venture of Williams and Walker, and yet again with new managers, opened at the Majestic Theatre on Broadway on February 3, 1908. The setting this time was in the

American South. **Bert**, **George**, and **Aida** received accolades from whites and blacks and from all the professionals who came to see the show to standing-room-only audiences. Here, too, **Aida Walker** performed in and choreographed the show. Lottie Williams, Bert Williams' wife, had retired from the stage.

**George Walker** suffered a stroke on stage in 1908. He also found that he had contracted syphilis and had to stop performing. After Walker's death in 1911, **Williams** joined the *Ziegfeld Follies* where he earned a lucrative salary. He was the first black star in that well-known and prestigious company.

**Aida Overton Walker** *(Photo Plate 9-3)* went on to choreograph for two black female dance groups, the Happy Girls and the Porto Rico Girls. She then performed on **vaudeville**, doing ballroom dancing based on African American material, the **maxixe**, the **southern drag**, and the **jiggerree** with a new partner, **Lackaye Grant**. Her elegant performances led to what was later known as a "class act," one with impeccable dress, manners, and sophistication.

The Broadway stage had seen the death of several of its favorite black performers: **George Walker, Bob Cole, Ernest Hogan**; and in 1914, at age 34, **Aida Overton Walker**, one of the great stars of the black American stage, died of kidney failure – she was very young.

The **Cohan and Harris Minstrels** (1909) *(Photo Plate 9-4)* was the last minstrel show to play Broadway. Minstrel shows were becoming more and more expensive to produce, with very large casts of sometimes more than one hundred performers and with audience expectancy of gorgeous costumes. Minstrel shows were later replaced by **vaudeville**, much less costly, in the early 1900's. **Blackface makeup** disappeared with the Civil Rights Movement.

The habit of portraying several racial or ethnic groups in disparaging terms had been prevalent earlier in **burlesque theater**, before minstrel shows appeared. Burlesque consisted of parodies of famous plays or performers in song, dance, or pantomime. The **burlesque extravaganzas** produced by comedians **Ed Harrigan and Tony Hart**, the *Mulligan Guard* series, in which Harrigan and Hart also starred from 1879 till 1885, dealt with caricatures of New York City life. These depicted such racial and national groups as blacks, Germans, and Irish with their individual mannerisms and speech habits in everyday situations – a picnic, an election, a ball. After **burlesque** came the **minstrel shows** (and after the **minstrel shows** came **vaudeville**) *(Photo Plate 9-2 and 9-4).* When minstrel shows became popular, and years later too, performers continued to portray several ethnic groups, very often their own, in demeaning terms. People were glad to see all of that finally being changed with the Civil Rights Movement of the 1960's.

**Minstrel shows** always had many dances of the type known as **animal dances**, from people's observances of life in the country: **snake hips**, **camel walk, buzzard lope, duck waddle**, the **snake**, the **squirrel, kangaroo hop, chicken scratch**, the **angle worm wiggle**, the **horse trot, chicken flutter, grapevine twist**, and **walking jaw bones**. (The skeletons of asses' jaws in which the loosened bones created a rattling sound were tried as an instrument when drums were forbidden by law in 1749). Some of these dances were developed solely for minstrel shows and had nothing to do with African dance.

Photo Plate 9-5

"La Calinda," dance of the Negros in America, 1783. Artist: François Aimé Louis Dumoulin (1753-1834, Swiss). Medium: Watercolor.

Slave Dance in the late 18<sup>th</sup> century painting "The Old Plantation" depicts African Americans dancing to banjo and percussion. It is an American folk art watercolor that was likely painted by John Rose, a South Carolina plantation owner, around 1790. Original painting is in the Abby Aldrich Rockefeller Folk Art Museum in Williamsburg, Virginia.

Sheet Music Cover: "I'm a Jonah Man," from the musical "In Dahomey," 1903. Music and lyrics By Alex Rogers. Vaudeville stars Bert Williams and George Walker shown on cover in formal portraits and in costume with blackface.
Publisher: New York: M. Witmark & Sons.

The **buzzard lope** was a **plantation animal dance** created around 1880. It was mentioned in the local newspapers from 1890 to 1915, as clubs were formed for those eager to learn and dance the buzzard lope. Arms were outstretched at the sides like a buzzard's wings; the dance consisted of a shuffling step, then a little hop or lope like that of a large buzzard getting ready to eat a dead mule or cow. This dance resembled a West African type of dance.

The **camel walk** was a ragtime animal dance that originally came from **vaudeville**. College kids and flappers did it in the 1910's and 1920's in a straight-up posture. However, the girls would often place their heads on the shoulders of their partners, which was considered very vulgar. The popularity of this dance revived in the 1950's and 60's. The left foot advanced while the pelvis was pushed forward (or contracted) and the right foot rose to the ball of the foot. Then the right foot advanced as the left foot went up to the ball (front) of the foot and the pelvis was pushed back (or released). These movements were repeated. This was meant to be a one-humped dromedary camel found in the Middle East.

Several of these types of dance appeared again later with new names as **rock and roll dances** and **disco dances**. Their titles were just as descriptive; the **bus stop dance**, the **hitchhiker**, the **fish**, the **alligator crawl**, the **monkey**, the **bunny hop**, and the **mashed potato** were a few. These were in the **challenge dance position** – no touching – of **plantation couples dances**, including the **Charleston.** Some psychologists suspected that this dance position showed the breakup of family life.

The old version of the **alligator crawl**, another animal dance, was as follows: The women would lift their skirts in back and show off their pretty petticoats. The grinding or the wiggling of their rear ends presumably looked a lot like alligators crawling up on the bank of the river. That dance was later called the **funky butt**.

Another type of dance common before the 1900's was the **barn dance**. It was a social gathering and was held in a rural community, often after the raising of a barn, or to celebrate a wedding or a birthday or someone's homecoming. These barn dances were popular with the common folk who were hardly likely to be invited to a fancy ball. This was their ballroom – the barn. The dances could consist of the **waltz**, the **jig**, the **buck**, the **Virginia reel**, the **square dance**, the **rag**, and the **schottische** and included country music, a singer and of course, a fiddler with a fiddle or an African banjo. The most popular fiddlers at that time were the black fiddlers.

The **square dance** *(Photo Plate 9-4)*, one of the types of dances done at **barn dances,** is the official state dance in nineteen of the states in the U.S. It is a **folk dance** with four couples. The head couple faces away from the music; then progressing clockwise, comes couple number 2, then 3, then 4. Couples 1 and 3 are the head couples; 2 and 4 are the side couples. Each dance begins and finishes with a call for "sets in order." A caller announces the steps to be done, and regardless of the country, France, Mexico, or Japan, they are always called in English. These are all steps taken from traditional folk dances such as **quadrilles**, the **Morris Dances**, and **English country**

**dances** done in 17<sup>th</sup> century England, France and other parts of Europe. In colonial United States, the **square dance** provided recreation and socialization, and having a caller eliminated the need to remember all the dances. In 1920 the New York City school system gave it a boost by making **folk dance** (including square dancing) a required activity. In the 1930's Henry Ford became interested in the revival of square dancing to counteract what he considered to be "the evils of jazz." By 1948 it seemed like a fad but it gained in appeal, with a growth of thousands of square dance clubs throughout the United States. **Square dances** are now danced worldwide.

# 10

# Jazz Music – Blues, Ragtime

## and More Dancing

The music and the dances resulting from jazz music advanced greatly and quickly. Jazz music was considered to be a folk music coming from the heart and soul, not from the mind. Jazz music started with the blues. The slight lowering of certain pitches like the thirds, fifths, and sevenths of the major scales, the use of a major or minor pentatonic scale, and the spirituals and the sad-toned slave work songs of blacks had much influence on blues.

The first blues piece to be published was *Memphis Blues* in 1913 (said to have inspired the creation of many of the steps for the **foxtrot** by **Vernon and Irene Castle** although the originator of the fox trot, danced worldwide in 2/4 or 4/4 time, was **Harry Fox**). However, *Memphis Blues* was actually written in 1906 by **W.C. Handy** (1873-1953), a black American and the self-nominated "Father of the Blues." He took the blues from little known folk material and made it a major force in American music. The trials and problems of the black man, his spirituals and work songs, together with European hymns, led to the blues. The blues were about mourning, unhappy love, and sexuality, together with the human emotions of jealousy, fear, lust, envy, and loneliness. The song of 1918 said it best: *Everybody's Crazy About the Doggone Blues* by Henry Creamer and Turner Layton. **Bert Williams**, a black American, first sang this instantaneous hit in the *Ziegfeld Follies of 1917-1918*.

At the end of the 19th century, New Orleans, Louisiana, was the place to be to hear all the new music, the blues, ragtime, and the brass bands. New Orleans was considered to be the birthplace of jazz music. From there jazz spread to the dancehalls and saloons of Storyville, a district created by a city ordinance in 1897. It was the only legal red light district in New Orleans.

In the early twentieth century many people bought player pianos and sheet music. **Ragtime** and **blues** were more popular than ballads and sold more sheet music. **W. C. Handy** did not really invent the blues. **Jelly Roll Morton** (1885 or 1890-1941) *(Photo Plate 10-5)* felt he was the one who had done that (although no one believed him); he preferred saying that he was born in 1885, since 1890 would have made him too young to be the originator of jazz. Still, Morton was the first arranger of jazz music. He was also a pianist, prolific composer (his best known works were *Wolverine Blues*, 1923, and *Black Bottom Stomp*, 1926), and bandleader of a group called Morton's Red Hot Peppers. He died of heart failure. But it was **W. C. Handy** who promoted the blues in the American music of the early 1900's.

In the 1920's there were several black female blues singers: Bertha "Chippie " Hill (1905-1950), Bessie Smith (1894-1937), "Ma" Rainey (1886-1939). There was one blues singer who was part Native American, Mildred Bailey (1907-1951), of the Coeur d'Alene Reservation. Small bands, solo piano or guitar accompanied these singers. *Ma Rainey's Black Bottom* (1984), a Broadway play with music, was acclaimed for depicting the era when "Ma Rainey" sang the blues.

When the blues later met the frantic pace and piercing sounds of city life it became rhythm and blues with electric guitar. When it then combined with gospel music it became soul music and rock music, which teenagers danced to in spite of the depressing lyrics. **Rock and roll** evolved from the 1930's black jump blues in the late 1940's and early 50's when it acquired its name, and it was energetic and danceable. The syncopated rhythm of its backbeat, produced by drums, led to the revival of the **jitterbug dancing** of the big band period and was popular from World War II through the 1950's. Home basement dance parties were in style, and teenagers watched Dick Clark's *American Bandstand* to catch up with the current dances. Some of the resulting **fad dances** were the **mashed potato**, the **hully gully (John Belushi** can be seen doing it in the film *The Blues Brothers*), the **bus stop**, and the **watusi**.

The **slow drag dance** was popular in the barrelhouses and juke joints in the South. Couples were hanging on to each other and barely moving except for grinding movements. In the early evening the music was up-tempo, but as night came the music became slow low-down blues. This was the type of slow drag dance that was featured in 1929 in an otherwise straight play on Broadway, *Harlem*, until the critic of *The New York Daily News,* several Harlem groups, and the authorities complained. Only then was the dance toned down.

Blues music later went on to inspire many modern dance choreographers in the 20th century: *Rainbow 'Round My Shoulder* (1950) choreographed by **Donald McKayle**, showing prisoners in a chain gang carrying a pick ax on their shoulders. The axes were shaped like a rainbow. **Alvin Ailey** created *Blues Suite* (1958); it depicted the era when jazz began. He showed us emotions in the South at the moment when jazz and brothels were closely connected. Some historians thought the word jezebel led to the word jazz belle, and then to the word jazz. A bluesy piece choreographed by **Eleo Pomare**, *Blues for the Jungle* (1966), had to do with life in Harlem. A favorite piece by **Alvin Ailey**, *Cry* (1971), soon won recognition through **Judith Jamison**'s exceptional portrayal of the emotions of black women.

**William Forsythe** (b. 1940) created *Love Song* (1979) for the Munich Ballet and recreated it for The Joffrey Ballet (1983). It was a sadistically bluesy dramatic ballet to recordings of Aretha Franklin and Dionne Warwick. In a 2008 article for the British newspaper *The Guardian,* Sanjoy Roy described the ballet as having "brutal emotion" and "bruising action."

**George Gershwin**'s (1898-1937) music was used for the movie *An American in Paris* (1951), starring **Leslie Caron** and **Gene Kelly**. It was an excellent mix of ballet and jazz, in a happier vein, and was choreographed by **Gene Kelly**. It seems incredible that George Gershwin created so much remarkable music in such a short life, having died of a brain tumor at age 39.

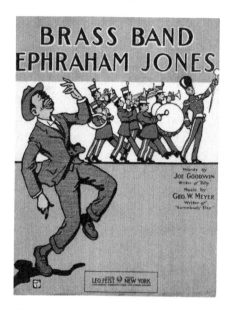

Sheet Music Cover: "Brass Band Ephraham Jones." Words: Joe Goodwin (1889-1943), Music: George W. Meyer (1884-1959), Pub: NY: Leo Feist, 1911. First line of text: Old Ephraham from Alabam; First line of chorus: Ev'ry time a band starts playing. Cover illustration: black American man dancing and a marching band in background.

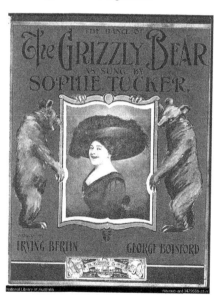

Sheet Music Cover: "The Grizzly Bear." Words: Irving Berlin. Music: George Botsford. Pub: NY: Ted Snyder Co., 1910 and D. Davis & Co. in Sydney, Australia, 1910-1913.

Sheet Music Cover: "The Angle Worm Wiggle." Composer: Harry S. Lorch; Lyrics: I. Maynard Schwarz. Publication: Chicago: Victor Kremer, c. 1910.

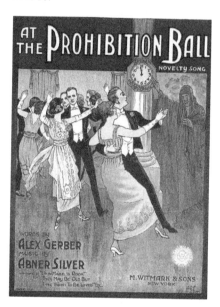

Sheet Music Cover: "At the Prohibition Ball". Lyrics: Alex Gerber, Music: Abner Silver. Pub. NY: W. Witmark & Sons, 1919. Cover illustrates a party that is taking place on Jan. 15, 1920, with the Grim Reaper pointing to a clock about to strike midnight when prohibition would begin. The 18th Amendment to the Constitution ratified on Jan 1, 1919, was not to take effect until one year later on Jan 16, 1920, and the partygoers were anxious about the future without any alcohol.

In the late 19th century, however, the French and Spanish popular songs with the rhythms of black marching bands shifted their accent from the strong beat to the weak beat and became ragtime *(Photo Plate 10-1)*. This shift in accent could be traced back to the hand clapping and foot stomping of southern Methodist revival meetings. Bands marched in New Orleans for every possible reason, advertising, holiday, death, among others. In 1881, more than a dozen bands marched in New Orleans in a procession to mourn the death of President Garfield (a fervent antislavery believer who rose from a log cabin to the White House). Marches were used for the **two-step**, which replaced the waltz. In ragtime the bass line consisted of a striding steady pattern, with a syncopated "ragged" upper melody line. (Stride piano is a jazz style characterized by a single bass note, octave, seventh, or tenth on the first and third beats and chords on the second and fourth beats.) Syncopation, an accent on the weak beat, or a shift of the accent from the expected beat, transformed these marches into the **grizzly bear**, the **bunny hug**, the **turkey trot**, or the **Texas Tommy,** which then became the **one step** (single steps to the beat with no change to the rhythm, performed to trendy music of the World War I era), the **Lindy hop**, the **Charleston**, the **black bottom** (a black-American dance, with stamps, kicks, swaying, and a slap on the backside), all to the fast music of the 1920's.

The **grizzly bear** *(Photo Plate 10-1)* was a rough, undignified, ungraceful, clumsy-looking dance. The **Castles** did it but did not enjoy doing it, and were glad to see the **fox trot** replace it later. **John Jarrott** and **Louise Gruenning** introduced the **grizzly bear** at Ray Jones' Café in Chicago, Illinois, in 1909. People danced it in San Francisco and also on the Staten Island Ferry boats in the 1900's. Broadway audiences first saw it in the show *Over the River* in 1910 in the song *Everybody's Doin' It Now*. The song's lyrics (by **Irving Berlin**) repeated the words "It's a Bear" many times. When doing the grizzly bear, one took a heavy step to the side while bending to that side. The dance was done in very close contact position of the cheeks and upper torso while the rear end of both partners stuck out. (Looked like two bears hugging.) It was a very popular dance, and the singers' interpretations of the songs made them all the rage. However, **Sophie Tucker** (1884-1966) was arrested for singing *The Grizzly Bear* and the *Angle Worm Wiggle (Photo Plate 10-1),* and the Chicago police ordered her to stop singing them.

The **turkey trot** was born in San Francisco in 1906. Before becoming a ragtime dance it had probably been a folk dance. Again dancers **John Jarrott** and **Louise Gruenning** were the ones who introduced this dance at Ray Jones' Café in Chicago in 1909. It had an up and down arm movement at the side that was considered offensive and demoralizing by some. The Vatican denounced it, thus increasing its popularity. Fifteen women were fired from a well-known magazine for dancing the turkey trot during a lunch break. **Vernon Castle** danced it in the Broadway show *The Sunshine Girl*, in 1913. That too increased its status.

**Scott Joplin** (1867-1917), a black American pianist and composer, was known as the "King of Ragtime." His compositions included forty-four ragtime pieces, one ragtime ballet, and two operas. His first rag, *Maple Leaf Rag (Photo Plate 10-2),* remained a hit during the 20th century and sold a half million copies. The cover of the original sheet music in 1899 depicted the famous vaudevillians **Bert Williams** and **George Walker**

with their future wives. Another popular piece of Joplin's, *The Entertainer*, was one of the "top 10" of the *Songs of the Century* as determined by the Recording Industry of America and the National Endowment of the Arts.

When Scott Joplin's opera *Treemonisha* (1911) was revived and presented at the Houston Grand Opera in 1975, **Louis Johnson** did the choreography. A black American, Louis Johnson had studied at the School of American Ballet in the hopes of a career in ballet. Although Johnson, an excellent dancer and choreographer, never became a permanent member of any ballet company, he had a fruitful career that included performing in several Broadway shows such as *My Darlin' Aida* (1952), *Hallelujah Baby* (1967), and *Damn Yankees* (1955 stage, and 1958 screen versions), choreographing the Broadway shows *Purlie* (1970) and *Cabin in the Sky* (1978), as well as becoming director of the Dance Department at the Henry Street Settlement in 1986.

A variety of rags were being written in the late 19th century and after. There was the *Eskimo rag*, *Harlem rag*, *Chinatown rag*, *German rag*, *Nobody Home rag*, the *Burglar rag*, the *Old Folks rag*, the *Virginia rag*, the *Mississippi rag*, the *Hawaiian rag*, the *Cowboy rag*, an endless array of every occupation, state, and nationality in honor of which anyone could do the many popular rag dances *(Photo Plates 10-2, 3 and 4)*.

The first original **ragtime waltz** was the best-known and well-liked composition of the gifted musician **Harry P. Guy** (1870-1950), *Echoes from the Snowball Club* (1898) *(Photo Plate 10-3)*, named after the nickname of the Detroit Musicians' Union, the Snowball Club, founded by the black American Harry P. Guy and the black Canadian composer **Fred S. Stone** (1873-1912, the first to use the word "ragtime" in 1898 in *Ma Ragtime Baby Two Step) (Photo Plate 10-2)*. Guy had studied the cello at the National Conservatory of Music in New York with Victor Herbert, had accompanied the Fisk Jubilee Singers, and he also founded the first Black American Music Academy.

Most ragtime musicians of that time could not read music. They did not use written music; they improvised. This was all right in Storyville, the only legal red light district in New Orleans until the United States Naval authorities got the government to close it down in 1917. Jazz had moved into Storyville because Storyville had provided jobs with pay. There had been an occasional move of jazz musicians to Chicago from New Orleans, but in 1917, when the musicians were deprived of their main source of income, Storyville, there was a general departure. There were other reasons that contributed to this. For one, the Slave Code (the laws developed in each state from the 1660's to the 1860's regarding an African slave and his owner) had never been either a written or an unwritten law in Chicago. And also, by 1921, when many were beginning to get their lives back together in the South after the closing of Storyville, the boll weevil came from the Rio Grande and ate half the cotton crops. It took three years for normality to return, and during that time hundreds of thousands of people, blacks and whites alike, moved away to seek jobs. In the north, in Chicago, Detroit, and New York, they could find work in the defense industry created by World War I. Jazz music followed them there from New Orleans.

Photo Plate 10-2

Sheet Music Cover: "The Ragtime Dance" Two Step.
Composer: Scott Joplin, black American; Publisher:
St. Louis, MO: John Stark & Son, 1906.

Sheet Music Cover :"Ma Ragtime Baby" Two Step.
Composer: Fred S. Stone, black American (1873-
1912); Lyricist: (his brother) Charles Stone. Pub.:
Detroit, Michigan: Whitney Warner Pub. Co, 1898.

Sheet Music Cover: "The Maple Leaf Rag".
Composer: Scott Joplin. Cover Illustrator: Vaistin;
The illustration depicts Williams and Walker with
their future wives. Publisher: Sedalia, MO: John Stark
& Son, c. 1899.

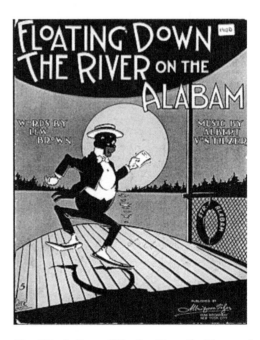

Sheet Music Cover: "Floating Down the River on the
Alabam." Composer: Albert Von Tilzer; Lyricists:
Lew Brown and Jack Lustig; Publication: NY:
Broadway Music Corp, 1912.

166

The Mississippi riverboats, paddle wheelers, were a stepping-stone to the north *(Photo Plates 10-2 and 10-4)*. During the slow months of November through April they were used for excursions and, with their large dance floors and a band, they provided entertainment. Many musicians found work on riverboats and some remained on them during their longer trips and spread the new jazz music and its dances to St. Louis, to Minneapolis, to Kansas City on the Missouri River, and to Pittsburgh on the Ohio River.

The 1927 musical *Showboat*, by **Jerome Kern** and **Oscar Hammerstein II**, depicted the life of entertainers on a Mississippi riverboat from 1887 to 1927. As the first dramatic musical on Broadway it influenced future musicals with its themes of racial marriage and racial injustice. It was not just a bevy of pretty girls. (*Showboat* required a large cast and so did not get revived often but in 1994 it was revived with spectacular choreography by **Susan Stroman** (b. 1959) and received rave reviews for a production with wonderful singing and dancing.)

These paddleboats carried people up and down the river and also furnished entertainment at the stopping places where the boat stayed for an evening, a week, or even two weeks. Blacks, who had worked at building railroads after the abolition of slavery in 1865, could now find work in St. Louis either on the railroads or in music.

The captain of the big riverboats, Captain Joseph Stekfun, had decided to assemble the finest musicians for his boats. Louis Armstrong, playing on the boat "Dixie Belle," said the audience loved the musicians and gave them additional gigs at parties in the city or as guest performers with local bands at big cabarets. St. Louis encouraged the growth of ragtime just as New Orleans had stimulated the development of jazz. Many ragtime composers got their ideas from the **cakewalk** *(Photo Plate 10-3)* of the blacks as well as from European dance tunes like the **polka**, the **mazurka**, the **waltz** and the **quadrille**. The St Louis atmosphere was that of gambling halls and drinking saloons packed with ostentatiously dressed pleasure-seekers of the naughty nineties.

At that time musicians moved to Chicago and then to New York to find work. Blacks and jazz dance followed the music. Where it went they went. Ragtime had been adapted into New Orleans Dixieland Jazz; it was made popular by white musicians and swept the country after the Original Dixieland Band chose *Tiger Rag* (transformed from an old quadrille) as its first piece of music to be recorded in 1917. The record-buying public did not yet own radios or use them to hear music. Many felt, however, that **Scott Joplin** (1869-1917) with his *Maple Leaf Rag* of 1899 (recorded in 1916) proved that he was Ragtime's master; he wrote almost fifty rags. *Maple Leaf Rag* was the first instrumental piece to sell over one million copies of sheet music. (In 1990, modern dancer **Martha Graham** choreographed her last work, a humorous dance to *Maple Leaf Rag*.)

In 1919, the newspaper *The New York Dramatic Mirror* made suggestions as to where the name jazz had come from: possibly it was the name of a widespread type of spasm band with washboards; or one of the players was called Jas, short for Jasper, or Chas, short for Charles. Or it came from Razz's Band, or it was of African derivation.

Tom Brown called the music he played jass – Tom Brown's Dixieland Jass Band. In 1919, Wendling (1888-1974) and Kalmar (1880-1947) named a piece of their music *Take Me to the Land of Jazz (Photo Plate 10-4)*. Now both the music and the dance had a name – jazz.

The atmosphere of the cities to which blacks and music moved was well represented later in dance choreography. **Donald McKayle** (b. 1930) captured that of Storyville in *District Storyville* (1962) for the Alvin Ailey Dance Company. **Robert Alton** (1906-1957) did the same for the gangster atmosphere of Chicago in the Broadway musical *Pal Joey* (1941) starring **Gene Kelly**. **Jerome Robbins** gave us Spanish Harlem in *West Side Story* in 1957 (an updated version of *Romeo and Juliet*). **Billy Wilson** (1935-1994) depicted the Harlem of the 1930's and 40's in *Bubbling Brown Sugar* (1976). **Michael Kidd** portrayed New York City's streets and nightlife in *Guys and Dolls* (1950). New York City in the 1930's was seen in *Wonderful Town* (1953) through **Donald Saddler**'s choreography, and Chicago's gangs and nightlife were shown through **Bob Fosse**'s choreography for *Chicago* (1975). And in 2001 the world of *The Producer* appeared in New York, choreographed by **Susan Stroman**. All these choreographers, directors, musicians, dancers, and singers were superbly talented.

There were many other changes around the time when jazz music and blacks were moving north. The Prohibition Party began in 1869 *(Photo Plate 10-1)*. The Women's Christian Temperance Union was created. The Women's suffrage movement was strong in the 1880's (and in 1920 the Nineteenth Amendment, which was passed in 1919, was ratified, giving women the right to vote). Women were gradually allowed to sit and to smoke anywhere in restaurants. If alone, they were no longer directed to the ladies' café, but they could still not enter a bar.

Harlem clubs and the Cotton Club were noticed for their music and dances. The **mooch** (a black-American dance of the 1920's and 30's with sensuous hip movements), the **shimmy** (shaking the shoulders continuously as **Gilda Grey** and **Mae West** used to do), **truckin'** (a dance popular in 1937 consisting of shuffling and at the same time shaking the index finger of one hand above the head; this was later added to the **Lindy hop**), the **Lindy hop**, and **jitterbug**, were popular with blacks and whites. **Earl "Snake Hips" Tucker** (1905-1937), **Bill Robinson** (1878-1949)**, Avon Long** (1910-1974)**,** and the **Nicholas Brothers** were hits, and so were musicians like Cab Calloway and Duke Ellington.

**Ted Koehler** (1894-1972) and **Harold Arlen** (1905-1986) wrote music and lyrics for about eight of the revues at the Cotton Club. Some of their well-known pieces of music were *Stormy Weather, I Gotta Right to Sing the Blues, When the Sun Comes Out*, and *Get Happy*. Koehler and Arlen wrote *Ill Wind* in 1934 for their last show at the Cotton Club. The performers at the Cotton Club were all excellent, and black; the customers were white; and the owners were mafia-backed and seeking an outlet for the bootlegged products that they sold. The Cotton Club music could be heard throughout the country due to numerous radio broadcasts. Moreover, the Cotton Club's bands and performers traveled to many parts of the country; consequently the shows with black

Sheet Music Cover: "Echoes From The Snowball Club," Rag Time Waltz; Composer: Harry P. Guy, black American. Publisher: Detroit, Michigan: Willard Bryant, 1898.

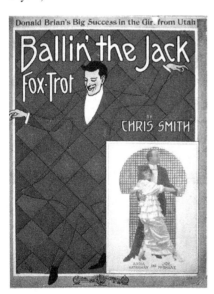

Sheet Music Cover: "Ballin' the Jack". Composer: Chris Smith; Lyrics: Jim Harris. Illustration of man dancing by Andre C. Takacs, Photo of Anna Hathaway and Joe McShane. Publisher: NY: Jos.W. Stern & Co., 1913. It introduced the very popular dance of the same name.

Leçon de Cake-Walk – L'Entrée. (Cake-Walk Lesson – the Entrance). A postcard of the 1900's.

The second verse of the: lyrics to "Ballin' the Jack" by Smith and Harris, 1914, goes like this:

*First you put your two knees close up tight*
*Then you sway them to the left, then you sway them to the right*
*Step around the floor kind of nice and light*
*Then you twist around and twist around with all your might.*
*Stretch your loving arms straight out into space,*
*Then you do the Eagle Rock with style and grace.*
*Swing your foot way 'round then bring it back.*
*Now that's what I call Ballin' the Jack*

talent were visible and seen by many blacks and by whites and thus promoted black performers. The Cotton Club moved later, and finally closed in 1940, having been plagued by problems from the depression, the end of Prohibition, and fines from the Federal Government for nonpayment of back taxes.

Music at eating-places was not new; in fact, restaurants competed for the best orchestras. *The Folies Bergères* opened in April 1911, using a new word, "cabaret," in their advertisements; the word was so new the ads had to tell everyone how to pronounce it. Then followed shows at roof gardens such as the Hotel Astor roof garden, and after this came package deals by vaudeville producer Jerry Lasky and theater producer Henry B. Harris. They offered shows that rivaled the *Ziegfeld Follies* while patrons also enjoyed excellent dining for $2.50, or fifty cents more than the most expensive seats for the *Ziegfeld Follies*. However, the Terrace Gardens at Lexington Avenue and East 58th Street offered a better deal: opera, dinner, then cabaret at an outdoor garden, and a free cab ride home, for just two dollars. The extravagant production numbers of the *Folies Bergères* caused Lasky and Harris to almost go broke. They went to Europe for a rest, but Harris had the bad luck to take the Titanic for his homeward journey.

The "Ziegfeld" Girls, an integral part of the *Ziegfeld Follies (Photo Plate 10-4)*, consisted of a group of tall, slender showgirls and a group of shorter girls called "ponies." Both were under the direction of **Ned Wayburn** who put together their tap and ballet routines. Ziegfeld chose the girls after auditioning thousands each year. They had to fit his standards of beauty – height, feminine form, and white skin.

The many new dances made their way to or from Broadway and were very popular. Blossom Seeley *(Photo Plate 10-5)*, "the Queen of Syncopation," sang a ragtime number in *Hen-Pecks* at a Broadway theater in 1911. The song was called *Toddlin' the Todalo* during which she shook and shimmied on a table and then did the **Texas Tommy**. Dancing stars from Europe as well as the team of **Irene and Vernon Castle** introduced the new dances: the **grizzly bear**, the **tango**, the **Castle walk**, and the **bunny hug**, Soon restaurants were hiring orchestras to play the latest music, and dancers to teach the latest fad dances in private or small group sessions, as a way to lure people to their eating-place. There were **tea dances**, **breakfast dances**, and of course **dinner dances**, with time for a dance between soup and the main entrée, and then again before dessert. The more courses the more dances *(Photo Plate 10-4)*.

In fact the restaurants even hired professional dancers in case the male guests had not learned the latest steps but the women had. One of the dancers, Maurice, opened "Chez Maurice," a restaurant and dance room. At another restaurant, the pianist Sigmund Romberg convinced the owners, the four Bustanoby brothers from France, to have a dance floor. They hosted an **Apache night** for this new and violent dance and decorated the room like a low-down type of Parisian nightclub; guests dressed like Parisian gangsters.

Some restaurants had professionals demonstrating the new dances and music so that everyone who wished to could try to do these dances. Any reasonably dressed person could go there and did. There was a mixture of people from all social classes, including married women, single women, women of the town, and debutantes. All danced with their partners in the new fashion, moving as one, held closely, and dancing sensuously like the Castles and other famous dancing pairs *(Photo Plate 10-4)*. The name for the type of men who hung around these places was **tango pirate**, a smooth talker, smooth dancer, not after sex, unless it was part of the game, but money. He danced with any woman and tried to get jewels or money from her. (A few unsolved murders were also attributed to a **tango pirate.**)

The **mooch** dance (the **fly**) was one of the fad dances of this period. As with all dances from the sub-Sahara African legacy, it was danced in a no-contact dance position since a closed dance position was thought to be in poor taste. This dance contained many hip movements, as did the **funky butt squat** and the **fish tail**. The **mooch** was later performed in the Broadway musical *Sophisticated Ladies* (1981). That particular number received a Tony award for Best Costume. The show was conceived by **Donald McKayle**, based on the music of Duke Ellington (1899-1974), directed by **Michael Smuin**, (1938-2007) and choreographed by **McKayle, Smuin,** and **Henry Le Tang** (1915-2007). The mooch dance consisted of high kicks, hip movements, and knees touching and opening to the sides while the elbows did a similar movement. (This could remind one of the leg movements of a fly cleaning its legs.) The costumes really complemented the dance. The show received seven other Tony nominations.

But in 1913 the main attraction was the *Darktown Follies* shown in Harlem's Lafayette Theatre; it drew in the crowds with its dancing. The black dance **Ballin' the Jack** *(Photo Plate 10-3)* at the end of Act One had the entire company moving in an endless chain before the footlights and behind the scenery while doing the movements from *Ballin' The Jack*. The motionless head and shoulders and movements only from the chest down resembled the **snake hips dance**. The show included some tap by **Toots Davis** (including **over the top** and **trenches**) and **Eddie Rector** (1890-1962), as well as a **cakewalk** finale and the **Texas Tommy** with a kick, three hops, and then a pulling or sliding movement. This was a show with some romantic interest too. *Ballin' the Jack*, both the song and the dance, were later used in 1942 in the **Judy Garland, Gene Kelly** movie *For Me and My Gal*.

The **Texas Tommy dance,** which started at a well-liked dance hall, the Thalia, in the Barbary Coast section of San Francisco, reached the peak of its popularity at Purcell's, a black cabaret also on the Barbary Coast, in 1912 at a time when countless fad dances existed that were made up of a modified **one step**.

The **Texas Tommy** then became a stage and social dance in New York. It included a **breakaway** (a time for the couple to separate and do their own thing before rejoining), a step-hop pattern and a running movement. Most of the fad dances traveled around the room, but not The Texas Tommy; it rotated around itself. It contained several of the later innovations of the **Lindy hop**. It was the first **swing dance** and had more impact on jazz dance than all the other rag dances.

Sheet Music Cover:" Take Me To The Land of Jazz". Composer: Pete Wendling (1888-1974), pianist, composer, and one of the favorite artists making paper rolls for player pianos; Lyrics: Edgar Leslie (1885-1976) and Bert Kalmar (1880-1947). Pub: NY: Waterson, Berlin & Snyder Co., 1919.

Sheet Music Cover: "12th Street Rag". It was one of the most popular rags ever written. Composer/ lyricist: Euday L. Bowman (1887-1949), American pianist and composer of ragtime and blues; arranged by C. E. Wheeler. Pub: Kansas City, MO: J.W. Jenkins' Sons Music Co, c. 1915.

Sheet Music Cover, "More Mustard" One-Step. RagTime Waltz, composed by Louis Mentel, 1914.

"Ziegfeld Follies," 1912, Sheet Music Cover," That Wonderful Tune," composed by Jean Schwartz, words by Grant Clarke, introduced by Elizabeth Brice at the Ziegfeld Moulin Rouge, created and published by Jerome & Schwartz Publishing Co., l912.

Each of the latest black shows had provided a break from minstrel tradition. Blackface makeup almost ceased being used. Women were included in the cast of *The Creole Show* (1891). A continuous story line was used in *A Trip to Coontown* (1898). Finally, in 1921 *Shuffle Along*, an excellent musical comedy, appeared and set the high standards by which musical comedies were judged in the future. It had *I'm Just Wild About Harry* by Eubie Blake and memorable Broadway stars: **Florence Mills**, **Josephine Baker**, the team of **Sissle and Blake** and the team of **Miller and Lyles**. *Blackbirds* (1926 and 1928) had high kicks, the **Charleston**, and the **staircase dance** to *Doin' the New Low Down* performed by **Bill Robinson**.

At about this time Steele Mac Kay (1842-1894) used electricity to light an American stage, and he also initiated overhead lighting. He bought the Lyceum Theater in 1884, and in 1885, with the assistance of Thomas Edison, this theater became the first completely electrically-lighted theater.

By the end of the twenties, chaperones were non-existent, automobiles were very popular, Boston had banned the **tango** as well as the **grizzly bear dance** with cheek-to-cheek dancing. Skirts had become shorter. In 1927 talkies appeared, and in 1929 the stock market crashed and the Great Depression made its presence felt.

In West Virginia, dance halls were considered by the church and by civic leaders to be unwholesome for the young. In Alabama an attempt was made to build skating rinks for young people to replace the dance hall activity. But young blacks liked music and dancing. Although dance halls in the South were segregated, there were jook houses where blacks went to dance, drink, eat, and gamble. These jook houses were where the new dances originated: the **black bottom**, the **big apple** (which **Arthur Murray** reassembled into a popular ballroom dance while still retaining the shaking shoulders and shanks).

Jook house, jook joint, juke house, juke joint, and barrelhouse were all about the same. They were found in rural areas in southeastern United States, had a bar with food and drinks, a dance floor, gambling in a back room, and perhaps a brothel. Jukeboxes to play music came later. By 1927 The Automatic Musical Instrument Company of Michigan had invented the first electronically amplified multi-selection phonograph. And so the colorblind jukebox was born to provide music by a variety of artists for dancing.

The **big apple dance** was thought to have originated from a religious observance called the "**ring shout**" before 1860 in African American plantations in South Carolina and in Georgia. The new dance had counterclockwise circling like the ring shout and high arm movements. A former synagogue in Columbia, South Carolina, had been converted into a juke joint called The Big Apple Night Club. Some white students, hearing the music, asked if they could come in. The answer was yes, but they had to sit in the balcony and pay twenty-five cents. They did and whenever the black dancers ran out of money for the nickelodeon the students dropped down some nickels, the music continued and the dancing too. The students came back many times. They named the dance they had seen The **Big Apple** after the name of the place. **Frankie Manning**, the lead dancer with **Herbert "Whitey" White's Lindy Hoppers** at the Savoy Ballroom in Harlem heard about it and, based on the description of the dance, he created a routine and taught it to the Lindy Hoppers who then performed it. This dance became very popular in New York. It contained many of the movements later found in the **Lindy hop**, which soon replaced it in popularity. The **big apple dance** also had an improvisational quality; couples wishing to improvise could go into the center of the circle. It is said that the nickname for New York State, The Big Apple, came from the name of the dance.

**Frankie Manning** (1914-2009) was an expert Lindy Hopper. There were clubs on almost every corner of New York in the early 1930's. He danced at the Renaissance, and at the Savoy in Harlem, the first club to allow both blacks and whites on the dance floor. Cab Calloway and Duke Ellington played the music, but the dancers stole the show. Those who were learning stayed at one corner of the ballroom, leaving space for other dancers to try out new steps. **Frankie Manning** was invited to join the select group that came to practice during the day with the bands that were booked there. In 2009 he was inducted into the Hall of Fame of the National Museum of Dance in Saratoga.

**Herbert "Whitey" White** so named for a streak of white hair that he had, was a black American bouncer at the Savoy who put together a group of dancers, "Whitey's Lindy Hoppers," from the young dancers who were going to the Savoy. He managed the group, and Frankie Manning did the choreography. It included one white couple, **Harry Rosenberg and Ruthie**, excellent dancers, as they all were. The Lindy Hoppers got experience performing everywhere, in feature films, Broadway productions, workshops, and at Lindy hop conventions, and they also got a place in which to practice – the Savoy. The craze lasted from 1935 to 1942. The **Lindy hop** was named after Charles Lindbergh's solo flight across the Atlantic in 1927.

.        From the 1920's through the 1940's the cultural Harlem Renaissance flourished. It was a blossoming of creative efforts in all fields – dance, art, music, literature, visual arts, and painting – by black Americans who had migrated to Harlem from 1914 through 1918.

Blacks were leaving the South with its lynching and poor crops and moving to Harlem. Jobs in New York were plentiful due to the defense industry in World War I. The population in Harlem went from 50,000 in 1914 to 80,000 in 1920, and 200,000 in 1930. In New York and Harlem the newest dances were created at Harlem ballrooms: the Savoy, the Renaissance, the Alhambra. These dances were the **camel walk**, the **mess around**, the **truckin'**, the **Lindy hop**, the **jitterbug**, the **shag**, and the **Suzie-Q.** The **Suzie-Q** was a dance of the 1920's, with the palms facing front and moving to the right as the knees and toes swiveled to the left, and then the palms and the heels moving to the left as the knees swiveled to the right, then the palms to the right and the knees and toes to the left, followed by a quick kick forward and a step in place with the right foot, after which all the steps were reversed. The entertainers at the Cotton Club, the Congo Club, Small's Paradise, and others were all outstanding dancers. Whites would go there to have a drink and watch the blacks dance. And the dances spread.

The **Carolina shag** originated in the Myrtle Beach area in the 1930's; it was then a mix of the **collegiate shag** and the **Charleston**. In 1984 it became the official State

Sheet Music Cover, "New York and Coney Island Cycle March" Two-Step, composed by E.T. Paull, Published by E. T. Paull Music Co., 1896.

Sheet Music Cover: "Way Down Yonder in New Orleans." Music: Joe Turner Layton (1804-1978), Lyrics: Henry Creamer (1879-1930), black American. Pub: NY: Shapiro, Bernstein & Co. Cover illustration has photo of singer Blossom Seeley. This song was performed at the Winter Garden Theater, Broadway, NY in the musical "Spice of 1922." In 1960 it reached No. 3 on the "Billboard" charts, and was used as a fundraiser after Hurricane Katrina in 2005, performed by Harry Connick, Jr.

Sheet Music Cover: "Jelly Roll Blues." Composer: Jelly Roll Morton (1885-1941). Cover illustration by Starmer has two people dancing on a huge jelly roll, the man plays the banjo and the woman plays the guitar. It says, on the jelly roll: By Ferd Morton, Author of "The 'Jelly Roll' Blues" song. Pub: Chicago: Will Rossiter, 1915.

Sheet Music Cover: "On The Mississippi.". Composers: Carroll and Fields; Lyrics: Ballard MacDonald; Cover illustrators: William and Frederick Starmer, photo of Carroll and Fields. Pub.: NY: Shapiro Music Pub. Co. 1912.

Dance of South Carolina. While dancing it, one had a smooth connected relation with one's partner. Some of the original steps were the **Cuban step**, the **shuffle**, and the **twinkle**.

The **mess around** was a black American dance first mentioned in a **Perry Bradford** song in 1912. But **Buddy Bradley**, a well-known dance coach to the stars, said it existed before then. The song became a hit when **Ethel Waters** sang it on the T.O.B.A. circuit. T.O.B.A. stood for the Theater Owners Booking Agency. The song suggested that the dance came from the Virgin Islands. With hands on the hips, pelvis, or backside, the hips moved in a wide circular movement while the dancer did a rhythmic bounce on the balls of the feet, keeping the rest of the body quiet. The dance became even better liked in the 1950's through the **Ray Charles** version of the song. The **swing dance version** was done with a partner; you had to lean forward and then away from your partner, each for eight counts, with hands as before.

T.O.B.A. Theaters were the only ones for black customers below the Mason-Dixon Line in the early 20th century, offering all-black acts for all-black audiences. This booking agency had thirty-one theaters when they started in 1903, all owned by white owners. At its peak in the 1920's the number of theaters was one hundred. Black and white vaudeville was less popular during the Great Depression. Vaudeville had black and white performers on the same stage since the 1890's, but most states did not permit blacks and whites to sit in the same theater in the South, while in the North the preferred seats were never sold to blacks. However, in the South at midnight, on Saturday nights, whites might be allowed in the balcony for the usual price of twenty-five cents. Some of the well-known performers who played on black vaudeville were **Bert Williams**, **Ma Rainey** and **Bill "Bojangles" Robinson**. Black performers who also played the standard vaudeville circuit for a higher wage would play the black circuit in order to be seen by black audiences. They had the same variety of acts, but the humor was a bit raunchier. T.O.B.A. was nicknamed "Tough on Black Artists," the pay was lower and touring arrangements were worse than in standard vaudeville.

Theater owners tried to add more than two shows a day, maybe three, four, or five during the depression, and also films, when the films were popular, to make up for their losses. This did not work out because the performers were exhausted. Some theaters offered films and vaudeville, or vaudeville only on weekends.

The Vaudeville Managers Association founded in 1900 led to the United Booking Office (UBO) in 1906. This was a clearinghouse for performers and theaters to make sure there was ample good talent for all the theaters. There were also many smaller theater circuits and a few theaters that were booked independently. Placement on a vaudeville bill was of the essence. Being the first or last act was the least desirable – customers were arriving or getting ready to leave. *Variety*, a trade newspaper, reviewed all the black acts as well as the white vaudeville. Vaudeville theater managers, for either black or white vaudeville, were only interested in getting customers. If the audience complained about an act, word got around and the act had trouble getting future bookings.

# 11

# Tap Dance

# During the 20<sup>th</sup> and 21<sup>st</sup> Centuries

It was not until 1902 that the term "tap" was used professionally. **Ned Wayburn** (1874-1942) created a show called *Minstrel Misses*. The young ladies in his show stepped onstage, sat at tables at the back of the stage, and put on dark makeup while the audience watched; then they proceeded to do a minstrel show. Wayburn called the dance they did *Tap and Stepping*. His dancers used light clogs with split wooden soles. Before that the dance was called "buck and wing," "flat-footed dancing," or "buck dancing." Aluminum heel and toe taps weren't commonly used until after 1910. Previously, most tap dancing shoes were made of leather uppers and wooden soles, while others had hobnails or pennies pounded into the toes and heels of the shoes. By the 1920's metal plates or taps had been added to leather soled shoes.

During the 20<sup>th</sup> century, Broadway revues (*Shuffle Along,* 1921, and *Blackbirds,* 1921 and 1928), the rise of vaudeville, and the traveling black road shows created more jobs for tap dancers. In spite of the Civil War (1861-1865), in which the 54<sup>th</sup> all-black Infantry Division had fought for the Union, and the First World War (1914-1918), when blacks and whites alike fought for the United States, it was embarrassing to have to admit that racism was still prevalent in the United States *(Photo Plate 11-1)*.

There were different theatrical circuits for minstrel shows and vaudeville – black performers for black audiences and white performers for white audiences. In the 1920's and 30's, black dance teams like the **Nicholas Brothers** (**Fayard** and **Harold**) added acrobatic movements also called flash acts and satirical acts to their routines. Well-known comedy-tap teams included **Slap and Happy** (Harold Daniels and Leslie Irvin), and **Stump and Stumpy** (James Cross and Harold Crome Slyder), and the song-and-dance team **Buck and Bubbles** (Ford Lee 'Buck' Washington and John 'Bubbles' Sublett) *(Photo Plate 11-1)*.

**Bill 'Bojangles' Robinson** (1878-1949) became the best-known tap dancer in the United States *(Photo Plates 11-1 and 11-2)*. He was the most highly paid black American performer in the world in 1929 and used up to twenty or thirty pairs of tap shoes a year just from practicing. He had a preference for wooden soled shoes and could produce nearly all the rhythmic sounds that a drum could create. His staircase dance, his signature dance, done to *Doin' the New Low Down* while making trombone sounds with his mouth, and his movie *The Little Colonel,* teaching tap to **Shirley Temple** (1928-2014), were favorites, and also *Stormy Weather,* starring Lena Horne (1917-2010), Cab Calloway

(1907-1994), **Katherine Dunham** (1909-2006), and the **Nicholas Brothers**. 'Bojangles' appeared on Broadway in the 1939 swinging production of *The Hot Mikado* based on Gilbert and Sullivan's *The Mikado*. His staircase dance originated from his dancing down the stairs from the stage to greet friends in the audience and dancing back up to the stage. Realizing that the audience loved this, he put it into his act by adding a few stairs as props. Jazz music added even more rhythmic complexity to tap and 'Bojangles' excelled all the time, both in the United States and abroad. His sounds were always clear, light, precise, and executed to the right and to the left, with an upright posture and few arm gestures – all very Irish, but with the addition of African syncopation which made it totally American tap.

The **Nicholas Brothers** (Fayard 1914-2006, and Harold, 1921-2000) were an amazing black tap dance act. Their specialty was a jump into a split, from which they got up to their feet without using hands to get down or to get up. **Gregory Hines** had commented that if ever anyone made a biographical movie of them, some of it would have to be computer generated because no one would be able to duplicate their movements. They appeared on television, in nightclubs, and theaters all over the United States. They received Honorary Doctorate Degrees from Harvard and in 2003 they were inducted into the Hall of Fame of the National Museum of Dance in Saratoga Springs, New York. One of the favorite films that the Nicholas Brothers made was *Stormy Weather*.

When **George Balanchine**, a renowned ballet master, choreographed for the Nicholas Brothers in a Broadway show, *Ziegfeld Follies of 1936*, he was so taken by the Nicholas Brothers that he put them into the Rodgers and Hart musical *Babes in Arms* (1937) also choreographed by him. Balanchine used the following method when choreographing for the Nicholas Brothers. He had them execute a few steps, slides, splits, etc., and then picked out the movement he wanted these brilliant tap dancers to do next. This worked extremely well. He had seen one of them jump and land in a split jump under the other's split leg stance and immediately decided to have them do that for a Broadway show under a line of eight lovely women standing with legs apart.

**Tap** was the performance dance of vaudeville and Broadway. (Vaudeville came after minstrel shows, was not expensive and was a family show.) A popular step in vaudeville in the early 1900's and still popular today was the **shim sham** or the **shim-sham shimmy**. It goes: shuf-fle, step, shuf-fle, step, shuf-fle, step, step, shuf-fle step (1+2, 3+4, 5+6+7+8, with the accent on counts 1, 2, 3, 4, 5, 6, 7, 8), or (+a1+a2+a3a+a4, with the accent on counts 1, 2, 3, 4), **shuffle** being a brush toward the front, followed by a brush toward the back. Then the step is reversed and started with the other foot. It was originally done at the Savoy ballroom to a song called *The Song of the Freaks*, written by Luis Russell. A shim sham routine can be seen in Cab Calloway's musical short *Jittering Jitterbugs* (1932-1934). It can be done solo, as a couples dance, or as a line dance with arms around the next person on each side and traveling sideways, to the front or to the back.

Here are some of the outstanding tap dancers of the 1920's and 30's, an inspiration to many who saw their performances.

Eleanor Powell (1912-1982), exuberant tap dancer and actress of the 30's and 40's. Photo 1936, unidentified photographer..

Sheet Music Cover: "Good Bye Alexander, Good Bye, Honey Boy". Composer/Lyricist: Henry Creamer (1877-1930) and Turner Layton (1894-1978). First Line: Alexander Cooper was a colored trooper, with his regiment he marched away. Publisher: NY: Broadway Music Corp, 1918. Illustration depicts France as a woman waving a French flag and leading a procession of black American troops. Cover illustration by E.E. Walton. At that time American troops were segregated; blacks and whites served in separate units.

Bill "Bojangles" Robinson, 1933; Photographer: Carl van Vechten (1880-1964).

Portrait of John W. Bubbles as Sportin' Life in "Porgy and Bess." Photographer: Carl van Vechten, 1936.

**Ananias** (1912-1951) and **Jimmy** (1914-1969) **Berry** - the **Berry Brothers** - a flash act and acrobatics team who performed in top hat and tails and never wore taps on their shoes. They became a trio when **William** (1922-1996), their younger brother, joined the act. They performed in *Blackbirds of 1928* and *Blackbirds of 1930* (choreographed by black dance director **Clarence Robinson**), toured with *Blackbirds of 1929*, and on December 27, 1932, they played for the opening of Radio City Music Hall. They frequently performed at the Cotton Club, as did many other exciting dancers and singers, under the direction of Leonard Harper, known for his theatricality and superb taste.

**Cora La Redd** (d. 1968) was a brilliant black female singer-dancer from the Cotton Club who performed in *Blackbirds of 1929*, in the black musical *Messin' Around* (1929), and in a 12-minute short *That's the Spirit* (1933). She was known for her fiery vitality and hard-hitting rhythm tap.

**Leslie 'Bubba' Gaines** (1912-1997), black, at 64 was still doing his jump rope tap routines for which he was famous. He had been a member of "The Three Dukes," also known as "The Aristocrats of Tap" in the 1930's, along with **Raymond Kaalund** (1913-1988) and **Leon Collins**. They did a synchronized jump rope tap routine and were celebrated for elegance and musicality.

**Leon Collins**' (1922-1985) signature piece was Rimsky-Korsakov's *Flight of the Bumble Bee*, an excellent piece for someone with his virtuosity. He also tapped to Bach's *Prelude and Fugue in C Minor* and to bebop standards; his feet could express what musicians played on their instruments.

**Ernest 'Brownie' Brown**'s (1916-2009) tap dancing style was fast and flashy, with syncopation and snake hips, and sudden drops into unexpected splits. Ernest 'Brownie' Brown died in 2009 at 93. He was the last of the Original Copasetics. His final performance was at the Tap City Festival in New York in 2008 with **Reginald McLaughlin,** his last partner during 16 years.

The Copasetics was a social club made up of a group of twenty-one musical artists, musicians and tap dancers, formed about a week after Bill Robinson's burial, to preserve Bill Robinson's name. It was a vital social club in Harlem with charitable performances and annual balls, and a pledge by its members to promote fellowship and strengthen character within the group. "Everything's copasetic," Robinson used to say for great, or okay.

**Charles 'Cookie' Cook** (1917-1991) was exceptional at performing beautiful soft shoe tap routines. **Cook and Brown**, both black Americans, were a comedy dance team. They also appeared as a specialty act on Broadway in the musical *Kiss Me Kate*.

"Showtime at the Apollo" is where all these excellent tap dancers appeared – at the Apollo Theater on West 125 Street – to an audience that expected great dancing. Besides these tap dancers, who all tried to outshine the other performers on the program, there were also excellent female dancers such as the team of **Edwina "Salt" Evelyn** (1922-2011) and **Jewel "Pepper" Welch** (**Salt and Pepper**), the **Edwards Sisters** (Ruth and Louise), and **Louise Madison,** as well as the superlative sixteen female tap dancers in the Apollo chorus line.

Later on, several big bands also included tap as part of their program. The tap dancers moved from vaudeville to movies and television. With the appearance of the **Lindy Hop,** new tap steps appeared. There were steps like the **flying swing outs** and the **flying circles**; these were Lindy Hop moves with tap footwork.

During the Depression years that started in 1929, movies became a national pastime and provided relief with the dancing of **Ginger Rogers** and **Fred Astaire.** Through them many Americans were introduced to dance.

During the 1930's and 40's the addition of movements from ballet, ballroom, acrobatics, and modern dance – turns and leaps – by dancers like **Fred Astaire**, **Ray Bolger**, **Paul Draper**, '**Buck**' and '**Bubbles**', **James Cagney**, and **Eleanor Powell** also stretched out the tap vocabulary; and in the 1950's **Gene Kelly** added new movements. Paul Draper did character sketches, such as a politician giving a speech, Ray Bolger did **legomania** (also called eccentric dancing or rubberlegging and involved flying kicks, exaggerated, rubber-like leg movements while tapping), and Hollywood films made tap popular worldwide.

'**Buck**' and '**Bubbles**' were a famous black song-and-dance entertainment team comprising **Ford L. 'Buck' Washington** (1903-1955) who sang and played the piano while **John William Sublett** (1902-1986), with the stage name of '**Bubbles**,' tapped. They were in the *Ziegfeld Follies of 1931* and were also the first black artists to perform at Radio City Music Hall. John 'Bubbles' emphasized a slower, more syncopated style of tap dance. He used percussive heel drops and slowed the rhythms in order to get more versatility into his taps. He was known as the "father of rhythm tap." In 1935 George Gershwin chose him to appear as Sportin' Life in *Porgy and Bess (Photo Plate 11-1)*. The team appeared in the films *A Star Is Born* (1937) and *Cabin in the Sky* (1943).

**Paul Draper** (1909-1996) was an inventive and unique tap dancer and choreographer who performed to classical music. He also studied at the School of American Ballet. He teamed up with a harmonica virtuoso, Larry Adler. Both were blacklisted in 1951 by the HUAC (House Un-American Activities Committee). Both careers suffered as did the careers of many others who were blacklisted, but Draper continued dancing and choreographing. He had previously appeared in nightclubs, in concert halls, and in Carnegie Hall, tap dancing to the music of Johann Sebastian Bach with much success. Draper also choreographed to music by Domenico Scarlatti (1685-1757), to Beethoven, to blues, and jazz. He was extremely creative in tapping sketches of various types of people, and he did it all in tap, without saying a word. It was fantastic – you could almost hear what he meant to say.

**Eleanor Powell** (1912-1982), an actress and exuberant tap dancer of the 1930's and 40's, danced in vaudeville as a child. Her film *Broadway Melody of 1936* was so profitable that it kept the studio from going bankrupt at that time. The Fred Astaire-

Eleanor Powell tap sequence to Cole Porter's *Begin the Beguine* is regarded as being in a class by itself. In *Ship Ahoy*, Powell's character tapped out a message to a secret agent in Morse code, while continuing to dance a tap routine. She was a perfectionist, but her hours of practice always made her intricate dancing look effortless (*Photo Plate 11-1*).

**Fred Astaire**'s (1899-1987) tap dancing was elegant, artistic and creative *(Photo Plate 11-5)*. As a child he had performed in vaudeville with his sister, **Adele**. When the team broke up he appeared in films, thirty of which had dancing. **Ginger Rogers** was his co-star in ten of these films. He or **Hermes Pan** choreographed most of them. Robert Benchley stated in 1938 that Astaire was the world's best tap dancer. In his films Astaire insisted that the dance routine be shot in a single take without any breaks and that it advance the plot of the story. **Ginger Rogers** was a favorite because she continued to act while in a dance routine and also because she conveyed the impression that dancing with Astaire was thrilling. (It probably was.)

Great dancers like Balanchine, the Nicholas Brothers, Rudolph Nureyev, Gene Kelly, Gregory Hines, and Bill Robinson all admired Astaire's artistry and perfectionism. Astaire said that if a dance was right there should not be a single superfluous movement in it.

**Hermes Pan** (1910-1990) choreographed fifteen of the Fred Astaire films as well as forty-five others, had no dance training but was inspired by music and things he saw, such as a fun house that he used in *Damsel in Distress* for which he won an Academy award. He picked up steps very quickly.

**Ruby Keeler**'s (1910-1993) singing and tap dancing in the movie musical *42nd Street* (1933) immediately made her a sensation as a tap dancer, especially so because this was followed by **Busby Berkeley**'s *Gold Diggers of 1933* and *Footlight Parade* (1933). In 1971 she appeared on Broadway in a successful revival of *No, No, Nanette*, a musical of the 1920's. The 1971 production was supervised by **Busby Berkeley** (1895-1976), directed by **Burt Shevelove**, choreographed by **Donald Saddler**, and won several Tony Awards.

**James Cagney** (1899-1986), an actor-dancer, played a hoofer and comedian in vaudeville until Warner Bros. hired him to do movies. He won an Academy Award for best actor in 1938 for *Angels with Dirty Faces*. Then in 1942 he won another for playing **George M. Cohan** in *Yankee Doodle Dandy (Photo Plate 11-2)*. He had begun tap dancing as a kid and even got nicknamed 'Cellar Door Cagney' because of his habit of dancing outdoors on the slanted cellar doors. His dancing skills helped him win that 1942 Oscar. He even performed a buck and wing dance followed by Cohan's signature move: running up the side of the proscenium arch, then flipping over backwards to be at the center of the stage for his bow. Cagney received a Lifetime Achievement Award from the American Film Institute in 1974 and in 1980 he was one of the recipients of the Kennedy Center Honors. He made many excellent films and was memorable in each of them. He was President of the Screen Actors Guild for two years.

Publicity poster for "The Band Wagon," MGM film, 1953.

Betty Grable (1916-1973). Promotional photo for 20th Century Fox's upcoming film "Pin Up Girl," photo by Frank Powolny, 1942.

Honi Coles in "My One and Only," Photo by Kenn Duncan, 1983.

Publicity photo for "Yankee Doodle Dandy," Warner Bros., 1942.

Jimmy "Slyde" Godbolt, tap dancer and NEA National Heritage Fellow, photo by Joseph T. Wilson.

Bill "Bojangles" Robinson. Photo: Carl van Vechten, 1941.

**Betty Grable** (1916-1973) starred in the Broadway show *Du Barry Was a Lady* (1940), winning great reviews, and also in numerous movies. *Down Argentine Way* (1940), *Moon Over Miami* (1941), *Pin-Up Girl* (1944), and *Mother Wore Tights* (1947) were some of the films that audiences loved. In *Moon Over Miami* she danced with **Hermes Pan**; this was his first screen appearance. Her dancing was rhythmic, excellent, and feminine. Her favored status with GIs during World War II helped her gain the leading role in *Pin-Up Girl* (starring the phenomenal, high speed tappers, the **Condos Brothers**) and also helped her earn a very lucrative salary. Her favorite co-star was **Dan Dailey**. The pose and angle in the photograph shown here hide the fact that she was pregnant and show off her gorgeous figure and the legs that Fox studios had Lloyd's of London insure for a million dollars *(Photo Plate 11-2)*. She was one of the top ten box office stars from 1942 to 1952.

**Gene Kelly** (1912-1996) appeared in the Broadway show *Pal Joey* (1940) and then in innumerable movies as the star, the choreographer and, in several, as the co-director. Some of the favorites were *Anchors Away* (1945), *On the Town* (1949), *An American in Paris* (1951), *Singin' in the Rain* (1952), and *Brigadoon* (1954). He tried to show a relationship between dance and athletics and received a *Dance Magazine* Award for directing and starring in the documentary *Dancing: A Man's Game* for NBC's *Omnibus*. He directed the Broadway musical *Flower Drum Song* (1958). He was the first American to choreograph and stage an original ballet at the Paris Opera, *Pas de Dieux* (1960, to George Gershwin's *Concerto in F*). He was made a Chevalier of the Legion of Honor by the French government in 1960, and in 1985. The American Film Institute awarded him a Lifetime Achievement Award for his work in motion pictures. At the Academy Awards ceremony in 1996, the director, Quincy Jones, gave a tribute to the deceased Gene Kelly and **Savion Glover** (more about him later) performed Gene Kelly's famous dance to *Singin' in the Rain*. When staging dance sequences on film, Gene Kelly thought of the camera as the eye of the audience.

Tap dance declined in the 1950's, especially in Broadway musicals, which were now more into ballet and modern dance due to **Agnes De Mille**'s influence.

With the popularity of rock and roll in the 1950's and the disappearance of former venues for tap dancers, the black tapper Charles 'Cholly' Atkins (1913-2003) nevertheless found work choreographing clever, synchronized routines to varied Motown singing groups like the Temptations. Earlier, on vaudeville, he had worked with **Charles 'Honi' Coles**. They were recognized for the precision, power, and elegance that they brought to their act; that was why they were called a "class act." Cholly Atkins was awarded a Tony in 1989 for his choreography for the Broadway musical *Black and Blue*.

**Jane Goldberg** and **Brenda Bufalino** in the 1970's started an effort to find the great tap dancers of the 1940's and revive their careers as teachers and performers so that young tappers could learn from them. Many of those great tap dancers – **Bunny Briggs** (1922-2014), **Steve Condos** (1918-1990), the **Nicholas Brothers**, **Sammy Davis Jr.** (1925-1990), **Howard 'Sandman Sims'** (1917-1980), and **Jimmy Slyde** (1927-2008, a jazz-influenced tap dancer whose style was reflected in his name); he also appeared in the movie *Tap* (1988) with Gregory Hines, where they did a typical tap challenge dance. *(Photo Plates 11-2 and 11-5)*

**Charles 'Honi' Coles** (1911-1992) *(Photo Plate 11-2)* started as a boy by tapping on Philadelphia streets in "cutting" sessions, jam sessions where you try to outshine and impress one another. From there he went on to dance in theaters, nightclubs, on Broadway and in Europe. He appeared in *Gentlemen Prefer Blondes* (1949) with his partner **Cholly Atkins**, the only blacks in the musical.

Suddenly tap dance in musicals ended and Honi Coles went on to become manager of the Apollo Theater from 1959 to 1974. As mentioned before, tap had lost its appeal in the 1940's with Agnes de Mille's modern dance choreography that integrated the story and the dance. However, in 1971 *No, No, Nanette* revived tap on Broadway. With the revival of tap dancing, Honi Coles then danced in *Bubbling Brown Sugar* in 1976 and toured Holland. He performed in *My One and Only* (1983) on Broadway, receiving a Tony Award for Best Supporting Actor, a Fred Astaire Award, a Drama Desk Award for his role as supporting actor, and a mention in the back of the program stating that the special material was by **Honi Coles**.

During the 1970's, with an assist in his career by **Brenda Bufalino**, Coles taught dance and dance history at Yale, Cornell, Duke, and George Washington Universities. In 1991 he was awarded the National Medal of the Arts by the first President Bush.

**Brenda Bufalino** (b. 1939) had been a protégé of Charles 'Honi' Coles. He was her mentor, partner, and collaborator. **Gregory Hines** *(Photo Plate 11-3)* considered her to be one of the great female tap dancers. She founded the American Tap Dance Orchestra and choreographed for them. She created tap workshops and tap dance festivals, received fellowships from the National Endowment for the Arts and from the New York Foundation for the Arts. She was awarded the Flo-Bert Award, the Tapestry Award, and the Hoofer Award for her lifetime achievement and her creative contributions to the field. As a master teacher, performer, author, and choreographer she has inspired many tappers worldwide. Her classes, workshops, and performances have taken place in Russia, Italy, Germany, France, Denmark, Australia, Turkey, Estonia, Latvia, Poland, Cyprus, Israel, Japan, and other locations.

Tap may have developed in the United States, but it certainly spread all over the world. Tours sponsored by the United States Department of State helped extend its popularity, especially when these tours included such creative and talented groups as **Brenda Bufalino** and her American Tap Dance Orchestra.

In the 1970's and 80's tap was considered to be not only entertainment, but also an art form. *No Maps on My Taps*, the PBS documentary (1979), won an Emmy award and helped start another tap revival. This documentary, by filmmaker George T. Nierenberg, focused on the old-time black American tap dancers: **Bunny Briggs**, **Chuck Green**, **Howard 'Sandman' Sims** and **John William Sublett**. It was a record of an American art form − tap dancing.

"Master Juba" (William Henry Lane) at Vauxhall Gardens, London. From "Dan Emmett and the Rise of Early Negro Minstrelsy" by Hans Nathan in The London Illustrated News, August 5, 1848.

Sheet Music Cover: "Raftero," by Ralph Rainger for the film "Bolero," 1934, starring George Raft and Carole Lombard.

Gregory Hines in "Sophisticated Ladies," 1981. Photo by Martha Swope.

"Dancing Dynamite", from Screenland Magazine piece on the movie "Colleen," Vol. 32, pages 512-53 (Nov.1935-Apr. 1936). Ruby Keeler and Paul Draper dancing.

The Lawrence Welk show on television – from 1955 to 1982 – had an excellent tap dancer. He was **Arthur Duncan**, the first black American to appear as a regular on a variety show on television. He was there for eighteen years, from 1964 to 1982, and was an inspiration to watch. He would record the tap sounds first, to be sure they would be easily heard above the music, then tape the dance routine, being extremely careful to match the sounds exactly. **Gregory Hines** (more about him later) claimed he would rush home to be sure to catch Arthur Duncan's tap routine on television every week.

With every reappearance of tap in a Broadway show, dancers would run to the nearest tap dance class to brush up their tap in time for a future audition and to learn the **Maxie Ford**, or the **time step** starting on the 8th count, and the one starting on the 1st count, and so on.

Tap dance had definitely returned to Broadway, film, and the concert stage in the United States, Japan, and Europe. Some of the Broadway hits were *Sophisticated Lady* (1981) with **Gregory Hines**, *The Tap Dance Kid* (1983) with a very young and extremely talented **Savion Glover**, *Black and Blue* (1989), and *Jelly's Last Jam* (1992). The films included *The Cotton Club* (1984) and *Tap* (1988).

**Tommy Tune** (b. 1939) appeared in several Broadway musicals, not only as a tap dancer, but also as an actor, director, and choreographer: *The Best Little Whorehouse in Texas* (1978), *Nine* (1982), and *My One and Only* (1983), for which he won a Tony. In his career he has won nine Tony Awards and seven Drama Desk Awards. He was inducted into the Dance Hall of Fame of the National Museum of Dance in Saratoga in 2009. He got his experience from choreographing a variety of styles of musicals for one-week musicals in summer stock. He said he got his best ideas just before waking in the morning and just before falling asleep at night.

A phenomenal female tap dancer was **Ann Miller** (1923-2004). Ann Miller was one-quarter Native American of the Cherokee tribe. She was a sparkling tap dancer and could do 500 taps a minute. Her turns and rapid-fire taps were amazing. Her films included *On the Town* (1939*)*, *Easter Parade* (1948), and *Kiss Me Kate* (1953). She appeared on Broadway in *Sugar Babies*, a smash hit, for three years (October 1979 to August 28, 1982). She and **Mickey Rooney** (in his Broadway debut) starred in *Sugar Babies* and then toured with it for four and a half more years *(Photo Plate 11-4)*. The show was done in revue style and honored the old burlesque era. Sugar babies were what members of a burlesque chorus used to be called. The choreographer, **Ernie Flatt**, had choreographed the **Ernie Flatt Dancers**, who were regulars on television on *The Carol Burnett Show*. He won two Oscars for *Sugar Babies* as choreographer and as director. The music was by Jimmy Mc Hugh, lyrics by Dorothy Fields, Al Dubin, and others, and book was by Ralph G. Allen and Harry Rigby.

During the 1980's and 90's there were numerous tap dance groups in the United States: **Lynn Dally**'s Jazz Tap Ensemble, **Linda Sol Donnell**'s Rhapsody in Taps, **Heather Cornell**'s Manhattan Tap, **Anita Feldman** and Company, **Acia Gray**'s Tapestry Dance Company, **Renee Kriethen** and **Yvonne Edwards**' Tappers with

Attitude, **Gene Medler**'s North Carolina Youth Tap Ensemble, and **Thelma Goldberg**'s Dynasty. Notice how many of these were started by women. Tap had previously been considered almost exclusively a man's dance.

A sensational contemporary female tap dancer is **Dormeshia Sumbry-Edwards** (b. 1976), who started tapping at age 3 and got into her first Broadway show *Black and Blue* with **Jimmy Slyde**, **Ralph Brown**, and **Lon Chaney** at age 13, and later appeared in *Bring in 'da Noise, Bring in 'da Funk*, the only female in the show, with **Savion Glover**. She is petite, graceful and feminine, and can maintain as much energy as a man when she taps, even or especially in heels. She married another tap dancer, **Omar Edwards**. They had three children, opened a dance studio in Harlem, and she has been the official tap spokesperson for Capezios, together with her family. She was elected in 2005 to the Advisory Board of *Dance Magazine* as the Tap Dance Advisor. She has taught on the International Tap Festival Circuit in New York, Los Angeles, Brazil, and Japan.

The tap virtuosos **Jason Samuels Smith and Company**, **Dormeshia Sumbry-Edwards**, **Chloé Arnold**, and **Michelle Dorrance** (recipient in 2013 of the seventh annual Jacob's Pillow Dance Award which included a prize of $25,000) gave a concert in July 2012 at the Joyce Theater to honor jazz saxophonist Charlie "Bird" Parker. It consisted of three pieces, the last of which, *Chasing the Bird*, was the premiere of a group work blending the sounds of bop and of tap. **Jason Samuels Smith** (b. 1980) is known for his use of intricate rhythms. **Sanuels Smith** has also performed with his tap dance group A.C.G.I. (Anybody Can Get It), made up of remarkable soloists, **Chloé Arnold**, **Sarah Reich**, **Melinda Sullivan** and his male co-dancer **Lee Howard**. They know how to establish a rhythm, embellish it, and keep it exciting with changes in the texture and in the emphasis of the varied meters. Samuels Smith is the recipient of both an Emmy Award and an American Choreography Award for "Outstanding Choreography" in 2003 for the opening number of the Jerry Lewis/MDA Telethon in a tribute to Gregory Hines who had died that year.

*Stomp*, which has been amazing audiences since 1991 when it opened in Brighton, UK, is a unique musical theatre of choreographed percussion, movement and physical comedy, and of tap. **Luke Cresswell** and **Steve McNicholas** created this very original show. The performers never utter a word; they use a variety of household items (plungers, garbage can lids, newspapers, plastic bags), and water to create rhythms and sounds. A very enjoyable family show, it opened at the Orpheum Theater, Off-Broadway, in New York in 1994 and won an Obie and a Drama Desk Award; it was still playing in 2015. In 1992 the show performed in Barcelona, Sydney, Dublin, and other locations, and it began touring the U.S. in 1995.

Tap dance jam sessions were hosted by the beloved tap dancer **Buster Brown** from 1997 until he died in 2002, at age 88. **Michela Marino Lerman**, a young teenage prodigy in those days, has been the host of her own tap dance jam session for a few years; it is held at Smalls Jazz Club in the West Village every Wednesday evening. Anyone who gets their tap shoes on can join, whether they are seven or seventy. Jam sessions are essential for the improvisatory skills of tap dancers. The trend has been for about half of the dedicated participating jammers to be East Asians: Taiwanese, Koreans, and Japanese who have come to New York for that purpose, to jam. The tappers find that the live musical accompaniment (a trio of jazz musicians, piano, bass and drums), and the possibility of hearing and seeing what the other jammers are doing are conducive to expanding their skills at improvisation.

Tap great **Gregory Hines** (1946-2003) *(Photo Plate 11-3)* was honored by the New York Public Library, which named its tap dance collection after him, together with that of the American Tap Dance Foundation of which Hines was a member. In 1992 Hines received a Drama Desk Award and a Tony for Outstanding Choreography for *Jelly's Last Jam*, a Broadway show about the life of Jelly Roll Morton. Gregory Hines and his brother, Maurice, had often appeared at the Apollo Theater when young. They were both in the musical revue *Eubie* (1978) and in *Sophisticated Ladies* (1981), a tribute to Duke Ellington. Gregory Hines appeared in the film *The Cotton Club* (1984) and also in *White Nights* (1985) with Baryshnikov. Hines had a smooth style in his tap solos. He was awarded the 1998 Flo-Bert Award for Lifetime Achievement in Tap Dance by the New York Committee in celebration of National Tap Dance Day. Gregory Hines had been instrumental in the selection of a date for National Tap Dance Day when, in 1989, Congress voted to proclaim National Tap Dance Day to be on May 25th, **Bill 'Bojangles' Robinson**'s birthday. This day is celebrated in many cities in the United States (and for a while even Macy's celebrated it outdoors in front of the store on 34th Street, New York City, with a large number of people coming to tap away). In 1988 Macy's Tap-O-Mania Day in 1988 set a Guinness record with 3,859 tappers.

There are Tap Dance Day Workshops going on in Iowa, Illinois, California, Hawaii, Japan, Canada, Germany, Netherlands, Argentina and other locations. By the 21st century one could find creative and excellent tap dancers in Finland – **Jussi Lindroos**, Estonia – **Alexander Ivashkevitsh** and **Anton Merkulov**, Brazil – **Christiane Matallo**, Taiwan, Austria, French Guiana, Germany, France, South Africa, and innumerable other countries that combined rhythm tap and their preferred music in a multicultural setting, incorporating them with American, Asian, and European traditions.

The main characteristics of tap dance are: syncopation, routines often starting on the eighth beat, or between the eighth and the first beat, and improvisations executed with music or a capella, without music. There exist a wide range of styles in tap dancing.

**Hoofers** use only their legs and make a loud, grounded sound, also called rhythm tap, percussive tap, and jazz tap; this style is often found in poor areas or cities, but not always. The emphasis is on the sound; music is not necessary.

Broadway tap is usually speedy and light, like the dancing in *42nd Street*. The **Berry Brothers** (Ananias, James and Warren) were a stylish flash act and used canes. **Hal Leroy** (1913-1985) looked like he had rubber legs; his legs flew all over the place (**legomania**) while he tapped. **Terry Hale** was an improviser; if he had five shows a day at the Apollo Theatre, they would all be great but different; he never did the same routine twice.

Photo Plate 11-4

"Sugar Babies," a revue-style musical starring Ann Miller and Mickey Rooney (in his Broadway debut).
Choreography: Ernie Flatt; Music: Jimmy Mc Hugh; Lyrics: Dorothy Fields; The show opened on October 8, 1979,
closed on August 28, 1982, and then toured the USA. Photographer: Helene Andreu.

**Steve Condos** performed in vaudeville, Broadway shows, and films; he was an expert at **rhythm tap**, and influenced **Gregory Hines**, **Savion Glover**, and **Marshall Davis, Jr.** Another hoofer was **Sammy Davis, Jr.**

Dancers like Fred Astaire gave tap a ballroom look; Gene Kelly used ballet together with tap. **Paula Abdul** did tap dance on her music videos.

**Alfred Desio**, in California, worked out a system called TapTronics or Zapped Taps. He inserted a device between the sole of the shoe and each tap to put the tap sounds through a synthesizer and create electronic music.

*Riverdance,* showcasing the traditional Irish dance mixed with Flamenco rhythms, was first danced during a 7-minute interval of the *Eurovision Song Contest* held at Dublin's Point Theatre in 1994. In 1995 it became a video – number one on the UK charts – and then a full-length stage production that was performed for 8 weeks at Radio City Music Hall and toured throughout the UK and Europe. It went to Broadway with a change of cast in 2000 and performed in Israel in 2011, in the interest of cultural interaction. After fifteen years of worldwide performances since 1998, *Riverdance* traveled on a farewell tour that included the Far East, Australia and Europe. Each of its production companies is named after a river in Ireland.

In 1996, *Riverdance* was produced, choreographed, and performed by **Michael Flatley** (b. 1958) and **Jean Butler** (b. 1971), both born in the United States of immigrant Irish parents. Jean Butler and Michael Flatley were both national and international dance champions. Flatley was the first non-European to win the All Ireland World Championship for Irish Dance. *Riverdance* was very popular and several versions of it have been presented, including *Lord of the Dance* (1996), *Feet of Flames* (1998), and *Celtic Tiger,* a creation of Flatley's that toured North America in 2005 and Europe in 2006.

The distinction between traditional Irish and the evolving black American tap is obvious and was made noticeable in a PBS television program of *Riverdance* as performed in Asia in 2010. It showed a "cutting" contest (as these types of contests are called in tap dance) between traditional Irish and black American tap dancers in which dancers attempted to outdo and impress their opponents.

**Savion Glover** (b. 1973), a gifted black tapper, first appeared on Broadway starring in the musical *The Tap Dance Kid* at age twelve. **Henry Le Tang** was the choreographer. In 1990 Savion joined *Sesame Street* on television and remained till 1995. His most recent film to date is the animated *Happy Feet* (2006) in which he tapped the penguin Mumbles and which he co-choreographed. Savion Glover appeared in the Broadway show *Bring in 'da Noise, Bring in 'da Funk* in 1996. In 2013 he presented his new show STePz.

After *Bring in 'da Noise, Bring in 'da Funk* Savion Glover started his own company called Not Your Ordinary Tappers (NYOT) for which **Glover** and **Ted Levy**, a Broadway tapper, could explore choreography and music as they choreographed a repertoire of thirty pieces, solos and group numbers for the group. In NYOT there was only one female, an outstanding tapper, **Ayodele Casel**, New York-born dancer, choreographer and actress. **Savion Glover** noticed her because of her obvious enjoyment of tap dancing plus her facility in picking up steps very quickly and her proficiency. She is one of the tappers in Glover's STePz.

Presidential Awards have been given to several tap legends for their lifelong contributions to the arts in the United States. These include **Charles 'Honi' Coles**, and the **Nicholas Brothers**.

Other famous tap dancers not yet mentioned in this chapter are (in no particular order) Eddie Cantor, Carlos Hess, Eddie Leonard, Patty Hughes, Eddie Foy, Charles Shelton, George Cohen, Sammy Dyer, Pat Rooney, Jim Diamond, Buddy Ebsen, Nick Castle, Marilyn Miller, Martha Raye, Avon Long - dancer-singer-actor, George Murphy, the Ritz Brothers, Earl 'Fatha' Hines, Pegleg Bates (an extraordinary tap dancer whose left leg was a wooden pegleg), Tad Bebblejad, Prince Spencer, Brian Petersen, Vera Ellen, Dianne Walker, Omar Edwards, Baakari Wilder, and Derick Grant.

Tap Dance in Films:

- *42ⁿᵈ Street* – 1933, with Ruby Keeler, Ginger Rogers, choreographed by Busby Berkeley
- *An American in Paris* – 1951, with Gene Kelly, choreographed by Gene Kelly
- *Anchors Aweigh* – 1945, with Gene Kelly
- *Bamboozled* – 2000, with Savion Glover, Dormeshia Sumbry-Edwards, Cartier Williams, Baakari Wilder, directed by Spike Lee
- *The Bandwagon* – 1953, with Fred Astaire, Matt Mattox *(Photo Plate 11-2)*
- *The Belle of New York* – 1952, with Fred Astaire, Vera Ellen
- *Born to Dance* – 1936, with Buddy Ebsen, Eleanor Powell, James Stuart
- *Brigadoon* – 1954, with Fred Astaire
- *Broadway Melody of 1936,* with Buddy Ebsen, Vilma Ebsen, Eleanor Powell
- *Broadway Melody of 1938*, with Buddy Ebsen, George Murphy, Eleanor Powell
- *Broadway Melody of 1940,* with Fred Astaire, George Murphy, Eleanor Powell
- *Cabin in the Sky* – 1943, with Bill Bailey, John (William Sublett) Bubbles, Henry Phace Roberts
- *Café Metropole* – 1937, with Bill Robinson, Geneva Sawyer
- *Colleen* – 1936, with Paul Draper, Ruby Keeler *(Photo Plate 11-3)*
- *The Cotton Club* – 1984, with Gregory Hines, Maurice Hines, Charles Honi Coles, James Buster Brown, Ralph Brown, Harold Cromer, Bubba Gaines, Deborah Mitchell, Henry Phace Roberts, Sandman Sims, Jimmy Slyde, Henry LeTang
- *Cover Girl* – 1944, with Gene Kelly, Rita Hayworth
- *Dimples* – 1936, with Shirley Temple, choreographed by Bill Robinson

Howard "Sandman" Sims, tap dancer and NEA
National Heritage Fellow; photo by NEA, 1984.

"Chocolat dansant," by Henri de Toulouse-Lautrec
(1864-1901). Chocolat dancing in the Irish and
American bar, from La Rire, 1896. Chocolat was a black
clown from Bilbao who toured Europe with an English
partner, Footit. Each night after their show at the
"Nouveau Cirque" in Paris they would go to the Irish
and American bar to sing and dance just for fun. The
barman (seen standing to the left) Randolphe, known as
Ralph, was of Chinese and Native American descent,
born in San Francisco.

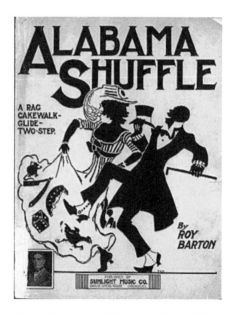

Fred Astaire in his famous routine with the hat rack
stand in MGM's "Royal Wedding," 1951, to Burton
Lane's composition, "Sunday Jump," choreographed by
Nick Castle.

Sheet Music Cover: "Alabama Shuffle." Composer: Roy
Barton; Publisher: Chicago, Ill.: Sunlight Music Co.,
1910.

- *Dixiana* – 1930, choreographed by Pearl Easton and Bill Robinson
- *Down Argentine Way* – 1940, with Betty Grable, Nicholas Brothers, musical numbers staged by Nick Castle and Geneva Sawyer
- *Easter Parade* – 1948, with Fred Astaire, Ann Miller, Jeni LeGon, Judy Garland, musical numbers staged by Robert Alton
- *Flying Down to Rio* – 1933, with Fred Astaire, Ginger Rogers
- *Follow the Fleet* – 1936, with Fred Astaire, Ginger Rogers
- *Footlight Parade* – 1933, with James Cagney, Ruby Keeler, choreographed by Busby Berkeley
- *For Me and My Gal* – 1942, with Judy Garland, Gene Kelly, directed by Busby Berkeley
- *Funny Face* – 1957, with Fred Astaire, choreographed by Eugene Loring and Fred Astaire
- *Go Into Your Dance* – 1935, with Ruby Keeler, Al Jolson
- *Happy Feet* – 2006; (an animated film about penguins and the environment) Savion Glover and the other tappers helping out on this film were wired and connected somehow to a computer so the animation people could get a very accurate sense of what the tappers were doing, and they were asked to keep their heads up, although many tappers prefer looking down, especially students)
- *Harlem Is Heaven* – 1932, with Bill 'Bojangles' Robinson
- *Hooray for Love* – 1935, with Jeni LeGon, Bill 'Bojangles' Robinson
- *It's Always Fair Weather* – 1955, with Gene Kelly, Dan Dailey, directed by Stanley Donen and Gene Kelly
- *Just Around the Corner* – 1938, with Bill 'Bojangles' Robinson, Shirley Temple
- *Kid Millions* – 1954, with George Murphy, Nicholas Brothers
- *Kiss Me Kate* – 1953, with Ann Miller, Bob Fosse, choreographed by Hermes Pan and Bob Fosse
- *Lady Be Good* – 1941, with Eleanor Powell, choreographed by Eleanor Powell
- *The Little Colonel* – 1935, with Bill 'Bojangles' Robinson, Shirley Temple
- *Little Miss Broadway* – 1938, with George Murphy, Shirley Temple
- *The Littlest Rebel* – 1935, with Bill 'Bojangles' Robinson, Shirley Temple
- *Look for the Silver Lining* – 1949, with Ray Bolger
- *Moon Over Miami* – 1941, with Condos Brothers, Betty Grable
- *My Sister Eileen* – 1955, with Bob Fosse, Tommy Raal, choreographed by Bob Fosse
- *New Faces of 1937* – 1937, with Ann Miller, Three Chocolateers
- *On Your Toes* – 1939, with Donald O'Connor, dance direction by George Balanchine
- *Orchestra Wives* – 1942, with Nicholas Brothers
- *Pin-Up Girl* – 1944, with the Condos Brothers, Betty Grable (*Photo Plate 11-2*)
- *Rebecca of Sunnybrook Farm* – 1938, with Dixie Dunbar, Bill 'Bojangles' Robinson, Shirley Temple
- *Reveille with Beverly* – 1943, with Ann Miller
- *Roberta* – 1935, with Fred Astaire, Ginger Rogers

- *Robin and the Seven Hoods* – 1964, with Sammy Davis, Jr.
- *Royal Wedding* – 1951, with Fred Astaire
- *The Seven Little Foys* – 1955, with James Cagney, Bob Hope
- *Ship Ahoy* – 1942, with Eleanor Powell, Stump and Stumpy
- *Silk Stockings* – 1957, with Fred Astaire
- *Singin' in the Rain* – 1952, with Donald O'Connor, Gene Kelly, directed by Stanley Donen and Gene Kelly
- *Six Hits and a Miss* – 1942, with Paul Draper, Ruby Keeler
- *Stage Door Canteen* – 1944, with Ray Bolger
- *Stand Up and Cheer* – 1934, with James Dunn, Shirley Temple
- *Stormy Weather* – 1943, with the Nicholas Brothers, Taps Miller, Henry Phase Robert, Bill 'Bojangles' Robinson, musical numbers staged by Nick Castle
- *Summer Stock* – 1950, with Judy Garland, Gene Kelly
- *Sun Valley Serenade* – 1941, with the Nicholas Brothers
- *Swing Time* – 1936, with Fred Astaire, Ginger Rogers
- *Tap* – 1988, with Bunny Briggs, Steve Condos, Sammy Davis, Jr., Arthur Duncan, Savion Glover, Jane Goldberg, Gregory Hines, Frances Nealy, the Nicholas Brothers, Sandman Sims, Jimmy Slyde, Diane Walker, Dorothy Wasserman
- *This Is the Army* – 1943, with Harold Cromer, George Murphy
- *Thousands Cheer* – 1944, with Judy Garland, Gene Kelly, Eleanor Powell
- *Top Hat* – 1935, with Fred Astaire, Ginger Rogers
- *Varsity Show* – 1937, with Buck and Bubbles
- *Wake Up and Live* – 1937, with the Condos Brothers
- *West Point Story* – 1950, with James Cagney, Gene Nelson
- *White Nights* – 1985, with Gregory Hines, choreographed by Twyla Tharp
- *Words and Music* – 1948, with Vera-Ellen, Gene Kelly
- *Yankee Doodle Dandy* – 1942, with James Cagney, dances for James Cagney choreographed by Johnny Boyle *(Photo Plate 11-2)*
- *Ziegfeld Follies* – 1936, with Fred Astaire, Gene Kelly.

Photo Plate 11-6

"Cool looking dancer makes a difficult jump." Photo by ayakovlevcom.

The Dance Theater "Young Tramps," choreography by Don Oscar Becque, music by Donald Pond, A Federal Dance Theater Project.

Sheet Music Cover "Tambourine Dance," composed by Joaquin Valverde, Spanish, 1917.

Balasaraswati in the classical Indian dance form Barata Natyam. Undated photo from the Jacob's Pillow Dance Festival, Beckett, Massachusetts.

Igor Stravinsky, composer of "Petrouchka" (1910-1911), "The Rite of Spring," and others.

# 12

# More Modern Dance –

## the Avant Garde

The early modern dance choreographers were often women, but by the 1940's and 50's most of the choreographers were men – **Alvin Ailey**, **Donald McKayle**, **Paul Taylor**, **Eleo Pomare**, **Rod Rodgers**, **Louis Johnson**, **Murray Louis**, **Merce Cunningham**, **David Parsons**, and **Alwin Nikolais**, to name a few. In addition, audiences and employment were increasing. (This, of course, was before the recession of 2008.) Grants were now obtainable from foundations, corporations, and the government. Dance could be seen at home on television, and there were many VCRs and then DVDs of dance concerts or of films with dancing, many of which could be obtained from public libraries free of charge. And since the creation of YouTube in 2005, snatches of new ballets, even from foreign countries, can also be seen on the Internet on YouTube videos. These are wonderful alternatives but there is nothing like a live performance.

Here are a few characteristics of modern dance. Creativity is encouraged. There is usually no turnout in the legs. The ground is used to move on in all sorts of ways, rolling or moving the whole body on it. The choreography for a company is often all done by the artistic director of the company, such as **Kei Takei** or **Erick Hawkins,** rather than by a variety of artists, as in the **Alvin Ailey** American Dance Theater. The music and dance may be independent of each other, as in the **Cunningham-Cage** collaborations, where the collaborators did not get together till the premiere of the new work.

**Donald McKayle** (b. 1930), a black American, was one of the many choreographers whose works were performed by the Alvin Ailey Dance Company. **McKayle** had won a scholarship to the New Dance Group that enabled him to study with **Pearl Primus, Jean Erdman**, and **Sophie Maslow** of the **Dudley-Maslow-Bales** Trio. Together with **Daniel Nagrin, Donald McKayle** started the Contemporary Dance Group for which he choreographed *Games* (1951), one of his best-loved pieces. In it he combined street games and play songs while exploring poverty and discrimination. Much of his choreography looked into the black experience in America. In the 1950's he performed with **Martha Graham** *(Photo Plate 12-3)*, **Merce Cunningham** *(Photo Plate 12-1)*, **Anna Sokolow**, and **Charles Weidman** *(Photo Plates 12-1 and 12-4)*. On Broadway he appeared in the original *West Side Story*. He directed and choreographed *Raisin* (1974), winning a Tony for best musical. He has choreographed works for companies in South America, Israel, Canada, and Europe. He was Professor of Dance and Artistic Director of the Dance Troupe at the University of California at Irvine. For all his work in dance he was named by the Library of Congress and the Dance Heritage Coalition as "one of America's Irreplaceable Dance Treasures."

**Eleo Pomare** (1937-2008), a Colombian-American, was another talented modern dance choreographer. He attended New York City's High School of Performing Arts and achieved acclaim for his choreography depicting the experiences of black people: *Blues for the Jungle* (1966, about life in Harlem), and *Narcissus Rising* (1968, a solo dance portraying the psychology of a member of a motorcycle gang), were two of his best.

The Alpha Omega Theatrical Dance Company, founded in 1972, has been since 1988 under the artistic direction of **Enrique Cruz DeJesus**, a former member of **Eleo Pomare**'s company. They occasionally perform some of Pomare's works. In 2012 they performed Pomare's *Radeau (Raft, 1994,* a depiction of 3 Haitian women leaving their previous life and journeying to a new one amid fears and the rhythm of the sea). The music is a collage by Johnathon Kabak. The performers were **Shauntée Henry**, **Donna Clark**, and **Brandi Stewart**. This appealing company performed at the Manhattan Movement and Arts Center and enabled us to appreciate Pomare's imagination.

The State Department of the United States sent the **Alvin Ailey** American Dance Theater to Asia and Australia in 1962 and then in 1970 to North Africa, Europe and the Soviet Union as cultural ambassadors. They were very well received.

The company survived after the death of its founder, **Alvin Ailey** (whom you read about in chapter 7) *(Photo Plate 12-4)*, and remained very strong under the artistic direction of **Judith Jamison** (b. 1943). As a performer with the company she was especially notable in *Cry* (1971) and *Masekala Language* (1969). She has choreographed many works for the Alvin Ailey Company – *Divining* (1984), *Forgotten Time* (1989), and *Hymn* (1993), among others. When Jamison retired in July 2011, she was elevated to artistic director emerita; choreographer **Robert Battle** became the artistic director; the associate artistic director is still Japanese-born **Masazumi Chaya**, a former Ailey dancer.

The first three revolutions in modern dance (mentioned in chapter 7) were the soloists, the new techniques, and then the techniques and companies of **Doris Humphrey**, **Charles Weidman**, **Jose Limon**, and **Martha Graham** in the 1920's and 30's *(Photo Plates 12-1, 3, and 4)*. The fourth revolution in modern dance was the avant-garde modern dance, also called postmodern dance. Many of the avant-garde choreographers accepted the techniques of the first modern dancers, but they were not interested in story-telling or in emotions; they usually wanted movement for itself. They wanted to extend their range just as modern art extended its range through the use of collage along with the usual paints and watercolors, permitting the use of buttons, wires, netting, and newspaper cutouts, while musicians used "prepared pianos," as **John Cage** did, or built their own instruments as did **Lucia Dlugoszewski**, **Erick Hawkins**' composer, or composed their own music on a Moog synthesizer, which is what **Alwin Nikolais** did. They wished to explore, for example, what to do with a cardboard box or with a skirt (sometimes nothing particularly interesting). They wished to extend their space to include parks, museums, and rooftops, following the examples of **Meredith Monk** and **Anna Halprin**.

Photo Plate 12-1

Portrait of Charles Weidman by Carl van Vechten, 1933.

Philadelphia Dance Company performs "Enemy Behind the Gates" by Christopher Higgins. From left to right are: Teneise Mitchell, Mora Amina Parker, Erin Barnette, Erin Moore, and Tracy Vog. Date: 2008. Photo by Lois Greenfield. This image is a work of the NEA. The company, also known as the Philadanco, is a professional dance company founded in 1970 by Joan Myers Brown.

Poster of Merce Cunningham and Dance Company, Brooklyn Academy of Music, 1969, Poster designed by Robert Rauschenberg.

Denishawn Dancers, created by Bain News Service, ca.1920.

Erick Hawkins (1909-1994) was the first male dancer in **Martha Graham**'s Company. They got married in 1948 but separated in 1950 due to artistic differences. He was very impressed by Mary Ellsworth Todd's book *The Thinking Body: A Study of the Balancing Forces of Dynamic Man*, which implied that almost no effort was needed to move if proper alignment was used; relaxation and concentration could assist in attaining this alignment. He believed that dance technique should never be harmful to the body and he had a huge following. His choreography was beautiful. His first piece, *Here and Now with Watchers* (1957), was a full-length work. He also choreographed *Eight Clear Places* (1960), *Black Lake* (1969), and *Plains Daybreak* (1979). He wanted his pieces to show cohesiveness between his imagination and nature and he often blended repetitious patterns with moments of stillness. His choreography bored some and fascinated others. He used music created specifically for his works. **Lucia Dlugoszewski** (1931-2000, who became his second wife) composed pieces to suit his works, using a "prepared piano," all sorts of sounds such as the tearing of paper, and many percussive instruments she had invented. Hawkins' company often used masks by Ralph Dorazio; they were very well designed, airy, and attractive; the dancers could easily see what was around while wearing one of them. When Hawkins died, **Lucia Dlugoszewski** took over the company and even did some choreography for it.

**Alwin Nikolais** (1910-1993) started to dance as a result of having seen a **Wigman** performance. He studied with **Hanya Holm** and eventually became co-director of modern dance at the Henry Street Playhouse in 1948 (now part of the Abrons Art .Center). He was against the psychological approach to modern dance (as best used by Martha Graham). He differentiated between the qualities of, for example, an arm movement reaching for a light feather or for a heavy stone. He then used these movements without reference to the feather or the stone. He referred to the following as "primary" emotions: heavy, light; thick, thin; large, small; fast, and slow. **Nikolais** preferred electronic sounds for music because they lacked emotional content. He himself created a total theatre of lighting, design, motion, props, electronic music, and costumes. His repertory included *Totem* (1960), *Imago* (1963), *Graph* (1984), and *Velocities* (1986). His choreography, as in *Tent* (1968), seemed to take into account the various fabrics and the lights as well as the dancers.

A successful European tour led to an invitation by the French Ministry of Culture to start a training program in France. He created *Scheme* for the Paris Opera in 1980. French critics praised him as being "the most original exponent of American contemporary dance."

Meanwhile, in the United States he received the Kennedy Center Honor in 1987 and was also inducted into the Hall of Fame of the National Museum of Dance in Saratoga, New York, in 2000.

**Nikolais** occasionally had the performers wear masks (*Masks, Props, and Mobiles*, 1954), or had a play of lights on the performers. He clad them in stretch material that covered several of the dancers. The performer was no longer an individual but a new unit. There were no star performers in this company. **Nikolais** believed that emotion did not cause a dance movement but was the result of the movement. The audience had fewer preconceptions and so looked at the movement with fresh eyes without bringing their own lives into the picture *(Photo Plate 12-5)*.

His ingenious imagination made his modern dance style appealing and entertaining. His inspired work influenced many, including the choreographers of Pilobolus and Momix. The Ririe-Woodbury Dance Company of Salt Lake City, for which Nikolais often served as guest teacher, has preserved many of his works.

**Murray Louis** (b. 1926), who worked with **Nikolais** from the start, had incredible muscular control and a sense of comedy as seen in his *Junk Dances* (1964). In 1969 he formed his own company. *Hoopla* (1972) was another humorous piece of his. Besides his dancing and choreography, he is also the author of several dance books, *Inside Dance* (1989), and *On Dance* (1995), and varied videos: a 5-part video, *The World of Dance* (1996), and *Dance as an Art Form.* He received honorary degrees from Ohio University (1999) and from Rutgers University (2000).

**Merce Cunningham** (1919-2009) used random chance to find new combinations of movements. Sometimes he wrote down each movement on a different piece of paper and chose the order by flipping a coin. Sometimes he used chance as a means of choosing the speed or direction of a movement or the length of time of a moment of stillness, or which parts of the body to move together or which segments from his works to place one after the other as Event No. 1, or Event No. 2 on a program. Naturally the choreographer had to intervene and make a choice if a performer was instructed, by chance, to lie down and then to leap up. As a dancer, Cunningham could do phenomenal jumps. He was the second male dancer to have been selected by **Martha Graham** to dance in her company.

To make sure that the music was not emotional, **Cunningham** choreographed without music. His long-time collaborator, **John Cage** (1912-1992), an influential, experimental, and controversial musician, composed separately. An ancient Chinese book, *The Book of Changes,* introduced Cage and Cunningham to the idea of chance as a way of organizing their dance and music. After they had agreed on the length of time of the music, say ten minutes, but before the basic beat was set, the instrumentalist could play as little or as much of the music as he wished as long as it lasted for the agreed length of time. Cunningham had excellent dancers in his company and they did not seem to mind being presented with the leg movements one day, torso the next day, and arm movements on the third day. At performances, Cage's sounds (he used "prepared pianos," with pieces of wood, metal, or rubber inserted between the piano strings to change the sounds) and Cunningham's disconnected motions startled audiences, and many walked out while others were captivated. But for Cage and Cunningham it was a way to escape from making the usual choices. Any movement was as acceptable as the next one, and audiences and the dancers themselves were continuously surprised.

The Neo-Dadaist artist **Robert Rauschenberg** (1925-2008), painter and printmaker who experimented with avant-garde ideas and techniques, collaborated with Cunningham beginning in 1954 and once designed a matching backdrop and costumes for *Summerspace* (1958) so that dancers and background all merged. The dance had lyrical movements, many classical steps as well as runs, skips, turns, and leaps against Rauschenberg's pointillistic backdrop of soft colors that he also used on the leotards and tights of the dancers. The score by Morton Feldman indicated the tonal range and timing, but not the exact notes to be played. **Cunningham**'s series called *Events* came about when the company visited Vienna and found that the required exits and entrances for a piece were nonexistent, so he simply changed the program by omitting the first dance, or at least the section that required the nonexistent exits and entrances, tacked miscellaneous sections of different works of his, one after the other, and called the new dance Event No. 1, and this led to others: Nos. 2, 3, 4. (For example, Event No. 1 might use the first section of *Antic Meet,* then include the middle section of *Duets* and finish with the ending of *Summerspace*.) The dancers found out about the sequence on the day of the performance. They were always excellent, talented, well trained dancers, and very adaptable. Cage died in 1992; Cunningham went on to choreograph for several years. They both changed the way people thought about dance and music. They gave dance complete independence from story, music, and set emotions *(Photo Plate 12-1)*.

Even the audience had to decide what to do at a **Cunningham** concert; one could listen to someone reciting jokes slowly, or quickly, or watch this person dancing, or that one. His choreography also included very long, demanding, slow balances to contrast with the fast sections. Some of his pieces were provocative enough for reviewers to worry that an audience might actually resort to throwing tomatoes and eggs at the performers when the booing was as loud as the hoorays, but it never happened.

Those of you who attended concerts of **Merce Cunningham**'s works in the year 2011 were the lucky ones because the company will not perform during any other year in the future. Cunningham issued an order that after his death his company would perform for two more years and then break up. However, the Merce Cunningham Trust, established in 2000, holds the rights to Cunningham's works (over 140 dances and 800 "Events"), and will, in the future, offer Cunningham classes in New York City, license works to dance companies and educational institutions all over the world, and will also present exhibitions, performances and projects at cultural sites, to honor the achievements of **Merce Cunningham**.

Cunningham died in 2009. In March 2011 the members of his company appeared at The Joyce Theater in a 1958 work that had last been seen in 1969, *Antic Meet,* costumes and décor by Robert Rauschenberg and music by John Cage. They received excellent reviews for all the performances of *Antic Meet* as well as for the piece *CRWDSPC*, considered by Roslyn Sulcas of *The New York Times* to be a "spellbinding" work. The Cunningham Company had been founded in Durham, NC, in 1953, and it performed in Durham for the last time in February 2011. One of the pieces seen there was *Duets* (1980). Cunningham duets are among the best in the dance world, with rules as intricate as those for the Olympic Ice Dances: no overhead lifts, partners cannot be more than a yard apart, sometimes the two must do the same steps at the same time, or she must dance separately but return to him for support. Two of the other works performed in Durham were favorites: *Sounddance* (1975) and *Biped* (1999). The dancers had rehearsed these with Cunningham himself but he had allowed them to give their own nuances to the Cunningham was a Kennedy Center Honoree in 1985 and that same year he was awarded a MacArthur Fellowship Award (nicknamed the "genius" award).

A MacArthur Fellowship Award has been given each year by The John D. and Catherine T. Foundation since 1981 to from twenty to twenty-five individuals a year who are passionate about and very creative in whatever their field or occupation happens to be. Each recipient is given $625,000 (till 2013 the stipend was $500,000) in a no-strings-attached support that is given to the recipient over five years. One does not

Photo Plate 12-2

Avant garde modern dance was often
involved with discovering new
things to do with, for example, a
wall, or a cardboard box, or as
shown here, a dance skirt. For some
choreographers this led to very
innovative ideas.
Dancer: Helene Andreu;
Photographs by Enia.

apply for this award; the recipients, who have ranged in age from 18 to 82, are nominated and then chosen by a committee of the MacArthur Foundation. Avant-garde modern dancers are creative by nature and vocation and have won an impressive number of MacArthur Fellowship Awards.

As a result of their approach to dance, some choreographers, especially the avant-garde choreographers such as **Nikolais** and **Cunningham,** were accused of dehumanization. They denied this charge. On the contrary, they felt they were letting the audience partake of the experience. In the 1940's they had found dance too similar to drama. Now the audience could see what they saw; if it was pure dance, good. If it was a story, it was the audience who assisted in forming it through their thoughts while watching the dance *(Photo Plate 12-5)*.

**Paul Taylor**'s first piece in a concert consisted of standing still on stage for a certain length of time, whereupon John Martin's review in *The New York Times* consisted of a certain amount of space without any print at all – empty. Taylor's work *Epic* was performed to telephone sounds such as "at the tone," or "the time will be." He also used sounds of rain instead of music for a dance for two girls.

**Paul Taylor** (b. 1930) *(Photo Plate 12-5)* was an art major at Syracuse University. He danced in **Martha Graham**'s Company for several years but left in 1962 to found his own company. His style was often humorous and light, but not always; it could also be cruel, dark, or witty. However, it has always been excellent. He has used music from Haydn, Bach, Offenbach, Vivaldi, the Andrew sisters, the tango, and popular fun songs such as *She Wore a Teeny Weeny Itsy Bitsy Yellow Polka Dot Bikini*. His dancers are always on the beat to whatever music he chooses for his choreography, and they point their feet and look ballet trained, are extremely talented, and able to do anything he gives them. He created *Aureole* (1962) for the American Dance Festival. It was not his favorite dance but everyone else loved it and it has been added to the repertoire of many ballet companies. His next piece, *Orbs* (1966), was about the planets. *Big Bertha* (1970) with **Bettie de Jong**, a tall, talented soloist from his original company, was about a typical American family and a malevolent, weird nickelodeon. (*Orbs*, *Esplanade* and *Aureole* were revived in 2011.) Taylor stopped dancing because of health problems but his creative choreography continued to be brilliant. In 1975 his best-loved work, *Esplanade (Photo Plate 12-5),* with **Carolyn Adams** (a petite black dancer and another one of the original members of his company who remained in Taylor's company as a lead dancer till she retired) was a presentation of movements called run, leap, get caught, cradled, and sent along. It was set to five movements from two Bach concertos. By the time this format was used in duets on the 21st century TV program *So You Think You Can Dance*, it had become: run, catch, and throw away – why the difference? It probably depended on whether the duet was about happy love or hate love.

**Taylor** has also played with going through a dance twice, as far as the choreography is concerned, while changing the mood, the music, or the dancers, as in *Airs* (1978) and in *Polaris* (1976). In April 2009 he presented a new and hilarious work called *Now Playing,* guaranteed to provide his audience with escapism from their depressing economic problems. His other new work for the season was *Beloved Renegade*, a beautiful piece to Offenbach's music. A new work for 2011 was *Three*

*Dubious Memories,* in which a sex-and-violence story was told three different ways as in the Kurosawa film *Rashomon,* with each character's account differing from the previous version; the dance included a chorus moving in a style of comment and reaction. The music, taped, was *Five Enigmas,* Movements 1, 3, 4, and 5, by Peter Elyakim.

Critics appreciate **Taylor**'s musicality and the great variety of his choices of music and steps. And so does his audience. The Paul Taylor Dance Company had a memorable season in 2012, its first time at Lincoln Center, at the David H. Koch Theater. Outstanding dancers in the company included **Michael Trusnovec, Amy Young, James Samson, Sean Mahoney, Eran Bugge, Parisa Khobdeh, Laura Halzak, Michelle Fleet, Francisco Graziano, Heather McGinley, Michael Novak, Jamie Rae Walker, Jeffrey Smith**, and **Robert Kleinendorst** in a season that incorporated many favorite pieces by **Paul Taylor**, some of which had not been performed by the company for a while. These were *Aureole* (1962), *Piazzolla Caldera* (1997, about the world of the tango), *House of Cards* (1981, integrating social dances of the 1920's), *Mercuric Tidings* (1982, pure dance to music from Schubert's first two symphonies), *3 Epitaphs* (1956, the oldest work in this repertoire and performed to jazz music), *Oh, You Kid* (1999, evoking the ragtime era), *Beloved Renegade* (2008, about a man's observations on love, war, pain, and death), *Troilus and Cressida* (2006, a comedy danced to Ponchielli's *Dance of the Hours*), *Big Bertha* (1970, a nasty sort of nickelodeon and its tragic effect on a family's life), *Roses* (1985, to music by Richard Wagner), *House of Joy* (2012, "shady ladies " of a brothel, to sleazy jazz music by Donald York who was the former music director of Taylor's Company), *The Uncommitted* (2012, a somber piece set to Arvo Pärt's *Fratres* and three other Pärt scores), *Gossamer Gallants* (2012, a comedy about mating insects, to music from Smetana's opera *The Bartered Bride* and with sets by Santo Loquasto), *Brandenburgs* (1988, to music from two of Bach's Brandenburg concertos). There is tremendous diversity in this repertoire. Paul Taylor was awarded a MacArthur Fellowship Award in 1985 and was a Kennedy Center Honoree for 1992.

An excellent documentary called *Paul Taylor Dancemaker* (1999) by Matthew Diamond shows rehearsals and a performance by **Paul Taylor**'s company

**Taylor**, at age 83, in 2013, and celebrating the 60th anniversary of his company, announced plans to restructure it so it could survive many more decades. The company, Paul Taylor's American Modern Dance, would present his works, but not exclusively. It would become a repertory company and include great American modern dance masterpieces of the past, by **Doris Humphrey, Martha Graham**, and others, as well as dances by choreographers of the future.

**Gus Solomons, Jr.** (b. 1940), a black American dancer and choreographer, danced with **Martha Graham, Pearl Lang, Donald McKayle, Joyce Trisler**, and **Merce Cunningham**. In his choreography his background in architecture can be seen in his use of space and dance patterns. He has also dealt with aspects of modern life that have had a negative effect on society. He is the artistic director of the dance group Paradigm.

Paradigm is a modern dance performance ensemble founded in 1998 by **Carmen de Lavallade** (b. 1931), **Gus Solomons Jr.** (artistic director), **Karen Brown, Michael Blake, Valda Setterfield, Dudley Williams** (d. 2015), and guest artists **Hope Clarke** and **Martine Van Hamel**. Paradigm offers new and previous audiences a chance to see these exemplary performers in recent works, such as *Tango With Ghosts*, **Kate Weare**'s *Idyll*, **Gus Solomons'** *Royalty Redux*, and *A Thin Frost*. They aim to promote the talents of mature stage artists and show the eloquence brought forth by years of experience, while at the same time developing the creativity of young choreographers.

**David Parsons** (b. 1971), a former member of **Paul Taylor**'s Company (1978-1987), founded the Parsons Dance Co. in 1987. He is a dancer-choreographer with a light, humorous touch. *Caught* (1987) is fun and looks like someone walking mid-air with the help of a strobe light and blackouts; another amusing piece of choreography is *Envelope Passing* (1986). He also choreographed for a New Year's Eve 2000 celebration and for a daylong celebration of New Year's Day in New York City's Times Square on January 1, 2001. Numerous companies worldwide have performed his works. He received a *Dance Magazine* Award for 2000. In 2001 he was appointed artistic director of dance for the Umbria Jazz Festival in Perugia, Italy, and choreographed *Aida* at the Arena di Verona, Italy, in 2007. His company performed at the Joyce Theatre in NY in 2014.

**Robert Battle** (b. 1973), a black American, studied at Juilliard and then joined David Parsons' company and danced and choreographed for them from 1994 to 2001. He creatods several works for the Alvin Ailey American Dance Theater and the Alvin Ailey Dance School since 1999. Some of these are: *Juba* (2003), *Love Stories* (2004, choreographed by Jamison, Battle, and Rennie Harris), *Unfold* (2005), and *In/Side* (2008). He is known for the variety in his choreography, his ability to attract audiences, and his excellent rapport with dancers. He was selected to replace **Judith Jamison** when she retired in July 2011 as the director of the Alvin Ailey Dance Theater. He knew the Ailey Company and was also expected to bring something different to it. His presence was acknowledged at the gala opening of the Ailey Company at the City Center on December 1, 2010, with a performance of his work *The Hunt*, which he created in 2001. It was a perfect choice for the Ailey Company, showing off the men's athleticism and virtuosity. His short speech made obvious that his charisma and ease were comparable to Ms. Jamison's. She chose an excellent replacement. For Robert Battle's inaugural season at the City Center, the Ailey dancers performed their first Taylor work, his masterpiece *Arden Court* (1981) set to baroque music by William Boyce. **Paul Taylor**, as well as **Carolyn Adams** (Battle's teacher at Juilliard and a former Taylor dancer) were both great inspirations to Robert Battle as a student. The six bare-chested males performing in *Arden Court* were the personification of Taylor's beefy male ideal and did such wonderful leaps that Taylor added an extra leap to the piece as an exit when he saw the rehearsal. Another new piece was the premiere of **Rennie Harris'** work *Home* to commemorate World AIDS Day and which was also in memory of Ailey who died of the disease on Dec. 1, 1989. Ailey had always envisioned his company as a repository for great works of earlier modern dance. **Robert Battle** seems to be keeping this in mind with his programming. The sexy dancing of the Ailey Company was brought out by his choice of **Lar Lubovitch**'s *Prelude to the Kiss,* danced by **Clifton Brown** and **Linda Celeste Sims**. *Chroma* (2006), by British choreographer **Wayne McGregor** was another very successful addition to the repertoire in 2013.

Ailey's second company, Ailey II, is full of talented dancers ready to advance into the main troupe. After 38 years as the nurturing artistic director of Ailey II, **Sylvia Waters** retired in June 2012 and was replaced by **Troy Powell** who has choreographed several successful pieces, including *Reference Point* (music by Mio Morales) for Ailey II.

**Anna Halprin** (b. 1920) is an avant-garde choreographer and teacher who used happenings and rituals that could look unpredictable or disorganized. She occasionally had an ad in the *New York Times* that a happening would go on at Central Park on two specified Sundays, at 2:00 pm; anyone could go to participate or just to watch. And of course, even if her dancers did some planned movements each time, the outcome always looked different depending on whether half of the people who attended the happening had decided to try her movements, or whether they had done their own movements, or they had sat in the center and watched.

With **happenings,** anyone could get into the dance field, and thus began the vocabulary of the pedestrian movement. In fact a few of the choreographers who started their companies told their dancers not to study with anyone, so as to achieve the look of untrained dancers for their works. This had definite limitations. Most dancer-choreographers taught, but now the dancers in their own companies could not study with them; this was not good for finances. Any of the dancers who started liking dance and wished to do more or do better could not remain in the company if they appeared to have been studying dance.

Eventually most of these dancer-choreographers saw the light, and some, like **Garth Fagan** (b. 1940), Jamaican-born, even insisted that the dancers in Garth Fagan Dance take company classes daily. As a result, Fagan has an excellent company that is well trained. He feels that the speed of movement comes from ballet, the rhythm and the movements from the Afro-Caribbean, and the center from modern. Interesting, because some think the centeredness comes from ballet. Many would agree that his best work is *Griot: New York* (1991), to a commissioned score by Wynton Marsalis. His work *Madiba*, to a score by Abdullah Ibrahim, which premiered at the Joyce Theater in 2011, and which honors Mandela's strength and perseverance, is meant to be an inspirational dance for survival and change rather than a documentary about Mandela's life. Garth's piece *No Evidence of Failure* (2013) to a recording of jazz and reggae by Monty Alexander, included a solo for **Natalie Rogers**, a dancer returning to Fagan's company and still brilliant after an eight-year break; his dancers all attribute their skill to Fagan's technique classes. **Garth Fagan** was also the choreographer of the Broadway show *The Lion King* that won the Outer Critics Circle Award and the Tony Award for Best Choreography for 1998. This musical, based on the animated film of 1994 by Disney, had music by Elton John and lyrics by Tim Rice. The Director, Julie Taymor, won a 1998 Theatre World Award for Best Director of a musical, and together with Michael Curry, Julie Taymor won an Award for Outstanding Costume Design of a musical.

. **Norwood Pennewell**, with Garth Fagan Dance for over 39 years, is the only other person to have choreographed for the company (*Liminal Flux*, 2011, set to music by Miles Davis and Chancha Via Circuito). It premiered on the same date as Fagan's *Madiba* and followed Pennewell's choreographic debut of 2010, *Hylozoic*, which was a success.

The Judson Dance Theater of the 1960's and 1970's was comprised of artists, composers, and dancers who felt that dance did not have to take place in the theater. It did not require sets, costumes, equipment, or training. The Judson Dance Theater came out of a class in dance composition given by **Robert Dunn**, a musician who had studied with John Cage. Performances took place in lofts, museums, parks, rooftops, or on a raft on a lake. Performers wore street shoes and, later, sneakers. The Judson Dance Theater

Photo Plate 12-3

Daniel Nagrin in his work, "Indeterminate Figure, 1957." Photographer unknown.

Martha Graham and Bertram Ross, Photo by Carl van Vechten, 1961.

Rudolf von Laban (1879-1958), unknown photographer.

Ruth St. Denis, photo by Arnold Genthe (1869-1947), taken in 1913.

had a great impact on postmodern dance. The focus was often on intellectualizing abstract dance and its creation. Its first performance in 1962 at the Judson Memorial Church was free of charge; at that time it was a co-operatively produced dance performance, but it eventually veered off in many different directions, led to post-modern dance, and even into doing choreography for ballet companies.

There were many postmodern dancer-choreographers like **Anna Halprin** (Happenings); **Twyla Tharp** (b. 1941, *Bakers' Dozen,* 1979); **Trisha Brown** (b. 1936, equipment pieces with ropes, pulleys and cables, and *Roof Piece,* 1971); **Yvonne Rainer** (b. 1934, *No Manifesto,* 1965; *The Mind Is a Muscle, Part I,* 1966).

Another postmodern dancer-choreographer is **Meredith Monk** (b. 1942, *Juice,* 1969). This piece involved the making of frozen condensed orange juice; the performing spaces varied in size and location. The first part of the dance was presented on a large stage, perhaps to represent the orange grove, the next one medium-sized and the third and last was very small to represent a can of frozen juice. Meredith Monk used both taped and live sound in her productions.

Some examples of improvisational dancers are: **David Gordon** (b. 1936)**,** a founding member of the improvisational group The Grand Union. His *Field, Chair and Rainbow* (1985) for American Ballet Theatre included ballet dancers who were partnering folding chairs. He also did performance art. **Laura Dean** (b. 1945) does spins without focusing. **Steve Paxton** (b. 1939) does contact improvisation. **Lucinda Childs**, **Deborah Hay**, **Judith Dunn**, and **Aileen Passloff** are other performance artists.

Performance art has no rules. The artist says it is art; that is what makes it art. It is live and may include sculpture, dance, music, film, photography, and singing, and it may be studied in college. It can possibly entertain, upset, or amuse.

Contact improvisation first appeared on the New York scene in 1922. It was a means of working past one's inhibitions, getting used to partner work, and also practicing lifting, falling, being lifted, and accepting responsibility for one's partner, mentally as well as physically. It became an important part of many modern dance courses.

The Judson Memorial Church, located on Washington Square in New York City, has long promoted the arts, They held workshops for dancers and choreographers, and in the 1960's and 70's participants in these workshops arrived at the conclusion that dance could be any physical movement *(Photo Plate 12-2).* Choreographers would draw ideas from any source. The world had gotten smaller, so foreign sources were also acceptable.

In contrast to the rigorousness of postmodern dance, large productions were a surprising outcome after the 1960's. **Robert Wilson's** (b. 1941) "operas" were appreciated for their visual aspects and were a welcome change from the postmodern dances. Wilson is known as an avant-garde stage director and playwright. A donation from the French government made possible the premiere of *Einstein on the Beach* at the Avignon Festival (1976), a five-hour opera by **Robert Wilson** with music by Philip

Glass. It was later sold out at the Metropolitan Opera House performances and revived at the Brooklyn Academy of Music in 1984, 1992, and 2012-13. *Einstein on the Beach* has no story line. **Lucinda Childs** (b. 1940), the choreographer for the 1984, 1992, and 2012 versions of the "Field Dances," and the other dances in the opera, and **Andy deGroat** (b. 1947), the original choreographer, were the choreographers for all the dances, but Robert Wilson is the one who choreographed everything else in the scenes, including the stagehands' dance as they slowly assemble the set pieces. Some of the movements were extremely slow. Wilson's was a theatre of visual images.

Two new groups started at about this time, Pilobolus and Momix. Pilobolus was another outcome of the 1960's Judson Church ideals, that is, to not demonstrate technical virtuosity and to not have a star system. Pilobolus was very imaginative and successful. Momix was equally if not even more imaginative, fanciful, humorous, and was much loved by children too. Pilobolus Dance Theater was among the winners of the 53rd annual *Dance Magazine* Award in November, 2010. (Other winners were **Deborah Jowitt**, dance critic and historian, **Matthew Rushing**, an astounding dancer with Alvin Ailey American Dance Theater, and **Irina Kolpakova**, a ballet mistress at American Ballet Theater.)

**Martha Clarke** (b. 1944), a former dancer of **Sokolow**'s company, a Guggenheim Foundation grant recipient, and a former Pilobolus member, has enjoyed choreographing dramatic works. Her *Garden of Earthly Delights* of 1984 was a dance theater piece that journeyed through the world of the Dutch painter Hieronymus Bosch (1450-1516), as shown in his painting of the same name. The dance depicted a medieval world of heaven and hell in scenes that were either sensual, or coarse, or out of a nightmare, but certainly unexpected. The score was by Richard Peaslee. Clarke's work brought the original paintings to life in striking visual tableaux. She had a multidisciplinary approach to theater, opera, and dance and was awarded a MacArthur Fellowship award as theater director in 1990. She received what is considered to be the greatest life achievement award for choreography – the 2010 Samuel H. Scripps/American Dance Festival Award for Lifetime Achievement. Her work was compared to **Robert Wilson**'s in theatricality and is considered to be very painterly.

A more recent 70-minute dance-theater work of **Martha Clarke**'s is *Angel Reapers* (2011), which gives us an impressionistic interpretation of the Shakers' custom of worshiping through dance and song, and of the life and struggles of its founder, Ann Lee (1736-84). The script is by Alfred Uhry and is sung by the cast. A 2013 work by **Martha Clarke** is *Chéri,* a rapturous love story based on a novella by Colette, to piano music of Debussy, Poulenc and Ravel, and with expressive dancing by **Alessandra Ferri** and **Herman Cornejo**, formerly of American Ballet Theater.

A few postmodern (also called avant-garde) choreographers such as **Molissa Fenley, Elizabeth Streb**, and **Susan Marshall** have not been involved with the visual aspects of dance movement, as **Robert Wilson, Alison Chase**, or **Martha Clarke** had been, but with the intensity of physical activity.

**Molissa Fenley** (b. 1954). Her piece *Energizer* (1980) required great stamina in running, skipping and spinning movements and in circle or chain formations using music with a hypnotic beat.

**Elizabeth Streb** (b. 1950) has been even more physical and her performers swung from cables, leaped off platforms, or threw themselves against mattresses. Streb replaced music with the sounds of the dancers' landings, their grunts, and the noise from the stage props. They did not perform in theaters but in gymnasiums, malls or beach boardwalks, like the one in Coney Island. For her inventiveness as a dancer and choreographer she was given a MacArthur Fellowship Award in 1997.

**Susan Marshall** (b. 1958) has used pedestrian movements such as running and walking combined with contact improvisation. (Pedestrian is the correct term in postmodern dance when referring to such movements as walking or running. These movements are not meant to be considered dull or unimaginative.) She combined weightless lifts with heavy plunging movements. She was awarded a Bessie Award for her work *Opening Gamet* (1985) and became a MacArthur Fellowship Award winner in the year 2000.

Another winner of a Bessie Award, in 1986, was **Anna Theresa de Keersmaeker** (b. 1960), a Belgian of Flemish descent who studied at Béjart's Mudra school in Brussels and also at New York University's Tisch School of the Arts. She used varying degrees of energy as well as electronic sound, melodramatic lighting, repetitive movement, and almost no dance steps. She won her Bessie Award after her company performed *Rosas danst Rosas* for the New Wave Festival at the Brooklyn Academy of Music (BAM), thus also ensuring her reputation in experimental dance in Europe.

The New York Dance and Performance Awards, better known as The Bessie Awards, named after the dance educator and mentor **Bessie Schonberg** (1906-1997), were geared mainly toward honoring dancers and choreographers in experimental noncommercial work. However, since 2010, **Lucy Sexton**, a performer, director, choreographer, and co-founder of the dance and performance duo, Dancenoise, has been the producer of the Bessie Awards. The span of these awards was broadened to include all those people who contribute in various ways to the field of dance – performance, music composition, visual design – as well as ballet, Indian dancing, Broadway, lifetime achievement, and so on. The Bessie Award Committee consists of dance presenters, producers, journalists, and academics.

**Twyla Tharp** (b. 1941) trained with **Martha Graham** and with **Merce Cunningham** and performed with **Paul Taylor** from 1963 to 1965. She uses ballet, jazz, and tap in her pieces, and has occasionally had quirky dance combinations making fun of some steps. Her company does not dance barefoot but wears jazz shoes since the feet can stick to the floor when barefoot. Her choice of music has run from Philip Glass, a contemporary composer, to the Beach Boys, Jelly Roll Morton, Sinatra songs, and a Haydn symphony for a ballet commissioned by The American Ballet Theater. She has often used very precise legwork together with an appearance of nonchalance through the upper torso and arms. In sharp contrast to her early days of modern dance choreography, her later works have much more emotion and theatricality. Her works have been highly praised. *Deuce Coupe*, created in 1973 for the Joffrey Ballet Company to music by the Beach Boys, a 1960's rock group, made ballet and rock seem compatible. Her next most popular piece, *Push Comes to Shove* (1976), was choreographed for The American Ballet Theater and **Mikhail Baryshnikov,** who caught all the nuances in the starts and stops of her choreography and thoroughly enjoyed dancing this piece which for him was a new way of moving. Tharp choreographed for her own company, for the Joffrey Ballet, for

American Ballet Theater where she became artistic director for a short time, and for the 2002 Broadway show with Billy Joel's music, *Movin' Out*, which she also directed and for which she received the Tony Award for Best Choreography and for best direction of a musical, as well as the Astaire Award for Best Choreographer in 2003. She had previously choreographed for films like *Hair* (1979), *Ragtime* (1980), *Amadeus* (1984), and *White Nights* (1985). The New York City Ballet gave the premiere of Tharp's *The Beethoven Seventh* in 2000, and Pacific Northwest Ballet premiered *Waiting at the Station* (2013) in a triple bill of Twyla's pieces. She was the recipient of a MacArthur Fellowship Award in 1992 and in 2008 she was named a Kennedy Center Honoree. She used Sinatra's music in several of her works, *Nine Sinatra Songs*, *Once More Frank,* and *Sinatra Sings.* Then in 2010 she choreographed the musical *Come Fly Away* (originally called *Come Fly With Me*) for Broadway with Sinatra's music. Like *Movin' Out,* it had no dialogue. The choreography and the dancers conveyed the emotions from love to rage. Tharp won the Drama Desk Award for Outstanding Choreography, and **Karine Plantadit** was nominated for best Featured Actress in a Musical. Deborah Jowitt of *The Village Voice* raved about it and especially about the dancers: **Keith Roberts**, **John Selya**, **Rika Okamoto**, **Holly Farmer** (a former Cunningham dancer), **Charlie Neshyba-Hodges**, **Laura Mead**, **Ashley Tuttle**, **Matthew Dibble**, and **Karine Plantadit**. Nineteen live instrumentalists and two additional alternating vocalists were on stage and backed Frank Sinatra's recordings in this dance musical about four couples seeking love in a New York nightclub. It opened on March 25, 2010, and closed on September 5, 2010.

**Yvonne Rainer** (b. 1934) belonged to the Judson Dance Theater group. She wrote the *No Manifesto* in 1965, a written statement that influenced many dancers in the Judson Dance Theater Group. It suggested that modern dancers say "No" to all sorts of things that one usually sees at ballet concerts: smiling, facing the audience, acknowledging applause, virtuosity, and spectacle. She began adding film segments to her dances and eventually concentrated more on film than on dance. She received awards and recognition for her film work and was a recipient of a MacArthur Fellowship Award as filmmaker and choreographer in 1990. After about 30 years in filmmaking she returned to the dance field in 2011 with a new work, *Assisted Living: Good Sports 2* performed by her small troupe, the Raindears, in counterpoint to her readings of texts by several authors: Cynthia Carr, William James, Louis Menand and others along with reconstructions of her 1960's works.

**Trisha Brown** (b. 1936), another Judson Dance Theater alumna, used repetition – repeat and add a phrase – sometimes outdoors with the dancers far apart, but just able to see the previous dancer's movement, as in *Roof Piece.* In 1970 she was a cofounder of Grand Union, an experimental dance collective. Several of her pieces, such as *Roof Piece* and *Walking on Walls,* were for specific locations. Brown's movements were often common everyday actions, from repetitive gestures to fluid and quick motions with the use of classical music, such as baroque composer Jean Philippe Rameau's music, side by side with American marches by Sousa played by a local marching band, or music of Monteverdi (*Orfeo,* 1980). Occasionally she collaborated with the artist Robert

Contractions, a new technique created by Martha Graham, and now in every dancer's vocabulary, is demonstrated here by Helene Andreu. Photo: Clotilde

Portrait of Alvin Ailey. Created by photographer Carl van Vechten.

Charles Weidman, modern dance choreographer with a rare humorous tendency. Photographer unknown.

Shen Wei, choreographer, Shen Wei Dance Arts, New York, N.Y. The Shen Wei Dance Arts combines dance with theater, art, architecture, philosophy, and Chinese opera.

Rauschenberg as in her large-scale ensemble piece, *Foray Foret* (1990), for which he created the costumes. She received a MacArthur Fellowship Award in 1991 for her choreography. She also began directing opera in 1998. One of her latest dances was called *Amour au Théatre* (2009). She choreographed her first piece for a ballet company (*O Zlozony / O Composite*, 2004), commissioned by the director of the Paris Opera Ballet, **Brigitte Lefeuvre**, because **Trisha Brown** was a pioneer whose works made one see dance in a completely different and new way. France honored her with the rank of Commander of the Order of Arts and Letters in December 2004. The August 2011 Jacob's Pillow Dance Festival in Massachusetts ended her 40th year of performances and included her recent work *Les Yeux et l'âme* (2011, to a dance suite from Rameau's opera *Pygmalion*), and *Set and Reset* (1983) and *Foray Foret* (1990), two of her best works, with loose jumps and silky-smooth transitions.

**Trisha Brown** received a Bessie award for Lifetime Achievement in 2011 for what the committee of the Bessies said (*NY Times*, Oct. 6, 2011) was "the influence of both her distinctive movement style and inquisitive choreographic drive." The Dorothy and Lillian Gish Prize, established in 1994 and named for the two silent film actresses, is awarded to artists for their pioneering impact on their chosen areas. In September 2011 it was awarded to Trisha Brown because she had "transformed" modern dance with "new vocabularies of movement." The Trisha Brown Dance Company Education Program has projects that extend to such diversified locations as China, London, Scotland, and Belgium.

**Meredith Monk** (b. 1942) is a composer, performer, vocalist, filmmaker, modern dancer, and choreographer. She received a MacArthur Fellowship Award in 1995 (for originality as vocalist, composer, and director), three "Obies," two "Bessie" Awards for Sustained Creative Achievement, the 1992 *Dance Magazine* Award, and innumerable other awards. She created theater pieces with a combination of movement, symbolism, her own composed music, or vocal sounds for music. *Vessel* (1971, about the life and death of Joan of Arc) was a much-talked-about dance piece of hers; it consisted of three sections, presented at three different places in New York, with the audience bused from one spot to the next, beginning in Monk's loft, continuing in the Performance Garage, and finishing in a parking lot. She has also made films, such as *Ellis Island*, and has written a symphonic work commissioned by the Kronos Quartet in 2005. She has been called "a magician of the voice" and "one of America's coolest composers."

**Reggie Wilson** (b. 1967) is another interdisciplinary artist who uses vocal sound and movement. In his autobiographical piece, *Introduction* (1996), he traces his life from Milwaukee to New York and Africa with speech, breathing techniques, and walking rhythms. The members of his Brooklyn-based company, Fist and Heel Performance Group, are adept at using their voices and bodies to impart rhythms. **Reggie Wilson** starts in an offhanded manner and builds up forcefully in his work. The sources are varied and include traditional songs and work songs. In his pieces Wilson blends contemporary and African traditions. His works include: *Tales from the Creek* (1998), *The Good Dance* (2009), and *Moses(es)* (2013). The singers, Rhetta Aleong, Lawrence Harding, and **Reggie Wilson**, excel in conveying Wilson's vocal arrangements a cappella, and the dancers, **Clement Mensah**, **Dwayne Brown**, **Malcolm Low**, **Paul Hamilton**, and **Raja Kelly** deliver the rhythms and counter rhythms in Reggie Wilson's choreography.

**Laura Dean** (b. 1945), a dancer-choreographer and composer, uses spinning in her dances, but without spotting, just focusing to the front with a blind gaze. Also, her dancers repeat a segment while moving forward, and then another line, and yet another line of dancers do this, and after a while that step is replaced with repetitions of a new movement. This repetition, together with the elimination of all non-essential features, is what makes Laura Dean a **minimalist**. She also likes to produce geometric figures and circles within circles, as she did in *Dance* (1976) and *Spiral* (1977), or an intricate mixture of geometric patterns and original movement (*Impact,* 1985, with commissioned musical score by Steve Reich) and with less emphasis than before on repetitive movements. She composed the music for many of her pieces (*Skylight,* an adaptation of a 1982 work, with lighting by Craig Miller and music by Laura Dean). For The New York City Ballet she crafted *Space* (1988, music by Reich), and for The Joffrey Ballet she created *Billboards* (1993, music by Prince). She also choreographed pieces such as *Reflections* (1993) for ice dance companies. In recognition of her accomplishments as choreographer and composer she has received many awards and in 2007 was awarded the Samuel H. Scripps American Dance Festival Award for Lifetime Achievement.

**Ronald K. Brown** (b. 1967) is a dancer-choreographer. In the choreography for his company, Evidence, he shows us the joys of dancing to music. He uses intricate and rhythmic movements that are based on a mixture of contemporary modern and traditional African movement in themes of community and spirituality. He has choreographed for other companies, for Philadanco as well as for The Alvin Ailey American Dance Theater. For his own company he created *Come Ye* (2003, to music by Nina Simone) and *On Earth Together* (2011) to Stevie Wonder songs and with a slightly new version for the opening in 2013 of BRIC House, a multidisciplinary arts organization in Fort Greene, Brooklyn. He has received a Guggenheim Fellowship and a Bessie Award.

Many modern dance choreographers such as **Laura Dean**, **Lucinda Childs**, **Molissa Fenley**, **David Gordon**, and **Karole Armitage** choreographed for ballet companies in the 1980's; their works served as novelties and usually lasted for only one season. **Taylor's** *Airs* and *Company B* (1991), however, were readily accepted into ballet companies' repertoires, as were **Limon's** *Moor's Pavane* and also **Cunningham's** *Duets.*

**Eiko** (b. 1952) **& Koma** (b. 1948) are a married team from Japan who use stillness and very slow movement in their work. This would be anguishing for some but on the other hand they have had a following of people who were enthralled by them, their philosophy and visual images. Their work emphasizes that humans are a part of nature. **Kazuo Ohno** (1906-2010), a butoh dance form pioneer, was one of their main inspirations although they do not consider their work to be butoh. They received a Bessie Award in 1984 and a MacArthur Fellowship Award as dancers and choreographers in 1996. In 2004 they received the Samuel H. Scripps/American Dance Festival Award for Lifetime Achievement in modern dance. Since 2009 they have celebrated their many years of living and performing in the United States with a three-year Retrospective

Project consisting of their performances, lectures, exhibitions, and installations at various universities .and art centers throughout the country.

The **Lar Lubovitch** (b. 1943) Dance Company, formed in 1968, is a modern dance group that can be relied on to present first-rate choreography to beautiful music and executed by talented dancers. **Elisa Clark**, formerly in the Mark Morris Dance Group, danced in Lubovitch's *The Legend of Ten*, (2010, to a Brahms piano quintet). **Clifton Brown,** previously in Alvin Ailey's Company, danced in Lubovitch's *Serenade,* to music by Dvorak. All Lar Lubovitch's dancers are strong and eloquent, as seen in his signature piece *North Star* (1978, to a score by Philip Glass). Numerous companies worldwide have performed **Lubovitch**'s works, including the San Francisco Ballet Company and the Paris Opera Ballet Company.

**Mark Morris** (b. 1956) opened the dance school at The Mark Morris Dance Center in Brooklyn in 2001 near the Brooklyn Academy of Music. It was the first permanent home for his company and included a dance studio with classrooms and rehearsal studios, outreach programs for children, and dance classes for all ages. In 2001 he celebrated the twenty years of performances at the Brooklyn Academy of Music by The Mark Morris Dance Group with presentations of his classic piece, *L'Allegro, il Penseroso, ed il Moderato* to music by George Frideric Handel. His other works include *Gloria* (1981, to Vivaldi), *Dido and Aeneas* (1989, to Henry Purcell's 1689 opera of the same name), and *Mozart Dances* (2006). In 2007 *The Hard Nut* (Morris' humorous and inspired version of *The Nutcracker*) was released as a DVD and shown on TV after a 15-year absence. Morris' artistic quality won him a MacArthur Fellowship Award in 1991 as dancer-choreographer. In 2010 the dance company made its first appearance in Russia with Mark Morris conducting his group's music ensemble for a performance of *Dido and Aeneas* at the Koldov Novaya Opera Theatre in Moscow.

After the March 2011 earthquake-tsunami in northeast Japan, the Japanese American Association Dance Project New York organized "Dance for Japan" (the proceeds to go to the Japan Earthquake Relief Fund). The performance, held at the Mark Morris Dance Center, featured both Japanese and American dancers performing works by **Alexander Ekman**, **Lar Lubovitch**, **Francesco Harper**, **Mark Morris**, and others.

Mark Morris opened his 2011 season with three new pieces presented at the Mark Morris Dance Center. The new pieces were: *The Muir* to Beethoven's arrangement of nine Scottish and Irish folk songs; a very exuberant *Festival Dance* to a piano trio by Johann Nepomuk Hummel (1778-1837); and a dance for eight women, *Petrichor,* to a string quartet by Heitor Villa-Lobos. All were danced barefoot to live music – five instrumentalists and three singers. Morris' three-hour-long production of *Romeo & Juliet* (2012) featured Prokofiev's original score from 1935 and the scenario by Prokofiev and Sergei Radlov in which the lovers do not die. **Maile Okamura** and **Noah Vinson** danced the roles of the lovers. The final scene shows them alone on a beautiful starry night as Romeo clasps Juliet tenderly and spins her around. Mark Morris has also choreographed for various ballet companies; for the San Francisco Ballet he has choreographed eight works since *Maelstrom* in 1994, his latest being *Beaux,* to music by Bohuslav Martinu, for an all-male cast of dancers.

In 1994 a trio of choreographers, two in dance, **Dana Reitz** and **Sara Rudner**, and one in lights, **Jennifer Tipton** (winner of a MacArthur Fellowship Award in 2008 as stage lighting designer), created a work, *Necessary Weather*, and revived it in 2010. The piece was saluted as an amazingly imaginative intermingling of lights and dance.

**Kei Takei** (b. 1946), a Japanese-American avant-garde modern dancer-choreographer, has performed many of the sequences of her ongoing work, *Light*, in New York with her company, The Moving Earth, founded by her in 1975. She was inspired by Japanese butoh and by Western contemporary modern dancers, such as **Trisha Brown**, **Merce Cunningham**, and **Alwin Nikolais**. Although *Light* is considered to be a single unit, it is much too long for all of it to be presented in one performance. In 1969 Kei Takei choreographed Part 1; by 1996 there were 31 segments in *Light*. In 1996 the company performed Parts 1-15 and it took eleven hours. Kei Takei has been choreographing the additional segments since she started in 1969. Some of them are very powerful theatrical pieces. She has used scores by **Yukio Tsuji** and **John Williams**. Her company has an international group of dancers from China, Japan, Peru, Israel, Germany, Spain, and Canada.

New experimental works lend an aura of excitement to each new season. There have been many performances of works by postmodern and also by post-butoh choreographers from many countries: **Angelin Preljocaj** and **Maguy Marin** (France); **Anna de Keersmaeker** (Belgium); **Birgit Akesson, Mats Ek** (Sweden); **Carolyn Cohan, Richard Alston, Siobhan Davies, Michael Clark** (Great Britain); **Kazuo Ohno, Tatsumi Hijikata, Min Tanaka**, and **Sankai Juku** (Japan, a butoh troupe with slow moving epics that completely hold the audience's attention); **Pina Bausch** Germany); **Bill T. Jones** (American); **Flemming Flindt** (Denmark); and **Shen Wei** (China).

**Angelin Preljocaj** (b. 1957), French of Albanian parentage, studied with a disciple of **Mary Wigman** and in New York with **Merce Cunningham**. He founded the Ballet Preljocaj in 1984. In his *Romeo and Juliet* (1990) he sets the scene in Berlin with the lovers killing themselves with razors. All his works, such as *Le Spectre de la Rose* (1993) and *Le Parc* (1994, music by Mozart) have a sinister aspect to them. He also choreographed a piece for the New York City Ballet, *La Stravaganza* (1997), to music by various baroque and modern composers: Antonio Vivaldi (1678-1741), as well as Evelyn Ficarra, Robert Normandeau, Serge Morand, and Ake Parmerud. In this piece he presented characters dressed in 17th century clothes dancing to modern music with unnatural steps, and modern characters dancing to baroque music with expansive steps, and with the two groups eyeing each other warily. Among his many creations are *Siddhârta* (2010, to original music by Bruno Mantovani) for The Paris Opera Ballet, and the controversial work *Annonciation* for the Cedar Lake Contemporary Ballet.

Photo Plate 12-5

Paul Taylor's American Modern Dance performing "Esplanade," Photo by
Lois Greenfield.

The Dancer, bronze sculpture by
PaoloTroubetzkoy, Italian, 1912.

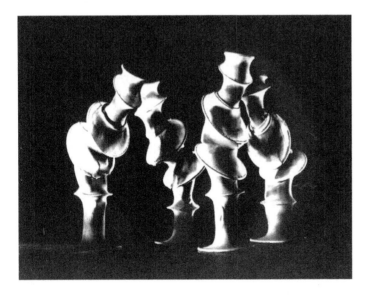

Alwin Nikolais in his 1959 work, "Allegory," Photographer unknown.

Poster for Federal Theater
Project Presentation of Myra
Kinch and Group, in concert,
between 1936 and 1941.

**Maguy Marin** (b. 1951), French, studied with **Nina Vyroubova** of the Paris Opera and at **Maurice Béjart**'s school in Brussels. Her work *Babel Babel* (1982) dealt with the outdoor camping craze of the French; there is some nudity at the beginning and the end of it. Marin's 1985 production of *Cendrillon,* to Prokofieff's music (which had previously been used for other versions of Cinderella by various choreographers) was for the Lyons Opera Ballet and was her most successful work. All the dancers were dressed as dolls; they looked like a childhood fantasy. Her works never resembled one another but were each individually inspired. Her piece *May B* (1981, choreographed in Angers, France) made her the most important choreographer of new dance in France. In 2003 she became one of the only non-Americans to be awarded the American Dance Festival Award. She also won a Bessie for her work *Unwelt* performed at the Joyce Theater in 2008.

**Robert Cohan** (b. 1925, American) a former dancer with **Martha Graham**'s Company, went to London to choreograph for the London Contemporary Dance Theatre founded by the restaurant owner and lover of modern dance, Robin Howard. Cohan used excellent production effects as well as passion and acrobatics in his pieces. **Robert Cohan**'s work *Stages* (1971), a full-evening work, was a huge success and traced a modern man through temptation and confrontation of self; *Ice* (1978) tackled fear, and *Class* (1975) was a representation of the Graham technique, with which he was very familiar.

**Butoh** is an expressionist form of modern dance that developed in Japan after World War II. It was a reaction against the dance scene in Japan, an imitation of Western dance and Noh Theater. Three of the people credited with the creation of the butoh style or "the dance of darkness," were **Kazuo Ohno** (1906-2010, who also performed modern dance) together with **Tatsumi Hijikata** (1928-1986), and **Akira Kasai** (b. 1943, who used more vertical movements and more humorous, clown-like elements than most in his particular butoh style).

**Sankai Juku** is the name of the best known of the Japanese troupes that perform in **butoh** style. This is the Japanese choreographer-dancer **Ushio Amagatsu**'s Paris-based butoh group; it has outstanding visual effects. The piece *Tobari – as if in an Inexhaustible Flux* explores, and makes visible in dance, the passage of life, birth, and rebirth, slowed down or speeded up.

**Butoh** eventually assimilated conventions from the theatrical styles of the Noh and from the Kabuki Theater. A **butoh** performance may include several of the following: the projection of grotesque body language, shaved heads, bodies painted white, elimination of identifying characteristics of individuals, use of a darkened stage, distorted faces, gaping mouth, extraordinary discipline in the slow pace of movement, convulsion of bodies, directing energy down toward the floor, use of sequence of falls with bodies crumpling, use of improvisation, metamorphosis onstage and off. The thought was that daily tasks were the basis of human gesture and of dance. The piece *Jōmon Shō* (*Homage to Prehistory,* 1982) had a theme related to evolution that went back to Japan's Jōmon era (ca. 10000-300 BC) and questioned man's capacity to adapt to natural laws. Many of the early followers of butoh studied with **Mary Wigman**.

**Pina Bausch** (1940-2009, German), was concerned with the problem of women as commodities; she explored her own experiences and those of her dancers. She accepted, in her dances, the new dynamics created through speech, movements, music, and scenery. She used memories and thoughts obtained from improvisational exercises for her dancers. These formed the basis of her new productions. One of her dancers' favorite pieces was *Vollmond* (*Full Moon* 2006, performed on a stage that is dominated by a huge boulder and rushing water), which asks intimate questions about love. The dancers jump, roll, and run through the water and over and around the large rock.

**Pina Bausch** attained an international reputation with her "Tanztheater Wuppertal." The minimalization of the dance and the exploration of the psyche in Pina Bausch's earlier works became less important. Dance in The Tanztheater (Dance Theater) discovered the use of collage, a system not previously used in dance. Bausch was not so much interested in how people moved as in what moved them. Bausch's dance universe is an extraordinary place, a combination of drama and dreamlike movement. She received many awards, including The United Kingdom's Laurence Olivier Award, Japan's Kyoto prize, and the *Dance Magazine* Award in 2008 as well as the Goethe Prize from the city of Frankfurt am Main, also in 2008. After Bausch's death in 2009 her son Salomon Bausch created a foundation to be in charge of her works. Wuppertal, Germany, home of Tanztheater, was committed to continue financing Tanztheater. Several of her works were staged for the Cultural Program preceding the 2012 Olympic Games in London. Pina Bausch originally created these while on a tour of 10 global locations from 1986-2009 and some had never been performed in London before 2012. There is a 3-D film about Pina Bausch by Wim Wenders that received wonderful reviews. It is called *Pina dance, dance, otherwise we are lost.* It is considered to be one of the top documentary films of 2011.

**Bill T. Jones** (b. 1952), a black American dancer, was another choreographer involved with social issues, racism, and AIDS. After touring extensively doing solos and duets with his partner **Arnie Zane**, a white dancer, the Bill T. Jones/Arnie Zane Dance Company was formed in 1982. Arnie Zane died of AIDS in 1988. Jones has created powerful works on the topic of AIDS, using spoken narrative and visual tapes, such as *Still Here* (1994), and *Last Supper at Uncle Tom's Cabin/The Promised Land* (1990). He received a MacArthur Fellowship Award in 1994 and numerous other awards over the years in recognition of his outstanding inventive choreography. He was awarded a Tony in 2010 for his choreography for the Broadway show *Fela!* (2009, based on the life of the Nigerian performer and activist Fela Anikulapo Kuti). This show had Fela Kuti's Afrobeat music and was co-created and directed by Jones. He also won the 2009 Lucille Lortel Award as Outstanding Choreographer. The Bill T Jones/Arnie Zane Dance Company merged in 2011 with The Dance Theater Workshop, an arts center that, from 1965 to 2011, gave over one hundred performances a year by a miscellaneous group of forty-five companies and artists who were exploring new ways of looking at dance. The place that used to be named Dance Theater Workshop is now called New York Live Arts and remains at 219 West 19th Street, Chelsea, New York, with no changes in its outward appearance. New York Live Arts is described as "an artist-led arts producing and presenting organization" that tries to "create a robust framework in support of the nation's dance and movement-based artists." The Bill T. Jones/Arnie Zane Dance

Company was the first to perform there in September 2011, with dancers of varied races, shapes and sizes and a few guest artists in revivals of *Body Against Body* (1977-1982 by Zane and Jones), *Continuous Replay* (1977, revised by Jones in 1991), and several Jones/Zane duets. **Bill T. Jones** received a 2013 National Medal of Arts award presented by President Obama.

In France, **Carolyn Carlson** (b. 1943), an American of Finnish descent, and formerly of Nikolais' company, had made quite an impression on the new director of the Paris Opera, **Rolf Liebermann,** with her dancing and choreography in her solo *Densité* in 1973, and Liebermann then offered Carlson the new position of Étoile-Choréographe (principal dancer-choreographer) at the Paris Opera Ballet (1974-1980) and gave her the right to create experimental works for a new small company. When she went to Venice in 1980 the Paris Opera created another new group made up of dancers from the ballet company to dance in new works, mostly by Americans. When Nureyev became director of the Paris Opera in 1983, groups of this sort were no longer necessary since experimental works were already appearing on the programs of the Opera Ballet itself. France awarded Carlson the title of Chevalier des Arts et des Lettres.

After an absence of five years Carlson returned to the United States in 2010 to perform with her company at Montclair State University and at the "Fall for Dance" series presented each autumn at City Center in New York. She presented her work *Double Vision*, on a multimedia approach to color, light, and movement, in collaboration with the artist Yacine Aït Kaci and architect Naziha Mestaoui,

The Fall for Dance Festival at the City Center is always varied and may include the **Nrityagram** company from India, a work by Swedish choreographer **Mats Ek**, a performance of *Devil in the Detail* by Britain's **Richard Alston** to music by Scott Joplin for the Richard Alston Dance Company, or **Robert Garland**'s *Gloria* (2012, to music by Poulenc, celebrating the rebirth of Dance Theater of Harlem).

In Denmark, under the direction of **Flemming Flindt** (1936-2009), modern works by **Murray Louis**, **Glen Tetley**, and **Paul Taylor** were included in various programs from 1966 to 1978, and dancers went barefoot for the first time. Flindt himself created *The Triumph of Death* (1972), a televised ballet in which everyone danced completely naked; then for his own company, which he formed in 1978, he created *Salome* with his wife **Vivi Flindt** as Salome. She danced the final scene of *Salome* completely naked (not as sensational as Flindt's televised nude ballet of 1972 had been). He was artistic director of the Dallas Ballet from 1981 to 1989 and freelance choreographer for the Cleveland Ballet. Subsequently he returned to the Royal Danish Ballet to choreograph *Caroline Mathilde* (1991, music by Maxwell Davis). He was made a Knight of Dannebrog (1994). In 2004 he choreographed *Out of Africa* for the Ballet San Jose of Silica Valley. It was an adaptation of Isak Dinesen's book about life in Kenya.

**Shen Wei** *(Photo Plate 12-4)* (b. 1968), Chinese dancer-choreographer, received a scholarship from the Nikolais/Louis Dance Lab in 1995 and moved to New York. He subsequently presented his pieces at the National Theater of Taiwan (1996), the Stockholm Dance Theater (1999), and the Edinburgh Festival Theater (2000). He founded the Shen Wei Dance Arts in 2000 and creates the sets, costumes, and make-up designs for his works. The company travels extensively, and **Shen Wei** has also received many commissions from ballet and opera companies in the United States. He has won awards world wide – in France, Australia, China, and the United States – including a MacArthur Fellowship Award (2007) for his works, which are a creative blend of Western ballet and performance art with Chinese dance, opera, and music. He helped to coordinate 16,000 performers for the opening ceremonies of the 2008 Olympics in the Bird's Nest Stadium in Beijing.

Over the years, new modern dance companies have constantly been springing up. Some have become popular and have lasted, while others have not. Since the 1980's, dance companies have found themselves spending more money in administrative departments than in the creative end. The cost of producing a Broadway show kept increasing, but nevertheless audiences continued to attend. At the same time, dance has proven to be very popular on television in shows like *Dancing With the Stars* and *So You Think You Can Dance*. These feature not only **tap, modern**, and **ballet**, but also **East Indian dance, Bollywood, bolero, Charleston, contemporary, disco, hip hop, rhumba, Argentine tango, Russian folk dance, Irish clog dancing** and **krumping**. Millions watch all of these shows and enjoy them, and many are inspired to take dance classes.

# 13

# Jazz Dance and Musicals

## – Stage and Films –

## from the Charleston to the Present

Everything was changing: the dances were faster; music was more energetic; women were more liberated and had jobs and looser garments; filmmakers were trying new techniques; dancing was everywhere. The Jazz age was really here.

The popularity of the **Charleston** dance was largely due to the black musical *Runnin' Wild* (1923) with the song *Charleston* by James P. Johnson *(Photo Plate 13-1)*. Everyone did the Charleston and many said they had invented it. The name of the dance did come from Charleston, South Carolina, although the title of one song goes *The Charleston Didn't Come from Charleston.*
The **Charleston** required endurance, high spirits, and vigor, with energetic movements involving all parts of the body. But everyone was ready for it. There had already been a dance craze with some new fad dances – over one hundred of them – in the United States in 1910. People got up to dance, as the food got cold, in restaurants and at teatime. Everyone danced regardless of color or class and enjoyed the new dances.

As for the **shimmy** and the **black bottom**, it was more or less the same story as for the Charleston. **Ethel Waters** (1896-1977) performed them both in the revue *Africana* (1927) but several other stage stars claimed to have invented them. These dances were very popular and so was the 1922 song by black composer **A. J. Piron**, *I Wish I Could Shimmy Like My Sister Kate.*

Women's greater freedom, due to factory and typing jobs, large cities, comfortable garments, and the example of **Irene** and **Vernon Castle** made it acceptable to do the new dances *(Photo Plates 13-1 and 13-2)*. However, dance halls and *Ten Cents a Dance* could be dangerous. Too much dancing at dance halls made both men and women get looked upon as low possibilities for both career and family. The Jazz Age stood for sex, speakeasies, and sin.

**Irene** (1893-1969) **and Vernon Castle** (1887-1918) were America's favorite ballroom team. Actually, Vernon was English and Irene was American. They made a career out of the many fad dances of the 1910's by dancing them at exhibitions, shows, vaudeville, and ballrooms.

The Castles hired a black American musician from Alabama, **James Reese Europe** (1885-1919), to be their accompanist because they found him to be almost intuitive about music. He became the most popular bandleader in the country. His "society orchestra" was well known nationally and abroad *(Photo Plate 13-2)*. He served in World War I. The musicians in the band from his regiment introduced the new music to France. He was well liked by Europeans, but upon his return to the U.S. he was killed by one of the drummers in his society orchestra.

The public adored the **Castles.** They set the trends in fashion and clothes. When she cut her hair, all women cut their hair. When she did away with corsets and wore loose garments, American women followed. The **Castles** brought grace, dignity, and good manners to ballroom dancing. When the Castles did all the new dances, men and women felt these were now proper and did them too.

In 1914 Vernon Castle enlisted in the Royal Air Force, and in 1918 he died in a plane crash while training a pilot. The Castles had performed together for four years and they popularized dance teams like **Fred and Adele Astaire**, and **Sally and Tony DeMarco.**

The puffed sleeves and tight corsets from the Victorian era were no more, at least not for the young or the young at heart who now wore the latest styles – short skirts, fringes and beads that shimmered and shook as they danced, close fitting hats over short bobbed hair for women "**flappers**" and a ukulele, raccoon coats and bell bottomed trousers for the men or "**shieks**" as they were called.

The dances and music of the 1920's were quick and energetic and provided a chance for people to release all their pent-up emotions produced by the horrors of World War I (1914-1918) and its demands and restrictions on their lifestyles. This was now a peaceful time. Dancing proved to be one of the favorite outlets of many, and the preferred dances were the **ragtime dances**, the **waltz**, and the **foxtrot**. Performers had steps named after them. There was the **Maurice walk**, the **Gaby glide** *(Photo Plate 13-1)* and, of course, the **Castle walk** first introduced by the Castles in 1913 at the Café de Paris in France and in New York in 1914. It consisted of a few elegant walking steps on the toes followed by a hop.

The standard of living was going up. Many homes had a piano or a player piano. There was appropriate music for the entire selection of new dances. The **Arthur Murray** dance studios and others published or sold "how to" books on these dances. (**Arthur (1895-1991) and Kathryn (1906-1999) Murray** were inducted into the Dance Hall of Fame of the National Museum of Dance in Saratoga, New York, in 2006.) The new dances could be seen and learned at the dance studios or could be seen in movies and then practiced at home with music on the phonograph *(Photo Plate 13-2)*. Dancing was a popular activity at school gymnasiums, at parties or nightclubs, at home, and also at churches; it appealed to the young. Schools taught the latest popular dances, and parents also sent their children to dance schools to learn ballet and tap.

Photo Plate 13-1

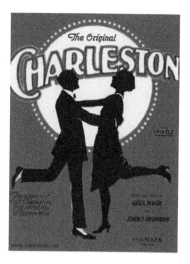

Sheet Music Cover: "Charleston" from the musical
"Runnin' Wild," a very popular show. "Charleston"
by the black composer/pianists James P. Johnson and
Cecil Mack became a more than favorite hit. The
musical ran from October 29, 1923 through June 28,
1924. The Charleston allows for many variations and
can be danced solo, with a partner, or in a group.

Sheet Music Cover: "Poor Butterfly" was the song
hit of the show "The Big Show at the New York
Hippodrome," staged by R. H. Burnside, words by
John L. Golden; music by Raymond Hubbell;
illustration and lettering by Burton Rice. Published:
NY: World Magazine, 1916.

Dancers Vernon and Irene Castle. Gelatin silver
print. Date: 1910-1918. Author: Frances
Benjamin Johnston, photographer and creator, 1864-
1952.

Sheet Music Cover: "The Gaby Glide." Lyrics:
Harry Pilcer; Music: Louis A. Hirsch; Publication
New York, Shapiro, 1911.

Many of the jazz bands in New Orleans and Chicago were comprised primarily of men. The pianist, however, if they had one, was usually a woman. It was assumed that a woman was able to do this and provide feminine attraction at the same time. Superior male piano players could probably get solo positions and would not want a band-rate salary whereas women would accept this lower pay scale.

The Chicago of the Roaring Twenties was the Chicago of Prohibition, 'speakeasies', liquor, rackets, dancehalls, nightclubs, 'dives', gangster patronage, and extravagantly spent money, with jazzy music playing from seven in the evening till seven in the morning and customers drinking, dancing, and gambling during those hours.

The New York Hippodrome, which had opened in 1905 with extravaganzas featuring scenic illusions like fires, floods, herds of elephants, and over 200 chorus dancers, all carefully staged, closed and was demolished in 1939 *(Photo Plate 13-1)*.

**Albertina Rasch** (1896-1967) *(Photo Plate 13-2)*, a Viennese ballerina, appeared at the New York Hippodrome in 1920. She subsequently studied **Wigman** modern dance and **Jacques-Dalcroze** technique while touring in Europe. She also opened a school in New York to teach the women who became the Albertina Rasch Dancers and appeared in revues and on vaudeville. In her choreography she combined **ballet**, **modern**, and **jazz**. She had incorporated **pointe technique** into Gershwin's jazzy stylistic *Rhapsody in Blue* and choreographed a Broadway production of *George White's Scandals of 1924* using ballet in her work rather than a solitary line dance. She also choreographed *Rio Rita* (1927), *Ziegfeld Follies* (1927 and 1931), *Show Girl* (1929), and *Three's a Crowd* (1930). It was rare for a woman to choreograph a show in the 1920's. One of her last works was *The Bandwagon* (1931) with lyrics by Howard Dietz, music by Arthur Schwartz, and starring **Adele Astaire**, **Fred Astaire**, and the stunning **Tilly Losch** (1903-1975) in distinct and attractive dance numbers. *The Beggar's Waltz* was a novelty at that time – a dream ballet, and *Dancing in the Dark* was outstanding, with **Tilly Losch** dancing on pointe.

Rasch worked constantly. In 1934 she staged **folk dances** and **ballet** for *The Great Waltz* starring **Alexandra Danilova** and a corps of fifty dancers. The choreography for *Lady in the Dark* (1941) proved a great success again with a fantastic and complex dream ballet. Before Albertina Rasch, men had predominated in the field; **Ned Wayburn** (1874-1942), for example, had provided many line dances with tap and other dance movements.

Meanwhile, the 1923 musical *Runnin' Wild* (lyrics and music by Cecil Mack and Jimmy Johnson) was the show that had caused everyone to go wild doing the Charleston. It was an overnight hit. The **Charleston** was becoming so popular that in 1924 the Roseland Ballroom in New York City held a marathon for twenty-four hours of **Charleston**. The *George White Scandals of 1925* had **Tom Patricola** (1891-1950) doing the Charleston along with sixty attractive girls.

**Josephine Baker** (1906-1975) *(Photo Plate 13-2)* sang and danced in the chorus of the first all-black musical, *Shuffle Along*, and was well liked. The musical opened at Daly's 63rd Street Theatre in midtown Manhattan on May 23, 1921. When Baker went to Paris with *La Revue Noire* in 1925 she was adored, and also in 1926 in the *Folies Bergère de Paris*. Paris' love for her was reciprocated. She introduced France and Europe to the new dances, the **black bottom** and the **Charleston**. She remained in Paris, a star, later joined the Resistance to help France against the Nazis during the German Occupation in World War II. She had become a French citizen in 1937, and adopted twelve children in France. Whenever she visited the United States she refused to perform for segregated audiences. France honored her with the Medal of the Resistance and named her a Chevalier of the Legion of Honor.

Many years later the **Charleston** appeared again in numerous Broadway musicals and movies: *Tea for Two* (1950, an adaptation of *No, No, Nanette* of 1925), with the insertion of the song *I want to Be Happy* from *No, No, Nanette* as well as the song *Charleston* from *Runnin' Wild*. Another successful Broadway musical with a Charleston dance was *The Boy Friend* (1954), starring Julie Andrews, with choreography by **John Heywood**. *Won't You Charleston with Me?* was the popular song in *The Boy Friend* with music, lyrics, and book by Sandy Wilson. *My One and Only* (1983), starring **Twiggy** and **Tommy Tune** with choreography by **Tommy Walsh**, **Tommy Tune**, **Mike Nichols**, and **Michael Bennett**, was an adaptation of *Funny Face* (1927), which had starred **Fred Astaire**, and had lyrics and music by Ira and George Gershwin. *My One and Only* had several original songs.

Audiences of the 1920's and 1930's were amazed by the splendor of the movies. In the United States the movie craze started with the Al Jolson movie *The Jazz Singer* (1927). Neither stage shows by **Ziegfeld** nor the *Earl Carroll Vanities* nor *George White's Scandals* could compare with the even more complicated movies of the **Ginger Rogers-Fred Astaire** musicals, with choreography by **Hermes Pan** and **Fred Astaire**, music by George Gershwin, Cole Porter, Irving Berlin, Vincent Youmans, Bert Kalmar and Harry Ruby (who also wrote *Three Little Words*, 1950).

The great **Busby Berkeley** (1895-1976) movies with intricate, multifaceted musical numbers and complex geometrical designs were entertaining and new and a distraction from the gloom of the Great Depression. Busby Berkeley had directed a Broadway musical, *A Connecticut Yankee* (1927), but what he did in films was shoot scenes from unexpected angles. He wanted the audience to see in films what would be impossible for them to see in the theater. (He later turned to drama and filmed one of the best John Garfield movies, *They Made Me a Criminal* (1939). The Great Depression audiences thoroughly enjoyed **Busby Berkeley**'s movies, especially the musicals *42$^{nd}$ Street* (1933, starring **Ruby Keeler**), *Footlight Parade* (1933, starring **James Cagney**, **Joan Blondell**, **Ruby Keeler**, and **Dick Powell**), *Gold Diggers of 1933*, and *The Gang's All Here* (1934), with **Carmen Miranda**'s *Lady in the Tutti Frutti Hat*. Busby Berkeley's work helped the movie musical become an important film category and also saved Warner Brothers from bankruptcy. When Berkeley moved to MGM studios he worked on such films as *Babes in Arms* (1939), *Strike up the Band* (1940), and *Girl Crazy* (1943) with songwriter-producer **Arthur Freed**, starring **Judy Garland** and **Mickey Rooney**. **Berkeley**'s choreography for *Lady Be Good* (1941) created a spectacular vehicle for **Eleanor Powell** with eight grand pianos and 65 partners with canes and tuxedos. In the 1940's he even provided some memorable movements for aquatic star Esther Williams.

Vaudeville had replaced minstrel shows, and a favorite act was *The Four Cohans* (**Cohan family**) with timely material and plots as the basis of dances and songs. It led to the popularity of song and dance men like **Donald O'Connor**, **Dan Dailey**, **Eddie Cantor**, and **Bob Hope**.

There were new stars on Broadway and in films. Ziegfeld's blonde dance star **Marilyn Miller** (1898-1936), who could do **tap** and **ballet** and had been inspired to dance after seeing **Adeline Genée** on vaudeville, appeared in Kern's *Sally* (1920) and in the *Ziegfeld Follies* (1918). Black shows like *Dixie to Broadway* (1924) and *Chocolate Dandies* (1924) did well at the box office. **Bill "Bojangles" Robinson** appeared in *Blackbirds of 1928* and taught **Shirley Temple** his famous **staircase tap dance** in the film *The Little Colonel* (1935). **Clifton Webb** (1889-1966) was a white performer who could perform any black dance, as he proved in the musical revue, *The Little Show* (1919, with lyrics by Howard Dietz) when he did a **snake hip** routine, gliding around on one foot while executing figure eights with his hips.

The priceless musicals by **Jerome Kern** (music) and **Guy Bolton** (lyrics) that appeared at the tiny Princess Theater in New York, *Very Good Eddie* (1915), *Nobody Home* (1915), and *Oh Boy!* (1917) could not possibly earn much from the sale of seats, so consequently the shows had simple sets and costumes but made up for it by having the songs' lyrics and Castle-type dance routines that advanced the story and appealed to the small intimate audience.

Star performers in minstrel, vaudeville, and extravaganzas had created their own routines up to now or had hired coaches to enhance their predominant skills when putting routines together. The coaches did the choreography but the performer got the credit for it. **Buddy Bradley**, a black American, was such a coach to **Clifton Webb**, **Pat Rooney**, **Mae West**, **Ruby Keeler**, and **Jack Donahue**. **Buddy Bradley** (1908-1972) would listen to various music records, their syncopation, and find suitable steps. Directors of the ensemble were in charge of the chorus girls who had been chosen for their good looks, kicks, and ability to do the easiest of steps.

Black musicals, superior in the 1920's, did not make a comeback until the 1970's with *Bubbling Brown Sugar* (1976, choreographed by **Billy Wilson**), *Ain't Misbehavin'* (1978, choreographed by **Arthur Faria**), and *Eubie* (1978, choreographed by **Henry Le Tang** with music by **Eubie Blake**). All of these had great jazz music and dances.

Jazz dance was gradually being taught in dance classes by 1915-1920. As technique improved, jazz was taken apart into exercises, isolations, walks, easy steps, and short routines. After that, jumps and pirouettes from ballet or contractions from modern dance were included in these short routines to enlarge jazz's vocabulary.

"Marathon dancers," 20 April 1923.

Josephine Baker (1906-1975) dancing the Charleston at the Folies Bergère, Paris – Revue Nègre Dance, 1928. Photographer: Walvery (1863-1933, French). Josephine Baker was a singer, dancer, entertainer who spent most of her career in France.

.

Sheet Music Cover: "The Castle Walk Trot & One Step," The dance that made Mr. and Mrs. Castle famous. Composed by James Reese Europe (1881-1919) and Ford T.Dabney (1883-1958). Photographer: George Moffett. Publisher: NY: Jos. Stern & Co, 1914.

.

Viennese choreographer Albertina Rasch, circa 1915. George Grantham Bain, photographer.

Edison Phonograph ad by Wendell Moore of Phonograph Monthly, page 16 Aug. 1907 issue.

**Ruth St. Denis** and **Ted Shawn** had been especially firm about opening dance schools all over the United States and about the importance of students learning all forms of dance. There were many ballet companies visiting from other countries; this too increased the importance of ballet and modern dance. The outcome of all this was dancers with better training and technique and the ability to do a choreographer's steps and routines.

There were a few bad years for musicals at that time. The worldwide flu epidemic of 1918 killed half a million people in the United Sate alone and theater audiences were scarce. Subsequently, in 1919, there was a strike by actors. Stagehands honored the strike, and producers, facing crippling losses, were forced to accept the demands of the Actors' Equity Association union.

The prosperity and elated optimistic mood of the 1920's came to an abrupt stop with the Stock Market crash on Black Thursday in October 1929. Many out-of-work people were now eager to take part in **dance marathons** in the hopes of winning some money *(Photo Plate 13-2)*. The length of time of these marathons could vary from several hours to several days. They often had doctors and nurses in attendance in case the participants became sick. Eventually dance marathons were outlawed; they were considered a health hazard.

However, the golden age of musicals in America that had started in 1925 continued despite the depression. Up to fifty new musicals opened during one season; by 1948 people were spending as much as $3.50 for a seat.

With the increased importance of ballet and modern dance in the 1930's came choreographers instead of dance directors. **George Balanchine**, who worked on several Broadway shows and was the choreographer for *On Your Toes* (1936), created a **ballet** on toe, and a **jazz ballet** in ballet shoes. He choreographed *Slaughter on Tenth Avenue* for Rodgers and Hart's musical *On Your Toes* starring ballerina **Tamara Geva** and hoofer **Ray Bolger**. Black choreographer **Herbie Harper** had assisted Balanchine with *On Your Toes*, and their combination of **tap**, **jazz** and **ballet** and the stars **Geva** and **Bolger** made this musical a huge success. (*Slaughter on Tenth Avenue* was later added to the repertoire of the New York City Ballet Company starring **Suzanne Farrell** and **Arthur Mitchell**.) **Balanchine**'s subsequent musical was *Song of Norway* (1944), with **Alexandra Danilova, Maria Tallchief**, and the **Ballet Russe de Monte Carlo**. After that came *Where's Charley* (1948) with **Ray Bolger**. All of the dances dealt with the show's theme and furthermore elevated the standards of dance on Broadway.

*Pal Joey* (1940) was choreographed by **Robert Alton** (1906-1957), formerly of the Mordkin Ballet Company and the choreographer of several other Broadway shows, *Du Barry Was a Lady* (1939), *Panama Hattie* (1940), *By Jupiter* (1941), *Hazel Flagg* (1953), and also numerous movie favorites. *Pal Joey* was not the usual type of musical. It was too serious and did not have a likeable hero. Although it starred **Gene Kelly** it was not successful; the audience at that time was not ready for a musical of this sort. However, when it was revived in 1952 with **Harold Lang** (1920-1985), formerly from the American Ballet Theatre Company, it was considered worthy of numerous awards. The stars of the dance section of this musical were also the stars of the rest of the musical. This too was a change.

**Jack Cole** (1911-1974), the creative originator of **modern jazz dance**, studied with Denishawn (**Ruth St. Denis** and **Ted Shawn)**, danced with Shawn's Male Dance Company, with the **Humphrey-Weidman** Dance Company, and studied the **Bharatanatyam** (also spelled Bharata Natyam) dance of India with **La Meri**. Cole's choreography was completely different from what had been seen before him. It was an astonishing blend of ethnic dance, Indian, Latin, Cuban, African American, modern, and ballet, combined with sharp precise body isolations and jazz rhythms *(Photo Plate 13-4)*. When Columbia Pictures, where he worked and had started a Dance Workshop, went on strike he took his group of superb dancers on the road. They included **Bob Hamilton**, **Buzz Miller**, **Carol Haney**, **Florence Lessing**, **Gwen Verdon**, and **Rod Alexander**. They performed his piece *Sing, Sing, Sing* in 1947 at the Latin Quarter. For Broadway he choreographed *Magdalena* (1948), *Kismet* (1953), and *Jamaica* (1957), among others. The glamour of exotic lands, and modern dancers' curiosity about East Indian dance led to this mix of **Hindu jazz**, **modern jazz** and **ballet jazz** in Jack Cole's choreography, as in *Alive and Kicking* (1950).

When the American Dance Machine company under **Lee Theodore Becker** was hoping to present *Jack Cole: Interface Project* in 1976, **Billie Mahoney** tried to put a few of his pieces and his technique in labanotation, using his dancers' recollections. She succeeded in notating *In a Persian Garden* and *Macumba* but the dancers could not recollect all of *Sing, Sing, Sing*. The notations are registered at the Dance Notation Bureau in New York. Cole also choreographed several unforgettable movies in which he incorporated his incredible jazz style and imaginative staging: *Moon Over Miami* (1941, with **Betty Grable**), *Kismet* (1944), *Gilda* (1946), *Meet Me After the Show* (1951, with **Rita Hayworth**), *On the Riviera* (1951, with featured dancer **Gwen Verdon**, who was Jack Cole's assistant for seven years), *Gentlemen Prefer Blondes* (1953), and *Les Girls* (1957). In movies **Cole** tailored his choreography to fit the particular strengths of the film stars. His work influenced many theatrical dance choreographers, **Bob Fosse**, **Gower Champion**, and **Jerome Robbins,** among others.

In 2012, *Heat Wave: The Jack Cole Project* emerged. **Chet Walker,** who assisted in the creation of *Fosse*, the bookless revue and Tony-winning best musical of 1999, conceived and directed *Heat Wave* with a singing and dancing cast of fifteen. It was presented in Queens Theater in the Park, in Queens, New York, in May 2012. The most successful numbers were the ones that were originally choreographed for the stage: *Sing, Sing, Sing*, and a dance for three men from the Broadway show *Carnival in Flanders*.

The modern dance choreographers, **Charles Weidman**, **Helen Tamaris**, **Hanya Holm**, **Jack Cole**, and **Agnes de Mille** had fresh ideas about choreography in Broadway shows, such as the dream ballet in *Oklahoma* and the bereaved woman's dance in *Brigadoon*.

Before them there had been **precision line** and **tap dancing** such as was performed by the **Tiller Girls,** with identical kicks and lines; subsequently **modern** and

**ballet** appeared. But chorus people were still practically identical, no distinctiveness. There was a singing chorus with pear shaped tones and a dancing group. The chorus opened the show, allowed latecomers to be seated, and reassured everyone that the girls in the show were beautiful. But they were not an impressive part of the story.

Musicals were changing. With **Agnes de Mille** *(Photo Plate 13-3)* the storyline had greater importance than before and was not to be interrupted by a crowd of handsome and beautiful men and women. Dance, book and music were of equal importance. Singers had to move well; dancers had to carry a tune.

In *Oklahoma* (1943), a musical adapted from Lynn Rigg's play *Green Grow the Lilacs* with music and lyrics by Richard Rodgers and Oscar Hammerstein II, choreographer **Agnes de Mille** used dancing substitutes for the principal singers and made the audience more aware of the characters' personalities. De Mille also presented us with the American West in her works.

*Carousel* (1945) followed *Oklahoma*, again with **Richard Rodgers, Oscar Hammerstein**, and choreographer **Agnes de Mille**, based on Ferenc Molnar's *Liliom*, a story from Hungary that was adapted to New England fishermen and townspeople for this musical. Here, too, a dance sequence presented the character of the girl (**Bambi Linn**) clearly to the audience.

**Latin dances** soon appeared on Broadway. This stemmed back to 1914 when one of the favorite dances in New York had been the **tango**, a fluid yet sharp, sensuous dance; it was denounced till an approved Parisian version appeared. It became known as the **tango** in Argentina, but was descended from the Moors, Arabs, gypsies, an early Spanish folk dance called the **milonga**, and the African slaves' **tangano**, and was danced in Mexico, Brazil, and Argentina.

The **Argentine tango** from Buenos Aires neighborhoods appeared at the end of the 19th century. The **Argentine tango** can be danced in various ways. Some variations are performed in an open embrace position at arm's length and executed with long elegant steps, involved figures and an even more open embrace to allow for the complicated positions and footwork. This style with the addition of lifts and drops was easily adapted to stage shows like the *Tango Argentino* that opened in Paris in 1983 before touring extensively. Another style was the very close chest-to-chest position, a dance with very small steps, a more intimate dance.

A variation of the Argentine tango was called the **Finnish tango** and was the version that the Finnish danced and loved. Traveling musicians had brought the tango to Finland in 1910 where it became so well liked that by 1930 Finnish musicians were composing tangos, and by 1940 its popularity spread to the countryside. **Finnish tangos** often include beguine and habanera rhythms, are usually in a minor key and have lyrics that mention love, sorrow, the countryside, and nature – spring signifies hope, and autumn rain, crushed hope. Since 1985 there has been an annual tango festival in Finland, drawing over 100,000 participants for the crowning of a tango king and queen, with media attention, and recording contracts for tango music.

The **Uruguayan tango** from Montevideo was also from the 19th century, and much later, in 1990, there was a newer style from Buenos Aires called the **nuevo tango**. **Ballroom tango** also developed in two styles, the **American** and the **International**. All Europe and also Japan enjoyed dancing the tango.

In August 2009 a Japanese pair, **Hiroshi Yamao** and his wife **Kyoto,** won the World Tango Championships held in Buenos Aires, Argentina. Forty-five pairs from all over the world had come to compete in the finals. Ballroom dancing had become very popular in Japan and especially so after the movie *Shall We Dance*, a Japanese-produced film.

The tango appeared in England in *The Sunshine Girl* (1913) *(Photo Plate 13-5)*. The Broadway version with **Vernon Castle** and **Julia Sanderson** made the tango a hit at tango teas, and so did the more sensuous versions seen after World War I in **Rudolph Valentino** movies (*The Four Horsemen of the Apocalypse*, 1921) and in several Broadway shows. There was *Tango Melody* in *The Coconuts* (1925, with dances by **Sammy Lee**, starring the **Marx Brothers),** and *Capt. Hook's Tango* in *Peter Pan* (1954, directed and staged by **Jerome Robbins**, starring **Mary Martin**). Other tangos in musicals were *Tango Ballad* in *The Threepenny Opera* (1955, with music by **Kurt Weill**), *A New Fangled Tango* in *Happy Hunting* (1956, starring **Ethel Merman**), *Pickpocket Tango* in *Redhead* (1959, starring **Gwen Verdon**, with director-choreographer **Bob Fosse** who was awarded a Tony citation), *Tango Argentino*, choreographed by **Claudio Segovia** (1983 in Paris, 1985 on Broadway, with many repeat performances for over 20 years), and **Luis Bravo**'s *Forever Tango* (1990 on the West coast, then on Broadway and a subsequent tour). These were all audience favorites.

Other Latin dances were likewise popular on Broadway. The **conga** in the Broadway musical *Wonderful Town* (1953), choreographed by **Donald Saddler**, achieved renown; this dance was also in the straight play movie version of 1942, *My Sister Eileen* (dance choreographed by **Bob Fosse**). The **conga** was a popular party dance of the 1930's and 1940's, and great for breaking the ice. It originated in Africa, followed by Cuba and Latin America, with lyrics commenting on social events. The dance progresses in a line with each dancer's hands on the waist of the person ahead. The **conga line** moves forward with 3 steps forward and a kick to the side.

An example of the love of dance in South America was seen during the 2014 World Cup games when the Colombian team broke out in well-choreographed, well-rehearsed, groovy and varied dances to celebrate its goals against Japan, Greece, and the Ivory Coast after having qualified for the first time for the quarterfinals. Millions saw this on YouTube.

The **samba**, **rhumba**, **cha-cha** (with a typical triple step – cha cha cha that goes quick, quick, quick, followed by slow, slow, it derived from the mambo and became popular in 1953), **merengue** (from the 1950's, with a sort of limping movement as one foot joins the other to the side), and **salsa** (a rhythm developed by Puerto Rican musicians and an extremely popular dance in the late 20th century) were also favored, but the one that influenced jazz dance the most was the **samba**. Playful and sexy with an infectious rhythm, it was popular in the 1940's and 1950's. Its sudden popularity began after the New York World's Fair of 1939, the many **Carmen Miranda** movies, and the dancing of **Irene and Vernon Castle**. The **samba** originated in Africa, was taken to Bahia, Brazil, by black slaves working in sugar plantations, and went to Rio de Janeiro with them for Carnival. The **samba** took over the holiday festivities in street dances, cafés, and

Jerome Robbins: Rehearsal for "West Side Story," 1960, unknown photographer.

Portrait of Agnes de Mille in "Three Virgins and a Devil," Created by photographer Carl van Vechten.

Sheet Music Cover: "The Kangaroo Hop." Composer: Melville Morris; Gus Kahn, lyricist. Publication: NY: Jerome H. Remick & Co., 1914.

Bob Fosse's all dance revue with a score of already existing music of all different styles. Poster designed by Bob Gill for the Broadway show directed and choreographed by Bob Fosse.

DanceBrazil performing "Ritmos," choreographed by NEA National Heritage Fellow Jelon Vieira, brings the art of Capoeira to the U.S. Photo by Tom Pich, 2009, for the NEA.

ballrooms until it became well established by the 1960's. In the movie *Black Orpheus* (1958) the music of the well-known Brazilian composers Antonio Carlos Jobim and Luiz Bonfá reflected both the sad and the lively emotions of Brazil.

When the jazzier musicals appeared on Broadway, there was no need for pear shaped tones in the singing. *West Side Story* (1957), for the chorus anyway, preferred the flat tones of dancers and non-singers and had no separate singing chorus. Choreographers like **Jerome Robbins** started to direct the whole show; performers, such as **Chita Rivera,** were expected to be able to act, to sing and to dance. *West Side Story* (music by **Leonard Bernstein,** lyrics by **Stephen Sondheim**, book by Arthur Laurents, choreography by **Jerome Robbins**) *(Photo Plate 13-3)* got especially great reviews for its dances, which were fully integrated into the musical. Robbins' next musical, *Gypsy* (1959, music **Jules Styne**, lyrics **Sondheim**) had **Jerome Robbins** as director-choreographer and starred **Ethel Merman.**

Being both choreographer and director allowed **Robbins** the freedom to reproduce his vision on whatever musical he was working. He inserted all types of dancing into this show, **burlesque**, **vaudeville**, **tap**, **jazz**, and **ballet**, anything appropriate to the story. His next show, *Fiddler on the Roof* (1964) was particularly attractive to him since his family was descended from Russian Jewish immigrants. His use of **folk dance** material *(Photo Plate 13-5)* was incredible and very appealing. Other outstanding shows with Robbins' choreography were *On the Town* (1944), *High Button Shoes* (1947, with a Mack Sennett-style chase ballet), *Miss Liberty* (1949), and *The King and I* (1953, using **Siamese dance** in the "House of Uncle Tom" sequence). Robbins was skillful in assembling dances from any era or style, whether comedy or dramatic. His musicals were all memorable. For his outstanding creativity he was inducted into the Dance Hall of Fame of the National Museum of Dance in Saratoga in 1989.

Syncopation, the pause and swing found in jazz music, could be seen in jazz dance, gave it vitality, and made people want to dance. It was that swing in the music that enticed people to dance. **Jelly Roll Morton** first used the word "swing" in 1928 in his song *Georgia Swing*, but Duke Ellington is credited with giving the name to that type of music in the lyrics to his song, *It Don't Mean a Thing* (1932), and, the lyrics go on *if it ain't got that swing*. By 1934-5 the word "swing" had come into common use.

**Swing** was transformed into energetic **jitterbug**, done to boogie woogie music, swinging the partner out and back, and throwing him or her up in the air. The Laurel and Hardy film *Hellzapoppin* (1941) has a great dance sequence choreographed by **Frankie Manning** (1914-2009).

**Frankie Manning**'s "specialty" and trademark were **aerial steps**, in which one partner jumped or was thrown over the other. He choreographed and danced in the movies *Hot Chocolate* (1941) and *Hellzapoppin* (1941). The latter movie is amazingly full of energy. It seems Frankie Manning wanted everyone to know what a happy dance **swing** was. Indeed, if you saw his movies, he looked very happy while dancing. He served in World War II and then worked for the U.S. postal service. In 1980, when **swing dancing** came back, **Frankie Manning** and his son traveled, danced, and taught the

**Lindy hop** around the world. He choreographed the Broadway show *Black and Blue* (1989) for which he received a Tony. In 2000 he was awarded a National Endowment for the Arts National Heritage Fellowship ($25,000). He has been called the ambassador for the **Lindy hop** and was still dancing and teaching the Lindy when he died at age 95.

The early 1930's were the years of the economic depression, and jazz musicians could no longer obtain lucrative employment in the Chicago clubs. Big "swing" orchestras could be found in the large ballrooms of New York that were well publicized. By this time jazz had lost much of its earthiness and improvisational quality. People danced to swing in a respectful manner. Hotel ballrooms had so-called "potted palm orchestras," because they were often to be found behind potted palms. "Swing and Sway with Sammy Kaye," or whichever was the popular orchestra of the day, was the rule. A few of the big bands of the 1930's and 1940's were the bands of Guy Lombardo, Shep Fields, Tommy Dorsey, Eddy Duchin, Fred Waring and Phil Spitalny.

Swing started more or less in 1936 and lasted about ten years; it led to the battle between swing and sweet sounds and subsequently to **jive** and **lindy**. The young generation took over the dance floor. They were sociable rather than political, a change from the depression teenagers of the early 1930's. **Bebop**, not as danceable, and **rock and roll** followed. With its no-contact **disco dances**, rock lasted for years.

The "King of Swing" was considered to be **Benny Goodman**. His band set the style for many years: sleek uniforms, initials BG on all the music stands, a showman drummer. And in spite of objections by Southern booking agents, he hired excellent musicians, both whites and blacks, and helped set those standards too.

The show *Wonderful Town* (1953, choreographed by **Donald Saddler**) depicted New York City life and swing in its *Swing* number. The Broadway musical *Ballroom* (1978, choreographed and directed by **Michael Bennetts** (1943-1987), with the **social dances** of the 1940's and 50's) represented the swing scene in the number *A Song for Dancing*.

A former American Ballet Theater dancer, **Michael Kidd** (1918-2007), became an outstanding director-choreographer of Broadway shows, using fast paced movements, handsprings, walkovers, ballet, and jazz with additional flavorings of all sorts – crapshooters, rural types, gangster types, and Parisian nightlife. His shows were *Guys and Dolls* 1951), *Can Can* (1953), *Li'l Abner* (1956), and *Destry Rides Again* (1959).

**Michael Kidd** also choreographed MGM's greatest film musical, *Seven Brides for Seven Brothers* (1954), directed by Stanley Donen and starring **Howard Keel**, **Marc Platt** (1913-2014), **Matt Mattox** *(Photo Plate 13-4)*, **Jacques d'Amboise**, **Russ Tamblyn**, **Tommy Rall**, and **Jeff Richards** as the Seven Brothers, performing spectacular **acrobatic dancing**. The men stole the show, or I should say the film.

**Bob Fosse** (1927-1987), quite the opposite from Kidd, incorporated his own particular way of moving and his own limitations into what became known as the Fosse jazz style. He used this in the *Steam Heat* number from *Pajama Game* (1954), in **Gwen**

**Verdon**'s numbers in *Damn Yankees* (1955, based on baseball), in *Sweet Charity* (1966), in *Chicago* (1974, with theatrical, eye-catching jazz numbers), and in *Dancin'* (1978, no plot, just dance) with **Ann Reinking** (b. 1949) and others. *Dancin'* was an outstanding show that ran for over four years (*Photo Plate 13-3)*. **Gwen Verdon** (1925-2000), Fosse's widow, and **Ann Reinking** put together the dance musical called *Fosse* (1999) as a tribute to **Bob Fosse**. It included dances from his stage and screen musicals. In 2007 **Bob Fosse** was inducted into the Hall of Fame of the National Museum of Dance in Saratoga, New York.

**Marge** (b. 1919) **and Gower Champion** (1919-1980) were a husband and wife dance team when Gower started doing choreography and directing Broadway shows. He used film projections and photos in the Broadway show *The Happy Time* (1968), and in *Hello Dolly* (1964) he installed a circular runway for the waiters and for **Carol Channing**. He was very resourceful. He won a Tony for *Bye, Bye Birdie* (1960), starring **Chita Rivera** (b. 1933) and **Dick Van Dyke** (b.1925). **Gower Champion** captured the **Elvis Presley** type idol perfectly in this very successful musical. In real life, Elvis's hip gyrations reminded many of the snake hip movements of an old black Southern dance. **Gower Champion**'s last work, *42nd Street* (1980), opened the same day on which he died of a rare blood cancer. He received many Tony awards for his exceptional dances.

Early **Lindy** steps could be seen in *Bubbling Brown Sugar* (1976, choreographed by **Billy Wilson** and dealing with Harlem from about 1930 to 1946) and in *Hallelujah Baby* (1967, choreographed by **Kevin Carlisle**, about black people in show business and the social problems of the times). The spirit of the 1950's, with the early **Lindy**, **jitterbug**, and the start of the **hair-combing gesture** by teenagers, is an integral part of *Grease* (Feb. 14, 1972, a long-running show – 3,388 performances) with both the movie and the musical choreographed by **Patricia Birch**. In *Sweet Charity* **Bob Fosse** choreographed the offshoot of the **Lindy**, the **frug** (with much arm and hip movement and little locomotion) that led to the **wobble**, the **watusi**, the **surf**, and the **swim**.

The **watusi** dance was almost as popular as the **twist**, especially with the surf boarding subculture of the 1960's. The watusi was a solo dance stemming from Southern Central Africa. In 1964 a cover of *TV Guide* depicted **Fred Astaire** and **Barry Chase** doing the **watusi**. Sand and surfboards took the place of ballroom floors for this dance. TV viewers who watched *American Bandstand* could learn all the new fad dances. The **watusi** started with knees bent, feet twelve inches apart, and strong side movements made with the hips as if swinging a golf club. The feet might take one or two small steps front or back. The head and upper torso bobbed with accentuated arm movements, and palms moved firmly right and left while being held flat vertically.

*American Bandstand*, hosted by **Dick Clark** (1929-2012) from 1957 until 1989, and *Soul Train*, beginning in 1970 and hosted by **Don Cornelius**, were both television musical variety shows that presented the favorite recording artists of the time and a group of excellent regular dancers to perform the latest dances. These shows also held auditions for extra dancers. They had to be properly dressed and look immaculate, with ties for the boys, skirts and blouses or a dress for the girls. Everyone in the country could tune in and learn the **jitterbug**, **swing**, **rock and roll**, the **twist**, the **hustle**, and the newer dances: **locking** (it looks robotic and mechanical as the dancer moves then freezes to hip hop music), **popping** (became popular in the 1970's), and **electric boogie** (an electric current seems to pass through the dancer's body as one joint after another is moved in **break dancing**).

Break dancing began on the streets of the U.S. *(Photo Plate 13-4)*. The **b-boys** or **b-girls**, as **break dancers** are called, must be able to improvise, to do spins on their heads, **power moves**, moments of **freezes**, **body popping**, footwork and sharp actions to contrast with the freezes and all the latest versions, such as **jookin** *(Photo Plate 13-4)*.

Several of the movements from **break dancing** and **jookin**, such as standing on one's head and dancing on the tips of the toes with the knees bent, can also be found in the **Scissors Dance**, a traditional challenge dance for two or more dancers performed in the southern and central highlands of Peru to test spiritual and physical strength.

All the versions of the **Lindy** were at one time frequently seen on television, but not anymore. There were the bobbysoxers jitterbugging while wearing bobby socks and saddle shoes, the ladies wearing small hats while dressed to kill, and the men wearing zoot suits, as well as the G. I. Joe in the USO Canteen version of the jitterbug. All of these versions were shown on *Dance Fever* or on the *PBS Ballroom Championship Exhibitions*, shows that are now rarely on TV.

With the arrival of rock 'n' roll (the term was coined and popularized by Alan Freed of WINS radio), pop singers also began to dance all sorts of jazz steps. Audiences at that time bought the records and tried to duplicate the dance steps. The title of the 1953 song *Rock 'Round the Clock* was exactly what many were doing.

In 1963, discos appeared. Whisky à Go Go, the first one, opened in Paris. By the mid-1970's thousands of them had opened in the United States. New York City alone had two to three hundred discos with people of all ages dancing as they felt the music. It was a comfortable atmosphere, with psychedelic lighting and couples dancing but not touching. People could communicate with their partner, the music, and their feelings, as they wished; and psychologists again pointed out all the harmful effects to the young of a no-contact position in dancing, as they had done in the 1920's. More fad dances appeared: the **wiggle**, the **rope**, the **spark**, the **bump** (dancers at discos would bump their own hip with their partner's hip on the beat of the music), the **bus stop**, and the **mashed potato**, among others. Luckily the discos (discotheques) had a DJ (disk jockey) to choose the records, to play them, and to teach the latest dance steps of these fad dances. In their way they promoted songs, singers, and arrangements much as the Tin Pan Alley pluggers had pushed songs and sheet music in the 1920's by playing them on the piano and seeing that they got played in stores and on amateur nights in theaters so everybody would hear them.

The 1950's had much in common with the 1920's and their dance halls: a dance craze, dancing in a no-contact position, trendy dances with descriptive names or animal names *(Photo Plate 13-3)*. Some of the dances with music from the 1950's and 1960's were: *The Hucklebuck* (1949), *The Fish* (1955), *Dance the Mess Around* (1958), *Mashed Potato Time* (1962), *Limbo Rock* (1962), *Walking the Dog* (1963), and *Do the Funky Chicken* (1969).

Photo Plate 13-4

Afro-Caribbean jazz: a Calypso Walk.
Dancer: Helene Andreu;

Dancer, Helene Andreu, demonstrates
the stretched jazz hand position used
by Matt Mattox.

Latin jazz: a Cuban Walk.
Dancer: Helene Andreu;

James Leon and Willa Mae Ricker,
photo by Gjon Mili, 1943.

Hip hop style dancer performing
against a white background. Photo
by Carlos E. Santa Maria.

Michael Jackson performing
"Billie Jean," photograper not
identified, 2001.

The **mashed potato** was a **rock and roll disco dance** done to Dee Dee Sharpe's song *Mashed Potato Time* and was popular in 1962. You started with your feet twelve inches apart. You swiveled your heels so your knees and toes were pointed in, then after that you swiveled so your knees and toes pointed out. You continued, but on the first swivel on which the toes pointed out, your weight went on the right foot and you lifted the left foot; you continued to swivel with toes in, next with toes out and now the weight went on the left foot and you lifted the right one. You did it with a kick or a bounce if you preferred. It took energy. The heel swivel dated back to the 1920's.

The Beatles' song of 1964, *Twist and Shout*, stayed among the top five on the *Billboard* charts for 1964. (*Billboard* has existed since 1894, with a magazine and charts to inform music fans about trends in music.) The **twist dance** originally came from **wringin'** and **twistin'**, an African-American **plantation dance** from the 1890's. By 1959 the **twist** reached the peak of its fame largely due to **Chubby Checkers'** *Do the Twist*, which had everybody doing the twist. It became number one on the singles chart of records in 1960 in the U.S. and again in 1961. In 1962 the twist peaked. The twist led to additional **rock and roll dances** to be done at discos: the **fish**, the **slop**, the **waddle**, the **monkey**, the **shake**, the **fly**, the **jerk**, and the **hully gully**.

**Go-go dancing** started in the 1960's when women at the Peppermint Lounge in New York City got up on the tables to do the twist. Many wore miniskirts and boots to nightclubs; hence this became the desired outfit when promoters decided to hire them in the 1960's to entertain patrons. The word go-go comes from the phrase "go-go-go" used for someone with lots of energy and was also derived from the French à gogo meaning in abundance. **Carol Doda** began dancing **go-go dancing** topless (after having silicone breast implants) and continued dancing go-go for 22 years at the Condor Club in San Francisco. Suspended cages in which **cage dancers** would perform began in 1969 at the Whisky à Go-Go in Los Angeles' Sunset Strip. Many go-go bars were to be found in Saigon during the Vietnam War to entertain U.S. troops. Moreover, **caged go-go dances** could be seen on TV in the final sequence of the show *Hullabaloo A-Go-Go* and in ABC's *Shindig*. **Madonna**'s music and her MTV music videos in which she included go-go dancing led to the renewal in the popularity of go-go dancing in the 1980's. There were also clubs patronized by transsexuals and gay men and these had male go-go dancers. Other clubs like the Xenon nightclub in New York City provided go-go boxes on which amateurs could go-go dance. The song in *Chorus Line* says *Dance: Ten; Looks: Three*. In other words, if three is what you have in the looks department, that is not enough. And, if what is most important on Broadway is *Tits and Ass* (as another song from *Chorus Line* says), it is even more so for a go-go dancer. What go-go dancing is all about is **jazz dance** with a very erotic element added. The variety of arm and body movements, as in all dancing, depends on the creativity and skill of the individual dancer and the choreographer.

**Michael Bennett** (1943-1987) was considered Broadway's greatest choreographer. He was a musical theater director, choreographer, and dancer. He danced in many Broadway musicals but soon realized that choreography was his thing. He received innumerable Tony awards. His principal shows were *Promises, Promises* (1968), *Coco* (1969), *Company* (1970), *Follies* (1971), *Seesaw* (1973), *A Chorus Line* (1975), *Ballroom* (1978), and *Dreamgirls* (1981). He began his dance career as a dancer in the European tour of Robbins' *West Side Story*.

*A Chorus Line* (music by Marvin Hamlisch, lyrics by Edward Kleban) opened at the Public Theatre, moved to Broadway's Shubert Theatre and remained there for fifteen years for a total of 6,137 performances. **Bennett** won the 1976 Pulitzer Prize for Drama for this show. Instead of commissioning a script for it, he let the story develop from his long interviews with the Broadway "gypsies" (as the chorus dancers are called), who were auditioning for the show. **Bennett**'s choreography was not distinguished by a particular style as **Fosse**'s was, but by the characters represented in each particular musical. In spite of dying at a young age, of AIDS, he created countless memorable musicals.

In the 1980's there was a revival of **swing,** with large dance bands at discos and at Roseland in New York, swing music on the radio, and closed social dance positions with partners touching.

A Broadway musical of 1981, *Sophisticated Ladies*, brought back Duke Ellington's songs with a twenty-piece orchestra conducted by his son Mercer Ellington, with choreography by **Henry Le Tang**, **Donald McKayle**, and **Michael Smuin**, and starring **Judith Jamison** and tap great **Gregory Hines**.

**Punk rock** was a response against the neat, nice look of American Bandstand attire. It was now tolerable to look disheveled and sloppy at discos. There seemed to be an effort at individualism and uniqueness on the dance floors of discos: Studio 54, Hurrah, Ritz, Irving Place, Danceteria, Palladium (previously renowned for **Latin dance** in the 1940's). Most of these discos left, due to new zoning and licensing regulations, violations, and also complaints about excessive noise, blocked exits, and alcohol being served to minors. By the 1990's, dancing was out and lounging was in. However, by 2000, clubbing with dancing was in again but in smaller, more elegant places, such as Spa, Conscience Point, and Centro Fly.

Forty-one years after it originally opened in 1967, *Hair, The American Tribal Love-Rock Musical* was revived and won a Tony for Best Revival of a Musical. It depicted the birth of the 1960's culture. It had lyrics by Gerome Ragni and James Rado and music by Galt MacDermot. Some of the memorable songs from the show were *Aquarius*, *Good Morning Starshine*, and *Let the Sun Shine In*. **Karole Armitage** provided her youthful ensemble with joyous hippie choreography that looked as though it had been improvised on the spot. The audience felt impelled to join the cast as the energetic group danced by them in the theater's aisles. The DVD (1979) of *Hair* also had appropriate hippie choreography, but this time by **Twyla Tharp**.

More popular dance films followed. The 1977 movie with John Travolta, *Saturday Night Fever*, was so well liked that **John Travolta** was soon known in every household and the film helped to do the same for disco music and the **hustle dance** in the 1970's. The choreography was by **Lester Wilson**. It was adapted for Broadway in 1999 with direction and choreography by **Arlene Phillips**; it featured the songs of the Bee Gees, was loved by old and young, and had a good deal of **disco dancing**.

Another favorite was the film *Fame* (1980), choreography by **Debbie Allen**, with many dances that teenagers saw and tried out. The television series (1982-1987) of *Fame* was based on the film. **Debbie Allen**, the recipient of several awards, was the director-choreographer for this popular series. It took place at the Fiorello H. La Guardia High School of Music & Art and Performing Arts in New York City.

In the 1980's, British musicals came to the U.S. but without much dancing, except for *Starlight Express,* choreographed by **Arlene Phillips**, and *Cats,* choreographed by **Gillian Lynne** and based on the poems from *Old Possum's Book of Practical Cats* by T.S. Elliot. It opened in Great Britain in 1981, in the U.S in 1982, and by June 10, 1997, *Cats* had become the longest running musical on Broadway with 6,138 performances; it closed on September 8, 2000, after 7,485 performances. It won a Tony for Best Musical, one for Best Score (Andrew Lloyd Webber), and one for Best Book for a musical. The director was Trevor Nunn. The choreography by **Gillian Lynne** was stunning, and included **ballet**, **jazz**, and **modern**, as suited the particular characters. (*Cats* was translated into over 20 languages.)

There were also a variety of novel productions for lovers of dance: *Dancin'* (1978), choreographed by **Bob Fosse** *(Photo Plate 13-3)*, with lots of dancing but songs and book were secondary and almost nonexistent. *Contact*, Tony Winner for Best Musical in 2000, choreographed by **Susan Stroman** and **John Weidman**, had no singing, just three short stories, excellent unforgettable dancing, almost no book, and no orchestra. But *Contact* had much originality.

The Broadway musical *Swing* (2000), choreographed by **Lynne Taylor-Corbett** and directed by Jerry Zaks, was a high-spirited mixture of new and old, with happy swinging music and dance, and was well liked by audience and critics.

There has been a revival of **swing dancing** in Manhattan since 2009. Since then there have been many swing dance clubs, instructors (some for free), bands, dancers, and events. *The New York Times Weekend Arts Section* of Dec. 3, 2011, listed them in great detail on pages 1 and 15 with names, locations, days, phone numbers, and web sites. Some of these included Frim Fram Jam, New York Swing Dance Society, Swing Remix, and Dance Manhattan. Apparently people of all ages and races participated in this swing revival and enjoyed the swing dance events *(Photo Plate 13-4)*.

If you are eager to get a DVD and learn the steps from a popular film and Broadway production, *Hairspray*, the musical film extravaganza of 2007, is an excellent choice. Everyone, and especially teenagers, wanted to learn the "hot new dance moves" that the star of *Hairspray* learned in the show. **Adam Shankman** choreographed this film. **Jerry Mitchell** choreographed the Broadway version of 2003 that is based on the original film of 1988, choreographed by **Edward Love** and assistant choreographer **Kiki**

**Sheppard**. A few more excellent films with dance include *Moulin Rouge*, *Chicago*, and *Dreamgirls*.

**Freeform jazz** uses all or any of the many forms of dance and jazz that came before it: **Afro-Caribbean** *(Photo Plate 13-4)*, **Latin dances, social dances, disco movements, ballet, modern, tap, isolations** (as in *Dreamgirls* 1981, by **Michael Bennett**, with a hip lift, a head swing, a turn or kick here and there, and winning a Tony for best director and for best choreography together with **Michael Peters**), **hip hop**, and the newest addition, **break dancing**.

**Break dancing** was performed to hip hop music or rap and was a sort of **street dancing** in the 1970's. The **b-boys** and **b-girls** did competitions called **battles**, as individuals or in groups, called **crews**. Each **crew** attempted to do more complicated movements than its opponents. The ability to turn on one's back or head and to balance in gravity-defying poses was extremely important, as was athleticism.

The 1980's movies, such as *Flashdance* (1983, choreographed by **Jeff Hornaday**), and *Footloose* (1984, choreographed by **Lynne Taylor-Corbett**, and revised in 2011), give the appearance of not having a choreographer but of having a cast who really just had to dance; it all looked improvised. In 1984 the films *Breakin'* and *Breakin'2: Electric Boogaloo* opened and presented **popping, breaking, locking**, and **electric boogaloo** to movie audiences worldwide. In 1987 the movie *Dirty Dancing* with **Patrick Swayze** was released. This was another audience favorite.

In the twentieth century there was much amplification, and synthesizers could imitate any desired sound. The music could be speeded up, or slowed down. Electro-acoustical engineering produced anything desired in sound, but the dancing was real, never artificial. And people turned to dance more and more. It became available free of charge in parks, outdoor spaces, and in some museums such as The Brooklyn Museum on the first Saturday of the month. Lincoln Center, among others, offered free outdoor dance participation with excellent bands playing salsa, Cajun, swing, Lindy, rhumba, and others.

Dance critic **Jennifer Dunning** wrote in 2001 that there were more male choreographers than female choreographers and that more articles had been written about male dancers than about female dancers. Pop singers and television dance contests had done much to make dance very acceptable for men, and so did the musical *Billy Elliot* (2009, choreography by **Peter Darling**) and the videos of **Michel Jackson**.

The person who had the most influence on popular dance, music and videos was "The King of Pop," **Michael Jackson** (1958-2009), who set the standard for excellence in music videos and invented the **moonwalk** to the front, the side, and the back that was copied by everyone, along with his **spins** and other moves *(Photo Plate 13-4)*. His music was loved worldwide and his sudden death was mourned worldwide too.

Sheet Music Cover: "The Argentine" (tango - dance) from "The Sunshine Girl." Lyrics: Paul A. Rubens & Arthur Wimperis; Music: Paul A. Rubens (1873-1917). Cover photo of Julia Sanderson and Vernon Castle by White Studios, NY. Publication: London: Chappell & Co., c.1912..

"Drawing in Two Colors" also published under the title "Interpretation of Harlem Jazz." Print on Japanese paper; offset lithograph and halftone in two colors. c. 1920. German artist Winold Reiss (1886-1953), NY, between 1915 and 1920.

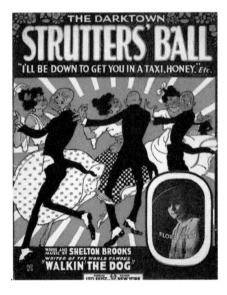

Three Russian Dancers, 1895, by Edgar Degas (1834-1917). Medium: pastel.

Sheet Music Cover: "The Darktown Strutters' Ball." (I'll Be Down to Get You in a Taxi, Honey.) Words and Music: Shelton Brooks (1886-1975), a child of black American and Native American parents; he wrote "Walkin' the Dog" and "Some of These Days;" he played the piano and organ. Well-known music cover illustrators, William Austin Starmer and Frederick Waite Starmer (brothers), depict couples dancing and a photo of Flora Stern. Pub: NY: Leo Feist, 1917.

Now in the twenty-first century the newest variety of **hip-hop** is **krumping**. Before that, a form of **krumping** known as **hip-hop clowns** existed in which dancers painted their faces in order to be better able to express themselves without feeling self-conscious. It has been the same throughout time whenever masks or excessive makeup were used; the dancer claimed he could dance more freely with his new identity. **Krumping** is an aggressive form of **hip-hop**. It is hard and intense and is danced either to rap music or to music with a heavy beat. It can look a lot like fighting. When done in a circular formation, it has a spiritual connotation, as did all **round dances** throughout history: in the middle ages, in **African dances**, in the **ring shouts** by the African Americans, and in **Native American dances**. Round dances, especially the open round dances, were meant to keep the good spirits in and the bad ones out. An example of **krumping** was danced in the latest *Nutcracker* by the group called Urban Ballet Theater under the direction of **Daniel Catanach** at the Abrons Arts Center in New York; he choreographed the rats doing **krumping**.

Several new musicals appeared, and as usual some did well but some did not. The musical *The Scottsboro Boys*, 2010, music by **Kander and Ebb**, direction and choreography by **Susan Stroman** and book by David Thompson, won the Outer Critics Circle Award for Outstanding New Off-Broadway Musical. There is no love interest in this musical. It is about nine young black boys accused of a crime – rape – in Alabama; they had not committed it and neither had anyone else. Perhaps an unusual subject for a musical but one that the producers, Barry and Fran Weissler and Jacki Barlia Florin, felt was a challenging and provocative subject and should be told. Kander and Ebb used the format of a minstrel show with satire to denounce injustice. While the musical did well Off-Broadway, at the Vineyard Theater, when it moved up to the Lyceum, on Broadway, it had a different type of audience and too small an audience to sell enough seats for the theater on Broadway. This musical dealt with the controversial and prejudiced Scottsboro trials of the 1930's, the third musical by Kander and Ebb based on a contentious subject (*Cabaret* and *Chicago*). *The Scottsboro Boys* was nonetheless entertaining. The entire cast was brilliant; all but one of the major characters were black Americans. Actors' Equity Association awarded *The Scottsboro Boys* the Fifth Annual ACCA Award for Outstanding Broadway Chorus in recognition of the distinctive talents and contributions made by the original chorus members of that musical. (The 12 Broadway musicals that opened in the 2010-11 season were eligible.) Kander and Ebb gave us a picture of corruption while giving us outstanding songs and lyrics. The musical won the Lucille Lortel Award for Outstanding Musical and the Drama Desk Award for Outstanding Lyrics. The lyricist, Fred Ebb, died before the completion of the musical, and so John Kander, the composer, finished the lyrics. **Susan Stroman** won the Lucille Lortel Award for Choreography. She used chairs to change the sets from a railway car to a cage-like prison cell, made an ingenious use of tambourines, and included lively dancing in a nightmarish electric chair dream routine. It closed on December 12, 2010, after 29 previews and 49 regular performances. There is an award-nominated DVD of this musical.

**Latin jazz dance** *(Photo Plate 13-4)* came back in 2007-2010 with the revival of *West Side Story*. Critics praised **Joey McKneeley**'s version of the original 1957 Tony-winning choreography by **Jerome Robbins**. **McKneeley**'s choreography still has the gangs performing fierce, prowling moves with the **classical ballet** style of the original, as well as the exuberant **Latin dance** of the girls and boys. Critics found **Cody Green**'s leaps and turns a standout performance and praised the contemporary use of a classic style by a cast of dancers soaring with talent.

*In the Heights*, a musical about Hispanic Washington Heights in New York, came out in 2008. It had a creative mix of **Latin jazz dance** and **break dancing** in a youthful, exuberant musical. The choreography by **Andy Blankenbuehler** and the songs and music by Lin-Manuel Miranda were vibrant with **salsa**, **Latin pop music**, and unexpected rap songs in a Broadway production, a plus. It was exciting and joyous and won the Tony Award for the Best Musical of 2008.

The economic situation since 2008 did not seem to have any immediate adverse effect on many of the Broadway musical productions. Maybe this was because the caliber of shows was so high, including the 2009 revivals: *Guys and Dolls, South Pacific, Hair, Hairspray, The Phantom of the Opera,* and *Mary Poppins*. In 2010, Broadway shows did exceptionally well. For those who could not afford the high prices, the Theater Development Fund, the nonprofit organization behind the TKTS theater discount service, had three TKTS outlets, two in Manhattan, at Broadway and West 47th Street, and at South Street Seaport, and one in Brooklyn at the MetroTech Center. Tickets there were sold at half price plus handling charges for the highest priced seats. Reasonably priced tickets for excellent shows are also available at Brooklyn College on Flatbush Avenue in Brooklyn, at BAM, on Lafayette Avenue near Atlantic Avenue, in Brooklyn, and at other locations.

Broadway made a lot of money in 2012 from some of the newer shows: *The Book of Mormon* and *Spider-Man: Turn Off the Dark, The Lion King* and *Wicked,* but also from aggressive ticket pricing, $477.00 for some of the best seats for *Mormon* and $197.50 for the best seats for *The Lion King*. By April 2012 *The Lion King* had grossed $850 million since opening in 1997, just surpassing *The Phantom of the Opera,* which opened in 1988.

Another successful musical was *Memphis*. It opened on Broadway in October 2009 and won the 2010 Tony Award for Best Musical as well as the Outer Critics Circle Award for Outstanding New Broadway Musical and the 2009-2010 Drama Desk Award for Outstanding Musical. **David Bryan** wrote the music and lyrics, **Joe DiPietro** wrote the lyrics and the book, and **Sergio Trujillo** did the choreography. The musical is based on the real-life story of a Memphis DJ, Dewey Phillips, one of the first white DJ's to play black music on the radio in the 1950's, and his love for his lead black singer, at a time when a mixed marriage would not have been acceptable. Critics were enthusiastic about the exuberant performances, singing, dancing, and acting of the cast and especially that of the leads **Montego Glover** (as the singer, Felicia) and **Chad Kimball** (as Huey Calhoun, the DJ). The rock'n'roll music and the imaginative staging showing the movements of the singing groups heard on the radio and later seen on TV were also a plus. A second company of *Memphis* began a first national US tour in 2011.

"The most entertaining musical in years," "A whole lot of song, dance, and acted glory," "hilarious and humane," "expert choreography by co-director **Casey Nicholaw**," and "exuberantly entertaining" were some of the reviewers' comments regarding the 2011 musical *The Book of Mormon*. It has book, lyrics, and music by Trey Parker, Matt Stone (creators of *South Park*) and Richard Lopez (*Avenue Q*), and choreography by co-director **Casey Nicholaw**. The story deals with two Mormon missionaries sent to a dangerous area in Uganda to spread the word. The songs are clever and easy to hum; the ensemble numbers are lively and surprising; the lead singer-dancer **Rory O'Malley** is excellent; and the ensemble is polished and enthusiastic. It won a Tony for best musical of 2011 and recouped its capitalization of approximately $11.4 million after 9 months of performances at the Eugene O'Neill Theater.

However, the Tony for best actor in a musical in 2011 went to **Norbert Leo Butz** for his absolutely outstanding performance and dance as the weary and wily detective Carl Hanratty, a frumpy FBI agent pursuing a con man in *Catch Me If You Can* (choreography by **Jerry Mitchell**). In 2005 Norbert Leo Butz won a similar award for his performance in the musical *Dirty Rotten Scoundrel*.

Television, especially in the past several years, has had wonderful dance contests with a diversity of dances. If you would like to study dance or go to dance concerts but are not too familiar with the variety, these TV programs are a good way to see what is around that might interest you. The *International Dance Contest* has presented the **Argentine tango**, traditional **Irish clog dancing**, **modern dance** by an Australian company, Russian **ballet**, Russian **folk dancing** *(Photo Plate 13-5)*, Chinese **Buddhist Monks Dancing**, **Traditional East Indian dance**, **Bollywood type of East Indian dance**, United States **break dancing**, and Australian **break dancing**, among others. Break dancing and variations of it with other names such as krumping, can be seen on television and on the Internet. These dancers can perform many intricate moves, turns on their hands and heads, and can also do ballet's tours jetés horizontally instead of vertically. Some of it is quite remarkable. It's definitely for the young.

Television's *Dancing with the Stars,* still popular today, first aired in 2003, has shown us the **Viennese waltz**, the **tango**, **swing**, **jive**, **cha-cha**, **samba**, **quick step**, the **bolero**, the **lambada** (from Brazil, and combining the passion, hips, and the zest of the **rhumba** and the **samba**), the **Charleston**, the **paso doble**, and the **fox trot**.

*So You Think You Can Dance* has numerous excellent choreographers responsible for putting the dances together, and some contestants have danced a **fox trot**, **samba**, **East Indian Bollywood type dance**, **Broadway jazz**, **break dancing**, a **ballet adagio**, **krumping**, **contemporary** or modern **expressive dance**, and **elegant ballroom dancing** a la Ginger Rogers-Fred Astaire – quite a challenge with such a variety of styles of dance to be performed by the contestants. The contestants seem to be getting better and better each year since the show started in 2005.

And don't forget DVDs. Libraries have many of your favorite dance companies and musical productions on DVDs and they can be borrowed like a book.

Remember to try some of the above to see enjoyable dance programs and to keep up with all the newest trends and the old favorites. Whenever possible, treat yourself to a live dance concert or a live Broadway or Off-Broadway musical.

# 14

# Ballet from the 1960's

## to the 21$^{st}$ Century

By 1960 the ballet situation in America had changed. Dance activity had greatly increased since the unsuccessful 1930's, with additional companies, superior regional companies, bigger audiences, new patrons of the arts, more dance students in private studios and in colleges, and greater possibilities for dance-related careers for non-dancers. The New York City Ballet and The American Ballet Theater companies each had over 100 dancers and large budgets. Ballet companies could be found in most major cities by the year 1960.

**George Balanchine** had created what became known as the American **neo-classic style** and developed the dancers trained to execute it. The style was a bold, flexible, quick, cool, and dignified one that included angularity, turned-in classical positions, interweaving of groups, and great energy. George Balanchine and **Lincoln Kirstein** had started small companies like Ballet Society for the students to perform abstract works such as *Mozartiana* (1934), *Concerto Barocco* (1941), and *Serenade* (1934) to the music of Tchaikovsky's *Serenade for Strings,* with simple leotards, tights, toe shoes for the women, and white T-shirts and socks, black tights and ballet shoes for the men. *Serenade* is still performed worldwide by many companies.

In 1946, after World War II, Balanchine, together with Kirstein who had just finished his military service, founded the New York City Ballet Company, which performed Balanchine's works primarily *(Photo Plates 14-1, 2, 3, and 5 )*. *Jewels* (1967), a three-act ballet with elaborate costumes, was an example of his neo-classic style. His use of angularity and dissonance was shown in *Four Temperaments* (1946), *Agon* (1957), and *Ivesiana* (1954). His classical style was seen in his version of *The Nutcracker* (1954). He also choreographed *Western Symphony* (1954), *Square Dance* (1957), and *Stars and Stripes* (1958), ballets with an American flavor. His type of movements, energy, and speed seemed very appropriate for the United States. Balanchine's ballets have also been staged by the Kirov Ballet, the Paris Opera Ballet, and the many regional companies scattered throughout the United States: **Helgi Tomasson**'s San Francisco Ballet, **Robert Weiss** and **Richard Tanner**'s Pennsylvania Ballet Company (later under the artistic direction of **Roy Kaiser**), **Peter Boal**'s Pacific Northwest Ballet, **Suzanne Farrell**'s Washington Ballet, **Edward Villella**'s Miami City Ballet, and **Ib Andersen**'s Ballet Arizona.

In 1959, **Balanchine** and **Martha Graham** had a collaboration of sorts in *Episodes*. Graham choreographed the first half using her own dancers and the ballerina **Sally Wilson** in a ballet with a plot; Balanchine choreographed the second half, without narrative, danced by his company and the modern dancer **Paul Taylor** from Graham's company (at that time). Modern and ballet were indeed finding some common grounds, as **Kurt Jooss** had wished (see Chapter 7), with modern dance choreographers now also choreographing for ballet companies, thus satisfying the ballet audiences' desire to see something new. Indeed, some ballet companies, such as the New York City Ballet Company, began to encourage ballet dancers to do choreography themselves through workshops like the Diamond Project. Furthermore, cities throughout the United States were building cultural centers similar to Lincoln Center.

In the 1960's several companies came to America on tour; the Moiseyev, a Russian folk dance company, and the Bolshoi Ballet from Russia were very popular. **Galina Ulanova,** looking remarkably like a sixteen year old in *Romeo and Juliet*, and **Olga Plisetskaya,** in **Fokine**'s *The Dying Swan,* were favorites, as well as **Carla Fracci**, from Italy, especially in *Giselle*. Everyone marveled at the fact that the men from the Moiseyev and the Bolshoi were large sturdy men and yet they could jump very high and looked so graceful.

The variety of other folk dance companies coming to the U.S. to perform was incredible. They came from Mexico (Ballet Folklorico), Israel (Inbal), Poland (Mazowsze), Argentina (Tango Argentina), the Philippines, Taiwan, China, India (with **Balasaraswati**, the Indian dancer celebrated worldwide for her rendering of the **Bharatanatyam Classical dance** style of India). The popularity of all these traditional dances from around the world showed people's need to connect with their roots.

It took us a while to realize that Americans were good dancers. Dancers did not have to be Russian. Soon Americans too started to travel: **Benjamin Harkavy** went to co-direct for the Nederlands Dans Theater, **Ted Shawn** became ballet master for the Cologne Company of Germany, **Todd Bolender** for the Turkish ballet and for a Turkish production of *Kiss Me Kate*. **Donald Saddler** choreographed musicals in Italy and received many Italian Awards (comparable to our Tonys) for these. The State Department of the United States sent several of our dance companies and musical theater classics abroad as cultural ambassadors. The Alvin Ailey American Dance Theater went to Russia, and the choreographer of The New York City Opera (no longer in existence since 2013), **Andrew Thomas**, went to Poland to choreograph *My Fair Lady*. American musicals became known worldwide.

**Maria Alba**, a flamenco dancer, and **José Greco** (1918-2000, flamenco dancer and choreographer), were both American and yet excellent Spanish dancers. Greco's family (Italians from Italy) had moved to Brooklyn, New York, when José was ten. In 1993 Greco received a Choreographer's Fellowship from the National Endowment for the Arts that enabled him to restage his most notable choreography and save it for posterity through labanotation.

In 1962 the State Department chose the New York City Ballet to tour the Soviet Union, and Balanchine saw his homeland again; the tour was a great success. In 1963 the Ford Foundation gave a total of $6 billion, $2 billion to the New York City Ballet and $4 billion to its affiliate, The School of American Ballet, giving scholarships to promising students like **Suzanne Farrell** and **Cynthia Gregory** as well as to specific local schools so that they too could give scholarships to deserving students.

Many of the other ballet companies, as well as the modern dance companies were not pleased that the New York City Ballet was the only company to have received a grant, and such a huge one at that. However, in 1965 President Lyndon Johnson signed into law the National Foundation on the Arts and the Humanities. This opened up another source of grants – the United States Government. The American Ballet Theater, in 1965, was the first to receive a federal grant – $350,000 from the National Endowment for the Arts (NEA).

In 1968, after the assassination of Martin Luther King, **Arthur Mitchell** (b. 1934) a superb black principal dancer of the New York City Ballet Company in the 1950's and 60's, felt challenged enough to start the ballet company The Dance Theater of Harlem *(Photo Plates 14-2)*, together with his instructor **Karel Shook**. They showed that blacks could also dance ballet if given a chance. Arthur Mitchell had studied at the Performing Arts High School in New York and had received a scholarship to study at the School of American Ballet. He became the first black principal dancer in the New York City Ballet Company and danced in *Bugaku, Midsummer Night's Dream*, among others, and also in *Agon*, created by **Balanchine** specifically for **Diana Adams** and **Arthur Mitchell** *(Photo Plate 14-1)*.

The repertoire of the Dance Theater of Harlem included **Agnes de Mille**'s *Fall River Legend* (1948), **Balanchine**'s *Bugaku* (1963), **Louis Johnson**'s *Forces of Rhythm* (1972), **Geoffrey Holder**'s *Dougla* (1974), **Garth Fagan**'s *Footprints Dressed in Red* (1986), **Alonzo King**'s *Signs and Wonders* (1995), the pas de deux from *Le Corsaire*, **Arthur Mitchell**'s updated renovation of *Giselle* (1984), staged by **Frederick Franklin** and occurring in the Louisiana Bayou (it was telecast nationally as the *Creole Giselle*), and **Michael Smuin**'s *A Song for Dead Warriors* (1999, from the 1979 original for The San Francisco Ballet) about the persecution of Native American Indians. It was a very diversified repertoire.

Problems with finances in 2004 put a halt to stage productions but the school on West 153rd Street continued. The principal ballerinas of The Dance Theater of Harlem were **Lydia Abarca** and **Virginia Johnson**. The male contingent included **Ronald Perry**, **Paul Russell**, and **Mel Tomlinson**. **Arthur Mitchell** was awarded the 12th annual Paul Robeson Award by Actors' Equity Association in 1986, the Kennedy Center Honors in 1993, a MacArthur Fellowship award in 1994, and in 1995 the United States National Medal of the Arts, presented by President Clinton. **Arthur Mitchell** was inducted into the National Museum of Dance at Saratoga Springs, N. Y. in 1999. He has been very dedicated and has certainly deserved all these honors and more.

In 1965 **Alexandra Danilova** *(Photo Plate 14-3)* and **Balanchine** instituted the annual School of American Ballet workshop performances. Occasionally the program showed pieces that had not been presented by the company for several years, such as *Bourrée Fantasque* in 2010 (not seen since 1993). These performances also gave balletomanes a chance to try to pick out the next ballet stars of the New York City Ballet.

251

Danilova received a Kennedy Center Award in 1989 for her contribution to the arts in the United States.

Balanchine had insisted on starting a school to train his future dancers, and it proved to be an excellent idea; many of the company's best dancers have come from the school. The teachers were and are inspiring and dedicated. When I attended the school they were **Felia Doubrovska**, **Elise Reiman**, **Muriel Stuart**, **Antonina Tumkovsky**, **Anatole Oboukhoff**, **Pierre Vladimiroff**, **Yurek Lazovsky** (character dance), and **Anna Sokolow** (modern dance).

**Edward Villella** (b. 1936) *(Photo Plate 14-5)* had exceptional artistry, energy, and virility, which helped to make male dancing admired in the United States. He had been a student at the School of American Ballet since the age of ten. Balanchine created many roles for him but the one for which he is best known is that of the *Prodigal Son* (a role that Balanchine recreated in 1960 from the original that he had choreographed in 1929 with **Felia Doubrovska** as the Siren, *Photo Plate 14-3*). In 1985 **Edward Villella** became director of the Miami City Ballet. He has honorary degrees and awards too numerous to even start listing them, including an award for Lifetime Achievement, and one for being one of America's Irreplaceable Dance Treasures. In 2012 the Miami Ballet had a new artistic director, **Lourdes Lopez**, a former principal dancer with the New York City Ballet, executive of the George Balanchine Foundation, and co-founder of Morphoses with **Christopher Wheeldon** in 2007, which she ran after Wheeldon left.

**Suzanne Farrell** (b. 1945) was likewise a student at the School of American Ballet. She was always outstanding. She received a Ford Foundation scholarship to study there in 1960, joined New York City Ballet in 1961 and became a principal dancer in 1965. She was Balanchine's last muse (he had several in the course of his career) and he choreographed many works for her: *Don Quixote* (1965) *(Photo Plate 14-3)*, the Diamonds section in *Jewels*, and numerous others. When she retired from performing, she taught Balanchine's repertoire throughout the world, including the Paris Opera Ballet, the Kirov Ballet, and the Bolshoi. In 2000 she started the **Suzanne Farrell** Ballet at Kennedy Center, Washington, D. C. The Kennedy Center, in recognition of her teaching skills, began a "study of ballet with Suzanne Farrell" for advanced-level students ages 13-17. By 2011 her small company of dancers was applauded for the musicality that she had conveyed to them. She has received many honorary degrees and is considered to be one of the most important ballerinas of the 20th century.

**Eliot Feld** (b. 1942), a brilliant young student of the School of American Ballet, was a modern ballet choreographer who started working professionally before his teens. At twelve he was the child prince in New York City Ballet's *Nutcracker*. He danced in the companies of **Donald McKayle**, **Pearl Lang**, and **Sophie Maslow**, performed on Broadway in *West Side Story* at sixteen, then performed for American Ballet Theater and choreographed for them *Harbinger* (1967, to Sergei Prokofiev's *Fifth Piano Concerto*) and *At Midnight* (1967, to songs by Gustav Mahler). Since 1967 he has choreographed over 140 ballets. Some of his most recent ones were performed at the Joyce Theater in 2009: *Dust*, *Radiance*, and *Spaghetti Ballet*. Steve Reich seems to have been his most inspiring composer.

Portrait of Violette Verdy (b.1933), taken on December 4, 1961. French ballerina and principal dancer of NYCB from 1958 to 1977, Balanchine created "Emeralds," "La Source," and "Sonatine" for her. She was awarded the French Legion of Honor (Chevalier) in 2009.

Frederic Franklin, ca. 1940, in costume for the Ballet Russe de Monte Carlo production of "The Nutcracker."

Mikhail Mordkin in the ballet "The Pharaoh's Daughter," 1900, St. Petersburg. The Mordkin Ballet Co. later became The American Ballet Theatre. Mordkin was Le Clercq's teacher before she went to The School of American Ballet.

Portrait of Hugh Laing (1911-1988), 1940. Laing danced in NYCB Co. from 1950 to 1952 in Tudor's "Jardin Aux Lilas" (Lilac Garden), Balanchine's "Prodigal Son " and in Robbins' "Age of Anxiety." He was a dramatic dancer; one of the finest of the 20th century. Photo: van Vechten.

Anna Pavlova. Photo by Arnold Genthe. He considered this to be one of the best dance photos he ever made.

Portrait of Arthur Mitchell, 1955. He was a principal dancer with the NYC Ballet and the founder of the Dance Theater of Harlem.

Portrait of Melissa Hayden (1923-2006). Hayden, a Canadian ballerina, joined NYCB Co. in 1948 and was prima ballerina from 1955 until 1973, often partnered by Jacques d'Amboise. Photo: Carl van Vechten.

Tamara Karsavina (1885-1978), a Russian ballerina in the role of Scheherazade, ca. 1915.

**Eliot Feld**'s works have been performed in ballet companies worldwide as well as in American ballet companies. He also studied at the New Dance Group and at the High School of Performing Arts in New York. He founded Ballet Tech (formerly called the NYC Public School for Dance) to give free classical ballet education to New York City public school students. Over 17,000 students have had this opportunity out of the innumerable thousands who auditioned. Ballet Tech arranged that as of the fall of 2014 its students would take their academic courses from eight through twelfth grade at the Professional Performing Arts High School and their dance classes at Ballet Tech. These students often go on to the School of American Ballet or companies like Cedar Lake Contemporary Ballet, NYC Ballet, or others. **Feld** is the recipient of an honorary doctorate degree from Juilliard as well as several well-deserved awards.

In 1982 **Eliot Feld** and art executive **Cora Cahan** founded the Joyce Theater. They felt that New York City needed an intimate space in which to showcase new and emerging contemporary dance. The former Elgin Theater is now a 472-seat theater with a sprung stage. (A sprung floor is one that absorbs shock, giving it a softer feel. These floors enhance performance and reduce injuries. Since the 1900's there are many ballrooms, dance studios, gyms, etc., that have been built with a sprung floor.)

Many of the wonderful Russian dancers who defected or later emigrated to the U.S. joined regional companies to teach, choreograph, or perform, and at the same time they enhanced these groups. Some of the early defectors were: **Rudolph Nureyev**, who appeared in London with the exquisite **Margot Fonteyn** to innumerable ovations, and also with the lovely **Karen Kain**, principal dancer of the National Ballet of Canada; Latvian-born **Mikhail Baryshnikov**, who danced with the New York City Ballet Company, The American Ballet Theater, the **Mark Morris** Dance Group and others; **Natalia Makarova** *(Photo Plate 14-4)* who danced and choreographed for The American Ballet Theater; and **Alexander Godunov** (1949-1995), a tall dramatic Russian-American ballet dancer who performed the classics with the American Ballet Theater and also danced with **Judith Jamison** in **Alvin Ailey**'s Company.

**Makarova** and **Baryshnikov** were recipients of the Kennedy Canter Award. This Award is given for lifetime achievement in the performing arts to recipients showing extraordinary talent, creativity, and tenacity over their careers.

The result of the influx of these phenomenal Russian dancers was a renewed interest in the classics and, in fact, in the full-length performance of the classics *(Photo Plate 14-3)*. After ABT (American Ballet Theater) received U.S. Government as well as private funds it started producing more classics: *Swan Lake* (1967), *Sleeping Beauty* (1976), *Don Quixote* (1978), and *Giselle* (first choreographed in 1841; the 1884 Petipa version is the one most frequently used), often with guest stars **Carla Fracci** (b. 1936), and **Erik Bruhn** (1928-1986). In 1980, the Board of Directors of ABT appointed **Baryshnikov** to succeed **Lucia Chase** (1907-1986) and **Oliver Smith** (1918-1994), as artistic director. ABT also acquired **MacMillan**'s ballets *Romeo and Juliet* (1965) and *Sleeping Beauty* (1976) and **Makarova**'s *La Bayadère* (1980). **Kevin McKenzie** became the artistic director when **Baryshnikov** left in 1989; in 1998 **McKenzie** produced a lavish, full-evening performance of *Le Corsaire*.

The ballet seasons now included classics in the grand manner as well as a repertoire of dances by a variety of important choreographers. American Ballet Theater had about six different full-length classics for their 2010 fall season; all were lavish productions. (And let's not forget that they already had *Coppèlia* and *Raymonda*). While **Ethan Stiefel** and **Angel Corella** may have retired in 2012 to concentrate on their own companies (New Zealand Ballet for **Stiefel** and Barcelona Ballet for **Corella**), ABT still had the formidable **Marcelo Gomez**, **Herman Cornejo** (who received a Bessie Award in 2013), and others.

The full length ballets were enjoying a revival worldwide and some choreographers were interpreting old and new stories in different ways: *Swan Lake* as a political story (1988) was created by **Rudi van Dantzig**; *Swan Lake* with hallucination (1976) was choreographed by **John Neumeier**; *Coppèlia* as a portrayal of a French roué (1975) was by **Roland Petit**; *Washington Square (1985),* a new full length ballet based on a short novel by Henry James, was choreographed by **Nureyev**; *Peer Gynt* (1985-87) and *King Arthur (1995)* were both created by **John Neumeier**; *Abdallah,* a 100-year-old-work done in **Bournonville** style, was performed by Ballet West of Salt Lake City in 1985.

**Rudoph Nureyev** (1938-1993), a defector from Russia in 1961, also helped to revive the classics. His performances with **Margot Fonteyn** in London were incredible. The two of them always drew a huge audience. They danced together as one entity. His animal magnetism, stage presence, and popularity were unprecedented.

Appointed director of the Paris Opera Ballet in 1983, **Nureyev** performed, directed, coached, and choreographed for them. He also included modern works in their repertoire. He put the Paris Opera back on the map internationally. His influence in having modern dance accepted for classical dancers was huge, too. He himself had appeared in a piece by **Martha Graham**. Although ill in 1992, he worked on a new full-length production of *La Bayadère*, similar to the one he performed in his youth at the Kirov in Russia. For this production for the Paris Opera Ballet he received a standing ovation and the highest cultural award from the French government, Commandeur de l'Ordre des Arts et des Lettres. He died of AIDS a few months later in 1993, mourned by all lovers of ballet.

**Mikhail Baryshnikov** (b. 1948) was one of the dancers who came from Russia eager to dance in works by **Balanchine** as well as by innovative choreographers such as **Glen Tetley**, **Jerome Robbins**, **Alvin Ailey**, **Trisha Brown**, **Twyla Tharp**, and **Martha Graham**. He danced under Balanchine with the New York City Ballet for 18 months. Then he became artistic director of American Ballet Theater and also appeared in numerous films as a dancer and actor. He was very creative, opened the Baryshnikov Arts Center in Manhattan (with a multidisciplinary residency program since 2005 that supports up to 30 artists a year), and published a book of his photographs of the **Merce Cunningham** Dance Company. He was awarded the National Medal of Arts in 2000. In 2011 he donated all his personal dance archives to the Jerome Robbins Dance Division of the New York Public Library so that young dancers could study how choreographers and dancers approach their work. The archives include 650 videotapes of Baryshnikov's dancing, starting when he was a boy of about eleven.

Exceptional dancers from Cuba were the next group to appear in the United States. **Alicia Alonso** (b. 1921) *(Photo Plate 14-4)*, a former star of American Ballet Theater, celebrated her 90th birthday on June 3rd, 1910, by returning to the Metropolitan Opera House from Cuba for the celebration of the 70th anniversary of American Ballet Theater. The event included a film retrospective of Alonso's career and a special performance of *Don Quixote*.

In Cuba she trained dancers, several of whom joined American Ballet Theater, a company that had dancers from many nations: Argentina, Cuba, Peru, Russia, Ukraine, Spain, Brazil, Italy, and Romania. (In 2013 seven dancers from the National Ballet of Cuba defected to the United State and immediately found positions in various companies, such as Ballet Arizona.)

The American Ballet Theater has a very varied repertoire: romantic ballets like *Eugene Onegin* and *Romeo and Juliet* from Russia, **Agnes de Mille**'s *Rodeo*, **Alvin Ailey**'s *The River*, **Paul Taylor**'s *Company B*, as well as *Interplay* and others by **Jerome Robbins**. The former co-directors of ABT, former dancer **Lucia Chase** and multiple-Tony-winning scenic designer **Oliver Smith**, who had served as co-directors from 1944-1980, had been greatly responsible for the company's rise to be one of the world's best dance companies. **Smith** had not only designed scenery for *Swan Lake* and *Giselle* for ABT and numerous **Robbins**' ballets, *Fancy Free*, *Interplay*, *Facsimile*, *Les Noces*, and *Age of Anxiety,* for New York City Ballet, but he had also been involved with Robbins for the musicals *On the Town* and *West Side Story*.

The prolific Russian choreographer **Alexei Ratmansky**'s new version of *Nutcracker* was presented for American Ballet Theater's Winter Season of 2010. The opening scene was in the kitchen of a nineteenth century home with hams and sausages hanging from the rafters; it was different, warm, and attractive. There were other changes, in excellent taste, well thought out, and enjoyable. The music followed the original score more closely than did some of the other versions of this ballet.

**Ratmansky**'s Ukrainian love story, *On the Dnieper,* was the showpiece of ABT's all-Prokofiev program in 2009, and in 2012 Ratmansky choreographed a new version of *Firebird* to Stravinsky's score for American Ballet Theater. In 2012, Alexei Ratmansky, ABT's artist in residence since 2009, choreographed three one-act pieces – a trilogy -- to Dmitri Shostakovich's *Symphony No, 9 (Chamber Symphony)* and ended with Shostakovich's *Piano Concerto #1 for Piano and Trumpet,* with all three pieces presented as an evening-length program by The American Ballet Theater on May 31 and June 1, 2013, at the Metropolitan Opera House in New York.

The Urban Ballet Theater at the Abrons Arts Center in New York, under its artistic director **Daniel Catanach**, has been performing a new version since 2002 of a full length *Nutcracker,* mostly to Tchaikovsky's music. This multicultural interpretation includes **krumping** rats, **popping** soldiers, **hip-hop**, **Chinese fan dancing**, a **salsa** festival for the party scene, and black and white women sur les pointes, as well as a racially mixed group in this production that represented the multilayered community of the Lower East Side. *The New York Times* reviewer, **Alastair Macaulay**, said the cast was "the most racially varied I've seen yet in a *Nutcracker*." (Dec. 9, 2010, pgs. C1 and C7.) If you missed this production, try to see it. The videos on the Internet look exciting.

**Mark Morris**, an American modern dancer-choreographer, updated *The Nutcracker* as *The Hard Nut* (1991), the last piece created by him during a 3-year residency as director of dance at the Théâtre Royale de la Monnaie in Brussels. Hence, for the holiday season in December there are now several completely different versions of *The Nutcracker* to add to the merriment. Mark Morris himself loves the music of *The Nutcracker* by Tchaikovsky, and has appeared in all of the performances of *The Hard Nut*. You just have to look to see if you can find him in his disguises. Sometimes he plays one of the guests, or Dr. Stahlbaum.

My favorite *Nutcracker* (besides that of the NYCB) of the ones I had seen by 2010 was choreographed by **Helgi Tomasson** (b. 1942, Iceland) for the San Francisco Ballet Company, of which he has been the director since 1985. There was an attractive outdoor opening scene with people shopping and walking home or visiting. This *Nutcracker* included a Chinese **dragon dance**, a larger than life Aladdin's lamp out of which came an exotic dancer, a colorful *Waltz of the Flowers*, and excellent, delightful dancing by the lovely **Yuan Yuan Tan** (Chinese) and her partner, **Artem Yachmennikov** (Russian), the King and Queen of the Snow, and the rest of the superb cast.

Two other full-length ballets performed by the San Francisco Ballet Company, and also excellent, are *Othello* and *The Little Mermaid* (the latter created for the Royal Danish Ballet in 2005 by **John Neumeier**, Hamburg Ballet director, who also did the ballet's lighting, set, and costume designs). *The Little Mermaid* is based on a story by Hans Christian Andersen and was given its U.S. premiere by the San Francisco Ballet Company in 2010. The film of this ballet showed a very poignant performance by **Yuan Yuan Tan** and by Hamburg dancer **Lloyd Riggins** as the lovelorn poet. The DVD of The San Francisco Ballet Company's performance of *Othello* (1997, music by Elliot Goldenthal) with **Lar Lubovitch**'s vibrant choreography, a blend of modern and ballet, features **Yuan Yuan Tan** as Desdemona, **Parrish Maynard** as the treacherous Iago, and the renowned black dancer **Desmond Richardson** as Othello.

**Desmond Richardson,** together with **Dwight Rhoden,** runs a New York-based company, **Complexions Contemporary Ballet,** founded in 1994, that performs regularly with excellent dancers, **Shuaib Elhassan**, **D. Gary W. Jeter II**, **Mark Caserta**, **Christina Dooling**, **Edgar Anido**, and **Tercell Waters**. Rhoden's choreography is set to varied music, including the Rolling Stones and songs by Nina Simone, and displays Richardson's star quality performances.

**Michael Bourne**, British, choreographed a different version of the classic *Swan Lake*, a new interpretation that premiered in 1996, in which the swans were male. (Even though the hero had a girlfriend, many people considered this *Swan Lake* to be a "gay" version.) As a part of his *Adventures in Motion Pictures,* Bourne presented *The Car Man,* a take on George Bizet's *Carmen.* In December 2012, in London, he presented *Michael Bourne's Sleeping Beauty, a Gothic Romance,* with a gardener as the prince and with vampires; this then came to the City Center in New York in October 2013.

The New York City Ballet Company also had a number of full-length ballets. **George Balanchine** choreographed the full-evening ballets *Don Quixote* (1965), as well

The Dance Theater of Harlem performs "Dialogues" by Robert Garland, 2006. Photo by Martha Swope. This image is the work of the National Endowment for the Arts and celebrates 40 years of NEA's support of dance.

Young dancers from the Dance Theater of Harlem perform during a dinner held at the White House on Monday, February 6, 2006. The Dance Theater of Harlem offers training to over 1,000 young adults annually. Photo by Shealah Craighead.

Edgar Degas: "Dancers practicing at the Barre," 1877, mixed medium on canvas; signed left of center, Degas. Painting includes a watering can used to keep the floor moist (so dust would not fly) and not slippery.

George Balanchine (1904-1983) was the foremost choreographer of the twentieth century. He choreographed hundreds of ballets, some in traditional style and many in a neo-classical style with costumes resembling practice clothes. Together with Lincoln Kirstein, he founded the School of American Ballet and the New York City Ballet. Photo 1959 by unknown photographer.

Maria Tallchief, 1946, ballerina with the New York City Ballet, was the first dancer to completely embody the style of Balanchine. Here she is performing the role of Sanguinic in Balanchine's "Four Temperaments."

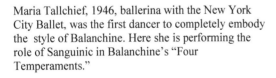

as *Midsummer's Night Dream* (1965) and *Jewels* (1967). **Peter Martins** choreographed *Sleeping Beauty* (1991), *Swan Lake* (1999), and *Ocean's Kingdom* (2011)

**Jerome Robbins** was a choreographer for the New York City Ballet Company. He had previously choreographed Broadway musicals such as *The King and I* (1951), *West Side Story* (1957), *Gypsy* (1959), and *Fiddler on the Roof* (1964) with great success. He even choreographed a ballet, *Moves* (1961), with no music. He was a genius and proved to be equally successful at choreographing ballets for the New York City Ballet Company. Some of the favorites were *Fancy Free* (1944), *The Concert* (1958), *I'm Old Fashioned* (1983, a tribute to Fred Astaire), also his rendition of *Afternoon of a Faun* (1958, completely different from Nijinsky's), and *The Cage* (1951, about insects whose habit it is for the females to eat up the male insects when they are no longer needed).

Another top-notch choreographer for the New York City Ballet is **Peter Martins** (b. 1946). His varied works have included *Calcium Light Night* (1977, to Charles Ives' music), *Ecstatic Orange* (1987, to Michael Torke's music), *The Magic Flute* (to Riccardo Drigo's music, in 1981 for The School of American Ballet, in 1982 for NYCB), *River of Light* (1998, created to music by American composer Charles Wuorinen), and *Morgen* (2001, a beautiful romantic reverie to Richard Strauss' *Songs for Soprano and Orchestra* with soprano Jessica Jones, costumes by Alain Vaes, lighting by Mark Stanley and dancers **Sterling Hyltin**, **Darci Kistler**, **Jenifer Ringer**, **Charles Askegard**, **Sébastien Marcovici**, and **Nilas Martins**). *Mirage* (2010, with Santiago Calatrava's string sculpture) was lit in rainbow colors by Mark Stanley, to Esa-Pekka Salonen's music, danced by **Jennie Smogyi** as the lead woman and with **Robert Fairchild** and **Kathy Morgan** in a tender duet, perfectly suited the New York City Ballet Company's Architecture of Dance festival. **Peter Martins**, a superb dancer, first danced the lead in George Balanchine's *Apollo* in 1967, but he retired from dancing in 1983 when he was chosen by Balanchine to be his successor as the next director of the NYCB Company. Together with Jerome Robbins, Peter Martins served as co-ballet master in chief from 1983 to 1989. In 1990 Martins became sole director and oversaw both the artistic and the business side of the company.

The New York City Ballet's mix of nationalities often included French, Russian, Spanish, Danish, and American. Their repertoire integrated works by Broadway choreographer **Susan Stroman** and **Twyla Tharp**, whose works were described earlier, and by **Christopher Wheeldon**, a highly applauded young British choreographer of thirty works in five years, considered to be a hot new choreographer in 2005, as well as works by the Russian choreographer **Alexei Ratmansky**.

**Christopher Wheeldon** (b. 1973) became the NYC Ballet's first resident choreographer in 2002. His works include *Polyphonia* (2001, music by Gyorgy Ligeti), *After the Rain* (2005, music by Arvo Pärt), *Mercurial Maneuvers* (2000, music by Dmitri Shostakovich) and *Variations Sérieuses* (2001, music by Felix Mendelssohn). He formed his own company, Morphoses, in 2008, but three years after doing so he quit his dance troupe and left the company's executive director, **Lourdes Lopez**, formerly of the NYC Ballet Company, in charge. (In 2012 she became artistic director of the Miami City Ballet.) Meanwhile **Wheeldon** choreographed for other companies: the San Francisco Ballet (*Cinderella*, 2013 premiere in NY, a joint commission with the Dutch National Ballet in Amsterdam, a previous December 2012 premiere there) and the Royal Ballet in London. His *Alice in Wonderland* (music by Joby Talbot) was sold out for the Winter of

2010-11. In 2015 he was director/choreographer of the Broadway musical "An American in Paris."

A recent addition to the choreographers for the New York City Ballet Company was **Justin Peck (b.** 1988), a member of the corps in that company. His work of 2012, *The Year of the Rabbit*, received excellent reviews. The piece was set to excerpts from Sufjan Steven's 2001 electronic album *Enjoy Your Rabbit*, reorchestrated for the occasion by the composer. Steven is also the composer of Peck's 2014 work *Everywhere We Go*. Justin Peck's first work for the NYCB, *In Creases*, to music by Philip Glass, was presented in 2012 at the Saratoga Performing Arts Center in New York State. His third ballet for the company was *Paz de La Jolla,* set to Bohuslav Martinu's *Sinfonietta La Jolla*, performed as part of the company's "New Combinations Evening," on January 3l, 2013. In 2013 he choreographed *Murder Ballads* for a new company, L.A. Dance Project.

**Alexei Ratmansky** (b. 1968), Russian, a recipient of the 2005 Prix Benois de la Danse for his choreography for *Anna Karenina* for the Royal Danish Ballet, has also choreographed for the New York City Ballet: the beautiful *Russian Seasons* (2006, music by Leonid Desyatnikov), *Concerto DSCH* (2008, music by Dmitri Shostakovitch) as well as *Namouna* (2010, to the score of *Namouna* by Édouard Lalo). He was the artistic director for the Bolshoi Ballet (2004 through the end of 2008) and has choreographed for many other companies: the Kirov Ballet, the San Francisco Ballet (*From Foreign Lands* in 2013), and the Dutch National Ballet. He became Artist in Residence at American Ballet Theater in 2008. In 2013 he was the recipient of a MacArthur Fellowship Award.

(The Prix Benois de la Danse is a ballet competition founded by the International Dance Association in Moscow in 1991 and takes place each year around April. It is a very prestigious competition. The categories are: lifelong achievement, ballerina, danseur, choreographer, composer, and designer. It is named after Alexandre Benois (1870-1960). Lifetime achievement winners have included **Alicia Alonso**, **Rudi van Dantzig**, **William Forsythe**, **Mikhail Baryshnikov**, **Maurice Béjart**, **Marina Semenova**, **Trisha Brown**, **Hans van Manen**, **Ohad Naharin**, **Peter Farmer**, **Ivan Vasiliev** *(Photo Plate 14-5)*, and **Toer van Schayk.**)

New York City Ballet's excellent dancers: **Wendy Whelan**, **Anthony Huxley**, **Daniel Ulbricht**, **Teresa Reichlen**, **Tiler Peck**, **Maria Kowroski**, **Charles Askegard**, **Janie Taylor**, **Jared Angle**, **Ashley Bouder**, **Robert Fairchild**, **Jennie Somogyi**, and **Sara Mearns**, to name just a few, are always a delight to watch. NYCB also had a black ballerina, **Aischa Ash**, for several years; her lovely arm movements were memorable. Then she went on to perform with Alonzo King's Lines Ballet in San Francisco.

**Misty Copeland**, a principal dancer with American Ballet Theater since her promotion in June 2015, is another lovely black American ballerina. She has performed numerous lead roles: in *Firebird*, in *Swan Lake,* and Swanhilda in *Coppelia*. **Copeland,** like many others, has been a source of encouragement to young aspiring ballet dancers. And, by the way, she has been a judge on TV's "So You Think You Can Dance."

**Jock Soto** (b. 1965) was a favorite dancer with the New York City Ballet Company and a product of the School of American Ballet. He is one half Navajo (Water Flowing Together is both the name of his Navajo clan and the name of a video made about him) and one half Puerto Rican. He was inspired to study ballet at five, after seeing **Edward Villella** dance in Balanchine's *Jewels* on television. Soto studied at SAB since he was twelve and became a member of the New York City Ballet Company in 1981. He was known to be strong, graceful, a very reliable partner, and an inspiration to many. He gave his farewell performance in 2005. Some of the pieces in which he danced were: *Ecstatic Orange* (1989) by **Peter Martins**, *Chiaroscuro* (1994) by **Lynne Corbett**, and *Polyphonia* (2001) by **Christopher Wheeldon**. After his retirement, Soto returned to the stage to dance as Lord Capulet in *Romeo and Juliet* (2007) by Peter Martins. **Jock Soto** is now a permanent member of the faculty at SAB, like many of the other former dancers from the New York City Ballet Company who have inspired the students and future dancers with their knowledge and love of dance. Soto also travels around the country to audition students for the School of American Ballet.

**Albert Evans** (1968-2015), a black American, was another former student of SAB, from 1986 to 1988, when he became a member of the New York City Ballet Company. He was a remarkable dancer who always stood out because his bearing was so elegant and poised. He performed in *Behind the China Dogs* by **William Forsythe**, *The Unanswered Question* (1988) by **Elliot Feld**, *Red Angels* (1994) by **Ulysses Dove**, *Fearful Symmetries* (1990) by **Peter Martins**, and many others. His farewell performance was in 2010. He then served as ballet master for the NYCB Company, under Peter Martins.

**Jock Soto** and **Albert Evans** have also both had another important role in the School of American Ballet and the New York City Ballet Company. Minority groups feel more accepted in the ballet field.

**Charles Askegard**, another excellent dancer and favorite partner from New York City Ballet, had a busy year in 2011, retiring from the company that year and forming a company, Ballet Next, with **Michele Wiles**, a former American Ballet Theater ballerina. Ballet Next initially used dancers that Wiles and Askegard both already knew; the company gave its first performance in 2011.

**Edward Villella** (b. 1936) is one of America's most beloved male dancers and the only American dancer ever to have been asked to perform an encore at the Bolshoi Theatre in Moscow. He studied at the School of American Ballet, interrupted his dance training to obtain a degree in marine science from the New York Maritime Academy, danced with the New York City Ballet as principal dancer in such notable roles as *The Prodigal Son*, *Jewels* (Rubies section), Oberon in Balanchine's *Midsummer's Night Dream*, and *Tarantella*, and in 1985, together with Toby Ansin, he founded the Miami City Ballet and was its artistic director until 2012. The company is energetic and precise whether in **Balanchine** ballets or in modern pieces such as excerpts of **Twyla Tharp**'s *The Catherine Wheel* (The Golden Gate section). The dancers have an international background and come from Cuba, Venezuela, Brazil, France, Argentina, Mexico, Switzerland, and the United States. In 2013 **Villella** choreographed *Reveries* for The Ice Theater of NY, a company known for dancing on ice. In 1997 **Villella** was a Kennedy Center Honors recipient and was also awarded a National Medal of Arts by President Clinton that same year *(Photo Plate 14-5)*.

In 1976 **Jacques d'Amboise** (b. 1934), former principal dancer of the New York City Ballet and the subject of the 1983 award-winning feature documentary, *He Makes Me Feel Like Dancing*, founded the Dance Institute of America. It brought dance, performance, and arts education to thousands of New York City public school students. He was awarded a MacArthur Fellowship in 1990 for his creative work in dance education and he received many other awards. In 2011 the Institute obtained a permanent home in Harlem as the National Institute for Learning & the Arts in a former school in NY City. It has four dance studios, a 175-seat performance space, art galleries, and it will revitalize the neighborhood by reaching out to other arts organizations, to seniors, as well as to preschool and afterschool children.

The many regional companies in the United States still retain the distinct American style. Graduates of the School of American Ballet and retirees from the New York City Ballet Company are now the ballet master, ballet mistress or instructors for these companies and schools.

**Colleen Neary**, former NYCB dancer, and her husband **Thordal Christensen**, also a dancer, founded the Los Angeles Ballet in 2006. The co-artistic directors of the company seem to be thriving with classes and performances. **Neary** is a Balanchine Trust répétiteur. (She, like **Suzanne Farrell** and others, has been approved to stage **Balanchine** ballets for companies desiring to perform them.) Los Angeles Ballet's performances have included Balanchine's *Symphony in C* as well as *Giselle*. They have also done *La Sylphide* and their own *Nutcracker* and plan to do works by more recent choreographers such as **Mandy Moore**, **Sonya Tayeh**, and **Travis Wall**, whose works have been seen on *So You Think You Can Dance* on television.

At the end of World War II, the G. I. Bill proved to be a great incentive for men wishing to continue their career in dance. Such was the case for **Gerald Arpino** (1923-2008), who danced, choreographed, and became assistant director, then director of the Joffrey Ballet..

In 1956 **Robert Joffrey** formed the Robert Joffrey Theatre Ballet (Joffrey Ballet since 1965 and The Joffrey Ballet since 2011) with **Gerald Arpino**, **Beatrice Tompkins**, **Glen Tetley**, **Brunhilda Ruiz**, **John Nelson**, and **Dianne Consoer**. Joffrey choreographed many opera ballets for them at the NY City Center. Gradually the school he had started in 1953 in New York City expanded. In 1962 The Rebekah Harkness Foundation sponsored the company's State Department tour of India, Pakistan, and the Middle East.

**Robert Joffrey** (1930-1988), born in Seattle of an Afghan father and an Italian mother, studied there with Mary Ann Wells and later in NY at the School of American Ballet. For the Joffrey Ballet he revived several of **Kurt Jooss'** masterpieces: *The Green Table, The Big City*, and *Pavane pour une Infante Défunte*. Joffrey also revived **Léonide Massine**'s works: *Les Présages, Parade*, and *Le Beau Danube*. For 1980, with **Nureyev** dancing with the Joffrey Ballet, Joffrey revived *L'Après Midi d'un Faune*, the **Yurek Lazovsky** staging of *Petrouchka*, and also *Spectre de la Rose*. He also commissioned many new ballets. Joffrey's works were known for having very imaginative effects. The most popular of the works choreographed by **Joffrey** was *Astarte* (1967), one of the first mixed media works in a ballet company's repertoire, with ear-splitting music by Crome Syrcus. **Trinette Singleton** and **Maximiliano Zomosa** were the main performers in it. Robert Joffrey died in 1988 at age fifty-seven.

**Gerald Arpino** (1923-2008,) American, studied ballet with **Mary Ann Wells** in Seattle under the G. I. Bill, having served in the U. S. Coast Guard from 1945-1948. He then studied modern and danced with **May O'Donnell**'s group; he also studied at the

School of American Ballet. The company that **Arpino** and **Joffrey** founded had a no-star policy and emphasized a variety of ballets. As resident choreographer, Arpino attracted a new public to ballet by providing the company with a wide range of subjects in his ballets: *Trinity,* a rock hit of 1970, his most popular work, *The Clowns* (1981, nuclear war), *Light Rain* (1981, Eastern music, mysticism), *Kettentanz* (1971, to Johann Strauss music), *Drums, Dreams, and Banjos* (1975, music by Stephen Foster), *Round of Angels* (1983, lyricism), and *Italian Suite* (1983). **Gerald Arpino** believed much could be accomplished through the unspoken word.

After Joffrey's death in 1988 Arpino became artistic director of the company; then in 1995 Arpino became director and moved the company to Chicago where it did much better financially. He stopped peforming due to an injury in 1963, but he then pursued an imaginative, prolific career in choreography. After his death in 2008, **Ashley Wheater** became the artistic director of the Joffrey Ballet. The Arpino Foundation handles all situations regarding the use of Joffrey's and Arpino's ballets by other companies.

The Joffrey Ballet appeared in the movie *Save the Last Dance* (2001), performing **Arpino**'s *Sea Shadow* and **Léonide Massine**'s *Les Présages*. The Joffrey Ballet was also the subject of the movie *The Company* (2003), with the majority of the roles played by company members. The Joffrey Academy of Dance, affiliated with the Joffrey Ballet, opened in Chicago in 2009. Previously the school had been in New York City.

Ballets often have an uncertain future after the death of their choreographer. **Frederick Ashton**, the British choreographer, did as **Balanchine** had done, and in his will he gave several ballets to each of his friends. This worked out well for some of his works but not for all, depending on who was authorized to stage the ballet for an international dance company. A ballet may be preserved by notation, such as Benesh or Laban, by film, or by the excellent memories of dancers. **Frederick Franklin**, who died in 2013 shortly before his 99th birthday, recreated many ballets from his incredible memory. His performances ranged from **de Mille**'s *Rodeo* to **Massine**'s *Le Beau Danube* and the classics *(Photo Plate 14-1)*. A few years after Balanchine's death, the **Balanchine** Trust was established to oversee the staging of his ballets, and almost all his ballets were passed on to the Balanchine Fund. Disagreements can, of course, arise over the choice of who should stage a ballet, but overall, this system works well.

**Virginia Johnson**, formerly prima ballerina of the Dance Theater of Harlem, was appointed as its artistic director in 2009. The company has all sorts of plans for creating a choreographic laboratory, reviving old works, and giving choreographers studio time, now that the company's debt has been reduced and the company has received some additional financing. The repertoire will include works by **George Balanchine, Alvin Ailey, Ulysses Dove**, and living choreographers: **Alonzo King, Alexei Ratmansky, Francesca Harper, Robert Moses** and by the resident choreographer, **Robert Garland**. A majority of the dancers are black American. The Dance Theater of Harlem hoped to reopen in 2013, and it did. The company had shut down in 2004. The school director of the Dance Theater of Harlem is **Endalyn Taylor.** The executive director is **Laveen Naidu. Keith Saunders** leads The Dance Theater of Harlem Ensemble, which consists of students on professional and fellows programs at the Dance Theater of Harlem School *(Photo Plates 14-2)*.

Many dance lovers now feel that there is not much difference between the ballet dancer and the modern dancer. Modern dancers are now slender, precise, and trained in ballet, so that they have the strength and lines of ballet dancers, but they miss the emphasis and thrust of the modern dancers' contractions that were so obvious in the early modern dance companies. Like it or not, just about every dancer trains in ballet nowadays. The works by modern dance choreographers that have survived well in ballet companies are those choreographed by modern choreographers knowledgeable in ballet and willing to intersperse ballet in a new way into their modern pieces so that ballet audiences see contemporary ballet – ballet for the 21$^{st}$ century – with a mix of modern in it.

Some of the contemporary choreographers have a style that has spread throughout Europe because it was one that several European companies wanted. It was not completely classical, nor was it completely modern. It was a blend of the two. Many of these choreographers had trained in classical and in modern. They also needed jobs and the companies needed new works. A few of these choreographers are mentioned here.

**John Alleyne** (b. 1960) was named artistic director of Ballet British Columbia in 1992. He was the first black student to go through the course of study at the National Ballet School of Toronto; he then choreographed for the Stuttgart Ballet in Germany, for the National Ballet of Canada, and for Ballet British Columbia. His works have blended ballet, modern, eroticism, and passion and have shown the influence of **William Forsythe.** His works include: *The Four Seasons* (2008, to Antonio Vivaldi's *Preludes), A Streetcar Named Desire* (2006, to music by Tobin Stokes), and *Septet* (1999, to music by Igor Stravinsky).

**Maurice Béjart** (1927-2007), French, is another choreographer who adhered to contemporary ballet, a mix of classical ballet, en pointe for the women, with modern. His showmanship and the originality of his works appealed to many and attracted new audiences for ballet. He completely changed the story of Stravinsky's *The Firebird* and *The Rite of Spring* when he did the choreography for these ballets. He could create very small works just for two people, such as *Webern Opus 5*, or colossal works like the one that the French Government commissioned him to create in the great hall of the Grand Palais in Paris for the bicentenary of the French Revolution. His version of Stravinsky's *Le Sacre du Printemps* (1959) was a favorite, as well as *Nutcracker* (2000), *Bolero,* to Ravel's music, *Songs of a Wayfarer* danced by **Rudolf Nureyev** (1971), and *Piano Bar* (1997) performed by **Mikhail Baryshnikov. Maurice Béjart** was trained at the Marseille Opéra Ballet, and he founded the Ballets de L'Étoile in Paris in 1953. He moved to Brussels, Belgium, to establish Ballet of the Twentieth Century in 1960, and to Switzerland in 1987, where he established the Béjart Ballet Lausanne. He also started the Mudra School in Brussels (1970-1988), The Mudra Afrique School in Dakar, Senegal (1977-1985), and the Rudra Béjart School in Lausanne, Switzerland (1992-present). He worked with abstract music, mystical sounds of the 1960's, and later with rock 'n' roll.

Photo Plate 14- 3

Suzanne Farrell and George Balanchine dancing in a segment of "Don Quixote" at the New York State Theater in 1965. Farrell, one of the most notable ballerinas of the 20th century, and Balanchine, the legendary choreographer, performed in "Don Quixote" at its opening night in May 1965. Photo by Orlando Fernandez.

Felia Doubrovska performing as the seductress in "The Prodigal Son;" choreography by George Balanchine, 1929.

,
Ballet Russes, scene from "Apollon Musagète" choreographed by Balanchine. Dancers: Serge Lifar, Danilova, Chernysheva, Doubrovska, and Petrova, ca. 1928.

Portrait of Alexandra Danilova as Fanny Cerrito in "Pas de Quatre." 1948. Photo by Carl van Vechten.

**John Butler** (1920-1993), American, was another influential choreographer. He had a small interracial company in 1955 comprising **Carmen de Lavallade**, **Glen Tetley**, **Mary Hinkson**, **Arthur Mitchell**, and himself. Well-known works of his were: *The Unicorn, the Gorgon, and the Manticore* (1956), *Portrait of Billie* (1960, about Billie Holiday and set to her records) for **de Lavallade** and himself and later restaged for **Ailey**'s Company, and *Carmina Burana* to Carl Orff's music based on 13th century poems and songs, with erotic dance passages of youth, and retrospective ones leading up to old age. His choreography was often on unconventional subjects. **Carla Fracci**, **Mikhail Baryshnikov**, **Natalia Makarova**, and **Judith Jamison** were some of the dancers for whom he created works.

**Birgit Cullberg** (1908-1999), Swedish, was a creative choreographer who was particularly interested in male-female relationships and often based her works on literary subjects: *Miss Julie* (1950, a Strindberg play), *Lady from the Sea* (1960, Ibsen), and *Medea* (1950, Euripides). **Martha Graham** had a great influence on Cullberg and, like her heroines, Cullberg's heroines were dramatic roles, but they also required the classical lines of basic ballet.

**Mats Ek** (b. 1945), Swedish, son of Birgit Cullberg, was a dancer-choreographer for the Nederlands Dans Theater from 1980-1981. He was the manager of the Cullberg Ballet from 1981 to 1985 when he took over his mother's role of artistic director of the **Cullberg** Ballet Company till 1993. His works include reworkings of the classics, *Swan Lake* in 1987 and, for the Hamburg Ballet, *Sleeping Beauty* in 1996, as well as *Casi-Casa,* which had its American premiere at the Hubbard Street Dance Chicago in 2012. He has won two Emmys for television adaptations of his ballets and was awarded the Prix Benois de la Danse in 2008. His work is known worldwide. He blends humor and psychology into his works, a mix of modern and ballet, and has also created theatre works such as *Don Giovanni* in 1999 and *Andromaque* in 2001 for the Royal Dramatic Theatre in Sweden.

**Ulysses Dove** (1947-1996), a black American, performed with **Cunningham**, **Sokolow**, **Pearl Lang**, and **Ailey**. As a freelance choreographer he created works for The NYC Ballet Company, American Ballet Theater, Dutch National Ballet, Dayton Contemporary Dance Company, and London Festival Ballet. His works were innovative and were noted for speed, force, and eroticism. *Night Shadow* (1982), *Bad Blood* (1984), *Vespers* (1986), *Episodes* (1987), *Red Angels* (1994), and *Twilight* (1994) were some of his works. He won the Primetime Emmy Award for Outstanding Choreography in 1995.

**Nacho Duato**, (b. 1957 in Valencia, Spain), is the first foreign-born dancer to lead a Russian ballet company in over 100 years, the Mikhailovsky Theater Ballet troupe in St. Petersburg, starting on January 1, 2011. Duato had been head of the National Spanish Dance Company for 20 years. His works were in repertoires as diverse as the Finnish Opera Ballet, the Paris Opera Ballet, the Deutsche Opera Ballet, the American Ballet Theater, the Hubbard Street Dance Chicago, and the Australian Ballet. His works include *Gnawa* for the Hubbard Street Dance Chicago, and *Jardi Tancat* for the Houston

Ballet. Vladimir Kekhman, the Mikhailovsky Theater's General Director, believes that Duato's unique dance style will inspire young Russian choreographers and dancers. In Spain **Nacho Duato** had mingled the classics with modern and with the Spanish heritage of spontaneity. Duato himself danced with the Alvin Ailey Company, with Béjart's Company and began choreography for the Nederlands Dans Theater under director **Jiři Kylián** before returning to Spain to choreograph. **Nacho Duato** is now the artistic director of the Berlin State Ballet.

**William Forsythe** (b. 1949), American choreographer and dancer, studied ballet, joined the Joffrey Ballet Company, and was invited by **John Cranko** to join the Stuttgart Ballet in 1974. After his first choreography he became resident choreographer for the Stuttgart and, later, ballet director for the Frankfurt Ballet. His creations included *Three Atmospheric Studies* (2005), *Human Writes* (2005), and *Yes We Can't* (2008). He used improvisation in innovative ways, and collaborative choreography.

**Alonzo King** (b. 1952), American dancer-choreographer, trained at excellent ballet schools and formed his Alonzo King LINES Ballet in 1982 with classically trained dancers. The women often dance en pointe. His choice of music is anything from Dmitri Shostakovitch, Henryk Mikolaj Górecki, Barber Samuel, and George Frideric Handel, to Astor Piazzolla, the Nubean music of Hamza al Din, and Japanese composer Miya Masaoka's original score played on an electric koto. He believes choreography can say more than words. He has worked with a variety of artists such as: Aka Pygmie, *The People of the Forest* (2001); musicians from North Africa, *The Moroccan Project* (2005); Hindustani vocalist Rita Sahai, *Sky Cloud* (2006); and the Shaolin monks of China, *Spring* (2007). He has received numerous awards for his choreography. His works are in the repertoires of many companies worldwide, both ballet and modern, including Dance Theater of Harlem, and Columbus, Ohio's BalletMet.

**James Kudelka** (b. 1955), Canadian, joined Les Grands Ballets Canadiens as a dancer and began to choreograph. His work for them, *In Paradisum* (1983), was an emotional work that showed the five stages in the acceptance of terminal illness. *Cruel World* (1994), for American Ballet Theater to Tchaikovsky's *Souvenir de Florence,* was also emotional and with unusual and somewhat risky partnering. Critics have liked the way his choreography relates to the music.

**Jiři Kylián** (b. 1947, Prague, Czechoslovakia) joined The Stuttgart Ballet in 1968 and became artistic director of The Nederlands Dans Theater in 1976. His joyful work *Sinfonietta* (1978) to music by Janáček became their signature piece. He explored space, shape, and humor in his movements. He contrasted flowing movements with staccato-sharp sequences. His best-known works are *Symphony of Psalms* (1978) and *Forgotten Land* (1981), which is based on a painting of women on a beach by Norwegian Expressionist painter Edvard Munch. The piece explored events and moments that are lost over time. In 1992 he founded a small chamber company for dancers over 40. This company lasted until 2006. All of his works look at universal themes and human relationships and are also filled with visual ideas and feeling: *Silent Cries* (1986), *Silent Cross* (1986), and *Tar and Feathers* (2005).

**Lar Lubovich** (b. 1943), American, created works possessing a seamless mix of ballet and modern dance. Some of these were simply visually beautiful, like his *Brahms Symphony* (1985). He founded the Lar Lubovich Dance Company in 1968. His works were especially popular in Europe. Some of these pieces are: *Vez* (a 1989 piece previously called *Fandango*, danced to Ravel's *Bolero*, reset in 2013 to a new score by Randall Woolf) and *The Time Before The Time After* (1971). He received commissions from England's Ballet Rambert, Israel's modern dance company Bat-Dor, and the Gulbenkian Ballet in Lisbon, Portugal.

**Brian Macdonald** (b. 1928), Canadian, choreographed a full-length ballet based on a Canadian theme, *Rose Latulippe* (1966), for the Royal Winnipeg Ballet. His *Ballet High* was the first rock ballet for Canada in 1970, while his *Aimez-vous Bach? (1962)* is a jive work to Bach. He has won many awards for his choreography, which is known worldwide.

**John Neumeier** (b. 1942), American, was influenced by modern dancer **Sybil Shearer** in the U.S. and by **Cranko** in Stuttgart, Germany. He was choreographer at the Hamburg Ballet since 1973, founded the Hamburg Ballet School, including a boarding school, in 1978, and in 1996 became ballet director of the Hamburg State Opera. He choreographed many classics with his own unique interpretations for the Hamburg Opera Ballet in Germany: *Firebird*, an outer space vision, *Sleeping Beauty* (1978) with updated flashbacks, *St. Matthew's Passion* (1981), a four-hour version, and several other works, including some to symphonies by Mahler. These ballets' collective effort was one of vision, with prop and scenery kept to a minimum. He held Ballet Workshops, a series of public lecture-demonstrations with his dancers. He has been considered Germany's unofficial "cultural ambassador." His works won him a long tenure at the Hamburg Opera Ballet.

**Choo San Goh** (1948-1987), American, began to choreograph in workshops at the Dutch National Ballet until invited to join the Washington Ballet by its director, Mary Day. For them he created *Fives* (1987) to music by Ernest Bloch, *Synonyms* (1987) to music by Benjamin Britten, and *Double Contrasts* (1987) to music by Francis Poulenc. He especially liked the works of **van Manen**, **van Dantzig** and **Balanchine.** Like the latter, he choreographed in the neoclassic style and loved energy and motion. He occasionally interspersed some modern movements or unexpected gestures, such as from the wrist, into his work, possibly a reflection of his Asian heritage. Modern and ballet companies all over the world wanted his works: the Paris Opera, the Royal Danish Ballet, Venezuelan, Chilean, and Hong Kong dance companies. He was a prolific American choreographer of over 50 works before his death at the age of 39. Before his death he had made plans to start a foundation, The Choo San Goh & H. Robert Magee Foundation, to further new choreographic works. It was formed in 1992. Many companies have received financial awards from the Foundation to create new dance works and develop choreographic talent *(Photo Plate 14-*5). The Foundation also looks after the licensing of Goh's ballets in performances by companies worldwide

**Glen Tetley** (1926-2007), American, was a performer in several modern and ballet companies and found himself able to combine classic and modern technique in such a way as to be a very desirable choreographer for many companies. One of the reasons why he went to Europe to choreograph was that dancers in the U.S. were used to studying either modern or ballet, whereas in Europe they often studied both. As a result, he has worked worldwide creating new works and restaging others for numerous companies. In 1977, **Nureyev** danced **Tetley**'s work *Pierrot Lunaire* (1962 to music by Schoenberg) very successfully with his group, Nureyev and Friends. **Makarova** danced his work *Voluntaries,* and the Ballet Rambert, having trained in **Graham** modern and in ballet, performed his two-act work, *The Tempest,* in 1979. He used movement to transmit his thoughts about a variety of ideas taken from myth, music, and literature.

    **Rudi van Dantzig** (1933-2012), a Dutch choreographer-dancer, was artistic director and resident choreographer of the Dutch National Ballet (1971-1991). His choreography related to hope, liberation, and complex homosexual relationships in the 21st century, abuses of power, classical elegance and modern energy. Seeing the film *The Red Shoes* obsessed him with the desire to dance and by 1955 he had choreographed his first dance, *Nachtieland,* to music by Debussy. He studied **Graham** technique and after seeing her perform he joined **Hans van Manen** and **Benjamin Harkavy** to found the Nederlands Dans Theater in 1959. His work *Movement to a Dead Boy* (1965) was **Nureyev**'s first performance in a modern work. *Sans Armes, Citoyens* (1987, with music by Berlioz) was about Liberty, Equality, and Fraternity without resorting to ammunition. He choreographed 50 more stimulating works before doing choreography for other companies and writing and publishing several books.

    **Hans van Manen** (b. 1932), Dutch, is a choreographer and dancer who believes in clarity in structure. He danced with the Roland Petit Co. in Paris and was choreographer for the Nederlands Dans Theater in 1960, then artistic director till 1971 for the Dutch National Ballet. Companies worldwide have presented his works. He was one of Holland's leading choreographers. He has used music by Beethoven, Satie, and Mozart. As a general rule he avoids narratives and dramatics, but prefers to explore relationships between men and women. He is also a professional photographer.

    **Toer van Schayk** (b. 1936), a third choreographer from The Netherlands, with a dark outlook as represented in several of his works, *Before, During, and After the Party* (1972), and *Pyrrhic Dances II* (1977). He danced with the Nederlands Ballet, under Sonia Gaskell, from 1955 to 1959 and later with the Dutch National Ballet (created in 1961 by combining the Amsterdam Ballet and the Netherlands Ballet) for which he was appointed resident choreographer. Earlier he had trained to be a sculptor and often used dancers as if they were moving sculptures. His works have a graphic quality. He is also well known for his designs for sets and costumes.

    Ballet companies have gradually sprung up all over the world. While some ballet companies, like the Kirov and the Paris Opera Ballet, do mostly classical ballet, others such as the Nederlands Dans Theater, Alonzo King's Lines Ballet, and The Forsythe Company have a blend of modern and ballet techniques to create a contemporary style of ballet. Companies throughout the world now present both classical works and contemporary works. Modern dancer-choreographer **Twyla Tharp** choreographed *Push Comes to Shove* for **Baryshnikov** and the American Ballet Theatre. In this piece as well as in *In the Upper Room* she combined modern dance, pointe shoes, and classically trained dancers to create very successful contemporary ballets. That is what many choreographers are doing now but with varying degrees of triumph.

Australian Ballet, with **David McAllister** as artistic director, is a classical dance company that celebrated its 50th anniversary season in 2012 by performing in Lincoln Center's David H. Koch Theater (formerly the New York State Theater) in New York. Ninety percent of their dancers are Australian; the others are from New Zealand, China, and Japan. Most of them have come up through the Australian Ballet School. One of the pieces they performed, titled *Warumuk – in the dark night,* was drawn from aboriginal stories and was choreographed by **Stephen Page**, the director of Bangarra, Australia's leading indigenous performance group. With this collaboration and the performance of **Graeme Murphy**'s 2002 *Swan Lake* showing their British heritage, they displayed a beautiful expression of Australian culture.

Les Ballets Trockadero de Monte Carlo, another ballet company that occasionally also does modern dance works, was formed in 1974 in the United States. It gradually attracted quite a following. The company's appeal lies in the imaginative mix of tutus and biceps, sylphs and hairy chests; the dancers are all men, with great names such as **Nina Enimenimynimova**, and **Olga Tchikaboumskaya**, and lots of personality. An example is **Robert Carter**, a black dancer who danced with the Dance Theater of Harlem, joined the Trocks (their nickname) in 1995 and received great reviews in *The New York Times* from **Jennifer Dunning** (August 19 1998) and from **Gia Kourlas** (Dec. 22, 2008). His stage name for female roles is **Olga Supphozova** and for male roles it is **Yuri Smirnov**. There is a mix of good humor, witticism, excellent technique and fun in the Trocks' performances of classics that have been choreographed by former dancers of the Kirov as well as by **Balanchine**, **Robbins**, and **Graham**. The Trocks seem to attract men who want a steady job (40 weeks a year), do not mind traveling constantly, and have excellent technique; they take a class daily like most company dancers.

The **Corella** Ballet was founded in Segovia, Spain, in 2008 by **Angel Corella**, principal dancer of the American Ballet Theater. In 2012 it became known as the Barcelona Ballet, based in Barcelona. It presented balletic ballets such as **Christopher Wheeldon**'s *For 4*, set to Schubert's *Death and the Maiden*, as well as ballet-flamenco-fusion pieces, such as *Pálpito*, by **Angel Riojas** and **Carlos Rodríguez** (directors of the flamenco troupe Nuevo Ballet Español), to an original score by Héctor González. The Barcelona Ballet was Spain's first classical ballet company in many years. **Corella** retired from the American Ballet Theater in 2012 to concentrate on his company. They performed in New York's City Center in 2012. Subsequently the company folded and Corella became the artistic director of the Pennsylvania Ballet in late 2014.

The Cairo Opera Ballet Company, associated with the Higher Ballet Institute at the Academy of Arts in Egypt, was established in 1966. Russian dancers helped to train the original members of the company. Their first ballet, directed by **Leonid Labrovsky**, former director of the Bolshoi ballet in Russia, was *The Fountain of Bakhchisarai*. The Cairo Opera House, where opera and ballet are performed, is now part of Cairo's National Cultural Center of Art and was Japan's gift to Egypt. (Egypt's previous opera house, the Khedivial Opera House, built in 1869, had been destroyed by fire in 1977.) The new opera house was inaugurated after three years of construction with the staging

Alicia Alonso, 1955. Cuban dancer, choreographer, and teacher.

Natalia Dudinskaya as Kitri in "Don Quixote," 1932-33. She was prima ballerina of the Kirov/Mariinsky Ballet in the 20th century.

Cherylyn Lavagnino Dance was formed in 2000. The company has performed at Danspace Project at St. Mark's Church, Jacob's Pillow, The Kaatsbann International Dance Center and New Dance Alliance, Inc. and has received excellent reviews from dance critics .

Little Dancer, Aged Fourteen, 1878, A young dancer posed for this, the only sculpture exhibited by Edgar Degas. He executed it in wax, and standing in fourth position, with real hair tied with a ribbon, and wearing a cloth bodice and tutu and silk ballet slippers. After Degas' death his heirs had it cast in bronze in 1922.

Natalia Makarova is welcomed at The White House as one of the 2012 Kennedy Center Honorees.

of a traditional Kabuki show with dancing and singing, a first in Africa. Since 1973, The Cairo Ballet Company has toured extensively in Europe and Asia. The classical ballets as well as creations by Egyptian choreographers and composers, such as *Osiris,* about the legend of Isis and Osiris, are part of their repertoire. **Dr Abdel Moneim Kamel,** chairman of the National Cultural Center, has also added to the company's repertoire his version of several classics, *Romeo and Juliet, Swan Lake*, as well as *Carmina Burana, Bolero*, and *Rite of Spring*. In 1998-1999 the company took part in a production of *Aida* directed by **Dr. Kamel** at the pyramid platform. **Erminia Gambarelli Kamel,** his wife, has been the artistic director since 2004.

The Cape Town City Ballet Company based in Cape Town, South Africa, originated from the UCT (University of Cape Town) Ballet Co. established by **Dulcie Howes** in 1934. It became the CAPAB Ballet Co. (Cape Performing Arts Board Ballet Co.) with **David Poole**, British, as artistic director and ballet master. This company presents versions of the classics reworked by resident choreographer **Veronica Paeper**, such as *Giselle, Les Sylphides*, and *Swan Lake,* as well as new works by her (a favorite is her *Carmen*) and other contemporary ballet choreographers. Guest artists have included **Margot Fonteyn**, **Carla Fracci**, and **Wayne Sleep** (b. 1948, British dancer-choreographer). **Wayne Sleep** established a world record in 1973 for doing **entrechat douze** (a jump with 12 beats). He danced with the Royal Ballet of London, studied at their school and received the **Carl-Alan Award** for outstanding contributions to dance.

The Cedar Lake Contemporary Ballet, located in New York City, does not perform en pointe but does present dances by several European choreographers who may be well known but are usually new to the U.S. These include **Crystal Pite,** a Canadian based in Frankfurt, Germany, **Alexander Ekman**, a former member of the Royal Swedish Ballet and a close affiliate of the style of **Mats Ek**'s Cullberg Ballet, **Regina Van Berkel**, Dutch-born choreographer who danced in Tokyo with **Saburo Teshigawara**'s company and with **Forsythe**'s Frankfurt Ballet, **Hofesh Shechter**, an Israeli-born, London-based choreographer, and **Jo Stromgren**, Norwegian. This was the brainstorm of **Benoit-Swan Pouffer** and made for a very interesting and varied repertoire for the Cedar Lake Contemporary Ballet, which was formed in 2003 by the Walmart heiress Nancy Watson Laurie. She appointed the French-born former **Alvin Ailey** dancer, **Benoit-Swan Pouffer,** as artistic director in 2005 just as the company moved into a new home with its own theater in the Chelsea neighborhood of New York City. Unfortunately the company closed in June 2015 for lack of funds.

Introdans, a small, polished Dutch contemporary ballet company founded in 1971 in Arnhem, eastern Netherlands, by **Tom Wiggers**, is under the artistic direction of **Roel Voorintholt**. The company commissions works by leading modern-ballet choreographers, like **Mats Ek, William Forsythe, Jiři Kylián, David Parsons, Twyla Tharp, Nils Christie** (*Fünf Gedichte, Five Poems*, 1996), **Ed Wubbe** (*Messiah*, 1988), **Lucinda Childs**, and **Alberto del Saz** (artistic director of the Nikolais Louis Foundation for Dance, for the staging of **Alwin Nikolais**' works for the company). Introdans company, with its eclectic repertory, is well known in Europe and finally performed in New York in 2012.

The Iranian National Ballet, founded in 1968 by the Iranian Ministry of Culture, was dissolved in 1979 after the Iranian revolution. The final director of the company was the Iranian **Ali Pourfarrokhan** (b.1938) who later became artistic director of the **Eglevsky** Ballet Company in Long Island, NY.

K-Ballet, a Japanese ballet company, was founded in 1999. The artistic director is **Tetsuyu Kumakawa**. The company gives approximately 50 performances annually, and involves 70 artists and dancers in its productions.

The Korean National Ballet Co., a South Korean ballet company, was founded in 1962. **Joo-won Kim**, one of its prima ballerinas, was the winner of the Prix Benois de la Danse in 2008. The Korean National Ballet was the first Asian company to perform **Yuri Grigorovich**'s *Spartacus,* in 2001. They also performed it in 2012, again under the KNB direction of **Choi-Tae-ji,** and featuring KNB's principal ballerina, **Kim Ji-Young**.

The National Ballet of China was founded in 1959. **Peter Gushev** from Russia laid an excellent foundation for classical ballet for this company, and several of its dancers have won gold, silver, and bronze medals at international competitions. In 2008 The National Ballet of China presented a premiere of a two-scene ballet adaptation of *The Peony Pavilion*, one of China's best-loved classical operas, originally written by Tang Xianzu in the Ming Dynasty. (The opera is long; it runs for 20 hours. The Lincoln Center production in 1999 was the first 20-hour, full-length staging in 300 years.) **Fei Bo** choreographed the two-scene ballet version of 2008, with music by Gus Wenjing. The opera director **Li-Liuyi** rewrote the story for the ballet version.

The National Ballet of Moldova in Chisinău, Moldova, survived and kept its ballet, opera, and orchestra after the collapse of the Soviet Union. In 1957 professional ballet began there with a group of dancers from Leningrad. Since 2001 it has presented **Yuri Grigorovich**'s *Nutcracker* in Spain and the United Kingdom and it has toured throughout Europe.

The Norwegian National Opera and Ballet was founded in 1957 by the great Norwegian soprano, **Kirsten Flagstad**. Like several other companies, it has a ballet school connected to the company. The teachers of the school have varied backgrounds so as to enable students to acquire the versatility demanded in the many operas and ballets in which they perform. Students dance in both the annual *Nutcracker* in school performances as well as in the annual Nordic-Baltic Ballet Competition in Sweden.

The Royal Ballet of Flanders in Belgium, one of the best companies in Europe, with **Assis Carreiro** as artistic director, succeeding **Kathyrn Bennetts** who had been artistic director since 2005, has top-notch dancers and a repertory that is well balanced between ballet and modern. Among its modern ballets are a few by **William Forsythe**, his full-length, very theatrical award-winning piece, *Impressing the Czar*, and *New Sleep*, and some pieces by **Balanchine** and by **Jerome Robbins**.

The Royal New Zealand Ballet, based in Wellington, New Zealand, presents an eclectic repertoire of classic ballets from the 19th century to contemporary ballets of the 21st century. **Ethan Stiefel** (formerly with the New York City Ballet, then with America Ballet Theater) became its artistic director in 2011 and retired from ABT in 2012. The Royal New Zealand ballet was featured in the TV3 series *The Secret Lives of Dancers*. The company is known for pushing the boundaries of ballet.

The Royal Swedish Ballet is one of the oldest companies in Europe, having been founded in 1773 by King Gustav III. Till then the only professional dancers in Sweden had been foreign groups. King Gustav believed in hiring dancers and teachers from France, Italy, and Belgium to perform and teach future dancers. During the 18th century the Swedish ballet had success with the ballet *Fiskama* (*The Fish*, by **Antoine Bournonville**). From the end of the 19th century till about 1913, however, ballet was performed in operas only, and not as a separate art form. The artistic director of the Royal Swedish Ballet is **Johannes Öhman**. This position was held by **Marc Ribaud** from 2008 to 2011. The company has a separate small chamber ballet company made up of dancers from the main company. It is called Stockholm 59° (degrees) North.

The Royal Winnipeg Ballet Company in Manitoba, Canada, was founded in 1939 and began touring in Canada in 1945. The company now tours approximately 20 weeks a year and produces four new ballets a year. **André Lewis**, the current artistic director, was chosen in 1996. Their best-known dancer is **Evelyn Hart,** who joined the company in 1976. She was awarded the bronze medal at the World Ballet Concours in Japan in 1980, and, that same year, the gold medal at the prestigious International Dance Competition in Varna, Bulgaria, where she also received the Exceptional Artistic Achievement Award. Canada honored her with the Order of Canada in 1983.

Sarasota Ballet, Florida, was founded in 1990, and since 2007 has been under the direction of **Iain Webb**, with his wife **Margaret Barbieri** as assistant director. Both are former dancers of London's Royal Ballet. Sarasota Ballet has several Ashton ballets in its repertoire as well as ballets by **George Balanchine, Antony Tudor, Agnes de Mille, Twyla Tharp, Michael Bourne,** and **Christopher Wheeldon**.

The Smuin Ballet, a San Francisco based company, was founded by Broadway and ballet choreographer **Michael Smuin,** who died in 2007. **Celia Fushille**, a dancer in the original troupe, is now its artistic and executive director. The company has appeared at the Joyce Theater in New York in Smuin's *Medea* (1977) to the music *Medea Suite* by Samuel Barber (the same piece that **Martha Graham** used for her dance about Medea, *Cave of the Heart*), and also in the resident choreographer **Amy Seiwert**'s *Soon These Two Worlds* (2009), to music for strings and drums from the Nonesuch recording, *Pieces of Africa,* performed by the Kronos Quartet. It also performed **Trey McIntyre**'s *Oh, Inverted World* (2012), set to songs by The Shins. This is an attractive and talented group.

The Stuttgart Ballet under the direction of **John Cranko** renewed the interest in ballet in Germany. In 1965 **Cranko** staged a three-act *Eugene Onegin*, based on Alexander Pushkin's poem, and in 1969, *The Taming of the Shrew,* based on

Shakespeare's play, perfect roles for both performers, **Marcia Haydée**, born in Brazil, and **Richard Cragun** (American, 1944-2012). Cranko's narrative ballets always made sense psychologically and suited the talents of his two stars. His ballets felt emotionally spontaneous. **Cranko** and his dancers encouraged new choreographers such as **John Neumeier, Maurice Béjart, Peter Wright, Kenneth MacMillan**, and **William Forsythe**. The latter employed unexpected solutions to put together his definitely contemporary pieces like *Love Song*. **Cranko** died in 1973 on a plane while returning to Stuttgart from a successful U.S. engagement. **Cranko**'s superior choreographic story-telling skills were also evident in the American Ballet Theater's new 2012 production of *Onegin*.

Besides the Paris Opera Ballet, France has many small companies outside of Paris, in Marseilles, Lyon, Toulouse, and Nantes. There is much contemporary dance in France and the many companies have received grants from the Ministry of Culture. The Ballet-Théâtre Contemporain was moved from Paris to Angers in 1972 in an attempt to decentralize the arts. An effort was made to establish a separate unit of the Paris Opera for experimental modern works under **Carolyn Carlson**, a Finnish dancer formerly with Nikolais' company, but when **Nureyev** took over the direction of the Paris Opera (from 1983 to 1989) he incorporated experimental works into the repertoire, making a separate group unnecessary. Nureyev is recognized as being the first director of this company since **Serge Lifar** to have revived the excellent standards that the company once had and to help it regain its international reputation. He continuously mounted full-length ballets for them and also commissioned works from modern ballet choreographers. By July 2012 their repertoire included both *Giselle* and a dance opera by **Pina Bausch**, *Orpheus and Eurydice,* as well as a rarely seen work by Serge Lifar, *Suite en Blanc,* when they performed at New York's Lincoln Center.

**Benjamin Millepied** (b.1977), former principal dancer of the New York City Ballet and choreographer of the movie *Black Swan* (2010), was chosen as director of the Paris Opera Ballet to succeed Brigitte Lefèvre in September 2014 upon her retirement. Millepied was born in Bordeaux, France, studied in France till he came to New York to study at the School of American Ballet at age 16. He became soloist at NYCB in 1998 and principal dancer in 2002. He has choreographed works for several ballet companies, among them, *Triple Duet* (2002), to music by J. S. Bach for Sadler's Wells Theatre, *Amoveo* (2006), with set design by Paul Cox for the Paris Opera Ballet, *Plainspoken* (2009), to music by David Lang for the NYCB, *Troika* (2011), for American Ballet Theater and *Reflections* (2013), for his L.A. Dance Project.

In Great Britain the former Sadler's Wells Ballet Company (founded by **Ninette de Valois** in 1931) became the Royal Ballet with **Frederick Ashton** and **Kenneth MacMillan** (d. 1992) as chief choreographers. Ashton's last ballet for **Margot Fonteyn** (1919-1991) and **Rudolph Nureyev** was named *Marguerite and Armand*, choreographed in 1963 to a score by Ferdinand Hérold; it was a huge success and they performed it together many, many times. (In 1964 Fonteyn had to go to Panama to care for her husband who had been injured by a bullet that paralyzed him. She gave her farewell performance at age 60 in London's Royal Opera House.) Ashton's *The Dream* (1964) based on Shakespeare's *Midsummer Night's Dream* was choreographed for **Antoinette Sibley** and **Anthony Dowell**. *Enigma Variations* (1968, music by Elgar), choreographed by Ashton, was another classical and very original piece by him. Many of Ashton's works have survived to the 21st century. The last presentation of artistic director **Monica Mason** before she retired had choreography by **Wayne McGregor** and **Christopher Wheeldon.** It was inspired by the London National Gallery's three great Titian "Metamorphoses" canvases and coincided with the London Summer Olympics of 2012. In July 2012, upon Monica Mason's retirement, **Kevin O'Hare** became the new artistic director with **Wayne McGregor** and **Christopher Wheeldon** joining the company's "senior artistic team."

**Sir Kenneth MacMillan** (1929-1992), just the opposite of **Ashton**, involved sociological and psychological aspects in his ballets, much like **Cranko**, thereby expanding the range of ballet. **MacMillan**'s *Romeo and Juliet* (1965) is usually the preferred version of *Romeo and Juliet* with its many lovely pas de deux. MacMillan also choreographed several full-length works that were quite different from the usual subjects: *Anastasia* (1971) included a hospital scene, revolutionaries storming at the door, and the execution of the last Russian Tzar and his family; *Mayerling* (1978) showed sordid characters; *Manon* (1974) showed greed, poverty, and passion, all danced in several pas de deux; *Different Drummer* (1984) showed the dehumanizing effect of war. MacMillan died in 1992 at age 62, backstage at the Covent Garden during the revival of *Mayerling*. His most lasting dances were *Romeo and Juliet* as well as *Manon*. He was knighted in 1983.

**Ninette de Valois** died in 2001, at age 102, seventy years after starting The Sadler's Wells Ballet Company.

**Anthony Dowell** (b. 1943) was artistic director of the Royal Ballet from 1986 to 2001. He is remembered for his dance partnership with **Antoinette Sibley** that had captivated many. He raised the dance standards, revised several of the works by **Ashton**, and updated the repertoire with works by **Balanchine, Twyla Tharp, Forsythe, Cranko,** and **MacMillan**.

The discovery of **David Bintley**, a former character dancer, was eventful. He choreographed an evening-long ballet, *Hobson's Choice* (1989). This period comedy was very successful and he was considered to be quite promising. He became the resident choreographer of the Sadler's Wells Royal Ballet from 1983 to 1985 and of the Royal Ballet from 1986 to 1993, then artistic director of the Birmingham Royal Ballet in 1995.

Meanwhile, Ballet Rambert had had financial problems during WW II and its Australian tour. It reorganized in 1966 upon the suggestion of **Norman Morrice** (d. 2008), a former Rambert dancer, to form a smaller group of dancers proficient in both modern and ballet. Morrice's mix of folk dance, classical, and modern appealed to audiences not yet ready for modern dance. **Christopher Bruce**, a dramatic dancer with the company, was the next choreographer to emerge. *Ghost Dances* (1981), regarding the Chilean dictator Augusto Pinochet, was a favorite, set to Andean folk songs and folk dances while showing the suffering of innocent people. **Robert North**, who had performed with **Graham** and became Rambert's artistic director in 1981, used a mix of Graham, classical dance, and jazz. His piece *Lonely Town, Lonely Street* (1981) was dedicated to American jazz dancer **Matt Mattox** (1921-2013) with whom he had studied. (Mattox was a versatile dancer and teacher, known for training students to use a wide,

276

Photo Plate 14-5

August Macke (1887-1914), expressionist painter who showed spectators as well as performers in his "Ballet Russes," 1914.

Ivan Vasiliev in "Spartacus" at the Bolshoi, Oct. 28, 2011.

Violette Verdy and Edward Villella performing at a State Dinner in Washington DC.

Wendy Whelan taking final bow, Oct. 2014, after 30 years with the New York City Ballet.

Jessica Lang Dance Company performing "Lines Cubed" at Jacob's Pillow Dance Festival, 2012. Dance Magazine called Ms. Lang "a master of visual composition."

Léon Bakst's design"for L'Après-Midi d'un Faune."

Natalia Osipova in "Flames of Paris" at the Bolshoi Theatre's reopening, Oct. 28, 2011.

tense hand in jazz for a strong manly look. He performed in many movies, including *Seven Brides for Seven Brothers*, choreographed by **Michael Kidd**.)

The Ballet Rambert became Rambert Dance Company in 1987 under **Robert Alston** and included in its repertoire works by modern choreographers such as **Merce Cunningham**. (The **Graham** modern dance technique was the recognized technique at another company, the London Contemporary Dance Theatre founded in 1967 under **Robert Cohan**, formerly with the Graham Company.) Since 2002 the artistic director of Rambert Dance Company has been **Marc Baldwin,** who was commissioned to choreograph *Constant Speed* to commemorate the centenary of Einstein's great ideas of 1905. Baldwin's later work of 2011, in a more humorous vein, was called *Seven for a secret, never to be told* and was choreographed to an adaptation by Stephen McNeff of Ravel's *L'enfant et les sortilèges.* The Rambert Dance Company is presently a touring contemporary dance company situated in Chiswick, London. They still have in their repertoire two works by **Antony Tudor**, *Dark Elegies* (1937) and *Judgment of Paris* (1938). **Marie Rambert** remained involved in the company until her death in 1982 at the age of 94.

There has been grief over the fact that several of the classical full-length ballets impart derogatory views of some cultures or races, especially noticeable in their character roles or dances, much as our early *Mulligan Guard* series in burlesque and the American minstrel shows used to do. This is not a good way to appeal to today's audiences. Modern dance has always been right on the mark with realistic dances portraying life. Ballet companies need to do what filmmakers do: read contemporary books and newspaper articles and ask themselves, "Could this story be adapted into a full-length ballet that would represent the world in which we live?"

Here are a few of the contemporary pieces that choreographers have created. It would be nice to see more of these.

- *Prodigal Son* by Balanchine (1950)
- *Frankie and Johnny* by Ruth Page (1938)
- *The Green Table* by Kurt Jooss (1932), deals with war
- *Dark Elegies* by AntonyTudor (1937), psychological mind-set
- *Qarrtsiluni* by Harold Lander (1942), dealing with a winter without sun, which is the usual in some countries
- *Fall River Legend* by Agnes de Mille (1948), about the ax murderess, Lizzie Borden
- *A Song for Dead Warriors* by Michael Smuin (1999), about Native American tribes
- *Washington Square* by Rudolph Nureyev (1985), based on a novel by Henry James
- *Spartacus* by Yuri Grigorovich (1967)
- *The Taming of the Shrew* by John Cranko (1985)
- *Ghost Dances* by Christopher Bruce (1981), regarding the Chilean dictator Augusto Pinochet and performed to Andean folk songs
- *Othello* by Lar Lubovitch (1991), performed by the multicultural/multiracial San Francisco Ballet with an Asian Desdemona and a black Othello
- *A Streetcar Named Desire* by John Alleyne (2006)
- *Lady from the Sea* by Birgit Cullberg (1960), adapted from Ibsen

- *In Paradisum* by James Kudelka (1983), about the five stages of terminal illness
- *Forgotten Land* by Jiři Kylián (1981), inspired by a painting by Edvard Munch
- *Different Drummer* by Kenneth MacMillan (1984), the effects that war has on people by depriving them of human qualities and spirit
- *Hemingway: The Sun Also Rises* by Septime Webre (2013), for Washington Ballet to original music by Billy Novick
- *Fancy Free* by Jerome Robbins (1944)

The latest hit musical with ballet dancing on Broadway was in 2009, *Billy Elliot*, imported from Great Britain. The three young boys who originally shared the role of Billy were all discovered in ballet schools in the U.S.: **David Alvarez**, **Trent Kowalik**, and **Kiril Kulish**; they were wonderful and, as one person, they won the Tony award for: "Best Actor in a Musical in 2009." **Peter Darling** was the choreographer of *Billy Elliot*. *The New York Times* called the musical "Intoxicating," *Time Out New York* said it was "Extraordinarily Uplifting," *The New York Post* said about Elton John's music: "His Best Score Yet." The book and lyrics were by Lee Hall; the director was Stephen Daldry. The musical also won the Tony awards for best musical director, best choreographer, best musical, best book of a musical, best lighting design, best featured actor, best scenic design, and others, for a total of ten Tonys. The dancing is outstanding, with wonderful turns, leaps, tap, and expressive, emotional dancing to suit the story. The musical was based on the film *Billy Elliot*. It was an incentive for boys and young men to study ballet. It lasted 2 years and 3 months, closing on Jan. 8, 2012, after a very successful run.

The television series *Dance in America*, directed and produced by **Merrill Brockway**, began on PBS in 1976; the whole country could now see ballets by **George Balanchine**, **Jerome Robbins**, and other choreographers. In 2011 Merrill Brockway donated his library of performance tapes to the N.D.I. (National Dance Institute) of New Mexico so that young people, their parents and teachers would be able to learn from these tapes.

There have been some excellent films and documentaries on dance. *The Turning Point*, 1977, an American film starring Shirley MacLaine, Anne Bancroft, ABT's **Leslie Brown**, **Mikhail Baryshnikov**, and **Alexandra Danilova**, directed by **Herbert Ross** with his wife, retired ballerina **Nora Kaye**, as co-director, was a success, and within the storyline there were lovely moments of classical dance. More recent films include *Margot* (TV 2009 DVD, directed by Tony Palmer) based on the life of **Margot Fonteyn**; Frederick Wiseman's *La Danse - Le Ballet de L'Opéra de Paris* (Dec. 2009) about the Paris Opera Ballet; and *Mao's Last Dancer* (2009, directed by Bruce Beresford). The latter was based on the best selling autobiography of **Li Cunxin**, Houston Ballet star, who rose from poverty in China during Mao's Cultural Revolution. Based on his proportions and flexibility, he had been chosen from hundreds of boys for training at the Beijing Dance Academy. **Ben Stevenson**, director of the Houston Ballet, invited Cunxin to come to the Houston Ballet to study at the school and to perform. You may also want to look for *The Black Swan*, a film starring Natalie Portman, not about the ballet *Swan Lake* as such, but as a fictional psychological study. It aroused enough filmgoers' curiosity to make it obvious at the NYC Ballet Co. box office that a great number of people want to see the ballet *Swan Lake* on stage. Another movie worth seeing is the documentary, *First Position*, produced and directed by Bess Kargman, released by Sundance Selects in 2012 in English, Spanish, French, and Hebrew, with English subtitles. It follows seven young competitors over a year as they prepare for the regional and finals of the Youth America Grand Prix, which awards scholarships and, for a few older students, company job offers. In 2013, *Gotta Dance,* a documentary, showed us a dozen or so senior citiaens of all sizes, shapes, and races, practicing and actually performing short dance routines at appropriate intervals during the New Jersey Net's basketball games.

In 2011, fifty years after Rudolph Nureyev defected to the West to dance, the Russians (more specifically, **Sergei Filin**, the artistic director of the Bolshoi Ballet of Moscow) reversed this trend by choosing a terrific romantic and classical dancer, **David Hallberg**, 29, who speaks no Russian, to be the first American to join the Bolshoi Ballet. Sergei Filin had seen Hallberg perform in Russia during a Ballet Theater visit and had been very impressed by his purity of line and phrasing. Hallberg was offered a position of premier (the Bolshoi's term for principal dancer) with the Bolshoi, was hired, and started at the Bolshoi Ballet in November, 2011, with *Giselle,* and with the possibility of even continuing to dance with American Ballet Theater at the same time during their May to July season at the Metropolitan Opera House at Lincoln Center. The Bolshoi also planned to have **David Hallberg** dance in *Don Quixote* and in *The Sleeping Beauty.*

Since the 1960's there has been a tremendous increase in paid attendance at dance performances in the United States. According to the National Endowment for the Arts and the Association of American Dance Companies, paid attendance in 1965 was one million; by 1975 it was 11.6 million. Companies throughout the country are performing their version of *Nutcracker* to large audiences that help them to pay their bills. By 1990 the number of paid attendance had gone up to 16 million. It may have gone down since 2010 due to the economic problems around the world.

Dance is a universal language, as old as man, and it is very much alive today, evolving, adapting and representing humanity and the changing world in which we live. There is a welcoming inclusiveness about multiracial, multiethnic, and multicultural companies, which communicates the message that dancing is indeed a universal language and is meant for all; nothing says this better than to actually see dancing on stage and in dance classes. Some of the choreographers who have seemed to welcome the variety found in humanity are: **Alvin Ailey**, **Brenda Bufalino**, **Daniel Catanach**, **Martha Graham**, **Lester Horton**, **David Parsons**, **Paul Taylor**, **Twyla Tharp**, and many, many more. Ballet may have started with King Louis XIV of France, but there are not many kings and queens around any more. Hence, ballet has become more inclusive. There are several musicals, films, TV films, and modern dance companies that have more than just a "token" black, Asian, Native American, and/or Hispanic performer; maybe it is still not a lot per show but the total adds up. Are ballet companies also trying to do this? Yes, but much more slowly.

Ballet and its choreographers have constantly learned much from other newer forms of dance, such as modern and jazz, and from trying to always stay in the present while honoring the accomplishments of the past. For example, the Paris Opera Ballet, a very large company, has successfully presented gems from the purely classical ballet field, as well as works by **Merce Cunningham, Pina Bausch**, and **Anna de Keersmaer**. **Balanchine** *(Photo Plate14-2 and 3)* created very classical ballets such as *The Nutcracker* and then choreographed others using the classic technique with a blending or a contrast of the newer elements: syncopation, jazzy hip thrusts, and modern contractions. Several dance companies have commissioned contemporary pop music for original ballets, to entice a completely fresh audience to attend ballet: Paul McCartney for the New York City Ballet (2011, *Ocean's Kingdom*, choreographed by **Peter Martins**, about a romance in a royal undersea court, with costumes designed by Paul's daughter Stella McCartney); the Pet Shop Boys' music with choreographer **Javier de Frutos** for Sadler's Wells Theater production in London of *The Most Incredible Thing*; and Joni Mitchell's music for the Alberta Ballet's 40th anniversary in Canada.

As a means of attracting a younger audience to the ballet, the New York City Ballet in 2014 commissioned *Les Bosquets.* by street artist JR (known for his large-scale photographs) for **Lil Buck** (Charles Riley), a specialist in **jookin** (a street style of dance which was born in Memphis, in which the artist very often dances on the tiptoes of his sneakers, and usually with bent knees). His partner in a pas de deux was **Lauren Lovette**, a soloist in the ballet company. *Les Bosquets* served its purpose.

American Ballet Theater's 2013 Fall Season included several modern dance pieces, Mark Morris's *Gong* (2001) and Twyla Tharp's *Bach Partita* (1983) as well as ballet favorites, Michel Fokine's *Les Sylphides* (1909), George Balanchine's *Theme and Variations* (1947), and Frederick Ashton's *A Month in the Country* (1978) with masterful choreography. All companies seek to find the most appropriate solution for themselves in order to endure and to attract a fresh audience as well as their loyal fans. Sometimes this includes promoting an outstanding soloist, such as **James Whiteside**, to the rank of principal. That is exactly what ABT's artistic director, **Kevin McKenzie,** did on October 30, 2013.

Ethnic dance was certainly well represented in the 21st century. **Madhavi Mughol** brought us the intricacies of Indian dance, **Soledad Barrio** and **Rocio Molina** entranced us with their flamenco, while **Gabriel Missé** reminded us why we love the Argentine tango.

Considering all the innovative and enterprising individuals around in the dance field, finding a fresh solution for keeping dance audiences loyal and discovering new audiences should prove to be a challenge but certainly not an impossible problem. All forms of dance: ballet, ethnic, jazz, modern, social, and tap have a promising anticipated future and an audience eager to see their performances.

# Bibliographies

**EARLY DANCE TO THE MIDDLE AGES – BIBLIOGRAPHY – Chapter 1**
**AND DANCE IN THE MIDDLE AGES – BIBLIOGRAPHY - Chapter 2**

Backman, E. Louis. *Religious Dances.* London: George Allen and Unwin Ltd., 1952.

Barber, David W. *Tutus, Tights and Tiptoes – Ballet History As It Ought To Be Taught.* Toronto, Canada: Sound and Vision. 2000.

Campbell, Joseph. *The Hero with a Thousand Faces. (1949)* New York: New World Library, 3rd edition, 2008.

_____*The Masks of God.* New York: Viking Press, (1959-1968).

De Mille, Agnes. *The Book of the Dance.* New York: Golden Press, 1963.

Ellis, Havelock. *The Dance of Life.* Boston: Houghton Mifflin Company, 1923.

Harris, Jane A. *Dance a While: Handbook of Folk, Square, Contra and Social Dance,* 6th edition. New York: Macmillan, 1988.

Hata, Michiyo. *Tradition and Creativity in Japanese Dance.* NY: Weatherhill, 2001.

Hughes, Russell Meriweather. *The Gesture Language of the Hindu Dance/ La Meri.* NY: Arno Press, 1979.

Kirstein, Lincoln. *Dance: a Short History of Classic Theatrical Dancing.* Princeton, NJ: Princeton Book Company/Dance Horizons, Anniversary Edition, 1987.

Kraus, Richard. *History of Dance.* Englewood Cliffs, NJ: Prentice-Hall, Inc., 1969.

Lal, Ruby. *Domesticity and Power in the Early Mughal World.* Cambridge, UK: Cambridge University Press, 2005.

Lane, Christy and Susan Langhout. *Multicultural Folk Dance.* Champaigne, IL: Human Kinetics Publishers, Inc., 1998.

Langer, Suzanne. *Philosophy in a New Key: A Study in the Symbolism of Reason, Rite, and Art.* New York: The New American Library, 1942.

Lawler, Lillian. *The Dance in Ancient Greece.* Middletown, CT: Wesleyan/New England Press, 2000.

Meerloo, Joost. *The Dance.* New York: Chilton Book Company, 1960.

Mukherjee, Soma. *Royal Mughol Ladies and Their Contributions.* New Delhi: Gyan Publishing House, 2001.

Petrides, Theodore and Elfleida Petrides. *Folk Dances of the Greeks.* Great Britain: Bailey Brothers & Swinefen, Ltd., 1961.

Sachs, Curt. *World History of the Dance.* NY: W.W.Norton, 1963.

Shawn, Ted. *Dance We Must.* London: Dennis Dobson, Ltd., 1946.

Vuillier, Gaston, with a sketch of dancing in England by Joseph Grego. *A History of Dancing from the Earliest Ages to Our Own Times.* D. Appleton & Co., 1898. (Google ebooks, Performing Arts, 446 pgs.)

*Wikipedia, the free encyclopedia.*

Wilford, John Noble. "In Dawn of Society, Dance was Center Stage," *The New York Times,* Feb. 27, pgs. Fl and F2.


**EARLY AMERICAN DANCE BIBLIOGRAPHY Chapter 3 - Alaska, Hawaii, and Native American**

Barbour, Baton H. *Fort Union and the Upper Missouri Fur Trade.* Norman, OK: The University of Oklahoma Press, Publishing Division of the University, 2001.

Buck, Elizabeth Benzel. *Paradise Remade: The Politics of Culture and History in Hawai'i.* Philadelphia, PA.: Temple University Press, 1993.

Butree, Julia M. (Julia M. Seton). *The Rhythm of the Redman in Song, Dance, and Decoration.* NY: A. S. Barnes, 1930.

Curtis, Edward Sheriff. *The North American Indian: being a series of volumes picturing and describing the Indians of the United States and Alaska,* Foreword by Theodore Roosevelt; field research conducted under the patronage of J. Pierpont Morgan. Washington, DC: Library of Congress.

De Mille, Agnes. *The Book of the Dance.* New York: Golden Press, 1963.

Fienup-Riordan, Ann. *The Living Tradition of Yup'ik Masks*. Seattle, WA: University of Washington Press, 1996.

Forbes, David W. *Encounters with Paradise: Views of Hawaii and its People, 1778-1941*. Honolulu, HI: Honolulu Academy of Arts, 1992.

Griffen-Pierce, Trudy. *The Encyclopedia of Native America*. NY: Viking, 1995.

Heth, Charlotte, ed. *Native American Dance: Ceremonies and Social Traditions*. Washington, DC: National Museum of the American Indian, Smithsonian Institution, 1990.

Highwater, Jamake. *Ritual of the Wind: North American Indian Ceremonies, Music, and Dances*. New York: The Viking Press, 1977.

Laubin, Reginald and Gladys. *Indian Dances of North America: Their Importance to Indian Life*. Norman, OK: The University of Oklahoma Press, 1977.

Nevell, Richard. *A Time to Dance: American Country Dancing from Hornpipes to Hot Hash*. New York: St. Martin's Press, 1977.

Paterek, Josephine. *The Encyclopedia of American Indian Costume*. NY: Norton, 1996.

Paul, Doris A. *The Navajo Code Talkers*. Pittsburgh, PA: Dorrance Publishing Co., Inc., 1973.

Radin, Paul. *The Story of the American Indian*. New York: Garden City Publishing Company, 1937.

Ray, Dorothy Jean. *Eskimo Masks; Art and Ceremony*. Photographs by Alfred A. Blaker. Seattle: University of Washington Press, 1967.

Seiden, Allan. *The Art of the Hula: the Spirit, the History, the Legends*. photography by A. Waipahu. HI: Island Heritage Pub., 2008.

Wagner, Ann. *Adversaries of Dance: From the Puritans to the Present*. Urbana, IL: University of Illinois Press, 1997.

**BALLET BIBLIOGRAPHY– Chapters 4, 5, 6, and 14**

Aloff, Mindy. *Dance Anecdotes – Stories from the World of Ballet, Broadway, Ballroom, and Modern Dance*. NY: Oxford University Press, 2006.

Amberg, George. *Ballet in America: The Emergence of an American Art*. New York: Da Capo, 1983.

Arbeau, Thoinot. *Orchesography*. Trans. Mary Stewart Evans. New York: Dover, 1967.

Balanchine, George. *Complete Stories of the Great Ballets*. NY: Doubleday & Company, Inc., 1954.

Bournonville, August. *Letters on Dance and Choreography*. Knud Arme Jurgensen (trans. and annotated). London: Dance Books, 1999.

Buckle, Richard. *Diaghilev*. London: Weidenfeld and Nicolsen, 1991.

Carter, Alexandra. *Dance and Dancers in the Victorian and Edwardian Music Hall Ballet*. Aldershot, Hampshire, UK: Ashgate Publishing, Ltd., 2005.

Clarke, Mary, and Clemont Crisp. *The History of Dance*. New York: Crown, 1981.

D'Amboise, Jacques. *I Was a Dancer – A Memoir*. New York: Alfred A. Knopf, 2011.

Davis, Mary E. *Ballets Russes Style: Diaghilev's Dancers and Paris Fashion*. Chicago, Ill: Reaktion Books, University of Chicago Press, 2010.

De Valois, Ninette. *Come Dance with Me: A Memoir 1898-1956*. Dublin: Lilliput Press, 1992.

Dunning, Jennifer. *Fifty Years of the School of American Ballet*. New York: Viking, 1985.

Grant, Gail. *Technical Manual and Dictionary of Classical Ballet*. Second Revised Edition. New York: Dover Publications, Inc., 1967.

Hamilton, Linda. *The Dancer's Way: The NYC Ballet Guide to Mind, Body, and Nutrition*. New York: St. Martin's Griffen, 2009.

Homans, Jennifer. *Apollo's Angels – A History of Ballet*. New York: Random House, 2010.

Karsavina, Tamara. *Theatre Street: The Reminiscences of Tamara Karsavina*. London: Constable, 1930. Revised and enlarged, 1948.

Kavanagh, Julie. *Nureyev: The Life*. New York: Pantheon Books, 2007.

Kent, Allegra. *Once a Dancer: An Autobiography*. New York: St. Martin's Press, 1997.

Kerner, Mary. *Barefoot to Balanchine, How to Watch Dance*. NY: Anchor Books a division of Bantam Doubleday Dell Publishing Group, Inc., 1991.

Kirstein, Lincoln. *Dance, a Short History of Classic Theatrical Dancing*. Princeton, NJ: Princeton Book Company/Dance Horizons, Anniversary Edition, 1987.

Kochno, Boris. *Diaghilev and the Ballets Russes*. Adrienne Foulke (trans.). NY: Harper and Row, 1970.

Koegler, Horst. *The Concise Oxford Dictionary of Ballet.* Revised ed. London: Oxford University Press, 1987.

La Gumina, Salvatore John, Frank Cavaioli, Salvatore Primeggia, and Joseph Varacalli, Eds. *The Italian American Experience: An Encyclopedia.* London, UK: Routledge, Taylor & Francis Group, 1999.

Makarova, Natalia. *A Dance Autobiography.* New York: Knopf, 1979.

Mason, Francis L. *I Remember Balanchine*. NY: Doubleday, 1991.

Moore, Lillian. *Artists of the Dance.* NY: Thomas Y. Crowell, 1938. Reprinted Brooklyn, N.Y.: Dance Horizons, 1976.

Nijinsky, Romola Pulszky. *Nijinsky and The Last Yeas of Nijinsky.* New York: Simon and Schuster, 1980.

Osato, Sono. *Distant Dances.* New York: Knopf, 1980.

Robertson, Allen. ”Glen Tetley” *International Encyclopedia of Dance,* Vol. 6, ed. Selma Jeanne Cohen. NY: Oxford University Press, 1998.

Schorer, Suki. *Suki Schorer on Balanchine Technique.* New York: Knopf, 1999.

Shook, Karel. *Elements of Classical Ballet Technique, as practiced in the school of the Dance Theatre of Harlem.* NY: Dance Horizons, 1977.

Smakov, Gennady. *Baryshnikov: From Russia to the West.* London: Orbis Publishing, 1981.

Stuart, Muriel. *The Classical Ballet: Technique and Terminology.* NY: Knopf, 1962.

Ulanova, Galina. *The Making of a Ballerina.* Moscow: Foreign Languages Publishing House, 1956.

Vaganova, Agrippina. *Fundamentals of the Dance Class.* NY: Dover, 1971.

## MODERN DANCE – BIBLIOGRAPHY – Chapters 7 and 12

Andreu, Helene. *Aerobic Razzmatazz: 12 Workouts of 2 Minutes Each.* Bloomington, IN: 1st Books Library (now AuthorHouse), 2000.

Andreu, Helene. *Dance, Movement, and Nutrition.* Bloomington, IN: Authorhouse, 2006.

Barnes, Sally. *Terpsichore in Sneakers: Post-Modern Dance.* Boston: Houghton Mifflin, 1979.

Barnes, Sally. *Writing Dancing in the Age of Postmodernism.* Middletown, CT: Wesleyan University Press, 1994.

Buonaventura, Wendy. *Something in the Way She Moves, Dancing Women from Salome to Madonna.* Cambridge, MA: Da Capo press, 2003.

Cheney, Gay. *Basic Concepts in Modern Dance, A Creative Approach,* 3rd edition. Pennington, NJ: A Dance Horizons Book, Princeton Book Company, Publishers, 1989.

Cohen, Selma Jeanne (ed.). *The Modern Dance: Seven Statements of Belief.* Middletown, CT: Wesleyan University Press, 1973.

Copeland, Roger, and Marshall Cohen. *What Is Dance.* New York: Oxford University Press, 1983.

Croce, Arlene. *Sight Lines.* New York: Knopf, 1982.

Duncan, Isadora. *The Art of the Dance.* Sheldon Cheney (ed.), NY: Theatre Arts Books, 1928, 1969.

Dunning, Jennifer. *Alvin Ailey: A Life in Dance.* New York: Da Capo Press, 1998.

Freedman, Russell. *Martha Graham, A Dancer's Life.* New York: Clarion Books, a Houghton Mifflin imprint, 1998.

H'Doubler, Margaret. *Dance: A Creative Art Experience.* Madison, WI: University of Wisconsin, 1990.

Horst, Louis. *Pre-Classic Dance Forms.* New York: Kamin Dance Publishers, 1953.

*International Encyclopedia of Dance.* Edited by Selma Jeanne Cohen. NY: Oxford University Press, 1998.

Jones Bill T. *Last Night on Earth.* NY: Pantheon, 1995.

Jowitt, Deborah. *The Dance in Mind.* Boston: David Godine, 1985.

Long, Richard A. *The Black Tradition in American Dance.* NY: NY Rizzoli International Publications, 1989.

Mazo, Joseph. *Prime Movers: The Makers of Modern Dance in America.* NY: William Morrow, 1977. Reprint, Princeton, NJ: Princeton Book Co., 1984.

McDonagh, Don. *The Rise and Fall and Rise of Modern Dance.* N.Y.: Outerbridge & Lazard, 1970. Reprint, Remington, NJ: a capella books, 1990.

McKayle, Donald. *Transcending Boundaries: My Dancing Life.* London: Routledge Harewood, 2002.

Nagrin, Daniel. *How to Dance Forever: Surviving Against the Odds.* NY: Harper Collins, Publishers, 1988.

Reynolds, Nancy and Malcolm McCormick. *No Fixed Points, Dance in the Twentieth Century.* New Haven, CT: Yale University Press, 2003.

Robertson. Allen, and Donald Hutera. *The Dance Handbook.* Boston, Mass.: G. K. Hall & Co., 1988.

Siegal, Marcia B. *Howling Near Heaven: Twyla Tharpe and the Reinvention of Modern Dance.* NY: St. Martin's Press, 2006.

Siegal, Marcia B. *The Shapes of Change: Images of American Dance.* NY: Avon, 1979

Silverman, Kenneth. *Begin Again.* New York: Alfred A. Knopf, 2010.

Sorell, Walter, Ed. *The Dance Has Many Faces.* 3rd revised ed., Pennington, NJ: a capella books, an imprint of Chicago Review Press, Inc., 1992.

Terry, Walter. *The Dance in America.* NY: Harper & Row Publishers, 1956. Rev. edition, 1971.

Thorpe, Edward. *Black Dance.* Woodstock, N.Y.: Overlook Press, 1990.

Wynne, David. "Three Years with Charles Weidman," *Dance Perspectives*, No. 60, Winter, 1974, pgs. 294-308.

## TAP DANCE – BIBLIOGRAPHY – Chapters 8 and 11

Audy, Robert. *Tap Dancing – How to Teach Yourself.* NY: Random House, 1976

Bordman, Gerald M. *American Musical Theatre*: A Chronicle. New York: Oxford University Press, 1978.

Brennan, Helen. *Story of Irish Dance.* Lanham, MD: Roberts Rinehart Publishers; Distributed by National Book Network, 2001.

Bufalino, Brenda. *Tapping the Source: tap dance stories, theory and practices.* New Paltz, NY: Codhill Press, (a Woodpecker Book), 2004.

Coffey, Michael, ed. *The Irish in America.* New York; Hyperion, 1997.

Erenbery, Lewis A. *Steppin' Out: New York Nightlife and the Transformation of American Culture 1890-1930.* Westport, Conn.: Greenwood, 1944.

Fletcher, Tom. *100 Years of the Negro in Show Business.* New York: Burge, 1954.

Frank, Rusty E. *Tap! The Greatest Tap Dance Stars and Their Stories 1900-1955.* Boston, MA: Da Capo, 1994.

Gershunoff, Max, and Leon Van Dyke. *It's Not All Song and Dance: A Life behind the Scenes in the Performing Arts.* Pompton Plains, NJ: Limelight Editions, 2005.

Glass, Barbara S. *African American Dance: an Illustrated History.* Jefferson, NC: McFarland & Co., 2007.

Glover, Savion. *My Life in Tap.* NY: William Morrow, 2000.

Hill, Constance Valis. *Tap Dancing America: A Cultural History.* NY: Oxford University Press, 2010.

Johnson, Anne E. *Jazz Tap - From African Drums to American Feet.* NY: Rosen Publishing Group, Inc.

Kislan, Richard. *Hoofing on Broadway; History of Show Dancing.* NY: Prentice-Hall, 1987.

Knowles, Mark. *Tap Roots: The Early History of Tap Dancing.* Jefferson, NC, and London: McFarland & Company, Inc., Publishers, 2002.

Mueller, John. *Astaire Dancing: The Musical Films of Fred Astaire.* NY: Knopf, 1985.

Quinn, Tom. *Irish Dancing.* Glasgow: HarperCollins, 1997.

Shipley, Glenn. *Modern Tap Dictionary.* Los Angeles, CA: Action Marketing Group, 1976.

Sonny Watson's StreetSwing, available at Streetswing.com.

"Tap Dance," Online Encyclopedia, *2000.*

## JAZZ DANCE BIBLIOGRAPHY – Chapters 9, 10, and 13

Altschuler, G.C. *All Shook up: how rock 'n' roll changed America.* Oxford: Oxford University Press, U.S., 2003.

Andreu, Helene. *Jazz Dance, An Adult Beginner's Guide.* Englewood Cliffs, NJ: Prentice-Hall Inc., 1983.

Andreu, Helene. *Jazz Dance Styles and Steps for Fun.* Bloomington, IN: 1st Books Library (now AuthorHouse), 2003.

Baker, Jean-Claude, and Chris Chase. *Josephine: The Hungry Heart.* NY: Random House, 1993.

*Ballroom, Boogie, Shimmy Sham, Shake! a Social and Popular Dance Reader.* Edited by Julie Mainig. Urbana, IL: University of Illinois Press, 2009.

Berlin, Edward A. *King of Ragtime: Scott Joplin and his Era.* New York, NY: Oxford University Press, 1995.

Blight, David W. *Union & Emancipation: essays and politics and race in the Civil War era.* Kent, OH: Kent State University Press, 1997. Editors: David W Blight and Brooks D. Simpson.

Collier, Simon, Artemis Cooper, Maria Susana Azzi and Richard Martin. *Tango! The Dance, the Song, the Story,* New York, NY: Thames & Hudson, Inc., 1995.

Curtis, Susan. *Dancing to a Black Man's Tune: A Life of Scott Joplin.* Columbia, MO: University of Missouri Press, 1994.

Dawson, Jim. *Rock Around the Clock: The Record That Started the Rock Revolution!* San Francisco: Backbeat Books, 2005.

Driver, Ian. *Century of Dance: A Hundred Years of Musical Movement, from Waltz to Hip Hop.* NY: Cooper Square Press, 2001.

Emery, Lynn Fauley. *Black Dance in the U.S. from 1619 to Today.* Second Revised Edition. Princeton, NJ: Princeton Book Co., 1988.

Forbes, Camille F. Introducing Bert Williams. *Burnt Cork, Broadway, and the Story of America's First Black Star.* New York, NY: Basic Civitas, A Member of the Perseus Book Group, 2008.

Garrett, Charles Hiroshi. *Struggling to Define a Nation: American Music and the Twentieth Century.* Berkeley, CA: University of California Press, 2008.

Giordano, Gus. *Anthology of American Jazz Dance.* Evanston, IL: Orion Publishing, 1975.

Gorer, Geoffrey. *Africa Dances.* Revised with a new introduction by the author. London: John Lehmann, April 25, 2005.

Kislan, Richard. *The Musical: A Look at the American Musical Theater.* Rev. edition. New York: Applause Books, 1995.

Loft, Eric. *Love and Theft: Blackface Minstrelsy and the American Working Class.* NY: Oxford University Press, 1993.

Malone, Jacqui. *Steppin' on the Blues: The Visible Rhythms of African American Dance.* Urbana, IL: University of Illinois Press, 1996.

Miller, Norma. *Swingin' at the Savoy: The Memoirs of a Jazz Dancer.* Philadelphia, PA: Temple University Press, 1996.

O'Neal, Michael. *America in the 1920's.* NY: Facts on File, 2006.

Ostransky, Leroy. *Jazz City, The Impact of Our Cities on the Development of Jazz.* Englewood Cliffs, NJ: Prentice-Hall, Inc. (a Spectrum Book), 1978.

Roan, Carol. *Clues to American Dance.* Washington, DC: Starrhill Press, Inc. 1993.

Smith, Karen Lynn. *Popular Dance From Ballroom to Hip-Hop.* New York, NY: Infobase Publishing (Checkmark Books), 2010.

Sonny Watson's StreetSwing, available at Streetswing.com.

Stearns, Marshall, and Jean Stearns. *Jazz Dance, the Story of American Vernacular Dance.* N.Y.: Da Capo Press, 1994.

Stephenson, Richard M. and Joseph Iaccarino. *The Complete Book of Ballroom Dancing.* NY: Doubleday, 1992.

Thomas, Helen. *Dance in the City.* NY: St. Martin's Press, 1997.

Thompson, Robert Farris. *Tango: The Art History of Love.* NY: Knopf, 2007.

Wagner, Ann. *Adversaries of Dance: From the Puritans to the Present.* Urbana, IL: University of Illinois Press, 1997.

Ward, Geoffrey C., and Ken Burns. *Jazz: A History of America's Music.* NY: Alfred A. Knopf, November 2000.

*Wikipedia, the free encyclopedia.*

Zanfagne, Christine. "The Multiringed Cosmos of Krumping / Hip Hop Dance at the Intersections of Battle, Media, and Spirit," in *Ballroom, Boogie, Shimmy Sham, Shake. A Social and Popular Dance Reader.* Julie Malnig, ed. Urbana and Chicago, IL: University of Illinois Press, 2009.

**DISCLAIMER**

The sheet music covers, lyrics, and art illustrations included in this book are presented as a part of the history of the dance. The illustrations and language display the attitudes and beliefs of earlier times. The author does not endorse the views expressed in the illustrations and in the language such as may have material that is offensive to some readers. They are typical of the art of the time they represent, and the author accepts no liability for their content.

# INDEX

288

290

303

*Figure des Sereines*, by Jacques Patin, 1581, Courtesy of Le Magazine de l'Opéra Baroque, http://operabaroque.fr/BEAULIEU_REINE.htm

*The Gavotte, a Country Dance*, pen drawing by Randolph Caldecott for *Breton Folk: an Artistic Tour in Brittany*, by Henry Blackburn, 1880, Courtesy of The Randolph Caldecott Society UK's page on *Breton Folk,* http://www.randolphcaldecott.org.uk/breton.htm

Morris Dancers with Maypole, page 631 of *Chambers' Book of Days*, Vol. 1, 1869, Robert Chambers, editor. Not in copyright, Courtesy of the Internet Archive, https://archive.org/details/bookofdaysmiscel01cham

### Photo Plate 2-3

Illustration of performances by acrobats, dancers, singers, and a tightrope-walker, from *Surname-i Vehbi*, (Book of Festival by Vehbi) illustrated by Abdulcelil Levni Celebi, Istanbul, 1720, Courtesy of Oslandi Araştimalari (Ottoman Studies) http://www.os-ar.com/levni/index-i0042.htm

*Le Fandango*, painted by Pierre Chasselat (1753-1814), ca. 1810, Courtesy Agora Vox, http://mobile.agoravox.fr/culture-loisirs/culture/article/le-joropo-un-fandango-tropical-58812

*Three Couples in a Circle Dance*, pen and brown ink with watercolor, artist unknown, German, c. 1515, Courtesy National Gallery of Art, Washington, NGA Images, Open Access Policy, Rosenwald Collection,
https://images.nga.gov/en/search/do_quick_search.html?q=three+couples+in+a+circle+dance

*La Bourrée d'Auvergne*, Postcard, Artist unknown, ca, 1906, Courtesy of Vitrifolk, Cartes Postales d'Auvergne sur la Danse Folklorique,
http://www.vitrifolk.be/cartes-postales/cartes-postales-france-auvergne.html

*Local Residents do Attan Dance*, Photo by Rahmat Alizada, Ghazni, Capital of Culture Vibe Section of Afghanistan-Today.org, an MICT project, Courtesy of Afghanistan Today, http://www.afghanistan-today.org/article/?id=467

### Photo Plate 2-4

*Peasant Dance in front of a Tavern*, etching by Adriaen van Ostade, 1652, Courtesy of The State Hermitage Museum, Inv. No. OG-133944, Photograph © The State Hermitage Museum, Photo by Leonard Kheifets, http://www.hermitagemuseum.org/wps/portal/hermitage/digital-collection/04.+Engraving/1491206/?lng=en

Performance of *Ballet Comique de la Reine*, Artist: Balthazar de Beaujoyeulx, 1581,Courtesy Store Norske Leksikon (CC-BY-SA),
https://snl.no/Ballet_Comique_de_la_Reine

Chennai, India - Indian Traditional Dance Drama, © f9photos | Shutterstock.com, http://www.shutterstock.com/pic-89469103/stock-photo-chennai-india-september-indian-traditional-dance-drama-kathakali-preformance-on-september.html?src=TgNSfQJ1BEAP6Rnz24AgnA-1-8&ws=1

### Photo Plate 2-5

*Negro Fandango Scene*, Campo St. Anna, Rio de Janeiro, watercolor by Augustus Earle (1793-1838), ca. 1822, out of copyright, Courtesy of the National Library of Australia, Rex Nan Kivell Collection NK12/98, http://nla.gov.au/nla.pic-an2822606

*The Whirling Dervish*, by Jean Leon Gérôme, 1889, Courtesy of The Athenaeum, http://www.the-athenaeum.org/art/detail.php?ID=15958

*The Peasant Dance*, by Pieter Bruegel the Elder, c. 1567, Courtesy The WebMuseum, (CC by-sa 3.0) http://www.ibiblio.org/wm/paint/auth/bruegel/

*Dance in the Garden*, illumination from the *Roman de la rose*, Toulouse, early 16th century, Free of known copyright restrictions, Courtesy The British Library (Harley 4425, f. 14v), http://www.bl.uk/catalogues/illuminatedmanuscripts/ILLUMIN.ASP?Size=mid&IllID=22381

*Round Dance at Aninoasa*, by Theodor Aman, Romanian, 1890, located in National Gallery, Bucharest, Courtesy Tom's Place,
http://www.tkinter.smig.net/romania/ArtGallery/Aman/Dance.htm

*The Allemande Dance*, by James Caldwell (1739-1819), printmaker, published in 1772, Courtesy of the Lewis Walpole Library, Yale University,
http://images.library.yale.edu/walpoleweb/oneitem.asp?imageId=lwlpr03282

### Photo Plate 3-1

Ptihn-Tak-Ochata, *Dance of the Mandan Women*, by Karl Bodmer, from Illustrations to Maximilian Prince of Wied's *Travels in the Interior of North America*, 1839, Courtesy of the Indiana Historical Society, Digital image © Indiana Historical Society, ,
http://images.indianahistory.org/cdm/ref/collection/dc015/id/30

*Buffalo Dance at Hano*, by Edward S. Curtis (1868-1952), 1921, Digital image courtesy of the Getty's Open Content program, Courtesy of the J. Paul Getty Museum. http://www.getty.edu/art/collection/objects/41244/edward-s-curtis-buffalo-dance-at-hano-american-1921/

### Photo Plate 3-2

*Snowshoe Dance at the First Snowfall*, by George Catlin, 1835-37, Courtesy of the Smithsonian American Art Museum,
http://americanart.si.edu/collections/search/artwork/?id=4382

*Dance to the Berdashe*, by George Catlin, 1835-37, Courtesy of the Smithsonian American Art Museum,
http://americanart.si.edu/collections/search/artwork/?id=4023

### Photo Plate 3-3

Nunivak Drummer, Photo by Edward S. Curtis, 1929, Edward S. Curtis Collection, Library of Congress, Reproduction No. LC-USZ62-46887, No known restrictions on publication, http://www.loc.gov/pictures/collection/ecur/item/2003652881/

Hamasilahi-Qagyuhl - (British Columbian ceremonial dancer), Photo by Edward S, Curtis, 1914, Copyright not renewed, Published in *The North American Indian*, by Edward S. Curtis, Library of Congress P&P Division, Curtis (Edward S.) Collection,
http://www.loc.gov/pictures/collection/ecur/item/2003652752/

Nunivak Maskette, Photograph by Edward S. Curtis, 1929, Copyright not renewed, Library of Congress, P&P Division, Edward S. Curtis Collection, Reproduction Number LC-USZ62-13913. Photo is from Edward S. Curtis' *The North Amerian Indian*, http://www.loc.gov/pictures/item/2003652889/

Thunderbird Transformation Mask, made by Namgis, Native American, Kwakwaka'wakw, British Vancouver, Canada, 19th century, Creative Commons-BY, Courtesy of the Arts of the Americas Collection of the Brooklyn Museum, Museum Expedition 1908, Museum Collection fund,
http://www.brooklynmuseum.org/opencollection/objects/19432/Thunderbird_Transformation_Mask#

Native American Dancer Competing in World Championship Hoop Dance Contest, © Paul B. Moore | Shutterstock.com,
http://www.shutterstock.com/pic-70658608/stock-photo-phoenix-az-feb-native-american-dancer-competing-in-the-st-annual-heard-museum-world.html?src=f40doD2pJTwOIqTrULgIsA-1-29&ws=1

### Photo Plate 3-4

A Hula Performed in Presence of Governor Kuakini at Kairua, from *A Narrative of a Tour through Hawaii, or Owhyhee*, page 75, by William Ellis, ca. 1827, Courtesy of the Hathi Trust Digital Library at the University of California,
http://babel.hathitrust.org/cgi/pt?id=uc2.ark:/13960/t5j968d3n;view=1up;seq=87

Sheet Music Cover - *Aloha Oe Farewell to Thee* (in Hawaiian and English), Composed by Queen Lili'uokalani, Published by The Popular Music Pub. Co., 1913, Courtesy of the Lester S. Levy Collection of Sheet Music, The Sheridan Libraries, The Johns Hopkins University,
https://jscholarship.library.jhu.edu/handle/1774.2/30702

Sheet Music Cover - *Fair Hawaii*, Composed by James F. Kutz, Artist L.E. Morgan, Published by Sherman, Clay & Co., San Francisco, 1914. Courtesy Lilly Library, Indiana University, Bloomington, Indiana, *Fair Hawaii* is in the public domain.
http://webapp1.dlib.indiana.edu/inharmony/detail.do?action=detail&fullItemID=/lilly/devincent/LL-SDV-221042

Lili'uokalani, Queen of Hawaii, unknown photographer, 1915, no known restrictions on publication, Courtesy Library of Congress P&P Division, http://www.loc.gov/pictures/item/2004679211/

### Photo Plate 3-5

*Pueblo Indian Eagle Dance, New Mexico*, Postcard published ca. 1930-1945 by Southwest Arts & Crafts, Santa Fe, New Mexico. "Tichnor Quality Views," No known restrictions on use. Courtesy of the Boston Public Library, The Tichnor Brother Collection, Boston Public Library, through flickr, https://www.flickr.com/photos/57362692@N00/7546141744/in/photolist-oeQLko-5AiGfN-vvgKuR-oeJonr-dhHf2Q-bXk68x-bPQeUB-oaoaN-6tS3ju-ot7RiK-74FiDD-8BBS9y-ow43Gg-odBXuY-cuPX39-6ZUAB6-74Fjat-8bXSyh-owe8aK-8PmxHx-2b2Vu1-6dgkfV-8PpRRf-8bXSvC-tEL9SH

*Bison-Dance of Mandan Indians in front of their Medecine [sic] Lodge,* in Mih-Tutta-Hankush., aquatint by Karl Bodmer, illustration in *Travels in the Interior of North America* by Prince Maximilian de Wied, London, Ackermann & Co., 1842, Courtesy of the DeGolyer Library of Southern Methodist University, http://digitalcollections.smu.edu/cdm/ref/collection/nam/id/165

*Hopi Corn Dance,* watercolor on paper by Louis Lomoyesva, Hopi Pueblo, Native American, Brooklyn Museum Photo, Courtesy of the Arts of the Americas Collection of the Brooklyn Museum, Creative Commons-BY, http://www.brooklynmuseum.org/opencollection/objects/50084/Hopi_Corn_Dance

Alutiiq Dancer, Photo by Christopher Mertl, Government Photo 59191, no date, Courtesy of the Federal Highway Administration, Washington, D.C., http://www.fhwa.dot.gov/byways/photos/59191

**Photo Plate 4-1**

*Mlle Sallé,* engraving and etching by Nicolas de Larmessin IV after Nicolas Lancret, French, 1732, Courtesy of National Gallery of Art, Washington, NGA Images, Open Access Policy, Widener Collection, https://images.nga.gov/en/search/do_quick_search.html?q=Mlle+Salle

*Claude Balon* or Ballon (1671-1744) of the Académie Royale de Danse, Engraving, artist unknown, from an article on Claude Ballon, *Vers les hauteurs! Le saut et la pointe,* by Juan Giuliano, in augustevestris.fr, A Society for the Advancement of the Ideas of Auguste Vestris, http://www.augustevestris.fr/article214.html

*Mademoiselle Subligny Dansant à l'Opéra,* Engraving, Artist unknown 169?, Courtesy of The New York Public Library Digital Collections, NYPLfor the Performing Arts, Jerome Robbins Dance Division, Cia. Fornaroli Collection, http://digitalgallery.nypl.org/nypldigital/dgkeysearchdetail.cfm?strucID=774032&imageID=1515987

The image Ballon is the property of Helene Andreu.

**Photo Plate 4-2**

*Trajes mexicanos, un Fandango,* Chromolithograph by C. Castro, Artist, and J. Campillo, Lithographer, 1869, publisher, L.Devrey, from *Mexico y sus Alrededores,* Courtesy of New York Public Library Digital Collections, No known copyright restrictions, http://digitalgallery.nypl.org/nypldigital/dgkeysearchdetail.cfm?trg=1&strucID=778520&imageID=1519708&word=col_id%3A208&s=1&notword=&d=&c=&f=&k=0&lWord=&lField=&sScope=images&sLevel=&sLabel=The%20Luso-Hispanic%20New%20World%20in%20Early%20Prints...&sort=&total=651&num=640&imgs=20&pNum=&pos=646

How to Dance the Minuet. This image, called *Conclusion or Presenting of Both Arms,* is from Kellom Tomlinson's *The Art of Dancing,* Book II, Plate XII, published in London, 1735, Courtesy The Library of Congress, Music Division, http://memory.loc.gov/cgi-bin/ampage?collId=musdi&fileName=158/musdi158.db&recNum=215&itemLink=r?ammem/musdibib:@field(NUMBER+@band(musdi+158))

Layout of Boree (bourée) steps, page 3 in *An essay for the further improvement of dancing, being a collection of figure dances, of several numbers, compos'd by the most eminent masters; describ'd in characters after the newest manner of Monsieur Feuillet.* by Edmund Pemberton, Published 1711, http://memory.loc.gov/cgi-bin/ampage?collId=musdi&fileName=134/musdi134.db&recNum=0035&itemLink=/ammem/dihtml/diessay4.html@1340036&linkText=3

Portrait of Françoise Prevost as a Bacchante, painted by Jean Raoux, 1723, located at the Musée des Beaux Arts in Tours, France, Photo by the Musée des Beaux Arts in Tours, Courtesy of Joconde, http://www.culture.gouv.fr/public/mistral/joconde_fr?ACTION=CHERCHER&FIELD_1=AUTR&VALUE_1=RAOUX%20Jean&DOM=All&REL_SPECIFIC=1&IMAGE_ONLY=CHECKED

**Photo Plate 4-3**

Ladies and Gentlemen Dancing, by Paul Grégoire, 1780, Courtesy of The Art Institute of Chicago, the Leonora Hall Gurley Memorial Collection, http://www.artic.edu/aic/collections/artwork/81210?search_no=54&index=94

Jean-Baptiste Lully (1632-1687), engraved by Henri Bonnart (1642-1711), Courtesy of Musicologie.org, http://www.musicologie.org/Biographies/lully.html

The Dancing Master, engraving by G.A. Delin, from Pierre Rameau's 1725 *Le maître à danser.* Translated by English dancer and writer John Essex in 1732, Courtesy The Library of Congress, Music Division, http://memory.loc.gov/ammem/dihtml/diessay4.html

The Position in Quadrille, by Theodore Wüst, Image plate between pages 20 and 21 of *The Dance of Society, a critical analysis of all the standard quadrilles, round dances. etc,* by Wm. B. de Garmo, published in New York, 1875, Courtesy of the Library of Congress, American Memory Collection, http://memory.loc.gov/cgi-bin/ampage?collId=musdi&fileName=181//musdi181.db&recNum=1&itemLink=r?ammem/musdibib:@field(NUMBER+@od1(musdi+181))&linkText=0

Beadle's *Dime Ball-room Companion and Guide to Dancing. Comprising rules of etiquette, hints on private parties, toilettes for the ball-room. Also synopsis of round and square dances, dictionary of French terms.* Published in New York by Beadle and Co. in 1868. http://www.loc.gov/item/musdi.101

**Photo Place 4-4**

The Waltz, Frontispiece to Thomas Wilson's *Correct Method of German and French Waltzing* (1816), showing nine positions of the dance, Courtesy of Dance's Historical Miscellany, the Wicked Waltz, http://www.danceshistoricalmiscellany.com/2014/05/the-wicked-waltz.html#sthash.qpxJcrwd.dpuf

Portrait of Auguste Vestris, by Adèle Romany, 1793, Courtesy of Le Creuset de la Danse, http://www.le-creuset-danse.com/nos-coups-de-coeur/danse-baroque/

Jean Philippe Rameau, painting by Jacques André Joseph Aved (1702-1766), Courtesy of Baroque Composers and Music, http://www.baroquemusic.org/bqxrameau.html

*The Fiddler,* illustration by E. W. Kemble for *Mrs. Stowe's Uncle Tom' At Home in Kentucky,* by James Lane Allen, published in *The Century Magazine* 34 (No. 6, October 1887). Helene Andreu owns this photograph.

**Photo Plate 4-5**

Louis XIV as Apollo, artist unknown, costume designed by Henri Gissey (1621-1673), Courtesy of Le Creuset de la Danse, http://www.le-creuset-danse.com/nos-coups-de-coeur/danse-baroque/

*Barbara Campanini,* by Antoine Pesne, 1745, at the Neues Palais, Potsdam, Courtesy of the Web Gallery of Art (www.wga.hu), http://www.wga.hu/html_m/p/pesne/campanin.html

*La Camargo Dancing,* Painted by Nicolas Lancret, c. 1730, Courtesy of National Gallery of Art, Washington, NGA Images, Open Access Policy, Andrew W. Mellon Collection, httpss://images.nga.gov/en/search/do_quick_search.html?q=la+camargo+dancing

*Merrymaking at a Wayside Inn,* Watercolor attributed to John Lewis Krimmel, 1811- 1813, Courtesy of the Metropolitan Museum of Art, OASC, Rogers Fund, 1942, Photo by Metropolitan Museum Photostudio, http://www.metmuseum.org/collection/the-collection-online/search/12728

*The Shepherds,* oil on canvas by Jean-Antoine Watteau, 1717-1719, at the Schloss Charlottenburg, Berlin, Courtesy of the Web Gallery of Art (www.wga.hu), http://www.wga.hu/index1.html

**Photo Plate 4-6**

Figure of a Dancer - bronze, ivory, marble base, designed by Demetre Chiparus, ca. 1925, Courtesy of Brooklyn Museum, Decorative Arts Collection, Gift of Benno Bordiga, CC -BY, Brooklyn Museum Photograph, http://www.brooklynmuseum.org/opencollection/objects/146472/Figure_of_a_Dancer/set/8e10b84198ecfb48abe64e5b535a1f68?referring-q=Chiparus

*A Dancing Couple Celebrating New Year's Day,* from *The London Illustrated News,* 1948, Artist unknown, Helene Andreu owns this image.

*The Elegancies of Quadrille Dancing,* etching by George Cruikshank, British, 1817, Courtesy of Brooklyn Museum, European Art Collection, Brooklyn Museum Photo, No known copyright restrictions, http://www.brooklynmuseum.org/opencollection/objects/25761/Moulinet._Elegancies_of_Quadrille_Dancing/set/e98079bf0438b76d1ad8d20edb66ae8f?referring-q=elegancies+of+quadrille

"Reverence" performed by a dancer. Helene Andreu owns this photograph.

**Photo Plate 5-1**

Carlota Grisi and Jules Perrot in *La Polka*, lithograph by Augustus Jules Bouvier, published 1844, scanned from *The Romantic Ballet from Contemporary Prints*, a Batsford Colour Book published by B.T. Batsford Ltd, 1948, with introduction and notes by Sacheverell Sitwell and 16 photo plates. Helene Andreu owns this book.

Fanny Cerrito in "Alma", from the Ballet *Alma ou la Fille de Feu* by Augustus Jules Perrot, lithograph by Jules Bouvier, published in 1842, scanned from *The Romantic Ballet from Contemporary Prints*. (See information in previous entry). Helene Andreu owns this book.

*The Three Graces*, representing the ballerinas Taglioni, Elssler and Cerrito, lithograph from a drawing by A. E. Chalon, 1844, scanned from *The Romantic Ballet from Contemporary Prints*. (See information in first entry for this Photo Plate). Helene Andreu owns this book.

Sheet Music Cover for *Valse de Giselle* from the ballet *Giselle*, danced by Carlotta Grisi and Marius Petipa, 1841, Courtesy of the Lester S. Levy Collection of Sheet Music, The Sheridan Libraries, The Johns Hopkins University, http://levysheetmusic.mse.jhu.edu/catalog/levy:186,065

**Photo Plate 5-2**

Giuseppina Bozzacchi as Swanhilda in the first performance of *Coppélia*, Paris, 1870, choreographed by Arthur Saint Leon, photographer unknown, Courtesy of Classical Ballet News, http://classicalballetnews.com/coppelia-with-royal-ballet/377px-coppelia_-swanilda_-giuseppina_bozzachi_-act_i-scene_2_-paris_-1870_-2/

Joseph Mazilier, ca. 1860, Artist unknown, Courtesy of Mediander, http://www.mediander.com/connects/4670249/joseph-mazilier/#!/

Sheet Music Cover *Melle Fanny Elssler's Quadrilles*, arranged for the piano by Ch. Jarvis, 1840, Courtesy of the Lester S. Levy Collection of Sheet Music, The Sheridan Libraries, The Johns Hopkins University, http://levysheetmusic.mse.jhu.edu/catalog/levy:185.037

Sheet Music Cover, *La Gitana* (The New Cachoucha), danced by Marie Taglioni, arranged for the piano by Charles W. Glover, ca 1838, Courtesy of the Lester S. Levy Collection of Sheet Music, The Sheridan Libraries, The Johns Hopkins University, http://levysheetmusic.mse.jhu.edu/catalog/levy:056.045

**Photo Plate 5-3**

The Five Positions of Dancing, from *An Analysis of Country Dancing*, by English dancing master Thomas Wilson, Illustrated with engravings by J. Berryman, published in London in1811, Courtesy of the Library of Congress, Music Division, http://memory.loc.gov/cgi-bin/ampage?collId=musdi&fileName=171//musdi171.db&recNum=5&itemLink=r?ammem/musdibib:@field(NUMBER+@od1(musdi+171))&linkText=0

Mercury - Bronze Statue, after Giovanni Bologna (c. 1780 - c. 1850), Courtesy the National Gallery of Art, Washington, NGA Images, Open Access Policy, from the Andrew W. Mellon Collection, https://images.nga.gov/en/search/do_quick_search.html?q=after+giovanni+bologna

Jean Coralli (1779-1854), French, artist unknown, Courtesy Encyclopedia Britannica, http://www.britannica.com/EBchecked/topic/137138/Jean-Coralli

Attitude Front Dance Pose, Photo owned by Helene Andreu

**Photo Plate 5-4**

Sheet Music Cover for *La Mazurka*, danced in *La Gitana* by Madame Taglioni, 1838, Music arranged for the piano by C.W. Glover, London, Courtesy of the Lester S. Levy Collection of Sheet Music, The Sheridan Libraries, The Johns Hopkins University, http://levysheetmusic.mse.jhu.edu/catalog/levy:185.046

Sheet Music Cover, *La Cracovienne*, showing Fanny Elssler dancing, Arranged for the piano by L. Gomion, published by A. Fiot, New Orleans,1840, Courtesy of the Lester S. Levy Collection of Sheet Music, The Sheridan Libraries, The Johns Hopkins University, https://jscholarship.library.jhu.edu/bitstream/handle/1774.2/7303/185.034.000.webimage.JPEG?sequence=7

Fanny Cerrito and Saint-Leon in *La Redowa Polka*, lithograph by J. Bouvier, published 1844, from *The Romantic Ballet from Contemporary Prints*, a Batsford Colour Book published by B.T. Batsford Ltd, 1948, with introduction and notes by Sacheverell Sitwell and 16 photo plates. Helene Andreu owns this book.

*Pas de Quatre*, ballet by Jules Perrot with the ballerinas Grisi, Taglioni, Grahn and Cerrito, lithograph by A.E. Chalon, 1845, Courtesy of Jerome Robbins Dance Division, The New York Public Library for the Performing Arts, Astor, Lenox and Tilden Foundations, http://digitalgallery.nypl.org/nypldigital/dgkeysearchdetail.cfm?trg=1&strucID=774240&imageID=1515900&total=7&num=0&word=pas%20de%20quatre&s=1&notword=&d=&c=&f=&k=1&lWord=&lField=&sScope=&sLevel=&sLabel=&sort=&imgs=20&pos=1&e=r

**Photo Plate 5-5**

*The Rehearsal of the Ballet Onstage*, oil painting by Hilaire-Germain-Edgar Degas, 1874, Courtesy of The Metropolitan Museum of Art, OASC, H.O. Havemeyer Collection, Gift of Horace Havemeyer, 1929, Metropolitan Museum Photo, http://www.metmuseum.org/collection/the-collection-online/search/436155?rpp=30&pg=1&ft=degas&pos=6

Poster showing a scene from the Kiralfy Bros production of *Black Crook*, lithograph created and published in New York by Central Litho. and Eng. Co, 1866, No known restrictions on publication, Courtesy of the Library of Congress, Prints and Photographs Division, Theater poster collection, http://www.loc.gov/pictures/resource/var.1527/

**Photo Plate 6-1**

Sheet Music Cover, *Down to the Folies Bergère*, Words and music by Vincent Bryant, Irving Berlin, and Ted Snyder, published by Ted Snyder Co., New York, 1911, Cover artist E. Pfeiffer, NY, Courtesy of the Lester S. Levy Collection of Sheet Music, The Sheridan Libraries, The Johns Hopkins University, http://levysheetmusic.mse.jhu.edu/catalog/levy:077.061

Nijinsky in *Danse Siamoise* from the ballet *Orientales*, Photographed in 1910 by Eugene Druet, French (1868-1917), Courtesy of The Metropolitan Museum of Art, OASC, Gilman Collection, Gift of the Howard Gilman Foundation, 2005, Photo by Metropolitan Museum Photostudio, http://www.metmuseum.org/collection/the-collection-online/search/286722?rpp=30&pg=1&ao=on&ft=nijinsky&pos=3

Helene Andreu doing a piqué, Photo belongs to Helene Andreu.

Photograph of Michel Fokine as Prince Ivan and Tamara Karsavina as the Firebird in *The Firebird*, 1910, Courtesy of the Library of Congress, Music Division, http://lcweb2.loc.gov/diglib/ihas/loc.natlib.ihas.200156311/default.html

**Photo Plate 6-2**

Sheet Music Cover, *Give us a Ragtime Tune* from *The Bachelor Belles*, Lyrics by Harry B. Smith, Music by Raymond Hubbell, Published by Jerome H. Remick & Co, New York, 1910, dancer Adelaide (Adeline) Genee in inset, Courtesy of University of Colorado Boulder Music Library, Digital Sheet Music Collection, Ragtime Sheet Music Collection, Digital image by UCB, http://libcudl.colorado.edu:8180/luna/servlet/detail/UCBOULDERCB1~78~78~1073270~137127:Give-us-a-ragtime-tune

Illustration from original Souvenir *Petroushka* Program, Paris, 1911, artist unknown, showing several dancers from the ballet, Courtesy of the Klavier Festival Ruhr Petroushka Page, http://www.petruschka-klavierfestival.de/index.asp?level1=6&level2=9&page=0&pdt=4&lang=2

Anna Pavlova as Nikiya in the *Grand Pas Classique of the Shades* from Act III of the Petipa/Minkus *La Bayadere*, ca. 1902, Courtesy of the New World Encyclopedia, (CC-by-sa 3.0), http://www.newworldencyclopedia.org/entry/Anna_Pavlova

Bronislava Nijinska as the Street Dancer in *Petroushka*, with Ludmilla Schollar, and Michel Fokine as Petrouchka, 1911, Courtesy the Library of Congress, Music Division, http://lcweb2.loc.gov/diglib/ihas/loc.natlib.ihas.200156314/default.html

Lubov Tchernichnova in *Petroushka*, ballet by Michel Fokine, photograph by Jean de Strelecki, 1916, Courtesy of the Library of Congress, Music Division, http://lcweb2.loc.gov/diglib/ihas/loc.natlib.ihas.200181859/default.html

**Photo Plate 6-3**

English Ballerina Alicia Markova in *Foyer de Danse*, photographed by Carl Van Vechten 1940, Courtesy of Library of Congress, P&P Division, Carl van Vechten Collection, http://www.loc.gov/pictures/collection/van/item/2004663269/

Photograph of Page 24 of the Official Program for May-June 1922 of the Ballets et Opéra Russes de Serge de Diaguilev, with portraits of the ballerinas Hilda Bewicke, Leocadia Klementovicz and Felia Doubrovska, Photographed by Swaine et Albin, 1922, Courtesy the Library of Congress, Music Division, http://www.loc.gov/resource/ihas.200156339.0/?sp=24

Photograph of Aurora's Wedding (*Le Mariage de la Belle au Bois Dormant*), 1921, choreographed by Marius Petita, ballerina Bronislava Nijinska, Courtesy of Library of Congress, Music Division, http://www.loc.gov/item/ihas.200156340

*La Troupe de Mlle Eglantine*, by Henri de Toulouse-Lautrec, printed lithograph, 1895, Courtesy of The Metropolitan Museum of Art, OASC, Harris Brisbane Dick Fund, 1932, Metropolitan Museum Photo, http://www.metmuseum.org/collection/the-collection-online/search/333988

Sergey Diaghilev, ca. 1916, photographer unknown, Courtesy of the Library of Congress, Music Division, http://www.loc.gov/resource/ihas.200156298.0

**Photo Plate 6-4**

Vaslav Nijinsky in *Le Spectre de la Rose*, by Emil Otto Hoppé, 1911, printed 1913, Courtesy of the Art Institute of Chicago, Photogravure from the portfolio "Studies from the Russian Ballet," Gift of Robert A. Taub, 2012.250.8, http://www.artic.edu/aic/collections/artwork/215401?search_no=1&index=8

Katherine Dunham in *Tropical Revue* (1943), at New York's Martin Beck Theater, photo by Alfredo Valente, there are no known restrictions to publication, Courtesy Library of Congress, Prints and Photographs Division, NY World-Telegram & Sun Newspaper Photograph Collection, http://www.loc.gov/item/ihas.200003770/

Photo of Marius Petipa, photographer unknown, 1899, Courtesy of the Library of Congress, Music Division, http://lcweb2.loc.gov/diglib/ihas/loc.natlib.ihas.200181848/default.html

Scene from *La Boutique Fantasque*, choreographed by Léonide Massine, photographer unknown, 1919, Courtesy of the Library of Congress, Music Division, http://www.loc.gov/resource/ihas.200156315.0

Great Russian Ball at the Academy of Music, New York, November 5, 1863, wood engraving by Winslow Homer, No known copyright restrictions, Courtesy of the Brooklyn Museum of Art, American Art Collection, Gift of Harvey Isbitts, Brooklyn Museum Photo, http://www.brooklynmuseum.org/opencollection/objects/159660/The_Great_Russian_Ball_at_the_Academy_of_Music_November_5_1863/set/?referring-q=russian+ballet+dancers#

**Photo Plate 6-5**

Photograph of Page One of the Official Program for May-June 1922 of the Ballets and Opéra Russes de Serge de Diaghilev, showing the costume by Natalie Goncharova for the ballet *Le Mariage de la Belle au Bois Dormant*, Photographer unknown, Courtesy of the Library of Congress, Music Division, http://www.loc.gov/resource/ihas.200156339.0/?sp=1

Bal à Bougival, by Auguste Renoir, oil painting, 1883, Courtesy of Museum of Fine Arts, Boston, Europe Collection, http://www.mfa.org/collections/object/dance-at-bougival-32592

Marcelle Lender Dancing the Bolero in *Chilpéric*, oil on canvas by Henri Toulouse Lautrec (1864-1901), French, 1895/6, Courtesy the National Gallery of Art, NGA Images, Open Access Policy, Collection of Mr. and Mrs. John Hay Whitney, https://images.nga.gov/en/search/do_quick_search.html?q=chilperic

Spanish Dance, *El Jaleo*, oil on canvas by John Singer Sargent, 1882, Courtesy of the Isabella Stewart Gardner Museum, http://www.gardnermuseum.org/collection/artwork/1st_floor/spanish_cloister/el_jaleo

**Photo Plate 7-1**

Ballet and Modern Dance both use the floor as a new level of action, Photo belongs to Helene Andreu.

Isadora Duncan in *La Marseillaise*, 1916, Photographer Arnold Genthe (1869-1942), Courtesy of Dance Heritage Coalition, 100 Dance Treasures Collection, http://danceheritage.org/duncan.html

Ted Shawn in *Invocation to the Thunderbird*, created 1919, unidentified photographer, Courtesy of New York Public Library Digital Collections, Denishawn Collection, Jerome Robbins Dance Division, http://digitalcollections.nypl.org/items/510d47df-86ef-a3d9-e040-e00a18064a99

José Limón, Photograph from the José Limón Collection, Dance Division, New York Public Library for the Performing Arts, Astor, Lenox and Tilden Foundations, Courtesy of the Dance Heritage Coalition, 100 Dance Treasures Collection, http://wwwColorado.danceheritage.org/limon.html

**Photo Plate 7-2**

Loie Fuller Dancing, Photograph by Samuel Joshua Beckett (British), ca. 1900, Courtesy of the Metropolitan Museum of Art, OASC, Gilman Collection, Purchase, Mrs. Walter Annenberg and The Annenberg Foundation Gift, 2005, Photo by Metropolitan Museum Photostudio, http://www.metmuseum.org/collection/the-collection-online/search/287806

Martha Graham and Bertram Ross, Photo by Carl van Vechten, 1961, Courtesy of Library of Congress, P& P Division, Carl van Vechten Collection, http://www.loc.gov/pictures/item/2004662952/

Ruth St. Denis (1879-1968), Photo by Bain News Service, no date recorded, Courtesy of the Library of Congress, P&P Division, George Grantham Bain Collection, htt p://www.loc.gov/pictures/resource/ggbain.05890/

Portrait of Martha Graham and Bertram Ross as Clytemnestra and Orestes, Photo by Carl van Vechten, 1961, Courtesy of Library of Congress, P&P Division, Carl van Vechten Collection, http://www.loc.gov/pictures/item/2004662956/

**Photo Plate 7-3**

Portrait of Alvin Ailey, Photo by Carl van Vechten, 1955, Courtesy of Library of Congress, P&P Division, Carl van Vechten Collection, http://www.loc.gov/item/2004662479/

Ruth St. Denis and husband Ted Shawn in *Yardbirds, 1920,* Photo by George Grantham Bain 1866-1944), of LOC P&P, George Grantham Bain Collection, Courtesy Shorpy, http://www.shorpy.com/node/3851

Ted Shawn in his work *Invocation to the Thunderbird*, 1931, Photograph by Robertson, Courtesy Library of Congress, Politics and the Dancing Body, Exploring National Roots, http://www.loc.gov/exhibits/politics-and-dance/exploring-national-roots.html

Pearl Primus, Photograph by Carl van Vechten, 1943, Courtesy of Library of Congress, Prints and Photographs Division, Carl van Vechten Collection, http://www.loc.gov/pictures/resource/van.5a52885/

**Photo Plate 7-4**

Katherine Dunham in the ballet *L'Ag'Ya* which premiered in 1938, Photograph from the Katherine Dunham Online Collection at the Library of Congress, Courtesy of the Dance Heritage Coalition, 100 Dance Treasures, http://www.danceheritage.org/dunham.html

Students of Modern Dance at CUNY - New York City College of Technology, ca. 1980, Photograph by Helene Andreu. Photo belongs to Helene Andreu.

Ruth St. Denis and Ted Shawn in *Dance of Rebirth* from *Egyptian Ballet*, 1916, from New York Public Library for the Performing Arts, Denishawn Collection, Jerome Robbins Dance Division, Courtesy Public Domain Images Online, Early Modern Dance, Denishawn Collection on Flickr Commons, https://imagespublicdomain.wordpress.com/category/historical/page//2/

Ruth St. Denis with Edna Malone, Betty Horst and Doris Humphries in *Greek Veil Plastique*, Photographer Witzel, 1918, from NYPL for Performing Arts, Denishawn Colletion, Jerome Robbins Dance Division. National Endowment for the Arts Millennium Project, No known copyright restrictions, Courtesy Flickr, http://www.flickr.com/photos/nypl/3110869088/

**Photo Plate 7-5**

Poster for Loie Fuller (1862-1928) at the Folies Bergère, painted by Jules Chéret, 1893, Courtesy Encyclopedia of Visual Artists, http://www.visual-arts-cork.com/famous-artists/jules-cheret.htm

Ruth St Denis and Ted Shawn in *The Abduction of Sita*, 1918, Courtesy NYPL Digital Collections, Photographer Lou Goodale Bigelow, Jerome Robbins Dance Division, Denishawn Collection, http://digitalgallery.nypl.org/nypldigital/dgkeysearchdetail.cfm?trg=1&flag=1&strucID=573302&imageID=den_0771v&word=Abduction%20of%20Sita%20(Choreographic%20work%20%3A%20Shawn)&s=3&notword=&d=&c=&f=2&k=1&lWord=&lField=&sScope=&sLevel=&sLabel=&sort=&total=2&num=0&imgs=20&pNum=&pos=2

Poster for Festival of American Dance, unknown artist, Los Angeles Federal Theater Project, WPA, 1937, Courtesy of the National Archives, Records of the Work Projects Administration, http://www.archives.gov/exhibits/new_deal_for_the_arts/rediscovering_america2.html

Ted Shawn and Ruth St. Denis, in costume for National Geographic Magazine, 1916, from New York Public Library for the Performing Arts, Denishawn Collection, Jerome Robbins Dance Division, Courtesy Public Domain Images Online, Early Modern Dance, Denishawn Collection on Flickr Commons, https://imagespublicdomain.wordpress.com/category/historical/page/2/

**Photo Plate 7-6**

*Geisha Holding A Fan*, by Edward Atkinson Hornel, 1921-25, Courtesy of the National Trust for Scotland, http://www.ntsprints.com/art/490591/a-geisha-girl-holding-a-fan-c1921-25

Matteo and Carola Goya performing Spanish dance at Jacob's Pillow, ca. 1950-59, Photo by John Lindquist (courtesy of the Harvard Theater Collection), Courtesy of the Dance Heritage Coalition, 100 Dance Treasures, http://www.danceheritage.org/matteo-goya.html

Sheet Music Cover to *Dar's Ragtime in Da Moon*, Maurice Shapiro (lyricist), Seymour Furth (composer), Sunday World Music Album Supplement to The New York World, Sunday, July 15, 1900, Courtesy of the Lester S. Levy Collection of Sheet Music, The Sheridan Libraries, The Johns Hopkins University, https://jscholarship.library.jhu.edu/handle/1774.2/3193

Poster, *Le Vrai Cake Walk au Nouveau Cirque*, ca. 1901-1902, lithograph by Franz Laskoff (German, 1869–1918), Courtesy Sonny Watson's StreetSwing.com, http://www.streetswing.com/histmain/posters/9le_vrai_cakewalk1.htm

**Photo Plate 8-1**

Baile por Bulerías, oil on canvas by José García Ramos, Spanish, 1884, Courtesy of the Museo de Bellas Artes de Sevilla, Spain, the D. Alfonso Grosso Collection, http://www.museosdeandalucia.es/culturaydeporte/museos/MBASE/index.jsp?redirect=S2_3_1_1.jsp&idpieza=10&pagina=5

Handbook of Irish Dances, Courtesy Caerde Rince Céilí na hÉireann, http://www.ceilidancing.com/shory_history.aspx

"Warspite" cadets dancing the hornpipe, photo by Associated Press, 1928, No known copyright restrictions, National Marine Museum reproduction ID H638, http://www.internetairship.com/2011/10/24/warspite-cadets-dancing-the-hornpipe/1219

Sheet music cover: *Africana*, composed by Leo Berliner, lyrics by Monroe H. Rosenfeld, illustrated by John Frew, 1904, Courtesy of the Lester S. Levy Collection of Sheet Music, The Sheridan Libraries, The Johns Hopkins University, http://lcweb2.loc.gov/diglib/ihas/loc.award.rpbaasm.0057/default.html

**Photo Plate 8-2**

William M. "Billy" Whitlock, as shown on sheet music cover of *Whitlock's Collection of Ethiopian Melodies*, published by C.G. Christman, New York, 1846, Courtesy of the Lester S. Levy Collection of Sheet Music, The Sheridan Libraries, The Johns Hopkins University, http://levysheetmusic.mse.jhu.edu/catalog/levy:020.093

T. D. Rice ("Daddy" Rice), 1832, singing *Jump Jim Crow*, Courtesy of broadwayscene.com, http://broadwayscene.com/tag/t-d-rice/

Blackface Virginia Minstrels, on sheet music cover of *The Celebrated Negro Melodies, Jim Crow Polka*, by A. F. Winnemore and Thos. Comer (composers), 1843, Courtesy of the Lester S. Levy Collection of Sheet Music, The Sheridan Libraries, The Johns Hopkins University, https://jscholarship.library.jhu.edu/handle/1774.2/17368

**Photo Plate 8-3**

*At a Georgia Camp Meeting*, composer Kerry Mills, published in Rhode Island and New York in 1897, Courtesy of the Lester S. Levy Collection of Sheet Music, The Sheridan Libraries, The Johns Hopkins University, http://levysheetmusic.mse.jhu.edu/catalog/levy:170.015

*Primrose & West's Big Minstrels*, created by Strobridge & Co., Lith., 1896, No known restrictions on publication, Courtesy Library of Congress, P&P Division, http://www.loc.gov/pictures/resource/var.1730/

**Photo Plate 8-4**

William Henry Lane, Master Juba dancing in New York's Five Point District, engraving from Charles Dickens' *American Notes for General Circulation*, engravings by Marcus Stone, 1842, Courtesy of Ephemeral New York, https://ephemeralnewyork.wordpress.com/tag/master-juba/

*The Baltimore Buck*, written by Harry Brown, published by Vinton Music Pub. Co., 1905, Courtesy of the University of Colorado Boulder Music Library, Digital Sheet Music Collection, http://libcudl.colorado.edu:8180/luna/servlet/detail/UCBOULDERCB1~78~78~1075345~136966:Baltimore-buck

Dancer Doing Toe Tip Tap to the Back. Helene Andreu owns this photograph.

**Photo Plate 8-5**

*Baile Andaluz* (Andalusian Dance), by Spanish artist José Villegas Cordero, 1893, Courtesy of Ciudad de la Pintura, http://pintura.aut.org/SearchProducto?Produnum=49735

*The Dancing Lesson, (Negro Boy Dancing)*, watercolor by Thomas Eakins, American, 1878, Courtesy of The Metropolitan Museum of Art, OASC, Fletcher Fund, 1925, Photo by Metropolitan Museum Photostudio, http://www.metmuseum.org/collection/the-collection-online/search/10821

**Photo Plate 9-1**

*Slave Dance, Cuba*, 1859, Source: Harper's Weekly (Jan, 29, 1859), vol. 3, p. 73 (Copy in Special Collections Department, University of Virginia Library), Image Reference HW0006, as shown on www.slaveryimages.org. compiled by Jerome Handler and Michael Tuite, and sponsored by the Virginia Foundation for the Humanities and the University of Virginia Library, Courtesy of the University of Virginia Library, Special Collections Department, http://hitchcock.itc.virginia.edu/Slavery/details.php?categorynum=12&categoryName=&theRecord=20&recordCount=54

*Love Song*, Artist E. W. Kemble, from Century Magazine, Vol. 31, 1886. Helene Andreu owns this photograph.

*The Bamboula Dance*, engraving by E.W. Kemble to illustrate the article "The Dance in Place Congo" by George Washington Cable, published in Century Magazine, February, 1886. Helene Andreu owns this photograph.

**Photo Plate 9-2**

*The Dance After the Husking*, engraving by Winslow Homer, published by Harper's Weekly on November 13, 1858, Courtesy of the Art Institute of Chicago, Prints and Drawings Collection, Gift of Arthur and Hilda Wenig, 2001.750, http://www.artic.edu/aic/collections/artwork/158351

Sheet Music Cover, *High Yellow Cake Walk*, F. Henri Klickmann (composer and lyricist), published by Frank K. Root & Co., Chicago, 1915, Courtesy of the University of Colorado Boulder Music Library, Digital Sheet Music Collection, http://libcudl.colorado.edu:8180/luna/servlet/detail/UCBOULDERCB1~78~78~1059715~137176:High-yellow-cake-walk-and-two-step

*Walking For Dat Cake Songster*, a collection of songs of the day of all kinds, compiled by Edward Harrington and Tony Hart, published by A.J. Fisher, New York, 1877, Courtesy Library of Congress, American Folk Life Center, Robert W. Gordon Songster Collection, http://www.loc.gov/folklife/guide/folkmusicandsong.html

**Photo Plate 9-3**

Sheet Music Cover of *Dancing On De Kitchen Floor*, by James A. Bland, published by White, Smith & Co., Boston, 1880, Courtesy Library of Congress, Music Division, http://www.loc.gov/resource/sm1880.13584.0/?sp=1

Geoffrey Holder and Carmen de Lavallade, Photo by Carl Van Vechten, 1955, Courtesy of Library of Congress, P&P Division, Carl van Vechten Collection, http://www.loc.gov/pictures/item/2004663018/

Ada (Aida) Overton Walker, 1912, Courtesy Library of Congress, P&P Division, NY World Telegram & Sun Newspaper Photograph Collection, No known restriction on publication, http://www.loc.gov/pictures/item/97502075/

Sheet Music Cover of *Darktown Is Out To-Night*, by Will Marion (composer and lyricist), published in 1898, Courtesy of the Lester S. Levy Collection of Sheet Music, The Sheridan Libraries, The Johns Hopkins University, https://jscholarship.library.jhu.edu/handle/1774.2/11276

**Photo Plate 9-4**

Photo of Sam H. Harris (left) and George M. Cohan (right), 1917, photographer not identified, Courtesy of the Library of Congress, P&P Division, Harris and Ewing Collection, http://www.loc.gov/pictures/item/hec2008007208/

*The Sandow Trocadero Vaudevilles*, lithograph in poster format created by Strobridge & Co., Lith., New York, 1894, No known restrictions on publication, Courtesy Library of Congress, P&P Division, Theatrical Poster Collection, http://www.loc.gov/pictures/resource/cph.3g12307/

Bent Creek Ranch Square Dance Team at Mountain Music Festival, Asheville, NC, (1938-1950), photographer unknown, No known restrictions, Courtesy of the Library of Congress, P&P Division, Lomax Collection, http://www.loc.gov/pictures/collection/lomax/item/2007660059/

*Great Ethiopian Songs*, a collection of minstrel show songs by James A. Bland, 1880, Courtesy of the Lester S. Levy Collection of Sheet Music, The Sheridan Libraries, The Johns Hopkins University, https://jscholarship.library.jhu.edu/handle/1774.2/28733,

**Photo Plate 9-5**

*Calinda*, dance of the Negroes in America, by François Aimé Louis Dumoulin, Swiss, 1783, Courtesy of the World eBook Library (CC-by-sa-3.0), http://ebook.worldlibrary.net/articles/Calinda

*The Old Plantation*, by John Rose, a South Carolina plantation owner, ca. 1785-1790, Image Reference NW0159, as shown on www.slaveryimages.org., compiled by Jerome Handler and Michael Tuite, and sponsored by the Virginia Foundation for the Humanities and the University of Virginia Library. Original painting in Abby Aldrich Rockefeller Folk Art Museum, Colonial Williamsburg, VA. Courtesy of the Virginia Foundation for the Humanities and the University of Virginia Library,
http://hitchcock.itc.virginia.edu/Slavery/detailsKeyword.php?keyword=dance&theRecord=24&recordCount=40

Sheet Music Cover of *I'm a Jonah Man*, composer: Alex Rogers, performers on cover: Bert Williams and George Walker, published by M. Widmark & Sons, 1903, Courtesy Brown University Library, African American Sheet Music: A Brown University Digital Collection,
http://library.brown.edu/find/Record/dc1093548719406250

**Photo Plate 10-1**

Sheet Music Cover, *Brass Band Ephraham Jones*, by George W. Meyer (composer) and Joe Goodwin (lyricist), published by Leo Feist, NY (1911), Courtesy Library of Congress, Music Division, http://www.loc.gov/item/ihas.100007253/

Sheet Music Cover, *The Dance of the Grizzly Bear*, Irving Berlin (composer) and George Botsford (lyricist), photo of Sophie Tucker in inset, published by Ted Snyder Co., NY, 1910, and by D. Davis & Co., Sydney, 1910-1911, Courtesy of the National Library of Australia, Digital Collections, Music, http://nla.gov.au/nla.mus-an13479569

Sheet Music Cover, *The Angle Worm Wiggle*, Harry S. Lorch (composer), I Maynard Schwartz (lyricist), photo of Will Philbrick in inset, published by Victor Kremer, Chicago, 1910, Courtesy of Baylor University, Frances G. Spencer Collection of American Popular Sheet Music, Digital images by Baylor University, http://contentdm.baylor.edu/cdm/ref/collection/fa-spnc/id/31699

Sheet Music Cover, *At the Prohibition Ball*, by Alex Gerber (lyricist) and Abner Silver (composer), 1919, Courtesy of the Lester S. Levy Collection of Sheet Music, The Sheridan Libraries, The Johns Hopkins University, https://jscholarship.library.jhu.edu/handle/1774.2/14597

**Photo Plate 10-2**

Sheet Music Cover, *The Ragtime Dance*, by Scott Joplin, (1868-1917), published by John Stark & Son in 1906, Courtesy of the Library of Congress Celebrates the Songs of America, Performing Arts Encyclopedia, http://www.loc.gov/item/ihas.200033246/#about-this-item

Sheet Music Cover, *The Maple Leaf Rag*, by Scott Joplin, published b John Stark & Son, 1899, Courtesy of the Lilly Library of Indiana University, DeVincent Collection, http://webapp1.dlib.indiana.edu/inharmony/detail.do?action=detail&fullItemID=/lilly/devincent/LL-SDV-202046

Sheet Music Cover, *Ma Ragtime Baby Two Step*, composed by Fred S. Stone, published by Whitney Warner Pub. Co., Detroit, 1898, Courtesy of the Lilly Library of Indiana University, Starr Collection, http://webapp1.dlib.indiana.edu/inharmony/detail.do?action=detail&fullItemID=/lilly/starr/LL-SSM-2-305-0176

Sheet Music Cover, *Floating Down the River on the Alabam*, by Albert von Tilzer (composer), Lew Brown and Jack Lustig (contributors), published by Broadway Music Corp., 1912, Courtesy of University of Colorado Boulder Music Library, Digital Sheet Music Collection, Ragtime Sheet Music Collection, Digital image by UCB, http://libcudl.colorado.edu:8180/luna/servlet/detail/UCBOULDERCB1~78~78~1058541~137109:Floating-down-the-river-on-the-Alab

**Photo Plate 10-3**

Sheet Music Cover, *Echoes From The Snowball Club*, by Harry P. Guy, published by Willard Bryant, Detroit, 1898, ID# 32278009988001, Digital publisher: Mississippi State University Libraries, Courtesy Mississippi State University Libraries, Special Collections Department, Charles H. Templeton, Sr. sheet music collection, http://digital.library.msstate.edu/cdm/ref/collection/SheetMusic/id/25698

Sheet Music Cover, *Ballin' the Jack*, Fox Trot, by Chris Smith (composer), James H. Harris (lyricist) 1914, Photo of Anna Hathaway and Joe McShane in inset, Courtesy of the Lester S. Levy Collection of Sheet Music, The Sheridan Libraries, The Johns Hopkins University, https://jscholarship.library.jhu.edu/handle/1774.2/8436

*Leçon de Cake-Walk*, postcard, 1900s, Courtesy of Archives Hub, http://archiveshub.ac.uk/blog/2015/01/2014-features-showcase/

Second verse of lyrics to *Ballin' the Jack*, by Smith and Harris, 1914, Courtesy of International Lyrics Playground, Song Lyrics from Around the World, http://lyricsplayground.com/alpha/songs/b/ballinthejack.shtml

**Photo Plate 10-4**

Sheet Music Cover, *Take me to the Land of Jazz*, lyrics by Bert Kalmar and Edgar Leslie, music by Pete Wendling, published by Waterson Berlin & Snyder Co., 1919, Courtesy of Charles H Templeton Sheet Music Collection, Special Collection, Mississippi States University Libraries, ID# 32278009344551, Digital publisher, Mississippi State University Libraries, http://digital.library.msstate.edu/cdm/ref/collection/SheetMusic/id/31193

Sheet Music Cover, *More Mustard One-Step*, Rag Time Waltz, composed by Louis Mentel, 1914. Courtesy of the Lester S. Levy Collection of Sheet Music, The Sheridan Libraries, The Johns Hopkins University, https://jscholarship.library.jhu.edu/handle/1774.2/6509

Sheet Music Cover, *12th Street Rag*, by Euday L. Bowman, published by J. W. Jenkins Sons Music, ca, 1915, Courtesy University of Colorado Boulder Music Library, Digital Sheet Music Collection, Ragtime Sheet Music Collection, Digital image by UCB, http://libcudl.colorado.edu:8180/luna/servlet/detail/UCBOULDERCB1~78~78~1054611~136881:12th-Street-rag

Ziegfeld Follies, 1912, Sheet Music Cover of *That Wonderful Tune*, composed by Jean Schwartz, words by Grant Clarke, introduced by Elizabeth Brice at the Ziegfeld Moulin Rouge, created and published by Jerome & Schwartz Publishing Co., 1912, Courtesy Library of Congress, Music Division, http://www.loc.gov/item/ihas.200004756/

**Photo Plate 10-5**

Sheet Music Cover, *New York and Coney Island Cycle March Two-Step*, composed by E.T. Paull (1858-1924), published by E,T, Paul Music Co., 1896, Courtesy Brooklyn Public Library, Brooklyn Sheet Music Collection, http://sheetmusic.brooklynpubliclibrary.org/detail.asp?card=sm-0021

Sheet Music Cover, *Jelly Roll Blues*, composed by Jelly Roll Morton, published by Will Rossiter, 1915, Courtesy of the Lilly Library, DeVincent Collection, Indiana University, http://webapp1.dlib.indiana.edu/inharmony/detail.do?action=detail&fullItemID=/lilly/devincent/LL-SDV-023048

Sheet Music Cover, *Way Down Yonder in New Orleans*, by Henry Creamer and Turner Layton, Blossom Seeley in inset, published by Shapiro, Bernstein & Co., NY, 1922, Courtesy of Bailor University, Frances G. Spencer Collection of American Sheet Music, Digital images by Baylor University, http://digitalcollections.baylor.edu/cdm/ref/collection/fa-spnc/id/35922

Sheet Music Cover, *On the Mississippi*, Carroll and Fields, (composers), Ballard McDonald (lyricist), Photo of Carroll and Fields in inset, William Starmer and Frederick Starmer (illustrators/artists), published by Shapiro Music Pub. Co., New York, 1912, Courtesy of Charles H Templeton Sheet Music Collection, Special Collection, Mississippi States University Libraries, ID# 32278011726837, Digital publisher, Mississippi State University Libraries, http://digital.library.msstate.edu/cdm/singleitem/collection/SheetMusic/id/30799/rec/4

**Photo Plate 11-1**

Sheet Music Cover, *Good Bye Alexander, Good Bye Honey Boy*, by Henry Creamer (composer) and Turner Layton (lyricist), cover illustration by E. E. Walton, published by Broadway Music Corporation, 1918, Courtesy of American Centuries, Memorial Hall Museum Online, First Person Oral Histories, Collection of Reba-Jean Shaw Pichette, http://www.americancenturies.mass.edu/centapp/oh/story.do?shortName=elliot1917

John W. Bubbles as Sportin' Life in *Porgy and Bess*, Photo by Carl van Vechten, 1935, Courtesy of Library of Congress, P&P Division, Carl van Vechten Collection, Portrait photographs of celebrities, http://www.loc.gov/pictures/item/2004662642/

Eleanor Powell, unidentified artist, 1936, Courtesy of National Portrait Gallery, Smithsonian Institution, gift of Alice B Levin, NPG.87.289, http://collections.si.edu/search/results.htm?view=&dsort=&date.slider=&q=tap+dance&tag.cstype=all

Portrait of Bill "Bojangles" Robinson, Photo by Carl van Vechten, 1933, Courtesy of Library of Congress, P&P Division, Carl van Vechten Collection, Portrait photographs of celebrities, http://www.loc.gov/pictures/collection/van/item/2004663520/

**Photo Plate 11-2**

Publicity Poster for *The Band Wagon*, MGM film, 1953, with Fred Astaire and Cyd Charisse, Courtesy FilmAffinity.com, http://www.filmaffinity.com/es/film355419.html

Publicity Poster for *Yankee Doodle Dandy*, 1942,Warner Bros. film directed by Michael Curtiz, Lyrics and music by George M. Cohan, Courtesy of IMP Awards, http://www.impawards.com/1942/yankee_doodle_dandy.html

Betty Grable, promotional photo for 20th Century Fox's upcoming film *Pin Up Girl*, photo by Frank Powolny, 1942, copyright not renewed, Courtesy of Pin Curl Magazine, http://pincurlmag.com/wwii-bomber-art

James "Jimmy Slyde" Godbolt, Tap dancer and 1999 NEA National Heritage Fellow, U.S. government agency photo by Joseph T. Wilson, , Courtesy of the National Endowment for the Arts, National Heritage Fellowships http://arts.gov/NEARTS/2006v1-moving-partnership-nea%E2%80%99s-40-years-support-dance/moving-partnership-nea%E2%80%99s-40-years

Honi Coles in *My One and Only*, Photograph by Kenn Duncan, 1983, Courtesy Dance Heritage Coalition, 100 Dance Treasures Collection, http://www.danceheritage.org/coles_honi.html

Bill "Bojangles" Robinson, Photo by Carl von Vechten, 1941, Courtesy of Library of Congress, P& P Division, Carl van Vechten Collection, http://www.loc.gov/pictures/collection/van/item/2004663516/

**Photo Plate 11-3**

"Master Juba", from *Dan Emmett and the Rise of Early Negro Minstrelsy* by Hans Nathan in *The Illustrated London News*, 5 August 1848. Helene Andreu owns this photograph,

Gregory Hines in *Sophisticated Ladies,* 1981, Photograph by Martha Swope, Courtesy Dance Heritage Coalition, 100 Dance Treasures Collection, http://www.danceheritage.org/hines.html

Sheet Music Cover: *Raftero*, from movie *Bolero* with Carole Lombard and George Raft, 1934, Courtesy of Carole & Co., http://carole-and-co.livejournal.com/554264.html

*Dancing Dynamite*, from a *Screenland Magazine* piece on the movie *Colleen,* with Ruby Keeler and Paul Draper, directed by Alfred E. Green, Vol. 32,pages 512-513 (Nov 1935 - Apr 1936), not in copyright. Helene Andreu owns digital version of Vol. 32 of *Screenland Magazine*, from which she copied this image. It is also at the LOC, Motion Picture, Broadcasting and Recorded Sound Divison.

**Photo Plate 11-4**

*Sugar Babies* Marquee, 1979, Photo belongs to Helene Andreu.

**Photo Plate 11-5**

*Chocolat Dansant dans un Bar*, from La Rire, by Henri de Toulouse-Lautrec, 1896, No known copyright restrictions, Courtesy of the European Art Collection of the Brooklyn Museum, Gift of Eileen and Michael Cohen, Brooklyn Museum Photograph, No known copyright restrictions, http://www.brooklynmuseum.org/opencollection/objects/158948/Chocolat_dansant_dans_un_bar_from_La_Rire

Fred Astaire in Hat rack dance from *Royal Wedding,* 1951, Courtesy of The Vintage Cameo, http://www.thevintagecameo.com/2015/01/royal-wedding-1951/

Howard "Sandman" Sims, Tap dancer and NEA 1984 National Heritage Fellow, Photo by NEA, a U.S. government agency, Courtesy of the National Endowment for the Arts, National Heritage Fellowships, http://arts.gov/honors/heritage/fellows/howard-sandman-sims

Sheet Music Cover of *Alabama Shuffle*, composed by Roy Barton, published by Sunlight Music Co., 1910, Cameo photo in inset of Harry L. Newman, Manager of the Sunlight Music Co., Courtesy of the University of Colorado at Boulder Music Library, Digital Sheet Music Collection, Ragtime Sheet Music Collection, Digital image by UCB, http://libcudl.colorado.edu:8180/luna/servlet/detail/UCBOULDERCB1~78~78~1054892~136900:Alabama-shuffle

**Photo Plate 11-6**

Cool looking dancer makes a difficult jump, © ayakovlevcom (/gallery-959 19p1.html / Shutterstock, http://www.shutterstock.com/cat.mhtml?lang=en&language=en&ref_site=photo&search_source=search_form&version=llv1&anyorall=all&safesearch=1&use_local_boost=1&search_tracking_id=p4kooUtu7wJF1NTVf70veg&searchterm=cool%20looking%20dancer&show_color_wheel=1&orient=&commercial_ok=&media_type=images&search_cat=&searchtermx=&photographer_name=&people_gender=&people_age=&people_ethnicity=&people_number=&color=&page=1&inline=16625515

The Dance Theater *Young Tramps,* choreography by Don Oscar Becque, music by Donald Pond, a Federal Dance Theater Project, 1936 or 37, No known restrictions on publication, Courtesy of the Library Congress, Prints and Photographs Division, http://www.loc.gov/pictures/item/98514968/

Sheet Music Cover of *Tambourine Dance*, composed by Joaquín Valverde, Spanish, 1917, Courtesy Johns Hopkins University, Levy Sheet Music Collection, https://jscholarship.library.jhu.edu/handle/1774.2/4496

Balasaraswati (1918-1984), born in South India, Photo from Jacob's Pillow Festival Archives, 1962, Courtesy of the Dance Heritage Coalition, 100 Dance Treasures, http://www.danceheritage.org/balasaraswati.html

Igor Stravinsky, composer of Petroushka (1910-11), The Rite of Spring, ca. 1913, and others, Courtesy of the University of North Carolina's UNC Digital Commons Project, the Stravinsky Compositions section of the Petrushka Web, http://petrushka.web.unc.edu/stravinskys-composition/

**Photo Plate 12-1**

Charles Weidman, Photo by Carl van Vechten, 1933, Courtesy of Library of Congress, P&P Division, van Vechten Collection, Portrait photographs of celebrities, http://www.loc.gov/pictures/resource/van.5a52775/

Poster of Merce Cunningham and Dance Company at Brooklyn Academy of Music, 1969, Poster designed by Robert Rauschenberg. The New York Public Library for the Performing Arts, Dance Division, Courtesy of the Dance Heritage Coalition, 100 Dance Treasures Collection, http://www.danceheritage.org/cunningham.html

Philadelphia Dance Company performance, Photo by Lois Greenfield for U.S. government agency, Courtesy of the National Endowment for the Arts, NEA Arts Magazine, the NEA's Partnership with the States, http://arts.gov/NEARTS/2008v2-nea%E2%80%99s-partnership-states/branching-out

Denishawn Dancers, photo by Bain News Service, ca. 1920, No known restrictions on publication, Courtesy of Library of Congress, P&P Division, George Grantham Bain Collection, http://www.loc.gov/pictures/collection/ggbain/item/ggb2006010516/

**Photo Plate 12-2**

Avant garde modern dance. Photos belong to Helene Andreu.

**Photo Plate 12-3**

Daniel Nagrin in his work, *Indeterminate Figure*, 1957, Photo from the collection of the Dance Notation Bureau, Courtesy of the Dance Heritage Coalition, 100 Dance Treasures Collection, http://www.danceheritage.org/nagrin.html

Rudolf von Laban (1879-1958), developer of Labanotation, unknown photographer, Courtesy of the German Digital Library, http://ausstellungen.deutsche-digitale-bibliothek.de/tanz/exhibits/show/das-gedaechtnis-des-tanzes/labanotation

Martha Graham and Bertram Ross, Photo by Carl van Vechten, 1961, Courtesy of Library of Congress, P&P Division, Carl van Vechten Collection, Portrait photographs of celebrities, http://www.loc.gov/pictures/resource/van.5a52058/

Ruth St Denis dancing, photo by Arnold Genthe (1869-1942), taken in 1913, No known restrictions on publication, Courtesy of Library of Congress, P&P Division, Arnold Genthe Collection, http://www.loc.gov/pictures/item/agc1996000002/PP/

**Photo Plate 12-4**

Contraction technique, Photo belongs to Helene Andreu.

Charles Weidman, 1931, Photograph from Dance Division, New York Public Library for the Performing Arts, Astor, Lenox and Tilden Foundations, Courtesy of Dance Heritage Coalition, 100 Dance Treasures Collection, http://www.danceheritage.org/weidman.html

Portrait of Alvin Ailey, Photo by Carl van Vechten, 1955, Courtesy of Library of Congress, P&P Division, Carl van Vechten Collection, Portrait photographs of celebrities, http://www.loc.gov/pictures/collection/van/item/2004662476

Shen Wei, choreographer, Photos are owned by the MacArthur Foundation and licensed under a Creative Commons License, CC-BY, Courtesy of John D. and Catherine T. MacArthur Foundation, http://www.macfound.org/fellows/840/

**Photo Plate 12-5**

Paul Taylor Dance Company performing *Esplanade*, Photo by Lois Greenfield, U.S. government agency photo, Courtesy of the National Endowment for the Arts, NEA Arts Magazine, American Masterpieces, http://arts.gov/NEARTS/2007v2-american-masterpieces-three-centuries-artistic-genius/american-masterpieces-dance

Alwin Nikolais in his 1959 work, *Allegory*, Photograph from the Dance Division, New York Public Library for the Performing Arts, Astor, Lenox and Tilden Foundations, Courtesy of the Dance Heritage Coalition, http://www.danceheritage.org/nikolais.html

The Dancer, bronze sculpture by Paolo Troubetzkoy , Italian, 1912, © Paul Getty Trust, Courtesy of J Paul Getty Museum, Department of Sculpture and Decorative Arts, Digital image courtesy of the Getty's Open Content Program. http://search.getty.edu/gateway/search?q=dancers&cat=highlight&highlights=%22Open Content Images%22&rows=10&srt=&dir=s&dsp=0&img=0&pg=2

Poster for Federal Theater Project presentation of Myra Kinch and Group, in concert, between 1936 and 1941. No known restrictions on publication. Courtesy of Library of Congress, P&P Division, Works Projects Administration Poster Collection, http://www.loc.gov/pictures/item/98507600/

**Photo Plate 13-1**

Sheet Music *The Original Charleston*, by Cecil Mack and Jimmy Johnson, 1923, Courtesy of Sonny Watson's StreetSwing.com, http://www.streetswing.com/histmain/posters/sheetmusic/charleston-the_original1.htm

Sheet Music Cover for *The Gaby Glide*, by Harry Pilcer (lyricist) and Louis A. Hirsch (composer), 1911, Courtesy of the Lester S. Levy Collection of Sheet Music, The Sheridan Libraries, The Johns Hopkins University, https://jscholarship.library.jhu.edu/handle/1774.2/24378

Sheet Music Cover, *Poor Butterfly, Big Show at NY Hippodrome*, staged by R. H. Burnside, words by John L. Golden; music by Raymond Hubbell; illustration and lettering by Burton Rice. Published: NY: World Magazine, 1916. Courtesy of Peter Spritzer Music Blog, http://peterspitzer.blogspot.com/2012/06/poor-butterfly-and-what-makes-good.html

Vernon and Irene Castle, photo by Frances Benjamin Johnston, between 1910 and 1918, no known restrictions on publication, Courtesy of Library of Congress, P&P Division, Johnston (Frances Benjamin) Collection, http://www.loc.gov/pictures/item/98506505/

**Photo Plate 13-2**

Josephine Baker performing the Charleston at the Folies Bergères, photo by Stanislaus Julian Walery, 1926, Courtesy Dance Heritage Coalition, 100 Dance Treasures, http://www.danceheritage.org/charleston.html

Albertina Rasch (1891-1967), published by Bain News Service, ca. 1915, Courtesy Library of Congress, P&P Division, George Grantham Bain Collection, No known restrictions on publication, http://www.loc.gov/pictures/item/ggb2006011811/

Marathon dancers, unknown photographer, 1923, no known restrictions on publication, Courtesy of Library of Congress, P&P Division, National Photo Company Collection, http://www.loc.gov/pictures/collection/npco/item/npc2007008259/

Sheet Music Cover, *Castle Walk Trot & One Step,* composed by James Reese Europe and Ford T. Dabney, published by Jos. W. Stern & Co., 1913, Photographer of Mr. and Mrs. Castle not identified, Courtesy of the Lester S. Levy Collection of Sheet Music, The Sheridan Libraries, The Johns Hopkins University, https://jscholarship.library.jhu.edu/handle/1774.2/24634

Edison Phonograph Ad, *Everybody Dances when the Phonograph Plays* by Wendell Moore of Edison Phonograph Monthly, page 16 of the August 1907 issue, from the Library of Congress, Media History Digital Library, Courtesy Lantern--Search, Visualize & Explore the Media History Digital Library, http://lantern.mediahist.org/catalog/edisonphonograph05moor_0130

**Photo Plate 13-3**

Jerome Robbins: Rehearsal for *West Side Story*, 1960, publicity photograph by United Artists; from the Dance Division, New York Public Library for the Performing Arts, Astor, Lenox, and Tilden Foundations, Courtesy of the Dance Heritage Coalition, 100 Dance Treasures Collection, http://www.danceheritage.org/robbins.html

Sheet Music Cover of *The Kangaroo Hop*, by Melville Morris (composer) and Gus Kahn (lyricist), publ. by Jerome H. Remick & Co., 1914, Courtesy of Sonny Watson's StreetSwing.com, http://www.streetswing.com/histmain/z5kngro1.htm

DanceBrazil Performs *Ritmos*, choreographed by NEA National Heritage Fellow Jelon Vieira, Photograph by Tom Pich, 2009, U.S. government agency photo, Courtesy of the National Endowment for the Arts, National Heritage Fellowships, http://arts.gov/NEARTS/2009v2-first-steps/presenting-life-philosophy

Agnes de Mille, in *3 Virgins and a Devil*, Photo by Carl van Vechten, 1941, Courtesy of Library of Congress, P&P Division, Carl van Vechten Collection, http://www.loc.gov/pictures/item/2004662788//

Poster for *Dancin'*, at the Broadhurst Theater, New York, 1978, choreographed and directed by Bob Fosse, photo designed by Bob Gill for the Broadway show, Courtesy Dance Heritage Coalition, 100 Dance Treasures, http://www.danceheritage.org/fosse.html

**Photo Plate 13-4**

Afro-Caribbean Jazz, Photo belongs to Helene Andreu.

Hip hop style dancer performing against a white background, © Carlos E. Santa Maria / Shutterstock, http://www.shutterstock.com/cat.mhtml?searchterm=break%20dancer&autocomplete_id=14287167693886425000&language=en&lang=en&search_source=safesearch=1&version=llv1&media_type=media_type2=images&search_cat=&searchtermx=&photographer_name=&people_gender=&people_age=&people_ethnicity=&people_number=&color=&page=1&inline=24512275

Demonstration of Stretched Jazz, Photo belongs to Helene Andreu.

James Leon and Willa Mae Ricker, Swing dancers, photo by Gjon Mili for Life Magazine, 1943, Courtesy Sonny Watson's StreetSwing.com, http://www.streetswing.com/histmai2/d2leonj1.htm

Latin Jazz, Photo belongs to Helene Andreu.

Michael Jackson performing *Billie Jean*, photographer not identified, 2001, Courtesy of Dance Heritage Coalition, 100 Dance Treasures Collection, http://www.danceheritage.org/jackson.html

**Photo Plate 13-5**

*Drawing in Two Colors*, by Winold Reiss (1886-1953), No known restrictions on publication, Courtesy of the Library of Congress, P&P Division, Winold Reiss Collection, http://www.loc.gov/pictures/item/97516539/

*Three Russian Dancers*, by Edgar Degas (1834-1917), Courtesy the National Museum of Sweden, Purchased 1916, http://collection.nationalmuseum.se/eMuseumPlus?service=direct/1/ResultDetailView/result.inline.detail.t1.collection_detailInline.$TspImage.link&sp=13&sp=Sartist&sp=SfieldValue&sp=0&sp=0&sp=3&sp=SdetailView&sp=0&sp=Sdetail&sp=1&sp=T&sp=0&sp=SdetailView&sp=3

Sheet Music Cover, *The Argentine (Tango)*, music by Paul A. Rubens, lyrics by Paul A. Rubens and Arthur Wimperis, photograph of Julia Sanderson and Vernon Castle by White Studio, NY, 1912, Courtesy of the Lester S. Levy Collection of Sheet Music, The Sheridan Libraries, The Johns Hopkins University, https://jscholarship.library.jhu.edu/handle/1774.2/24468

*The Darktown Strutters' Ball*, Shelton Brooks (composer), Flora Stern (in inset), Leo Feist Inc. (publisher), 1917, Courtesy Library of Congress, Music Division, http://www.loc.gov/item/ihas.100004308/

**Photo Plate 14-1**

Portrait of Violette Verdy, photograph by Carl van Vechten, 1961, Courtesy of Library of Congress, P&P Division, Carl van Vechten Collection, http://www.loc.gov/pictures/resource/van.5a52737/

Frederick Franklin, in Ballet Russe de Monte Carlo production of *The Nutcracker*, c. 1940, Photo by Maurice Seymour, from the Jacob's Pillow Dance Festival Archives, Courtesy of Dance Heritage Coalition, 100 Dance Treasures, http://www.danceheritage.org/baryshnikov.html

Hugh Laing, in *Lilac Garden*, Photo by Carl van Vechten, 1940, , Courtesy of Library of Congress, P&P Division, Carl van Vechten Collection, http://www.loc.gov/pictures/collection/van/item/2004663162/

Arthur Mitchell, photo by Carl van Vechten, 1955, Courtesy of the Library of Congress, P&P Division, Carl van Vechten Collection, Portrait photographs of celebrities, http://www.loc.gov/pictures/resource/van.5a52422/?co=van

Mikhail Mordkin in *The Pharaoh's Daughter*, St. Petersburg, 1908, Courtesy of 50 Years in Dance, http://50yearsindance.com/2011/09/17/marius-petipa-part-iii-the-pharoahs-daughter/384px-pharoahs_daughter_-taor_-mikhail_mordkin_-1908-jpg/

Melissa Hayden in ballet costume by Kariaska, Photo by Carl van Vechten, 1956, Courtesy of the Library of Congress, P&P Division, Carl van Vechten Collection, Portrait photographs of celebrities, http://www.loc.gov/pictures/collection/van/item/2004662995/

Anna Pavlova, photo by Arnold Genthe (1869-1942), ca. 1915, Courtesy of the J. Paul Getty Museum. Digital Image Courtesy of the Getty's Open Content Program, http://www.getty.edu/art/collection/objects/44899/arnold-genthe-anna-pavlowa-american-about-1915/

Tamara Karsavina, Bain News Service, publisher, ca. 1915, No known restrictions on publication, Courtesy Library of Congress, P&P Division, George Grantham Bain Collection, http://www.loc.gov/pictures/collection/ggbain/item/ggb2005019551/

**Photo Plate 14-2**

The Dance Theater of Harlem performing *Dialogues*, photo by Martha Swope, 2006, Courtesy of the U.S. National Endowment for the Arts, http://arts.gov/NEARTS/2006v1-moving-partnership-nea%E2%80%99s-40-years-support-dance/moving-partnership-nea%E2%80%99s-40-years

*Dancers Practicing at the Barre*, by Edgar Degas, 1877, Courtesy of the Metropolitan Museum of Art, OASC, H.O. Havemeyer Collection, Bequest of Mrs. H. O. Havemeyer, 1929, Photo by Metropolitan Museum Photostudio, http://www.metmuseum.org/collection/the-collection-online/search/436139

Young Dancers from the Dance Theatre of Harlem perform during a dinner held at the White House, White House photo by Shealah Craighead, 2006, Courtesy of White House Photos, http://georgewbush- whitehouse.archives.gov/news/releases/2006/02/images/20060206-10_p020606sc-0255jpg-515h.html

George Balanchine, 1959, Photo by Henri Cartier-Bresson, Magnum Photos, Courtesy of Dance Heritage Coalition, 100 Dance Treasures, http://www.danceheritage.org/balanchine.html

Maria Tallchief in George Balanchine's *Four Temperaments* photo from the Ann Barzel Dance Research Collection, The Newberry Library Chicago, ca. 1946, Courtesy of the Dance Heritage Coalition, 100 Dance Treasures, http://www.danceheritage.org/tallchief.html

**Photo Plate 14-3**

Suzanne Farrell/George Balanchine, New York World Telegram & Sun photo by Orlando Fernandez, 1965, no copyright restrictions known, Courtesy of Library of Congress, P&P Division, New York World Telegram and the Sun Newspaper Photograph Collection, http://www.loc.gov/pictures/item/2001701679/

Ballet Russes scene of *Apollon Musagete* by Balanchine, 1928, Photographer unknown, from the publication *Rozpravy Aventura*, vol. 5/1929-1930, issue 13-14, page 150. Digitized by the Czech Language Institute, ASCR, Courtesy of the Czech Language Institute, http://archiv.ucl.cas.cz/index.php?path=RozAvn/5.1929-1930/13-14/150.png

Felia Doubrovska performing as the seductress in *The Prodigal Son*, Photo by Sasha ?, 1929, Courtesy of Gallica, Bibliothèque National de France, Département Bibliothèque-Musée de l'Opéra, Album Kochno Fils Prodigue-3, http://gallica.bnf.fr/ark:/12148/btv1b7002662p.r=doubrovska.langEN

Portrait of Alexandra Danilova as Fanny Cerrito in *Pas de Quatre*, Photograph by Carl van Vechten, 1948, Courtesy of Library of Congress, P&P Division, Carl van Vechten Collection, http://www.loc.gov/pictures/collection/van/item/2004662772/

**Photo Plate 14-4**

Natalia Dudinskaya as Kitri in *Don Quijote*, c. 1932-33, Courtesy Natalia Mikhail Dudinskaya Website, http://dudinskaya.narod.ru/gallery.htm

Cherylyn Lavagnino Dance company members in *Triptych*, June 2012, Photo by Ella Bromblin, Courtesy of ArtsJournal, Dance Beat--Deborah Jowitt on Bodies in Motion, Making Ballet New, August 2012, Published under Creative Commons License | Share, http://www.artsjournal.com/dancebeat/wp-content/uploads/2012/08/AJ-women-Trip-CLD-06-26-2012-photo-by-Ella-Bromblin-176.jpg

Natalia Makarova is welcomed at The White House as one of the Kennedy Center Honorees for 2012, taken from official White House video, Courtesy of The White House Blog posting by Colleen Curtis, https://www.whitehouse.gov/blog/2012/12/03/president-and-mrs-obama-welcome-2012-kennedy-center-honorees-white-house

Alicia Alonso, Cuban dancer and choreographer,1955, Courtesy of the Library of Congress, New York World Telegram and Sun Collection, , http://www.loc.gov/pictures/item/95522322/

*Little Dancer, Aged Fourteen*, by Hilaire-Germain-Edgar Degas, sculpture executed in wax1878-1881, cast in bronze by the foundry Adrien Hébrard, Paris, around 1922, Courtesy of the Philadelphia Museum of Art, European Painting Department, The Henry P. McIlhenny Collection in memory of Frances P. McIlhenny, 1986, http://www.philamuseum.org/collections/permanent/82565.html?mulR=53010258|2

**Photo Plate 14-5**

*Russian Ballet*, painted by August Macke (1887-1914), in 1912, Photo by Lars Lohrisch, Courtesy Kunsthalle-Bremen, http://www.kunsthalle-bremen.de/sammlung/online-katalog/

Ivan Vasiliev in *Spartacus* at the opening gala of the Bolshoi Theatre after reconstruction, 28 October 2011, official Russian government photograph, CC Attribution 4.0 International, Courtesy of the website of the President of Russia, http://en.kremlin.ru/events/president/news/13260/photos

Violette Verdy and Edward Villella performing a Pas de Deux during the entertainment portion of a State Dinner Honoring the Prime Minister of Singapore, 5/8/1975, photo by White House Photographic Office (under President Ford (1974-1977), Courtesy of the GRF-White House Photographic Collection (Ford Administration), http://research.archives.gov/description/7518579

Wendy Whelan taking final bow after 30 years with New York City Ballet, photo by Paul Kolnick, Oct. 2014, Courtesy of ArtsJournal, Dance Beat--Deborah Jowitt on Bodies in Motion, Creative Commons License | Share, http://www.artsjournal.com/dancebeat/2014/10/a-ballerina-moves-on/

Jessica Lang Dance company at *Lines Cubed* dress rehearsal for first time performance of ballet at Jacob's Pillow Dance Festival, 2012, Photo by Taylor Crichton, Courtesy of ArtsJournal, Dance Beat--Deborah Jowitt on Bodies in Motion, Making Ballet New, August 2012, published under Creative Commons License | Share, http://www.artsjournal.com/dancebeat/wp-content/uploads/2012/08/AJ-pose-jessicalang_dressrehearsal_2012taylorcrichton_012.jpg

Natalia Osipova in *Flames of Paris* at the opening gala of the Bolshoi Theatre after reconstruction, 28 October 2011, official Russian government photographs, CC Attribution 4.0 International, Courtesy of the website of the President of Russia, http://en.kremlin.ru/events/president/news/13260/photos

Léon Bakst's Costume design for the faun in *L'Après-Midi d'un Faune*, 1912, Courtesy of the National Gallery of Australia, 2011 Exhibition *Ballet Russes, The Art of Costume*, http://nga.gov.au/exhibition/balletsrusses/Default.cfm?IRN=199403&BioArtistIRN=19455&mystartrow=37&realstartrow=37&MnuID=4&GALID=19455&viewID=3&DTLVIEW=TRUE

CPSIA information can be obtained at www.ICGtesting.com
Printed in the USA
LVOW05s2003260815

451693LV00021B/205/P

9 781504 920469